ISLAND IN THE STRI   MW00577164

An Ethnographic History of Mayotte

Island in the Stream introduces an original genre of ethnographic history as it follows a community on Mayotte, an East African island in the Mozambique Channel, through eleven periods of fieldwork between 1975 and 2015. Over this forty-year span Mayotte shifted from a declining and neglected colonial backwater to a full *département* of the French state. In a highly unusual postcolonial trajectory, citizens of Mayotte demanded this incorporation within France rather than joining the independent republic of the Comoros. The Malagasy-speaking Muslim villagers Michael Lambek encountered in 1975 practised subsistence cultivation and lived without roads, schools, electricity, or running water; today they are educated citizens of the EU who travel regularly to metropolitan France and beyond.

   Offering a series of ethnographic slices of life across time, *Island in the Stream* highlights community members' ethical engagement in their own history as they looked to the future, acknowledged the past, and engaged and transformed local forms of sociality, exchange, and ritual performance. This is a unique account of the changing horizons and historical consciousness of an African community and an intimate portrait of the inhabitants and their concerns, as well as a glimpse into the changing perspective of the ethnographer.

(Anthropological Horizons)

MICHAEL LAMBEK is a Canada Research Chair and professor in the Department of Anthropology at the University of Toronto Scarborough.

ANTHROPOLOGICAL HORIZONS

Editor: Michael Lambek, University of Toronto

This series, begun in 1991, focuses on theoretically informed ethno-graphic works addressing issues of mind and body, knowledge and power, equality and inequality, the individual and the collective. Inter-disciplinary in its perspective, the series makes a unique contribution in several other academic disciplines: women's studies, history, philosophy, psychology, political science, and sociology.

For a list of the books published in this series see page 335.

Island in the Stream

An Ethnographic History of Mayotte

MICHAEL LAMBEK

With a foreword by MICHAEL JACKSON

UNIVERSITY OF TORONTO PRESS
Toronto Buffalo London

© University of Toronto Press 2018
Toronto Buffalo London
utorontopress.com
Printed in the U.S.A.

ISBN 978-1-4875-0391-8 (cloth)   ISBN 978-1-4875-2299-5 (paper)

♾ Printed on acid-free, 100% post-consumer recycled paper with vegetable-based inks.

(Anthropological Horizons)

Library and Archives Canada Cataloguing in Publication

Lambek, Michael Joshua, author
Island in the stream : an ethnographic history of Mayotte / Michael Lambek.

(Anthropological horizons)
Includes bibliographical references and index.
ISBN 978-1-4875-0391-8 (cloth).   ISBN 978-1-4875-2299-5 (paper)

1. Ethnology – Mayotte – History – 20th century.   2. Mayotte – Social life and customs – 20th century.   3. Mayotte – History – 20th century.   I. Title.

GN661.M3L27 2018   305.8009694'5   C2018-903464-5

This book has been published with the help of a grant from the Federation for the Humanities and Social Sciences, through the Awards to Scholarly Publications Program, using funds provided by the Social Sciences and Humanities Research Council of Canada.

University of Toronto Press acknowledges the financial assistance to its publishing program of the Canada Council for the Arts and the Ontario Arts Council, an agency of the Government of Ontario.

Canada Council   Conseil des Arts
for the Arts   du Canada

ONTARIO ARTS COUNCIL
CONSEIL DES ARTS DE L'ONTARIO
an Ontario government agency
un organisme du gouvernement de l'Ontario

Funded by the   Financé par le
Government   gouvernement
of Canada   du Canada

Contents

Part Three: Dancing to the Music of Time, through 2001

Part Four: Contingent Conviviality, through 2015

Figures

Foreword

No one has lived in the past and no one will live in the future. The present is the form of all life, and there is no means by which this can be avoided. Time is a circle that is endlessly revolving. The descending arc is the past and the ascending arc is the future.

Jean-Luc Godard, *Alphaville*

There are several remarkable things about Michael Lambek's ethnographic corpus: the empirical depth and philosophical subtlety of his understanding, born of more than forty years' fieldwork among the people of Mayotte; the breadth and intellectual range of his anthropological expertise – encompassing hermeneutics, ritual, ethics, historicity, medicine, spirit possession, mytho-praxis, and religion; and his insistence on the complexity, multiplicity, and continual alternations that characterize life-as-lived. His refusal to reduce any way of knowing or way of being to a single defining characteristic, a single story, not only reflects the heterogeneity of the lifeworlds in which he has lived and worked, where incommensurable worldviews (Islam, astrology, and spirit possession) are resources to be drawn upon to varying degrees and in different situations rather than seen as mutually exclusive; it reflects a temperamental aversion to either-or thinking, and an intellectual restiveness that makes him sceptical of knowledge claims, fascinated by the ways in which human perspectives change through time, and convinced that despite the manifest differences between cultures and individuals, a shared humanity can be brought to light through our immersion in other lifeworlds and the intimate relationships we form with individuals in them. In *Island in the Stream*, Lambek makes this existential tenet his point of departure for exploring the question of how intellectual certainty is possible when both the anthropologist and the society of which he seeks an understanding are not so much culturally different as constantly changing. According to Heraclitus's famous aphorism "everything is in flux" (*panta rhei*), one cannot step into the same river twice, for neither self nor river stay constant over time. Michael Lambek's response to this shifting and indeterminate relationship between observer and observed is not to attempt a historical ethnography of Mayotte but to write an ethnographic history, comprising portraits or "cuts" that provide, in effect, a series of ethnographic presents, each one of which affords insights into the lives of Mahorais at a given moment in their history, but most importantly captures pivotal moments in the *relationship* of the anthropologist to the Mahorais – multiple perspectives that are juxtaposed without, however, admitting any final synthesis. In many respects, this method, which Michael Lambek compares to using a "series of still photographs moving at a certain pace [to provide] the illusion of cinematic movement," exemplifies Adorno's negative dialectics, in which the indeterminate relationship between life as lived and life as theorized, or between our immediate sense of the passage of time and the calibrated time of clocks and epochs, is acknowledged but deliberately not resolved.

For Lambek, there is an intimate connection between an ethnographer's attentiveness to an interlocutor, one's presence-to-another, and the question of ethics. What originally drew me to Michael Lambek's work, and continues to fill me with admiration, is not only this attentiveness to others but the way it encourages us to see that the *quality* of our relationships with interlocutors or collaborators in the field determines the *character* of our anthropological understandings. Anthropology is a social science; as such, its worth is to be evaluated not on intellectual grounds alone, but in terms of our social life in the field and the repercussions of our findings for those whose hospitality we enjoy and whose lives benefit us.

I am reminded of John Berger's preface to *Pig Earth*, his ethnographic-cum-fictional account of a French Alpine peasant community, published about the same time that Michael Lambek was embarking on his first fieldwork in Mayotte. "To approach experience," Berger writes, "is not like approaching a house. 'Life,' as the Russian proverb says, 'is not a walk across an open field.'" Indeed, Berger goes on to say, experience is always metaphorical – "continually comparing like with unlike, what is small with what is large, what is near with what is distant," like a shuttle on a loom (1979: 6). The way consciousness moves constantly between past, present, and future is crucial for both Berger and Lambek. Berger recounts how he was walking in the mountains with a friend of seventy. As they walked along the foot of a high cliff, the French peasant remarked that a young girl had fallen to her death there whilst haymaking on the *alpage* above. "Was that before the war?" Berger asked. "In 1833," his friend replied. What Lambek calls ethnographic history resonates with Berger's view that our sense of time is intimately connected with critical events and practical activities. When we recount a story or write ethnographic history we are instantly in time, but it is seldom the time of the historian (a matter of objective, datable chronologies); rather, it is the time of our lives, in which we are engaged in earning a living, raising children, cultivating fields, going to work, performing rituals, telling stories, coping with crises, and, sometimes, trying to render the world intelligible. This, for Lambek is the domain of sociality and ordinary ethics, and it is, in a sense, timeless. It refers to what human beings have been doing since time immemorial, regardless of the regimes under which they have lived, the cosmologies and faiths they have embraced, the languages they have spoken, the histories written about them in retrospect or, for that matter, their own ever-changing historical awareness.

François Hartog speaks of "regimes of historicity" in describing the ways in which our experience of the present involves a continual and alternating movement between different ways of understanding our relationship to what we conventionally call past, present, and future. Hartog's notion of presentism, however, brackets out such categorizations, since our consciousness is shifting its focus so continually between various objects, others, images, interests, emotions, and practical tasks that the distinctions between near and far, present and past, here and there, become blurred or annulled. Lambek's extensive writing on spirit possession captures this lived historicity with phenomenological precision, showing how former rulers or spirit beings come to life in the bodies and minds of living people, speaking and acting through them. This "poiesis of the past," as Lambek calls it, illuminates not only the nature of historical consciousness but the multiplicity of the self. Rather than deploy the language of identity, conceptualizing the person as a seamless, stable, skin-encapsulated monad, Lambek is sensitive to the ways in which we constantly change, like chameleons, according to our surroundings, possessing an extraordinary capacity to shift and adjust our self-state in response to who we are with, to what circumstance demands, and to what our well-being seems to require. "Horizons are mobile," Lambek writes, "expanding or retracting in response to social and political circumstances; changing as we move towards or away from them." These horizons are at once temporal, geographical, social, and psychological. Thus, Lambek brilliantly describes human improvisation, experimentation, opportunism, and existential mobility, and shows that individuals often struggle not to align their lives with extant moral or legal norms but to find ways of negotiating *the ethical space* between external constraints and personal imperatives. "Over time," Lambek writes, "I have come to understand that the critical units of analysis are not rules but acts, and that the ethical dimension of life, and of engaged citizenship, is as critical as the jural, the material, or the political – although these are all abstractions and need not appear as discrete forms or domains in actual life." Focusing on the time-old ethical question "How best can we live?" (rather than "What ought we to do?") means sensitizing ourselves to the strategic shape-shifting, both imaginative and actual, that is constantly occurring in everyday life. A corollary of this notion of *phronesis* (social adroitness, practical skilfulness, and moral judgment) is that the ongoing mutual adjustments we make in the course of our everyday lives happen without forethought or intentionality, and do not necessarily follow from what we think or believe. The philosophers on whom Lambek draws have abandoned the Cartesian prioritization of the *res cogitans*; they are fascinated by intuitive action, mimetic learning, risk taking, and the forming and unforming of habits. What Lambek does, however, is to show that living life "as if it matters" involves unending oscillations *between* unpremeditated *and* conceptually mediated actions. Although he sets great store by empirical detail, thick description, and lived experience, every foray into the everyday inspires theoretical reflections and digressions that always lead back to particular individuals, actual relationships, and critical events. Key concepts such as horizon and historicity are treated as hypotheses to be tested against empirical reality in much the same way that people who are neither scientists nor academics are constantly testing, checking, evaluating, and revising their assumptions, goals, and associations. Thus, we read of the structure and destructuring of the local exchange system (*shungu*) and correlative changes to cultural constructions of the life cycle and the life course (a dynamic shift from an ideology of equality to a more competitive market-based individualism), debates about correct Islamic practices or the relationship of Islam to art and spirit possession, and the vexed question of Mayotte's relationship to France as relatively plotless, Chekhovian "slices of life" rather than variations on a single theme, chapters in a lineal history, or refractions of a general thesis. What is disclosed at every turn is the creative ingenuity, imaginative vitality, and active engagement of Mahorais in their own unfolding history. As in his earlier book on historical labour and historical consciousness among Sakalava in northwest Madagascar (*The Weight of the Past*), Lambek is not only sensitive to the vernacular images local people use in expressing their sense of temporality; he takes pains to write *with* their images – of history as a burden to be borne and endured, to which one is subjected, but also as a source of empowerment and revitalization.

In the life of a Mayotte spirit medium called Nuriaty Tumbu, whose career Lambek has followed closely for many years, these elements are conspicuously present. "Nuriaty engages in a virtuoso poiesis (crafting) of history, complete with plot, character, scene, and so on ... Hers are acts of dignity and indignation, of courage, imagination, concern, and respect for herself and for others, of recognizing the indebtedness of the present to the past, of integrity. She speaks for collective values, for what, in her understanding, makes life meaningful and fruitful. Her means are traditional; her end is human flourishing (*eudaimonia*)." Reading this passage, itself an island in the stream of this book, I felt that no better summary could be made of Michael Lambek's own career, and of the ethnographic depth, historical sensibility, and practical wisdom that he has brought to anthropology, providing a powerful and persuasive corrective to the theoretical excesses, Eurocentric bias, and obscurantist tendencies of our discipline.

Michael Jackson
Distinguished Professor of World Religions
Harvard Divinity School

Note on Orthography

The orthography is somewhat mixed, borrowing from traditions for transcribing into French or Malagasy, but more often based on what makes most sense for an English reader. Sometimes, therefore, words do not look identical to the sources or cognates in Arabic, Comoran, French, or Malagasy. In the text "ñ" is used to indicate the guttural "ng" as in "si*ng*" when it appears in the middle of a word. What in Spanish is rendered as "ñ" here is written as "gn" or "ny."

Kibushy nouns do not distinguish singular from plural.

Where the word "cow" is used throughout the text the sex and age of the animal is not specified – it could be a female, a steer, an ox, or a bull.

Glossary

añala: bush, fields, countryside, forest

angivavy: father's sister

añumby: generic cow, including ox, bull, steer, heifer (etc.); cattle

asa: work, formal event, ceremony, or affair

baba: father

be: big, large, adult, senior

commune: municipality, in the French administrative system comprising several communities

dadilahy: grandfather, elderly man

dady: grandmother, elderly woman, often used as part of a personal name

Daira: men's dance in a circle, chanting God's name, associated with the Shathuly brotherhood

fady: taboo, prohibition

fihavañana: kinship

fomba: cultural practice, custom, also used as habit

fundi: expert, teacher, healer, learned person, especially of Islam

havaña, hava: kin, and used metaphorically, friend, companion

jaula: Muslim reform movement and ideology

kely: small, young, junior

Kibushy: the dialect of Malagasy spoken in Mayotte

kufungia: the Muslim act of marriage

kurmidza: the act of engagement

lahy: male

lalahy: man

lulu: spirit (general term)

mahery: difficult, tough, strong

Mahorais: *noun* – person of Mayotte; *adjective* – pertaining to Mayotte

mama: mother

mandeving: a large ceremony to pray on behalf of a deceased parent

manzaraka: a wedding celebration, often held long after the fact, focused on a procession of the groom to the bride's house accompanied by a performance of verses of the *Mulidy*

Maore: Mayotte

Maulida: an ode in honour of the Prophet; it can be recited or sung and danced

Maulida shengy: a popular version of the *Maulida* in which women sing and dance

mraba: compound, extended family, kin group, fence, fenced enclosure

mshia: a wooden box used to measure rice; and a unit of measurement of rice

mukary: cake, pastry, cookie (baked or fried)

Mulidy: a version of the *Maulida* that is sung and danced by a line of men, associated with the Qadiry brotherhood

nindry: mother

razaña: ancestor

razaña raiky: common ancestor (i.e., relation of genealogical descent)

shikao: formal age group, *équipe*

Shimaore: Bantu language of Mayotte; attributes of speakers of the language

shirika: a shared, undivided piece of land held collectively

shungu: a formal system of balanced exchange and its obligation or payment

silam: Islam, Muslim

socié: a group that purchases and owns a piece of land in common (Fr. *société*) *soma*: play, entertainment

tahalil: first verse of the *Shahada* ("There is no God but God"), performed multiple times at a *mandeving*

tanana: residential community, village, as both residential and social unit, city,

tany: land, country

tompin: owner, sponsor, principal, agent

tompin tanana: citizens, full members of a community

tranu, trañu: house, and implicitly the conjugal unit that inhabits it

trumba: Malagasy spirit, frequently a deceased member of the Sakalava royal clan

ulu: person, people

ulu be: elder, adult

ulun'belo: human being

vady: spouse

vavy: female

vazaha: European, French person

viavy: woman

vola: money

Preface

> Historical thinking has its dignity and its value as truth in the acknowledgment that there is no such thing as "the present," but rather constantly changing horizons of future and past.
>
> Hans-Georg Gadamer,
> *Truth and Method* (1985: 484)

This statement could perhaps have been written only at a certain age. Hans-Georg Gadamer was sixty when *Truth and Method* was first published in German in 1960, and I draw on it at some years older as I try to conceptualize and compose an account of life in a community of Kibushy speakers in Mayotte, an island in the Comoro Archipelago of the western Indian Ocean where I have conducted fieldwork over a forty-year period. I have been concerned with how best to depict this period with respect to structure, change, and lived experience – how to write an "ethnography" that spans forty years. I conceptualize this book as what I call an ethnographic history (*not* a historical ethnography), composed of successive portraits or analyses written at different times in a series of ethnographic presents, each with their changing horizons of future and past.

This book has been a long time in the making. It draws from articles written across the period of research, partially revised to fit an emerging whole. The delay in producing that whole is due less to idleness on my part (though there is plenty of that) than to a desire to wait and see how things continued to unfold in Mayotte and because I was unable to make any of my visits a last one. Taking the story to the firm instauration of Mayotte as a *département* within the French state, a goal for many Mahorais (as the people of Mayotte are called) since before my first visit, seemed as good a stopping point as any. Moreover, forty is a round number, even a biblical and Muslim one, and I may no longer be competent by the time the span reaches fifty.

I first conducted fieldwork in Mayotte over a period of fourteen months in 1975–6, a time of intense engagement that still remains vivid in my imagination despite the doubtless supersession of various screen memories. I stayed the first few weeks in 1975 in Mamoudzou, the community that was closest in size and function to being a town and capital.[1] It was then a small and sleepy place whose two main attractions for me became the post office and the island's only bakery. I lived those first weeks in the compound of the bakery and can attest that bread is one thing for which French colonialism need not be ashamed. There was one bar, catering to the last of the Creole population; its shrewd leathery owner was known as Madame Foucault, presumably unrelated to Michel, but who knows? The residents of Mamoudzou were mostly Shimaore speakers, but I learned some Kibushy vocabulary from a member of the bakery household.[2] I toured a few villages, selected one, and moved in, staying on that first visit for close to thirteen months. I returned in 1980, and then with a wife and two-year-old daughter for four months in 1985, and with my wife and two children in 1995.[3] I have made several other trips alone, for usually around a month or less, a total of eleven visits in all. The most recent was for three weeks in July/August 2015. Visits are intense, and I take reams of notes. Since the first visits I always go in the cooler and drier (post-harvest) season, a season that corresponds to the northern summer and to the period now called *vacances*, when the many Mahorais who reside in La Réunion or metropolitan France themselves return for visits and when most collective ritual events take place. Migrants still return home to conduct the major life-cycle ceremonies.

I always return to the same village and reside with the same family. I have visited other villages, of course, but my perspective on Mayotte is entirely through one village – or what is actually a pair of closely related adjacent villages. If I can brag about the length and depth of my study, I have equally to emphasize its limitation of breadth; the perspective I offer comes from a pair of villages and cannot speak to the experience of town and therefore of either the elites or the underclass who now reside in the urban strip, nor of those in the distinctive villages elsewhere on Mayotte.[4] The community I selected was relatively, but not excessively, far from town, now a forty-five-minute drive, depending on traffic, but a much longer trip in the days before the road was extended. In those years, the village was reached either by a steep trail through dense forest or by canoe, and on the return journey, once the road to town was reached, transport was infrequent, haphazard, and slow. We sat crammed into the back of pickup trucks climbing their way through endless hairpin turns.

Once I started composing the book, a further slowdown appeared; I was caught in a hermeneutic circle, enmeshed in the thicket of what I wanted to say and in what manner to say it. How to do justice to thousands of pages of field notes? (I can't.) How to distinguish the experience of one field trip from another? In what manner to draw on what I had written along the way? To what audience to pitch the book? Did I want an anthropological "bestseller," a narrative so direct it could stand for and exemplify "Africa," "social change," or some other broad topic? (Such books are generally highly misleading.) Conversely, should it portray as clearly as possible what I saw, without a moral or a general lesson for the discipline or the general public, or simply document as much detail as possible for some future historian to draw their own conclusions? These are questions any serious ethnographer asks, but they seemed particularly acute because of the time span the research covers, the interest of readers from Mayotte in what is past, and the increasing sense that comes with my own age and with the times that the present is always and all too soon already past.

An anthropologist collecting notes for a year has a hard enough time trying to compress and distil them into a book. Across forty years the challenge is greater. It is not just the quantity of notes but whether and how to specify and differentiate the years from which items are extracted or to which they speak. How to forefront change while preserving continuity, or forefront continuity while following change? There is also the balance to be found between comprehensiveness and cohesion. I could develop a plot, but that would render history unduly consistent. I could present narrative accounts of several lives, but that might not do explicit justice to structure. I could focus on big events, but there aren't so many and that doesn't capture the ordinariness – say the continuity – of change. I could turn incidents from my field notes into events of my narrative, and to an extent I have done so, but they are not exactly consequential actions of the scale or force that with hindsight inevitably initiate a revolution or lead to war. In the end, I have written chapters that approach the material somewhat differently from one another, some with an eye to structure, others more to experience. I want to grasp something sociologically valid about the lived experience of change without privileging linearity or teleology, without deferring unduly either to the modern frame of empty time or to the various Western myths of progress and decline, or some other story that readers will find simply justifies their expectations.

Some people would dismiss the study of a community as old-fashioned, limited, and unable to capture the globalized world in which we all live. I hope that my account dispels such opinions. This book is both a study of two related villages and an account of subjects – historicity, ethical life, sociality, marriage, exchange – that manifestly transcend them. Some readers will approach the book eager to know about life in Mayotte, others for how the ethnography speaks to broader questions of theory and methodology, or simply to our common historical existence. I hope no one will be completely unsatisfied.

Island in the Stream draws from what one can learn through close fieldwork. So a large caveat: the title is misleading. There are strong parallels between life as I describe it in the communities I call Lombeni and in other villages, and ultimately in the entire island. However, this is emphatically not a study of Mayotte as a whole. And it differs from much recent work, especially by French political scientists and journalists, in not being fixated on the political status of Mayotte. Though partially chronicling Mayotte's shift from marginal colony to *département d'outre mer* (i.e., a fully integrated and equivalent unit within the French state), that shift is not the core of what the book is about. Insofar as I am interested in that transformation it is in how the transformation was anticipated and received in the community and not about a political elite. It is neither a complacent nor a triumphalist account, nor, as is currently more common among French observers, does it wring its hands about the wisdom of having acquiesced in the desires of the island's citizens and incorporated them into the state and nation of France.

I stay, as I said, in the same village and with the same family. In previous work I have always called the village and the family members – as well as other people – by pseudonyms. The names were somewhat arbitrary and have always felt a bit silly. I have debated whether to abandon them for the real ones. The practice in the discipline of (oral) history is to be punctilious about recognizing each of one's sources; the practice in anthropology is generally to be careful to conceal them. The identity of the village will be fairly obvious to people who know Mayotte well, and I want now more than ever to acknowledge people for who they are. Yet I am mindful of potential embarrassment and find that what I want to say often touches on intimate matters. So I continue not to acknowledge individuals directly, despite all the insight, instruction, friendship, and assistance they have offered me and despite the fact that it is their lives that I describe and, in a sense, live with.

In a way, what I write is akin to biography, the biography of a community. With that comes a sense of the great privilege I have been given, from the first offers of hospitality, to trust, kinship, and appreciation. The community has opened itself to my investigation, put up with my incessant note taking, shared with me – and yet of course has gone on with its life in disregard of me. I am immensely grateful.

One of the peculiarities of long-term fieldwork is that, even more than a single intensive year or two, it becomes a part of the ethnographer's life as well, part of what Germans call *Erfahrung*, experience in the sense of a life's journey, an accumulation of knowledge and perhaps some kind of maturity, and in later life, field notes notwithstanding, also a kind of selective and unconscious forgetting.[5] I feel this more strongly with each visit, especially when I compare how my life has unfolded, my *Erfahrung*, with the various lives and *Erfahrungen* of my peers in the community. I was particularly struck with such existential concerns during my most recent visit. While there are continuous threads in what I have inquired about over the years and what I have learned, the tone of the encounter is changing. This is a result of both social change in the community (many people now speak French and a few even know English) and my own aging and historical position. This will be evident in the last chapters, which are newly written. I leave it to future scholars to discern whether there is a "late style" evident in aging writers of ethnography.

This is not to say that I know more now than I did earlier. If anything, I was more replete with knowledge following the first long stay, and it is that first stay, when everything was fresh and exciting, that I often revert to in my head. I knew then every member of the community and how each person was related to each of the others. Subsequent visits have undermined my knowledge – during my absence life goes on; new children are born and grow up; new residents move in; interests, ambitions, rules, and routines change. Each time I arrive I am confronted by how little I know. This is a healthy Socratic position in which to find oneself. I now often speak French with younger people, but just as at home, I find myself least connected to the world of adolescents, a world shaped now in Mayotte, as in Canada, by cell phones, Facebook, and the like. To young people I am a distant old man. On the other hand, to those of my age, or those of an age where they can consider me a younger or older brother, brother-in-law, father, mother's brother, or friend, time itself has deepened our intimacy.

What is it one can know or say about a span of forty years (and, to be clear, let me restate, based on intermittent visits, *not* forty years of residence)? Certainly, the answer cannot be a fine-grained synchronic structure-functional analysis of the kind that originally inspired me, and not only for the reason that theoretical tastes have changed in anthropology. The ethnographic present, that peculiar, problematic, and necessary fictional device, has already been refracted, fractured through my repeated visits and successive publications. The multiple visits also preclude, I am glad to say, a simple before-and-after story of the kind created by the single restudy. The restudy is distorted insofar as it pivots around the return of the ethnographer rather than the progression of the community. That is to say, the central event in such a narrative is the ethnographer's return, the salient experience is that of the ethnographer, and the study is not in any real sense historical.

One of the problems of that kind of study is that it implicitly puts too much weight on the ethnographer's immediate experience, as though a door closed on the ethnographer's first departure only to reopen on their return. It is as if nothing happens if the ethnographer doesn't witness it; no sound as the tree falls in the forest. It goes along with the implicit assumption found in many older works that the community under study was timeless until the ethnographer's first arrival. Things only begin to happen from that point on.[6] Repeat visits lessen these effects, and they are further mitigated (though never entirely neutralized) as people talk about their lives and what has transpired in the intervals of my absence. Return visits also lessen the strangeness of the ethnographer's presence, domesticating the practice, even if they also might partially disguise it.

The more significant problem with a before-and-after model is that it is conducive to a simplistic picture of change and tempted by overly simple or mechanical models of cause and effect. I want to highlight instead the density, texture, and experience of change itself. I want to do justice to the change that happened, but also to change *as* it happened, or happens, change or history in the intransitive as well as transitive mode. One cannot capture change in motion, but, just as a series of still photographs moving at a certain pace provide the illusion of cinematic movement, so these essays, emerging at different periods of fieldwork may capture something like the tone or tempo of change and the ongoing interpretations of life by members of the community that successively *are* that life as it changes. Change itself is anticipated yet indeterminate; conclusive yet conditional; shot with optimism yet shadowed with regret; simultaneously irreversible and ambiguous. Change is no less than life as it is lived, the product of multiple interpretive acts, layered against and overlapping one another on the part of successive generations and historical cohorts. Perhaps one of the transformations in change itself is that these cohorts have become shallower, succeeding each other more quickly, such that people only a few years apart in age have faced very different circumstances from one another and respond in different ways. We know this as the compression of space/time in modernity.

It is not possible to capture what I have in mind without metaphor, I hope neither excessively trite nor over-determining. I have called the book "Island in the Stream" to evoke the tension between identity understood as constancy and as movement.[7] "*Tsy tany mandeha, fa ulun belu*. It is not the land that moves, but people," the islanders used to say. In fact, Mayotte lies in an ocean not a river, and the flow is not linear. The better metaphor is of a moving craft on the restless ocean where the horizon stretches 360 degrees. In fact, it is the horizon that forms a central metaphor in the book. Horizons capture what is actually a double movement insofar as they recede or approach, raise or lower, widen or narrow, while people move towards them or turn to approach them from a different direction. If overused as the title for a book, the horizon has a distinguished history in German thought, extending from Husserl through Heidegger and then to Gadamer and Koselleck. My central reference point will be Gadamer, but my intentions are also captured in Koselleck's (2004) depiction of the tension between what he calls the "space of experience" and the "horizon of expectation."

Over the years I have published two books on the community, one addressing spirit possession (Lambek 1981) and the other detailing what I called the social organization of knowledge (Lambek 1993), concerning the articulation in thought and practice of Islam, astrology, and spirit possession. I also published many articles. Each publication was based on my knowledge and my ethnographic visits up to the point at which it was written. My idea for this book has been to layer some of these articles successively, according to when they were written and the time periods they each describe. The composition is one of a succession of ethnographic portraits or presents that, taken as a whole, makes up a history. Hence it is a history constituted by means of ethnography, an ethnographic history. It is a series of overlapping slices of life; a somewhat disjunctive rather than smoothly linear or narrative history. Yet it is not like a collection of short stories either.

Because the articles were written for different audiences and occasions and because my knowledge is cumulative, there is some overlap between them, like successive waves on a beach. Originally I thought to preserve the articles as they were, but the need for a tidier narrative won out. I have retained the discrete theoretical frames that index concerns at the time they were written but have pruned some empirical and contextual redundancy and added some continuity between the chapters, as well as removing infelicities and occasionally updating references.[8]

I selected articles that focused on a number of intertwined themes, notably community citizenship, the system of exchange, and the production of life-cycle ceremonies that are prominent in Mayotte. The articles also each addressed historical consciousness, the ways people situated their action with respect to past and future in an ever-moving present.

While I anticipated a relatively quick project, I soon complicated it for myself. First, I realized that I needed to clarify how the slices were connected to each other. Second, I needed to write additional essays (chapters 11, 12, and 13) about circumstances transpiring since the last articles were written. Some changes are quite significant, and they also provide reasons for writing the book at all, and for writing it now. Third, I was uncertain how to begin the book, and eventually I broke my own rule about using only writing contemporaneous with the time written about by drafting three new chapters (2, 3, and 4) concerning the period of my first visit and the history of the community before that visit. The newly written chapters, including the introduction and previously unpublished chapter 10, now make up well over two-thirds of the book.

By presenting the central chapters more or less as they were written, I avoid seeing the past exclusively through the present as it is now. If the ethnographic presents of these chapters are themselves already in the past, so are the presents at which I wrote and some of the theoretical arguments in which I framed them. To the degree that, like any work of history, this book has a presentist slant or bias, at least it is refracted across a few decades. It is composed of "presents past" (cf Koselleck's title, *Futures Past*), hence of presentist "biases past." Rereading the older essays now, I see what is dated most evidently in the somewhat moralistic way I closed a number of them. In any case, I wish to avoid conflating, condensing, and homogenizing "the past" (as though it were a single homogeneous object) and to try to see past, present, and future always transforming from and into one another, as the epigraph from Gadamer suggests.

Ethnographers too are historically located, their lives not simply unfolding in time but entangled in it. In his introduction to a debate on whether "the past is a foreign country," Tim Ingold argues that the ethnographic present "robs the life of ... people of its intrinsic temporality ... For the ethnographer there is life after fieldwork, and for the people too, life goes on" (1996: 149). Speaking for myself (as a "native" to ethnography) I am not so sure there is (full, autonomous) life after fieldwork; ethnographers get caught in the ethnographic present as well and become subject to their experience and their notes. As Ingold himself goes on to say, "As with the dreamlike world of our childhood recollections, where time stood still, the ethnographic present is the projection, onto another place and another people, of our own past" (ibid.). This continues into the ethnographer's future. My first period of fieldwork was the longest and most deeply immersive (well prior to cell phones and the Internet), and it is the period that remains clearest and most distinctive in my mind. Subsequent visits, other than the last, tend to blur into each other, their distinctiveness saved only by the fact that my field notes are dated and that I wrote and published after each visit. But if all this is my accumulated "experience," it is complemented, as Koselleck suggests, by moving horizons of expectation.

One thing the layering of chapters shows is the changing corpus of theorists, models, and concepts that I draw on, providing a kind of undertow to the present theoretical concepts engaged in the work. Some of the references appear only once, relevant at the time I was writing a particular piece, while others continue. This is not the place for intellectual autobiography, but I will say that if Geertz is present throughout, perhaps my understanding of his ideas has deepened over time. In the introduction I link my particular interpretation of Geertz to that of Gadamer.[9]

A change in my life that casts its reflection on later chapters is that, beginning in the early 1990s, I also conducted intensive fieldwork in north and northwest Madagascar. There is considerable cultural and historical connection between these places and Mayotte, and the local dialects of Malagasy are similar to one another. Research in Madagascar, along with the reading of scholars like Rita Astuti, Maurice Bloch,

Gillian Feeley-Harnik, Sarah Gould, Lesley Sharp, and Andrew Walsh, has helped place the ethnographic material in Mayotte in context, assisting me in seeing it from another angle. This is further enhanced by sharing experiences with people from Mayotte and Madagascar who also travel between the two places. What I learned of Sakalava historicity (Lambek 2002c) has shaped how I understand time in Mayotte and has further drawn me to the stream of German thought that affords the best way to translate Malagasy experience and conceptions.

Ethnography is premised on the presence of the ethnographer. This is often and misleadingly phrased as participant observation. It is perhaps better to say that presence implies attention and relation. It is a form of ethical engagement, even if the ethics are somewhat murky insofar as engagement is premised on the ethnographer's ability and, indeed, horizon, of departure, the expectation that they will decamp (Lambek 2012). I found that people engaged me; on my first trip, they instructed me concerning the kind of acknowledgment they expected, and they made it evident that I would be asked to leave if I did not show it. The kinds of relations expected of me were not homogeneous. I became particularly close to a couple, Tumbu Vita and Mohedja Salim (pseudonyms), who took me as their son and communicated with me as intimate equals. In 2005 I joined their biological children in conducting a mortuary ceremony on their behalf (Lambek 2018). This event recognized a mutuality we had not hitherto fully realized, and it transcended what had been an expected reticence between siblings of opposite sex.

On recent trips, I have become somewhat less obsessed with "observing" and readier to acknowledge our life in common. I intervened and became implicated in conflicts among the siblings. I also discovered a feeling of equanimity and solidarity with men my age, reflecting on how we had lived our adult lives in parallel and what each of us had faced or done. Some of these men I have considered friends, others not, but each of us has led distinct lives, shaped by our respective social environments, but also by the contingencies of work, marriage, parenthood, illness, and the ability to exercise our respective capacities. Two of the men I was close to on early visits died young, and I have distinctive relationships with their widows and with their oldest children, who were born when I was in Mayotte and who see me as a link to their fathers. In chapter 12, I give more space to other voices than I have in the rest of the narrative and, correspondingly, have less urge to impose a theoretical framework.

Ethnography is often conducted at a young age, and the immaturity of the ethnographer is rarely taken into account. The aging of the ethnographer approaches its own horizons. My stage in life affects both what I see and how I see it. On my last visit, certain responses on my part were undoubtedly shaped both by the fact that the membrane of difference had thinned and by the habit of speaking my mind that has grown alongside my age and status in the profession and increasing impatience with what I consider stupidity. Of course, that can entail stupidity of one's own.

ISLAND IN THE STREAM

An Ethnographic History of Mayotte

PART ONE

Prelude

The chapters that make up part one are all new to the volume and were composed during the academic year 2016–17. In the first chapter I lay out my theoretical approach and my aims in fashioning the book in the way I have done. I propose a particular way to approach historical experience or historicity, as I call it, and a particular way to combine ethnographic and historical approaches to the life of a community. This is a genre that is possible only after researching a community over a period of several years. Pieces of the introduction first appeared in various talks I have given since 2015 but are reorganized and further developed here.

The title of the book is slightly misleading insofar as this is an ethnographic history not of Mayotte as a whole but of a pair of neighbouring communities within it. The second chapter offers a portrait of the communities as I first encountered them in 1975. Although the chapter was composed in 2016, it draws on field notes taken in 1975–6. With respect to the overall schema of the book it thus represents something of a hybrid: ethnography primarily but not exclusively from 1975–6 and framed in theory I have come to since. The joke made by the old lady has had a long life, holding a stock place in my undergraduate lectures. I don't recall meeting her again, but I remain friends with two of her grandchildren, a brother and sister about my age, who each combine a sharp wit and irreverent sense of humour with an active devotion to Islam. In the chapter I begin to lay out what I mean by citizenship and why the village has been such a significant social unit.

The third chapter reconstructs the founding and history of the communities up to my arrival. The broader historical context is drawn largely from secondary sources, while the events and persons are as I learned about them through conversations with older residents. The exploration was not systematic, and the reconstruction is not comprehensive, but it does depict the structural basis of ownership of village property and the way residence developed, and it provides short portraits of some of the key figures in community life.

1   Introduction: The Presence of History

To exist historically means that knowledge of oneself can never be complete.

Hans-Georg Gadamer,
Truth and Method (1985: 269)

History is one of those words that will defeat anybody who wants to define it
or who wants to say something different about it.

Greg Dening, "Challenges to Perform: History, Passion
and the Imagination" (n.d.)

This book is based on a central conceit – namely, that it is an ethnographic history. This is a relatively uncommon term among anthropologists.[1] What I mean is simply this: the book is history insofar as it follows a community across a period of time, describing what transpired during that time. It is ethnographic insofar as it tells the story by means of successive, relatively holistic and synchronic portraits of the community and successive analyses of aspects of its life as they took place and were written over time. It is present rather than past oriented in that each chapter but one is about a given present and some were first written shortly after that present and partly in that mode of thinking that is called the "ethnographic present." But if each chapter hangs suspended in time, it overlaps with the others, moving forward historically, and today what they all speak about is past. Moreover, each chapter attends to historical consciousness and change, and to expectation and retrospection at the time about which it is written.

The present is evident in an additional sense, since the method in which the facts and impressions were collected has been ethnographic, and in ethnography, unlike mainstream history, that method is based on the presence of the ethnographer. This is a full and lived presence and present, unmediated by archives, shaped by the tempo of the events themselves, as they happen. And yet this book is also history in the sense that it is compiled now, long after many of the events described, and hence my field notes have become my archive. The observations sit there, innumerable, and like any historian or anthropologist, I must submit them to the heavy work and violence of selection and abstraction. Moreover, the history of their collection and analysis has become my history.

The book follows a community, the way the people in it have lived and have understood their historical presence in and passage through the world. The community I call Lombeni is a small place, on a small island, but the way of life and the things that transpire there are significant. They are by no means "typical" of anything; rather, as an account of continuous historical experience in a specific African and Indian Ocean community, this book is unique.

To write a book that characterizes the life of a community is out of fashion in anthropology, but the way I do so is to some degree original. The book departs from the older social structural literature, the many wonderful studies of African communities from the heyday of British social anthropology that have inspired me, in two main ways. First, it is historical in a deep sense. As indicated, it puts a series of synchronically developed pictures, written at different times and in response to different phases of fieldwork and different debates in the discipline, alongside each other to produce a hybrid that is neither pure ethnography nor pure social history but what I call ethnographic history.

Second, while attending to structure, the book approaches social life primarily in terms of activity. Activity, as I develop it, is not quite any of the movements that followed structural-functionalism, neither practice theory nor the addition of agency to structure. Its intellectual sources are threefold: first in Aristotle, insofar as he talks about human activity and develops it as doing (action, practice), making (production, creation), and contemplating (thought, reflection). A second source is a Weberian-inspired Geertzian cultural anthropology in which the meaning, or rather the meaningfulness, of what people do is central, even or especially in the face of aporias or the threat of anomie. Aristotle, as developed in Gadamer, and Weber, as developed in Geertz, come together in emphasizing that it is not only ethnographers or historians who interpret what people do: what ordinary people (our subjects) themselves do is interpret their world and actions. Interpretation is itself activity, and it is activity central to human existence; or rather, it is a dimension of, or manifest in, the three forms (ideal types) of activity I have just called doing, making, and thinking.[2] Acting in the world is a form of interpreting the circumstances, and interpreting the world is a form of action. Third, then, with respect to action itself, my account is inspired by Austin and Rappaport concerning the centrality of performative acts and acts of performance (not quite the same thing) and their consequentiality for social life.

For all these thinkers, there is a profoundly ethical dimension to action and interpretation as people respond in various ways (both tacit and explicit) to the fundamental questions of how to live and what to do in given circumstances. I attempt to bring to light the historicity of ethical life, particularly the ever-moving ways in which people exercise their judgment with respect to present contingencies and future goals and expectations but also draw from and acknowledge past commitments in the face of present change.[3] This could equally be stated the other way around, as the ethical dimension of historical action. This has strong affinities with the approach of Sherry Ortner (1989), who examines how people draw on inherited scenarios for action to make sense of the present and orient their projects within it.

Hence when I speak of history in what follows, it concerns historical consciousness and interpretation no less than objective change, and the reflective, tacit, and deliberate, creative, and agentive ways in which people engage in new commitments and release themselves from older ones, no less than ways in which they are subject to structure and change.

A further departure from pure social structural accounts is attention to the tone and tune of life, its musicality. This is something found in many older works, notably those of Malinowski and Benedict, as well as in new works that centre on experience or affect. What I am after is the pace and feel of life; I picture this in Mayotte harmonically and polyrhythmically, with respect to contrast and counterpoint. As will become evident, musical and dance performances in the literal sense are frequent occurrences in community life in Mayotte, punctuations and intensifications and also a means to temporarily withdraw from egocentricity (Tugendhat 2016). But I apply musicality metaphorically as well – for example, in the counterpoint of conviviality and competition that induces both joy and anxiety.

If Geertz (1973a) famously said that anthropologists could interpret cultural forms like texts along the lines that literary scholars do, he also noted that they "read" over the shoulders of their ethnographic subjects. So we ought to recognize local "readings" or interpretations as enactments and materializations of these forms. Over time, successive "readings" of a given "text" (form, figure, cultural scenario) constitute history of a kind. Such a history would be a history of being (in this case, of being Mahorais). It would also manifest a tradition, meaning by tradition something not static but unfolding, a long conversation composed of successive and diverging interpretations of a common and emerging corpus, much as contemporary thought in the humanities draws from successive readings of ancient tragedy and philosophy that become its own history. Such interpretations are palimpsestuous, piling up and rustling against each other, like the onionskin sheets of my typewritten (pre-laptop) field notes, according to the biological time of the lifespan, the social time of action, and the historical time of generational cohorts.

Viewed synchronically, the layering of successive interpretations according to disparate rhythms produces what German historiography describes as "a conjuncture of heterogeneous dimensions – the *Gleichzeitigkeit der Ungleichzeitigen*, or the contemporaneity of the noncontemporaneous" (Tribe 2004: xvii). This perception – the contemporaneity of the non-contemporaneous – is central to my interpretation of life and history in Mayotte, and it is a phrase that applies precisely to the composition of this book. I will return explicitly to it in later chapters.[4]

Classic ethnography was and is generally written in the present tense, and it is common to speak of the ethnographic present. Yet ethnography is closely akin to history; anthropologists recognize that their work is historical insofar as it is located in time, and insofar as their subjects are historically constituted – subject to time and living in history. The ethnographic present can be criticized for appearing to ignore this and for constituting the subjects of the monograph as timeless. In a way, this is the fate of any monograph. Thus, when anthropologists speak of "the Nuer" it is as likely that they are speaking of Evans-Pritchard's book of that name, or of Nuer life as it was depicted therein, as that they are speaking of Nuer as present-day actors in South Sudan or working in meat-packing plants in western Canada. In this sense, a work of ethnography functions like any other well-known text, as when we speak of *David Copperfield* or *War and Peace*, or, for that matter, of *The*

Republic or *Being and Time*. It is at once its timeless self and the series of influential readings (interpretations) that have followed from it (the contemporaneity of the non-contemporaneous).[5]

The alternative in ethnographic writing to the timeless present is not much better. I cannot speak for other languages, but in English, verb tense is necessary both for the construction of any given sentence and for weaving sentences and paragraphs into a coherent text. In English, the only reasonable alternative to the present tense is the past. Of course, whatever ethnographers describe lies in the past by the time they publish, but writing in the past tense makes it appear as though the people written about and their way of life are dead and gone; they might as well have lived in ancient times as in 1975 or 2015. Hence the past tense appears to dismiss the people we have known and interacted with and, more to the point, it obscures what is continuous in culture and social life. Thus, it appears to deny or obliterate structure. Finally, the past tense obviates what is and has been central to the ethnographic method, namely that our knowledge and insights emerge from our presence as ethnographers. As already noted, the ethnographic *present* is premised on (and an index of) the ethnographer's *presence*.

An additional problem the ethnographic present generates is the perception that things were static and timeless before the ethnographer's arrival and only began to change, and change dramatically, afterwards. *Après moi, le déluge.* This is sometimes redressed by drawing on historical sources – oral and archival – in the first chapter or two to tell the story of life before the ethnographer (as indeed I do in chapter 3). Another way to historicize ethnography is by conducting a restudy. But a restudy hinges on the moment of return, creating a kind of before-and-after scenario premised again precisely on the (re)appearance of the ethnographer.

In sum, the tense in which we write is not simply a matter of style but speaks to matters central to both methodology and theory; it shapes how we think about how the material has been acquired and with what authority and how it is received. It also makes assumptions concerning relations between structure and event, in other terms, between continuity and change.

The book at hand does not claim to solve these problems of linguistic bias. I recognize the point made by Lévi-Strauss (1966) that no pure temporal flow is possible when thinking or writing historically; everything must be structurally framed and parsed. Neither the theoretical nor the methodological tensions between structure and history can be fully resolved, only partially mediated and acknowledged. I do not wish to throw out the structural baby with the ahistorical bathwater. My experiment is to write in a series of successive ethnographic presents.[6] That is, I address the problem of the ethnographic present not by discarding or denying it but by multiplying it. The "present" of each chapter is (indexically) distinct and different from the one before.

I see ethnographic history as primarily neither an event history nor a structural history (the reproduction, transformation, collapse, or emergence of structures) – though both are relevant. It is historical chiefly in the distinctive sense of following life across time rather than merely looking back at it. It is therefore also an attempt to grasp history as it happens, based on an almost day-to-day chronicle, somewhat like the case histories of the Manchester school. However, this book is not constituted by following specific individuals or conflicts. Rather I aim for a history of activity, of ongoing practice, periodically marked by what seemed at the time or in hindsight signs of decisive change, shifts of gear. In the main, this is practice slowly changing as it goes, life caught in the act of its own continual transcendence, as Simmel (2010) might put it. It is best glimpsed at moments when participants catch themselves in the mirror or when they deliberately institute change. Hence, *this ethnographic history is also an ethnography of history*, a community's instantiation, awareness, and understanding of change, with its moral anxiety and its hopefulness, its active, frontal engagement, peripheral contemplation, and retroactive critique, its unique and mobile juxtaposition of experience and expectation (Koselleck 2004) but also recollection. In sum, it is a kind of interpretive chronology of interpretations that inhabitants of Mayotte have made with respect to their lives in the course of living them.[7]

Thus, one way in which this book is an ethnographic history is that I try to portray local historical consciousness, that is, to provide a sense of how people at each of the times about which I write understand themselves in history, how they see the present, what they aim for or expect of the future, and how, in going forward, they articulate their relations with the past. I am interested both in the ways individuals address these matters and in the underlying structures and particular cultural ideas and practices that shape and inform historical consciousness, much as the calendar and the work of professional historians and the news media shape historical consciousness in Europe.

The broad issue here is one of historicity. As Sahlins succinctly puts it, "Different cultures, different historicities" (1985: x). While modes of historicity may differ from a linear or empiricist conception of history (e.g., see Lambek 2002c, Stewart 2012), it is evident that we do not need to make an exclusive choice between (professional) historiography and historicity. Both are indispensable. On the one hand, Western historicism is one form of historicity; on the other (evidence permitting), forms of historicity themselves can be traced according to the linear and empiricist fashion of professional historians. As Matt Hodges concludes, "a study of 'historicity' does not exclude the incorporation of historiographical perspectives" (2015: 11).[8]

In other words, attention to local forms of historicity does not preclude examining how they change or the fluid ways they are drawn upon over time and from generation to generation. One institution found in the western Indian Ocean region that shapes historical consciousness is spirit possession, a cultural practice in which some people are engaged by other beings, notably deceased former rulers or non-human inhabitants of Mayotte, and periodically displaced by them. These beings, translated inadequately as "spirits," speak and act through the bodies of living people, whom I call their mediums or hosts, and sometimes they speak as the past or on behalf of the past.[9] But equally, as will be seen, they address and are addressed by the present. The spirits play a role in chapters 7 through 9 of this book. I also describe the ways in which other institutions, including the system of exchange and celebrations of marriage (discussed in chapters 4, 5, 6, 9, and 11), both shape historical consciousness and themselves have histories.[10]

Horizons

I approach history not by phrasing it as a before-and-after story, let's say, one of tradition in contrast to modernity (terms that are in any case ambiguous and misleading), but rather by means of moving horizons. Horizons point to the fact – and are implicit in the understanding – that the human condition is a historical condition, one in which acting in the present always supposes orientations with respect to past and future. Our horizons describe the extensions of the worlds we inhabit, not only in space but in time and in understanding. They are outer limits but they are not limitations. Horizons are mobile, expanding or retracting in response to social and political circumstances; changing as we move towards or away from them or as they begin to merge with those of new conversation partners. Our respective worlds are not mutually closed off from one another but overlap to the extent that they share an arc or portion of a horizon. In speaking of horizons in this manner, I draw from the thought of Hans-Georg Gadamer (1985).

Gadamer's horizon describes the nature of historical experience and understanding. If the hermeneutic project begins with how we understand people, especially texts and voices from the past, from both within our tradition and beyond it, it necessarily expands to the question of understanding one's own situation and acknowledging the fact that the human situation is a radically historical one.

Gadamer derives the concept of horizon from Husserl but sees it as the historical extension of the Husserlian "life-world," such that, as Georg Simmel put it, "Life at any given moment transcends itself" (Simmel 2010: 8).[11] Simmel speaks of the "protrusion of the past into the present" and the "immediate carryover of present will – and feeling and thought – into the future" (ibid. 7). "Psychic existence projects out beyond its narrow present, so to speak; ... the future is already encompassed within it" (ibid. 8). For Simmel, this is specific to *life*: "Life is truly both past and future; these are not just appended to it by thought, as they are to inorganic, merely punctual reality" (ibid. 8). This is the case for all living beings but amplified in human consciousness. This is not Heraclitic flux but manifest through the individual being, "a bounded form that continually oversteps its bounds ..." Simmel continues: "Insofar as life's essence goes, transcendence is immanent to it (it is not something that might be added to its being, but instead is constitutive of its being)" (ibid. 9). If this applies to the individual being, the point of immanent transcendence applies also to collective (historical) consciousness.

The horizon, says Gadamer, is "the antithesis of all objectivism. It is an essentially historical concept, which does not refer to a universe of being, to an 'existent world' [but rather concerns] the infinite progress of human-historical worlds in historical experience" (1985: 218).

The historical movement of human life consists in the fact that it is never utterly bound to any one standpoint, and hence can never have a truly closed horizon. The horizon is, rather, something into which we move and that moves with us. Horizons change for a person who is moving. Thus the horizon of the past, out of which all human life lives and which exists in the form of tradition, is always in motion. It is not historical consciousness that first sets the surrounding horizon in motion. But in it this motion becomes aware of itself. (Gadamer 1985: 271)

As Jason Throop has recently put it, "time's very unfolding opens outward toward anticipated horizons that are still undetermined" (2010: 272).

A significant feature of Gadamer's account of historical understanding is that it applies not only to the work of historians or ethnographers but more fundamentally to the lived situation of all human beings and the nature of historical existence (albeit within particular forms of life bearing different affordances or means for expressing historical consciousness). The horizon, as Gadamer explains it,

is the range of vision that includes everything that can be seen from a particular vantage point. Applying this to the thinking mind, we speak of narrowness of horizon, of the possible expansion of horizon, of the opening up of new horizons, etc. ... A person who has no horizon is a man who does not see far enough and hence overvalues what is nearest to him. Contrariwise, to have an horizon means not to be limited to what is nearest, but to be able to see beyond it. (1985: 269)

Gadamer continues that historical understanding takes an effort, that "to acquire a horizon means that one learns to look beyond what is close at hand – not in order to look away from it, but to see it better within a larger whole and in truer proportion." I take this to be one mode of attention within ordinary life.[12] One could ask when and in what social contexts it manifests itself.

Gadamer's formulation of horizons elucidates what I can say about the historicity of people in Mayotte and moves my project beyond an account of successive ethnographic presents or slices of structure (as though laid out on laboratory slides), and even of the transformations between them, towards a depiction of history in the happening. This is the moving horizon insofar as it is recognized in Mayotte, within the limits of how that recognition is in turn recognized by me.

I note three further points in Gadamer's argument. First, he observes that the horizon of the present is not fixed but is continually being formed or tested, in part through a fusion with horizons of the past (1985: 273). It is this continuous and moving formation of past, present, and future I seek to grasp in and as my historical account of the community. Second, Gadamer says that interpretation of the past or present happens not in some abstract intellectual realm but practically, by means of application, and not only in law or theology or in the work of the professional historian but in what he calls "reproductive interpretation," in modes like music or theatre, to which I add performances like curing rituals and weddings. He adds that cognitive, normative, and reproductive interpretation are not distinct but "constitute the one phenomenon" (277). Third, Gadamer suggests that historical consciousness or interpretation is not a matter of "'knowledge as domination' [citing Max Scheler], ie an appropriation as a 'taking possession of,' but rather a subordination to the text's claim to dominate our minds" (278). If true in general, this is particularly evident in the performance of spirit possession.

In sum, Gadamer's argument moves from an account of the fusion of horizons that characterizes the work of understanding on the part of the historian or anthropologist to an account of historical existence more broadly. It suggests that if not all change is initiated or received consciously, deliberately, or willingly, it is the case that often change is consciously and judiciously undertaken, received, recognized, acknowledged, or appraised. Put another way, historicity – historical apprehension – is simultaneously and intrinsically *ethically* informed and inflected, concerned with *how to live* and with *living as if it matters*. It is a matter both of finding the world we think we want and of understanding what we owe ourselves, our contemporaries, our predecessors, and our successors as we proceed.

The significance of Gadamer's departure from standard European notions of historicity (as famously depicted in Walter Benjamin's reading of Paul Klee's angel of history looking back at the ruins) can be highlighted by comparison with Reinhardt Koselleck, the leading German historiographer to draw from Gadamer.

Koselleck captures the movement of horizons in his recounting of a political joke (2004: 261). Khrushchev declares that, "Communism is already visible on the horizon." A comrade asks "But what is a horizon?" and is told to look it up in the dictionary. There he learns that "horizon [is] an apparent line separating the sky from the earth, which retreats as one approaches it."

No doubt this is true of any utopia. But I suggest it illustrates that one should distinguish the horizon from the objects on it. The horizon continues to recede, but we may indeed reach some of the objects we have anticipated; and we can then ask how their acquisition changes both experience and ensuing expectation. Koselleck, however, uses the story to argue that in contrast to expectations, which always need to be revised, the experiences one has collected are stable.

Koselleck departs from Gadamer insofar as he wants to restrict the horizon to the open future in contrast to what he considers the fixity of the past. Koselleck defines experience as the "present past, whose events have been incorporated and can be remembered" (2004: 259); this appears to be the sedimentation of discrete experiences rather than something continuous and mobile. He deliberately describes it as a "space" and uses the metaphor of the glass-fronted washing machine "behind which various bits of the wash appear now and then, but all are contained within the drum" (ibid. 260). By contrast, expectation is grasped in the metaphor of the ever-moving horizon. "Cultivated expectations can be revised; experiences one has are collected" (ibid. 261). Koselleck's book is about the history of the future – the ways in which expectations of the future have been revised over time and, more broadly, how the very nature of what can be expected has changed historically in Europe, such changes themselves shaping the way we understand the shift in epoch from the Middle Ages to modernity. In a sense, then, he treats experience as a set of past expectations; "former futures," his translator, Keith Tribe, tells us, was the title originally proposed for the book (Tribe 2004: xi, n13).

As a metaphor, the open horizon stands in sharp contrast to the closed box of the washing machine, and in Gadamer's view it applies as well to the ongoing interpretation of the past, as it also does in Mayotte with respect to an ongoing interpellation *from* the past (see chapter 8).[13] The horizon also stands in contrast to structure, not hidden below ground, as Lévi-Strauss approvingly compared Marx and Freud to geology, but open and visible; not synchronic, stable, and within, but diachronic, shifting, and surrounding (immanent transcendence); not generating or determining but affording, inviting, or enticing (and at times limiting or repelling).

The concept or metaphor of horizon is a happy one insofar as it indicates that we exist within worlds of given quality, substance, and circumstance and that such worlds have limits, but equally that such limits are always in motion. The metaphor suggests that we are always already located, but equally that we are always already in motion; that we have scope, vision, and mobility from and towards frontiers. This is doubly unstable in that as we move towards or away from a horizon, so the horizon itself shifts. This could be frustrating, like heading towards a mirage in the desert or losing one's way in a foreign city; but it could also be exhilarating, rendering life dynamic and adventuresome.

I draw on the concept of horizon in part to avoid having to choose between ethnography and history (or synchrony and diachrony); to catch the present in the act of transcending itself; to evade a simple before-and-after story, with its inevitable moral teleology or metanarrative; to grasp a form of historicity different from the dominant European model; and to finesse oppositions between structure and experience or structure and event.[14] The concept of horizon also places the anthropologist, qua interpreter, on the same footing as the ethnographic subject – within partly different horizons, to be sure, but on the same plane and hence with greater fusion of our respective horizons imminent.

Above all, I want to emphasize temporality. As Gadamer says, "Every experience has implicit horizons of before and after, and finally merges with the continuum of the experiences present in the before and after to form the one flow of experience" (Gadamer 1985: 216). That flow is the stream of this book's title. Moreover, "A horizon is not a rigid frontier, but something that moves with one, and invites one to advance further" (ibid. 217).

If hermeneutics understands people engaged in actively interpreting their worlds, this is not an idealist position insofar as interpretations are understood as acts, hence as consequential.[15] Each interpretive act provides the ground, conditions, or context for subsequent interpretive acts, ones that may be consistent or in conflict with those that preceded. Moreover, such acts are available to the professional historian or ethnographer (Ricoeur 1971).

Georgia Warnke summarizes what Gadamer takes as the hermeneutic situation and what I describe as interpretation qua action:

For Gadamer, following Heidegger, the hermeneutic situation signals the way in which as human beings, we are "thrown" into a history or set of stories that we did not start and cannot finish, but which we must continue in one way or another. We must always act in one way or another, because not acting or acting to end the necessity of continuing to act is itself a form of action. Yet, in order to determine how to act, we must also understand ourselves and the set of stories in which we find ourselves. If we have to act, we have to understand, in some better or worse way, who and where we are and who and where we want to be. From the beginning then, we are involved in the practical task of deciphering the story or stories of which we are a part so that we know how to go on.

The actions we take also react back upon our action-orienting understanding. They become part of what we understand when we understand
our past and ourselves as well as part of how we anticipate our future.
Hence, not only are we always deciphering the story or stories of which
we are a part so that we know how to go on, but also we are always already in the process of going on. To this extent, our understanding ... is
an understanding from the middle of an ongoing narrative. (2002: 79–80)

This is history as the rolling along of the hermeneutic circle of part
and whole, individual act and comprehensive narrative. It rolls over
"rough ground" (to shamelessly mix philosophical metaphors) and occasionally is halted at a rocky patch, suffers a puncture, or falls over
(stories collapse). This is also history understood as (a product of) practical reason rather than theoretical reason (Warnke 2002: 82). In other
words, interpretation takes place through practical application and the
temporality of action. The hermeneutic circle, traditionally understood
as a description of the interpretation of fixed texts by means of the
movement between part and whole, is also and intrinsically temporal
and historical, each successive interpretation part of a rolling, spiral-
ling, or wavelike sequence of interpretive acts and the reformulations
of the texts they manifest. Conversely, "history," in the sense of historical activity, is intrinsically hermeneutical. Texts and stories are not
fixed but continued in the course of their interpretation. As I noted
with respect to Geertz, the interpretation of cultural texts in practice by
those to whom they pertain is the way culture moves along.

Gadamerian hermeneutics is sometimes criticized for being at once conservative and overly optimistic about reaching understanding. Thus,
where Gadamer focuses on the achievement of understanding texts
and traditions, Derrida attends to the ways misunderstanding looms.
As Richard Bernstein, whose argument I follow here, writes, Derrida

seeks to expose the irreducible undecidable internal tensions and apo-
ria. His logic is a "both/and logic" where we uncover heterogeneities
for which there is no satisfactory fusion. Like Hegel (whom Derrida also
greatly admires), Derrida is a master in bringing forth internal conflicts
and contradictions, and in showing how at the heart of what we take to
be the same is already otherness and difference. But unlike Hegel (and
Gadamer), Derrida is skeptical that we can reconcile these contradictions
in an encompassing synthesis. Derrida's "world" is one in which we

never quite achieve the moment of coherence and fusion that is the aim of hermeneutics. (Bernstein 2002: 277)

For Derrida, "undecidability is the very condition for the possibility (and impossibility) of deciding and acting. A decision is not an *ethical* decision if it can be calculated, programmed, or "deduced" from some universal rule. Ethical decision is a possibility that is sustained by its impossibility. Or to make the point in a less paradoxical manner, an ethical decision requires confronting its irreducible undecidability" (Bernstein 2002: 279–80). By contrast, Gadamer draws on Aristotelian virtue ethics and argues that interpretation and ethical (practical) judgment are interdependent and perhaps not fully distinguishable from one another.

Bernstein suggests that Gadamer and Derrida are similar insofar as both reject technological or instrumental thinking, as well as the idea that one could "'deduce' specific decisions from universal principles alone" (2002: 280). Moreover, each can be a corrective to the other (278). "Derrida does not do 'justice' to the type of practical judgment that Gadamer highlights. At the same time, Derrida makes us painfully aware of something that Gadamer does not sufficiently emphasize – that even in practical judgment at its best, there is an element of irreducible risk and undecidability" (280).[16] Bernstein concludes, "In the fusion of horizons, there is a tendency to gloss over the heterogeneities and abysses that confront us. But there is also a danger of becoming so fascinated with impossibilities and undecidables that we lose any sense of coherence and unity in our lives" (281).

What I ask of my account is that it should be neither overly optimistic nor overly sceptical but take into consideration the way people in Mayotte have continued to seek historical understanding and exercise practical judgment in the face of risk and undecidability.

A further challenge concerns the depiction of the historical subject. Gadamer can be criticized for ignoring the respective power or authority of diverse interpreters. Without ignoring power, I do not focus on it insofar as the communities whose history I recount were not internally divided by overt differences of class or ridden with conflicts of interpretation. I do address such conflicts when they arise and situate specific subjects with respect to gender, age, and other relevant social criteria.

That said, I do not want to homogenize the historical subject or sharply distinguish it from other subjects either. Here is where a distinction between ethnographic history as I practice it and the well-recognized genre or discipline of ethnohistory is relevant. "Ethnohistory" is a term that encompasses both objectified, arm's-length historical accounts of specific "ethnic groups" that lacked their own practice of written historical documentation *and* accounts of the histories of such groups as they themselves explicitly constitute them. A danger here concerns the hypostatization of an "ethnos" (or a nation) "striving to realize itself."

If, as Nietzsche says, "Only that which has no history is definable" (*Genealogy of Morality* LL.13, 1887), then to acknowledge history is to relinquish attempts at defining a stable historical subject. Nietzsche distinguishes history conducted as pedigree and as genealogy. As Raymond Geuss elaborates, pedigree starts from a singular origin and traces through an unbroken line of succession (1999: 2–3), thereby constructing (and assuming) a coherent singular subject. Genealogy works backwards to multiple distinctive sources rather than forward from a single origin, since for Nietzsche, the historical subject (any historical subject) is a contingent synthesis of multiple elements, acts, and struggles over interpretation (Geuss 1999: 12–13). Geuss describes Nietzsche's history of Christianity as depicting successive attempts "to take control of and reinterpret a complex of habits, feelings, ways of perceiving and acting, thereby imposing on this complex a 'meaning'" (ibid. 12). Each reinterpretation is a struggle between imposing and resisting new meanings. "Christianity at any given point in time will be a 'synthesis' of the various 'meanings' imposed on it in the past and which have succeeded in remaining embedded … There will be nothing necessary or even particularly 'coherent' about such a 'synthesis.'" (ibid. 13).

I want to evade the hypostatization inherent to the pedigree and perhaps to ethnohistory. Nevertheless, I cannot write strictly in the genealogy mode either. People do not lead their lives or conceive of their history as though it were genealogy in Nietzsche's sense; the subjects of my ethnography have lived their lives forward and so have I. I propose something in between that works forward from a known, if arbitrary, beginning (the founding of a village) to the present but understands the subject as open and as contingent on the struggles over interpretation in which it engages. Through their recursive interpretations people do seek to find, and sometimes to make, cohesion and to establish reasonably stable definitions of themselves, their actions, and their communities, even in the face of knowledge that such attempts are, in the longer run, illusory. This claim to relatively continuous identity in the face of change is precisely what is offered through the performances of life-cycle and public events to which the following chapters attend.

Situating Mayotte

Mayotte is an island of some 375 square kilometres in the Comoros, an archipelago of four inhabited islands of the western Indian Ocean, between northern Mozambique and Madagascar (see *figure 1.1*). In 1975 I was *en route* from North America to Madagascar for doctoral fieldwork when the Malagasy president was assassinated and North Americans were abruptly made unwelcome there. Mayotte became an alternative destination, since about a third of the population were Malagasy speakers, with historical connections to Madagascar, yet the Comoros were under French rather than Malagasy dominion.

In fact, the Comoros were just moving towards independence. This was not without controversy. In the lead-up to independence, the Mahorais, as the inhabitants of Mayotte are called, were concerned about their weaker position vis-à-vis inhabitants of the other islands in the archipelago, notably Ngazidja and Nzwani, both of which were more stratified and more densely populated, and which benefited from a more educated elite who dominated in the late colonial administration. When referenda for independence from France were held in 1974 and again in 1976, the majority across the four islands in the archipelago were in favour of independence; counted island by island, the majority in Mayotte rejected it (see chapter 7).

By playing to French interests and esteem, the anti-independence movement convinced the French government to accept their decision for Mayotte. After 1976 the French responded with slow but incremental development of infrastructure, linked to enhanced forms of regulation and surveillance through both overt means and subtler disciplinary ones. Roads were built to make penetration of the communities easier, and new forms of housing were imposed. A market was established in Mamoudzou, imports increased, and European shops and wholesalers began to develop beyond the handful of enterprises run by South Asians. Investment in education preceded that in health, though some sanitary measures were taken. The elaboration of the formal sector was eventually accompanied by an infusion of social services and a big new hospital.

Mayotte moved in stages to full integration with France, until in 2011 the transition from a sleepy and neglected colonial backwater to a full *département* of the French state was officially completed. Mamoudzou and its surrounds grew into a bustling urban centre, with a population now more than double that of the entire island in 1975. The population of

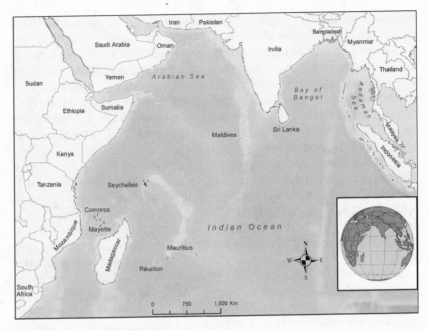

Figure 1.1 Map of the western Indian Ocean.
Source: Adapted from *Reefs at Risk Revisited*, 2011, World Resources Institute,
http://www.wri.org/resources/maps/reefs-risk-indian-ocean.

Mayotte itself has grown steadily, from 32,000 in 1966, to 48,000 in 1978, 86,000 in 1990, until in January 2017 it reached approximately 250,000 (United Nations Department of Economic and Social Affairs 2017). Despite a demographic transition among Mahorais women, for reasons of age distribution, immigration, and high birth rates among migrant women the population will continue to grow. Population density has reached 669 per square kilometre, six times that of 1975. Unemployment has risen significantly, and the urban strip is characterized by high rates of crime and drug use; these are less prevalent in rural areas and not directly a subject of the book.

Insofar as this is a history of Mayotte, it is very different from the way most historians would write it. I make no mention of the prefects who governed the island. I say nothing about how the politics of the French presence in Mayotte played out in Paris or Moroni (capital of the Comoros) or at the Organization of African Unity, and I do not indulge in speculations as to why the French stayed or describe in any specificity the investments they made or the value invested and extracted. There could be a book to write about the history of the French colonial imagination as it has applied to Mayotte, but that is not mine. Nor is this a book about key local players in the struggle for departmentalization or in instituting change.[17] Instead it concerns the history of the social and historical imagination of the inhabitants of two adjacent villages, concerning their own lives. It addresses how the lives of the villagers have played out within the broader horizon of expectation. It is "multi-sited" with respect to time rather than place.[18]

From an underfunded and neglected colony, in which the villages I first encountered had no running water or electricity, no French schooling, and grossly inadequate health care, there is now access to all these things, plus paved roads, passports, and regular travel to the metropole. Today – note my use of an ethnographic present – many villagers have indoor plumbing, washing machines, private cars, and laptops. Their occupation has shifted from a subsistence economy supplemented by cash cropping to one in which they have become either wage-earning commuters or recipients of social assistance, and in which they migrate temporarily to distant places inside France and receive "informal" migrants from neighbouring islands outside the European Union (EU).

As an article in *Le Monde* in 2011 states, "More than half the population is under 20. Mobile phones, satellite TV, air conditioning and traffic jams are increasingly commonplace. 'Between me and my daughter, a whole century has passed,' says Soulaïmana Noussoura, head of the local branch of the CGC trade union, noting that the gains have not been evenly spread. 'Inequality is more striking. Through contact with the outside world, we've found out we're poor,' she says."[19]

Needless to say, this has been an unusual "postcolonial" trajectory and an experiment in North/South relations with mixed effects. Many goals envisioned in 1975 have come to pass, albeit with paradoxical consequences. The questions I inevitably ask include what sorts of changes in social relations, village institutions, and practices accompany them – and what people make of what has happened, of the historical temporality ("a whole century has passed"), and the new opportunities and challenges they face.

Life on the other Comoro islands has taken a different path. In 1975 the Comoran government refused to accept the break up of the archipelago and declared France's continued presence in Mayotte illegal. France retaliated by abruptly withdrawing financial support. The Comoros subsequently experienced a series of coups, beginning with the Maoist-inclined Ali Soilih. Ali Soilih became notorious in the French press for shooting dogs – animals that had been abandoned by their French owners abruptly leaving their colonial posts. Dirty and dangerous for Muslims, and often fed more protein per day than most Comoran children, the dogs and their fate offered a complex symbol of the arrogance of colonialism and the shamelessness of its rapid termination. More significantly for Comorans, Ali Soilih attempted to dismantle social hierarchy and hence the complex institution in Ngazidja known as the *grand mariage*. It survived and has thrived despite decades of political and economic turmoil.[20] Moreover, as I describe in chapter 11, a transformation of the *grand mariage*, the *manzaraka*, has recently become fashionable in Mayotte. Ali Soilih was assassinated in a conquest of the Comoros by the rogue French soldier Bob Denard and his band of mercenaries, who imposed rule characterized subsequently by an unsavoury alliance with apartheid South Africa that used the Comoros as a weapons depot in the Mozambique war.

As residents of Mayotte gained French and EU citizenship and were gradually reaping social benefits and a vastly improved educational and medical system, almost on par with the metropole, the inhabitants of the other islands were increasingly impoverished and frustrated, yet culturally and socially relatively autonomous. Wanting what they perceive as a better life, in recent years many have taken the dangerous night-time passage to Mayotte, some seventy kilometres by boat from Nzwani.[21] Migrants come from Madagascar and coastal East Africa as well.

Many of the current immigrants are related by means of kinship to citizens or are busy recovering or creating such links through marriage and reproduction. Inter-island mobility was common in the past, and when the first post-independence migrants arrived they were often able to renew relationships with citizens. Villagers were hospitable and offered them informal jobs, but inevitably below the official market rate, thereby exploiting their labour to build new houses or look after their cattle, often while they themselves were temporarily away in La Réunion collecting the higher social benefits that were available there (see chapter 10). Despite a French law forbidding polygyny, many male citizens of Mayotte take immigrant women as second or third wives, recognized by Islam. Once children are born and registered in Mayotte they have *droit du sol*, residency and access to schooling and eventual citizenship, and their mothers do as well. Hence while many migrants are routinely shipped back to the Comoros, others are *en route* to citizenship. Collective identities are in flux, and the lines between who is and who is not Mahorais are difficult to draw.

As noted, population density is extremely high, and the presence of vast numbers of migrants – seeking livelihood, kin, marriage, papers, social benefits, and perhaps ultimately sojourn in continental Europe – has become perhaps the most troubling social fact, shadowing or overshadowing full encapsulation within the French state, the penetration of its laws and mores, and the influx of privileged teachers, doctors, bureaucrats, tourists, and entrepreneurs from the metropole. Interestingly, some of the metropolitans themselves have origins in former French colonies and may be Muslim or dark-skinned.

In sum, as Mahorais became mobile French and EU citizens, Mayotte itself became a southern gateway to fortress Europe, overflowing with people who are unrecognized by the state. An irony is that the current influx forms a counterpoint to the 1840s when, immediately after the French takeover of Mayotte, migration went the other way as inhabitants fled the French. But the greater irony is that if the Mahorais initially voted to stay with France out of fear of being inundated by people from the other islands, that is exactly what has transpired. However, the imagined hierarchy has reversed; it is a stratified system in which Mahorais have full rights and access to resources and migrants do not.

My aim in this book is to give neither a straightforward chronicle of events nor a political economy of transformation. Nor is it about the present contradictions and evident colonial features of this ostensibly European society. Rather, I try to grasp history as it has been lived and understood. As explained, I do so by setting out tranches of life observed and written about at different moments during a forty-year period. Each slice taken by itself is a kind of synchronic analysis in a seemingly motionless ethnographic present, yet each also speaks to change; at each period people are thinking historically, exercising judgment, and oriented to horizons of past and future. Together the slices add up to an ethnographic history. In the form of this book, it is a history ultimately orchestrated and interpreted by me, but one composed, performed, and enacted by the people I write about, albeit, to paraphrase Marx, not always with the staging or instruments of their own choosing.

As chapter 3 will show, the villages were formed within broad historical processes outside the inhabitants' control – mercantilism, the slave trade, colonialism, and plantations and their decline. And yet, as indicated in chapter 2 and elsewhere, the villages had a kind of relative autonomy; formed by migrants who chose to live there and who organized their internal affairs and participated in a political movement to transform their external affairs. Hence the account focuses on positive social activity and imagination, on a way of life, a form of sociality as it unfolds through time. To place a value judgment on it ("progress," "entrapment," etc.) is not my intention. What I want to show is how life was and is lived, richly and in the round, and how change has been undertaken and understood as central to the course of living it.

The chapters are produced by discontinuities, and in a double sense. First, in respect to their content, they offer a somewhat arbitrary selection of practices, events, and years. And second, they were written discontinuously. Written "ethnographically," they become "historical" by being placed in chronological sequence, according to the period each is about, the order in which each was composed, and the fact that their composition precedes your reception. "History," says Lévi-Strauss, "is a discontinuous set" (1966: 259) and "the facts are no more given than any other. It is the historian, or the agent of history, who constitutes them by abstraction and as though under the threat of an infinite regress" (ibid. 257).

Any consideration of temporality might turn for inspiration to music, considering its tempo and rhythm, its play of theme and variations, its insistence and beauty. In imagination, I liken the historical horizon to Wagner's prelude to *Tristan und Isolde*, a ship moving steadily forward, a horizon in which sea and sky blend into one another, the waves of music washing over each other, each taking the craft a little farther. Rather than being fully linear, the chapters here wash over each other as well.

Historical experience is not necessarily configured only within a linear, syntagmatic, melodic mode but is also simultaneous, paradigmatic, harmonic, repeated, and alternating. Historicity comprehends not only linear, unidirectional time but what Lévi-Strauss called reversible time, which includes the transformations among a set of myths or the complex sequences of social reciprocation, in conjunction with the irreversible events of reproduction and death. Together, human practices produce characteristic tempi of life, with rhythms and melodies that may be perceived as distinctive, sequential, or overlaid together disharmonically. To recognize this rhythm, sonority, dissonance, and disruption is also what an ethnographic history proposes. So, in fact, the chapters can be read in any order and chapter 3 describes events prior to those of chapter 2. The "ethnographic present" differs from chapter to chapter.

Historicity includes times of creation, beginning, and pause, set outside regular structure, practice, or time, in ritual acts that impose digital distinctions on analogic process (Rappaport 1999) and in the moments or intervals described by Victor Turner (1969) and Bruce Kapferer (2005) as liminal or transcendent. If metaphorically comparable to music, intervals often contain and are shaped by actual musical performance. In Mayotte, ordinary sociality is punctuated frequently by musical interludes, successive performances (interpretations) of classic compositions. The interludes could be called liminal, but this is liminality that is less outside of time per se than set in musical time. Prayer is like this as well; indeed, in Mayotte prayer and music overlap extensively.

In sum, if history as told is, or must be, a form of narrative, history as lived, life as it goes on, might be equally conceived in terms of music. It slows down or speeds up, has rhythm and repetition, rises to climaxes, swells, and calms. Above all, there is an improvisational quality like that of jazz. As lyrics are part of some musical compositions, so historical narrative forms one element of historicity, but only one. If music can be appreciated as more or less beautiful, unlike narrative it has no impulse to reach an ending or provide a moral. One way to think of this book is an attempt to capture the music, the "dance to the music of time" in Mayotte, the recomposition of life as lived by a series of overlapping historical cohorts over a forty-year period of great outward change.[22]

2 Village Life: Kinship, Community, and Islam, 1975 and After

I conducted fieldwork in a pair of villages, and this book is an ethnographic history of those villages. On one side, the villages offer a trajectory along which the large history of Mayotte can be examined. On the other side, they offer a lens for understanding local practices, ideas, and constructs whose particularity contributes to discussion of broader principles and questions of human sociality and historicity, comparatively and generally.

The communities I selected had a single name on the map and in the eyes of the French administration, but I eventually discovered that they were distinct to their inhabitants, each with its own history. They were adjacent to one another and in some respects identified themselves as a common place. But at times they engaged as separate units in reciprocity with one another or with other communities. I refer to them by pseudonyms as Lombeni Be and Lombeni Kely, Big and Small Lombeni, because of their relative size (*figure 2.1*).[1]

On my first arrival, at the beach of Lombeni Be ("Big Lombeni"), on 21 May 1975, I asked to speak to the chief. A young man led me up the hill. We eventually reached the end of the houses, but he kept going up the path, crossed a ridge, and descended over a stream and up the opposite hill to another cluster of houses. This was Lombeni Kely ("Small Lombeni"), where Tumbu Vita, the chief at the time, happened to live. The two villages rotated the office of chief between them, selecting able middle-aged men. The office had largely external reference; it brought little internal status, authority, or power. In truth, the government itself expected little of the village chiefs either. From the villagers' point of view, the main role was to deflect as much as possible the eyes of the colonial government. For example, if the police came looking for a

Figure 2.1 Lombeni, 1975. In 1975 houses were constructed with raffia palms (on the left) or by wattle and daub. A compound fence is visible on the right. Public areas were carefully weeded, a practice that removed vermin but encouraged erosion. A woman brings water from the tank at the upper end of the village, and a boy plays with a hoop and stick, as one might in France. Smoke rises from a cooking fire. The logs in the background are for seating; the fronds in the foreground are drying in preparation for basket weaving.

villager it was the responsibility of the *chef de village* to say that he had not seen the person in question, that the person either didn't live there or hadn't been around for some time. As I will show in chapters 3 and 4, the village had its own internal authority figures.

Tumbu was expected to deal with me. When I asked permission to return and live in Lombeni he acquiesced, thinking both that he had little choice and that my return was unlikely. His wife Mohedja Salim silently fed me a delicious meal of freshly cooked field rice topped with sesame seeds, and they sent me on my way. On my return, I inevitably moved into Lombeni Kely, where they resided. Tumbu and Mohedja were hospitable; they were the kind of people who often incorporated others into their family. And, unbeknown to me, they had consulted diviners and the spirits who possessed each of them. Reassured, they assumed responsibility both for my welfare and for the consequences of my as-yet-unknown actions. I rented a small wattle-and-daub house where one of Tumbu's brothers stored his vanilla, and I began to eat my meals with Tumbu and Mohedja.

Tumbu and Mohedja took a significant risk. What they did not tell me until years later was that most villagers (from both communities) were originally opposed to my residence and threatened to hold Tumbu responsible for any negative consequences. I was suspected of planning to appropriate land or women, and some feared me as a "liver thief," a foreign sorcerer who killed at night. My next-door neighbour, Tumbu's irascible mother, was more afraid of me than I of her and confessed to not sleeping. Some of the young children ran screaming when they saw me (while others were among the first to accept me).

Tumbu eventually told me I had been lucky no infant had died shortly after my arrival. But I was lucky in a much deeper way. Tumbu and Mohedja were simply amazing people. Not only were they highly intelligent, kind, reflective, serious, and sensitive, but they were patient with my stumbling Kibushy and, unlike most of their neighbours, never laughed at me or lied to me – absolutely the best people I could have landed with. I have written about their curing activities elsewhere, and this book is not primarily about them. If they appear in what follows it is both because I discussed almost everything with them and because it seems easier on readers to limit the number of personal names and to identify only a few people. In fact, I had a large number of interlocutors, and I went out every day to talk informally with people. Indeed, other residents of Lombeni Kely became quite miffed that I spent so much time in Lombeni Be.

Works and Principals

In an examination of how people lived together in the countryside of Mayotte in 1975, three broad structural fields become evident, ones that I call kinship, community, and Islam. In this chapter I focus primarily on kinship, but as I will show throughout the book, they are each abstractions from the larger whole that constitutes society or sociality in Mayotte. Kinship, community, and Islam articulate with one another such that in practice and in experience they are indissociable, each forming a dimension or necessary aspect of the others. This is particularly evident when I shift from structure to practice and explore the ways in which persons and relations are initiated, renewed, reproduced, and transformed through deliberate acts. These acts, of which the most explicit and elaborate are performed in ceremonies, are the subject of many of the chapters that follow. The acts and ceremonies have histories, shaped by changing ideas and practices as well as by material and political constraints and opportunities.

In both villages, it seemed as though ceremonies were being conducted almost continuously. People were either planning them, working to produce them, enjoying them, recovering from them, or travelling to other communities for similar events. It is a commonplace of anthropology to say that life in smaller-scale societies is constituted through kinship. Kinship is salient, but the ceremonies have a civic dimension that transcends kinship, whether understood as a relatively private phenomenon of domestic relations or as public and political (Fortes 1969). This was especially evident – and richly elaborated – in the communal organization and enactment of life-cycle ceremonies – especially circumcisions (exclusively male), weddings, funerals, and remembrances of the dead. These were also simultaneously Muslim rituals. Hence, a striking characteristic of life in Mayotte, and a major theme of this book, is the manner in which Muslim practice, kinship, and citizenship – by which I mean active and formal participation in community life, with attendant rights and responsibilities – were mutually embedded in one another and how their articulations have changed, and been understood to change, over time.

Each village regulated its ceremonial order autonomously but always with an eye to what other villages were doing. Ceremonies were and are salient in people's lives. In this book, I am less interested in their formal properties qua ritual than in their outward forms qua celebrations, their social production and entailments, and their qualities of festivity and reflexivity. For example, the central transformative act in which one goes from being single to being married occurs as a performative utterance under certain conditions. But what interests me here is all the things that happen around this act – the manner of announcing and celebrating marriage in the conduct of what translates loosely as "weddings."[2] As Rappaport has argued (1999), the liturgical core, the fundamental means of contract or sanctification, changes more slowly than what it sanctifies. The relation bears some resemblance in this respect to that between deep and surface structure. Viewed over the forty-year period, it is the outer parts that change more than the inner ones and hence that serve as indices of other circumstances.

Ceremonial events are locally understood as the carrying out of *work*, and they are known individually as *works* (*asa*). They are also understood as forms of play or entertainment (*soma*). From both the organization of work and the expressiveness of play much can be learned about the relations they draw and reflect upon, produce, reproduce, and simply mark. In one respect the works are texts in the sense that Geertz described cultural performances (1973a). Like Geertz, I consider that the interpretation of culture that I do as an anthropologist must comprehend the interpretations of culture that individuals and communities themselves perform through the selective enactment of the elements that make up the repertoire available to them (Lambek 2014a). I understand these interpretations less as bounded, fixed, or static texts than as live acts or performances. "Interpretation" here is comparable to that of the musician who *interprets* a score each time she plays it or the actor who interprets a role. So, while in one sense the interpretations that a culture produces of itself and its situation are found in the scripts or symbols of a ceremony, in another, more dynamic sense, they are found in the performances themselves. Each performance is an interpretation of a given script or scenario. Interpretations change over time and may lead to changes in the script itself. Culture as lived and as it continues in time may be conceived as the ongoing enacted interpretations of itself.

Over time I have come to understand that the critical units of analysis are not rules but acts, and that the ethical dimension of life, and of engaged citizenship, is as critical as the jural, the material, or the political – although these are all abstractions and need not appear as discrete forms or domains in actual life. Acts are intrinsically ethical insofar as they demand judgment and the application of criteria, in the first instance whether or not to carry them out, and also how, under what circumstances, with or in respect to whom, and so forth. They can always be left undone or done otherwise. They are intrinsically ethical in a second, related sense insofar as they are products of attention and care. Ethics in these senses is ordinary and it consists in the first instance of following through on what people care about, with respect to themselves and to others. It is not in the first instance a matter of objectified rules or abstractions like "freedom" or "justice" (Das 2015, Lambek 2015a, 2015b; cf Laugier 2015).

My understanding of the ethical cannot be readily separated from the practices I observed in Mayotte or my reflections on them. Thus, for example, it is significant that the word *tompin* means "owner," not just in the sense of owner of property, but owner (sponsor, initiator) of an act. *Tompin* in one sense distinguishes members of the community with greater rights from those with lesser rights, but in another sense, it refers to the responsible agent or sponsor of an *asa*. Here it is akin to what Erving Goffman (1981) refers to as a "principal," "someone whose position is established by the words that are spoken, someone whose beliefs have been told, someone who is committed to what the words say" (1981: 144). Hence in response to the question "Who did that?" the response might be "*za' tompin*," "I myself" – that is, "I am responsible." In everyday life, ethical responsibility for one's acts subsists in some tension with politico-jural considerations of ownership; but in the end the former trumps the latter as community members publicly enact their ceremonies of reproduction, reciprocation, prayer, and care.

In order to understand and contextualize these acts it is easiest to begin by abstracting the domains of kinship and community and the principles that underlie them.

Kinship as Sociality

From my first full day in Lombeni Kely (7 June 1975) I observed how civil people were and the importance of small acts like greeting one another or going daily to each other's homes to inquire about the well-being of the inhabitants, especially grown children greeting their parents. People also visited the sick. After my first few days in Lombeni Kely, Mohedja used this as justification to take me through Lombeni Be where I was not sure how to introduce myself and where she was not sure whether I would be welcome. We crossed the stream and climbed the short hill. On the crest, there was a view of the sea; at night you could see the glowing lamps of the fishing canoes in the lagoon and during the day the white line of the distant reef. In the daytime young men gathered there to relax and cut each other's hair.

That morning Mohedja and I moved in a zigzag path down through Lombeni Be. We stopped by various homes of her kin and then, on a very steep bit of exposed hillside, at a small mud house to greet an old woman who had broken her hip. We entered the single dark room where the woman lay on a narrow bed, surrounded by daughters and granddaughters. At the time, young women received nice two-room houses made of wattle and daub or raffia palm on marriage, often displacing themselves when their own daughters married, and moving to smaller or more decrepit huts when very old and widowed. People lived as married couples, but a compound often included the dwelling of an elderly person. Indeed, adjacent to Mohedja were rooms inhabited by her elderly mother and her mother's older, childless sister. Mohedja and Tumbu themselves had moved into her mother's small house to leave their house to a married daughter whose own dwelling was incomplete.

I had yet to enter one of the smallest houses (though my own was not much bigger). I knew virtually no Kibushy, and as we ducked through the doorway I was somewhat abashed to be intruding on an intimate and presumably abject scene. Mohedja greeted the old lady, and the younger women pushed me forward. The old woman looked me in the eye and pointed first to me and then to herself. Raising her skinny arms above her so that her bangles rested on her elbows and placing one thumb and forefinger together in a circle she thrust the index figure of the other hand vigorously in and out. Everyone burst into peals of laughter before I grasped what she was saying.

This was my introduction to a significant mode of sociality and a dimension of kinship anthropologists call joking relations. In Mayotte, they are significant between people of every second generation. By her gesture, the old lady put our relationship under description, indicating that it was one of grandmother to grandson and incidentally implying that her actual granddaughters might be appropriate marital partners for me; that I might become an in-law. In enacting the relationship, she established who we were as persons to each other. Her act also illustrated the saliency of sexuality for personhood in general and for configuring cross-sex relations in particular. It was also a piece of self-mockery concerning her age and incapacitated condition; if the infirm can't laugh at themselves they become victims of others' laughter. Fundamentally, the joking acknowledges the non-linear, looping, or alternating quality of social life as the generations replace each other, grandchildren being in some sense the renewal, reappearance, and replacement of their same-sex grandparents.[3]

The playful banter in which grandparents addressed young grandchildren as their fiancés or sweethearts and proposed or assumed marriage with them was common, but as I gradually became aware, not everyone drew on it to the same degree. Sexual joking was particularly characteristic of this family. I recall the old woman's son-in-law, a man of about sixty then, whom I came to like very much, depositing himself with a happy grin on top of his granddaughter as she lay on her marriage bed. Some older women also did this with grooms. The joking could get a bit aggressive. Men sometimes reached for the breasts of young girls, to which the girl would retort with a remark about the man's old age and unattractiveness.

Joking was ubiquitous and sexual remarks common, but only in certain kinds of relations and within certain limits, as I discovered whenever my retorts and eventually my overtures misfired. In particular, relations between siblings of opposite sex were expected to be devoid of any sexual connotations, and a grown brother and sister should not even be alone in a room together. For the first year or so I mistakenly considered Tumbu and Mohedja's grown daughters as either dull or standoffish, as my sisters appeared to me, whereas a surprising and happy consequence of the friendships I developed with men of my age was the very easygoing relations that developed with their wives, understood as my sisters-in-law.

Civility is thus made up not simply of respectful courtesy but of joking and teasing as well as direct and intimate conversations, each correctly distributed. When people encountered one another on the path they would inquire about each other's well-being and the well-being of their spouses and perhaps their children or elderly parents. They would then ask "What's new?" or "What's up?" People might respond "Nothing new," or they might say that things were "*moramora ndraiky maréré*," that life was "both slow and easy *and* fast and intense," a phrase I have often found to fit my own experience. People also asked each other direct questions like, "Where are you going?" or "Where are you coming from?" These questions invited elaborate responses, but it was always possible to reply with the circumlocution, "I'm just going for a stroll" (*mitsangatsangana*) or "wandering about" (*miriuriu*). In semi-public places like the backs of the pickup trucks that served as *taxi-brousses*, people could talk raucously or intimately with strangers. Silence was not a generally approved mode of interaction, though there were plenty of topics and occasions for which discretion was valued. People who were *tsantsaña*, lively and extroverted, were appreciated, while those described as *miavung*, introverted, withdrawn, or sullen, were not. To get ahead in life and be appreciated you had to be a good talker and quick with repartee. This held equally for women as for men and across gender lines as within them.

Joking expressed and signified the quality of specific kinds of relations as indexed by pairs of kinship terms like "grandmother" and
"grandson," "mother's brother" and "sister's son," and "brother-in-
law" and "sister-in-law." Other relationships emphasized solidarity,
respect, care, and restraint. Everyone applied the range of kin terms
to, hence predicated relationships with, all others in their community
and network, and the predications could be extended to strangers, as
the old woman did with me. Because people were often genealogically related to one other in multiple ways, there was some flexibility
in how the terms were applied in any given context. This flexibility,
even playfulness, was expanded by the fact that in many situations one
could address someone deliberately by a term that did not in fact apply
genealogically.

The multiple ways in which solidarity could be expressed were increased and elaborated by spirit possession. When spirits are present
they develop specific relations with their human hosts and the hosts'
close kin as well as having some kinship connections with one another. Thus, a man might refer to a male spirit inhabiting his wife as his
brother-in-law, and a client who had a relationship of dependency with
a spirit who rose in one medium would in principle maintain or renew
the relationship when the same spirit rose in a different medium. The
relationships between two mediums who were both possessed of the
same spirit or where one was possessed by the son of the spirit who
possessed the other were tinged accordingly.

In all these respects kinship formed the substance and quality of
most relationships. Kinship as a system implies systematic diversity in
the kinds of relationships that pertain among people, but in Mayotte
(as in many societies) mimesis, multiplicity, and indexical shifts were
significant aspects of kinship in practice.

At the same time, relations of parenthood were primary. Parents had
to be treated with respect. This applied also to the same-sex siblings of
one's actual parents, even where circumstances might have expected
one to overlook it. I recall two little girls being raised together, the older
of whom was the daughter of the sister of the younger; from an early
age, she was expected to show respect to her younger playmate. Although there was considerable circulation of children, people raised by
an aunt or grandparent would often turn back in the end to their genealogical parents. Tumbu and Mohedja's youngest son was raised from
birth by their oldest daughter, whom he called mother. But once he
heard from his playmates what the "real" genealogical relations were

he subsequently shifted his use of kin terms. As he grew up, the woman he had called *mama* (mother) became "older sibling" (*zuky*), also a term of respect, and he developed filial attachment to, and respectful relations with, the parents he had once known as grandparents.

Tecknonymy also emphasizes parenthood and the priority of the relation over the individual. Mohedja was known throughout her adult life as *nindry ny* Nuriaty, mother of Nuriaty, her first born, even though Nuriaty was raised by her paternal grandmother, Dady ["grandmother"] Nuriaty, after whom she had been named. Childless adults received respectful tecknonyms as well, according to the first child they raised. Since the terms "mother" and "father" refer equally to the siblings of one's mother and father respectively, the distinction was often unmarked, though some people were known by tecknonyms beginning with "older sibling of-" or "father's sister of-."

Personal names themselves were composed of two parts, the first, like Nuriaty, individual, though possibly reproduced within the family in alternate generations, like the joking relations, and the second part being the first name of the father, thus Nuriaty Tumbu. Some people, especially the elderly and children, were called by nicknames. One old woman was Sokolon ("cyclone"), after her somewhat explosive temperament, and an elderly man of particularly dark skin was Sharbon ("charcoal").[4] With the imposition of French documents many years later, people had to add family names. Almost every adult selected the father's name as their family name; people rapidly discovered that international travel was easier when family members shared a last name, but married women selected their father's rather than their husband's name. To my knowledge, no one used a woman's personal name as a family name.

Constructs and Practices of Kinship

Kibushy speakers drew on three terms to cover the sorts of things anthropologists talk about when they use the word "kinship." These terms signify three distinct but related and overlapping concepts, each of which offers a particular perspective on the whole. In no order of priority, there is the matter, initially, of genealogy, summarized in the word *razaña*, which means in the first instance "ancestor" but which I took to mean also common descent from any given ancestor, shared ancestry. When people said they were *razaña raiky*, "one ancestor," they meant that they shared an ancestor or ancestors in common, that they were related genealogically. Such connections are cognatic, with a patrilineal bias supported by Islam and a matrilineal bias supported by living arrangements, but with a strong emphasis on siblingship, both same sex and cross sex. Ancestors were remembered three or so generations back, but Mohedja often remarked that people she recalled as genealogically connected to her had themselves forgotten, or at least no longer acted like kin, *havaña*.

To say that people are of one ancestor also implies that they are *havaña*. *Havaña* is the most general term of the three, equivalent roughly to "kin" or "kinship" in the sense of having relations of diffuse enduring solidarity. To call someone *havaña* indicates a relationship of mutuality, with implications of commitment, trust, and care. *Havaña* refers both to kin and to the principle of kinship; it is a quality of relationship rather than (like *razaña*) a basis for assuming a relationship, and it does not refer to a grouping, as the third term, *mraba*, does, though all members of a *mraba* will be each other's *havaña* ("kin"). *Fihavañana*, "kinship," is refracted in all the relationships indicated by the kin terms, with the qualities of respect, joking, and care mentioned above. *Havaña* can also be used to refer to "companion," and one spouse will sometimes refer to the other spouse as *havaku*, "my kinsmate" or "my companion," although in other contexts spouses might deny they were related by kinship.[5]

Kinship could be deliberately predicated, whether informally and of the moment, as in the old woman's joke with me, or formally and on a more permanent basis irrespective of genealogy. I became Tumbu and Mohedja's son and Tumbu and Mohedja had each established cross-sex sibling relationships of their own. Tumbu had such a relationship with a woman in another village who subsequently asked for one of his daughters to raise. Mohedja engaged in such a relationship with a man in town, at whose house she could always stop on her infrequent visits there. A sibling relationship of this kind enabled solidary bonds on the order of friendship while specifically precluding sexual relations between the parties.

Third, is the concept of *mraba*, referring to the units of people closely connected by means of *razaña* who have common interests and do things collectively. *Mraba* means also "compound," "fence," and "enclosure." As both material enclosure and as social unit, the *mraba* is more inclusive than a single house, identified as the locus of a married couple and their unmarried children. But despite the association with a fence or boundary, in the social sense the *mraba* is open, including all extended kin who come together regularly to support events held by the members of the house. It is perhaps best translated as "family," as the boundaries are significant yet simultaneously amorphous, flexible, and porous, much like "family" in North American or European kinship. Like the word "family," depending on context it is the exclusivity or the openness that is emphasized. The *mraba* can be conceived as the network of close kin of one member of a marital union or the other, or of both together, as it would certainly be for their children. It can denote the practical network of effective members of the descent line but can also include people who do not have a common ancestor with one another.

There are no permanently named or formally bounded kin groups. Named units are pieces of land or places, and the relatively permanent corporate entities are villages. The *mraba* is sometimes named for a senior member, and people talk about the *ulu be* or elders of the *mraba*, even sometimes of the *chef* or head of the *mraba*; but *mraba* do not have fixed or exclusive memberships, and everyone experiences themselves as the members of multiple and overlapping *mraba* through their parents and, indirectly, their spouse. If forced to consider the question, people might say that spouses are members of one another's *mraba* though other affines are less so. The *mraba* could be conceived in reference to a deceased ancestor; but if, as more commonly, a living person is pointed to, it need not be the person most senior in a genealogical sense but the one most influential socially. On the demise of parents, an oldest sister may be called "mother" or an oldest brother become the *mraba* head. In effect, *mraba* are always contextually configured, and everyone is in some respect the indexical origo of their *mraba*, in the sense of kindred.

In sum, people use three terms to consider kinship, respectively marking genealogy, mutuality, and active grouping. Anthropological debates about kinship might learn from these distinctions, as our arguments are often based on their conflation or on category mistakes engaged in choosing among them.

Underlying each of these modalities of kinship are ideas about sex and gender. Parents are conceived to contribute equally to the makeup of the child, and children are conceived to be equally the offspring of both parents and affiliated equally with both of them. People of either gender can serve as a nodal ancestor. Gender complementarity is emphasized in the idea of the married couple, known simply as spouses (*vady*). Some kin terms are sex specific and some indicate same or cross-sex relations. Cross-sex relations are distinguished as to whether they anticipate or preclude flirting and sexual intercourse. Personal pronouns are unmarked by gender, and the same is true for terms for spouse and older and younger sibling. Where gender is marked, it is often the male side that is distinguished from something more general. Thus *akohu* is chicken, *akohulahy* a rooster. *Dady* is the term for grandmother; grandfather is specified as *dadilahy*. As the old lady's act suggests, gender dualism was salient and universal heterosexuality assumed.[6]

There is no single word for the concept of affines or affinity, or for distinctions between wife givers and receivers. Affinal kin terms are such that it looks as though sets of siblings are exchanging marriage partners with one another, although in fact there is no rule to this effect nor is the practice marked or common. Affines may share *razaña*, as in cross-cousin marriage; may in certain contexts be understood as being within the same *mraba*; and may be people with whom one expresses diffuse solidarity (*havaña*).

There are no rules of postmarital residence, but because fathers are responsible for building houses for their daughters when they marry as virgins, it is likely the daughters live close by. But equally, because women own their houses they are more likely to stay in their natal villages. Hence the common pattern is for men to move in with their wives.[7] Uxorilocality is not detrimental to a man's status, though for social and practical reasons men sometimes prefer marrying within their own communities. Occasionally they convince their wives to follow them to their own village, and the women either settle there permanently or eventually return home.

I will have a lot to say about marriage in later chapters. Suffice it to mention here that in 1975 marriages were arranged, and girls were often married young, some even before menarche. Parallel-cousin marriage was frowned upon and opinion about cross-cousin marriage divided, some appreciating it for conserving proximity and status and reducing costs, others shunning it for leading to quarrels among kin.

Marital unions were quite fragile; stability was the exception. Marriage was initiated by the Muslim rite of *kufungia*, a performative act before witnesses, but it often ended in unmarked fashion, the husband either leaving or being asked to leave by his wife. The most salient feature about marriage was that each woman should marry the first time as a virgin and each man should at some point in his life undertake to marry a virgin. Other marriages were more easily established. Men engaged in polygynous unions, but these were generally impermanent, and only a minority were married polygynously at any given time. Co-wives rarely lived together, not even within the same village. It was common for both women and men to engage in successive marriages over the course of their lives. This meant as well that most people had both maternal and paternal half-siblings and that many people who were not kin to each other had kin in common. A frequent marriage pattern was *hava ny havaña*, marriage between "kin of kin," that is, between people who have kin in common. Widows were strongly urged to remarry though not all chose to do so, and it was expected that late-in-life marriages might dissolve when neither party could look after the other any longer.

One of the attractions for me of being associated with Mohedja and Tumbu was that their marriage was an unusually stable and harmonious one. Mohedja had only one husband throughout her life and Tumbu only one wife, with the exception of a single brief attempt at polygyny. Tumbu's mother, Dady Nuriaty, sometimes urged Tumbu to divorce Mohedja and take a different wife, but Tumbu and Mohedja saw their interests as very much in common. By contrast, Tumbu and Mohedja's oldest daughter, Nuriaty, has had (by 2005) some seven husbands, including remarriage in midlife to someone she had been married to when she was young.

Kinship in all respects – as *havaña*, as *razaña*, as *mraba*, and as affinity – extends across linguistic, residential, and citizenship divides. Early in my stay people in Lombeni Kely told me they were one big family. But genealogy aside, people often spoke of *havaña an tanana*, of being kin to one another as a function of sharing village residence and long interaction. This was used to refer to fellow villagers who did not share an ancestor or were not part of the same extended household. Conversely, community ownership cross-cut kinship and created relations of inequality, as I describe in the next chapter.

Household Economy

In 1975 villages were composed of houses of two rooms each, known as the male side and female side, the former facing the street and the latter the courtyard. Houses were materially simple, constructed of rectangular wood frames covered either by wattle and daub or panels of raffia poles. They had earth floors and roofs of woven coconut leaves. Inside were several beds made of wood frames and crisscrossed rope "springs," with kapok-stuffed mattresses, embroidered sheets and pillows, and high box frames over which mosquito nets were hung. Houses were built for newly married daughters or else passed on to them. Houses were each occupied by a married couple, never more than one, along with young children and unmarried daughters. Adolescent boys built their own one-room houses and lived either singly or with a friend. These were on the outskirts of the village and often decorated with painted designs and surrounded by pretty gardens. As noted, elderly single people also lived in one-room houses, usually adjacent to a married daughter. The courtyards behind houses contained raised granaries and smaller fenced enclosures for bathing. Women wove mats, and people mostly sat on mats laid on the ground. Each village also contained a mosque constructed of more durable materials.

The household, composed ideally of marital partners and their unmarried children was the unit of production. In 1975 virtually every household was cultivating dry rice as well as a variety of other crops, some interspersed in the rice fields. Most households had plots in several places and under various use rights. Land was inherited along bilateral lines and generally shared with siblings and cousins rather than individually owned.[8] Other land was lent by close kin or sharecropped. Some people, like Tumbu and his brothers, were actively trying to purchase land. Many people had rice fields quite far from the village and spent the agricultural season dispersed on them. People slept in very simple houses in the fields and returned to the village periodically and for communal events.

Had I arrived a few years earlier I might not have met Tumbu and Mohedja. They were living then mainly a long day's walk away in distant fields owned by Mohedja's mother and the mother's older sister. Mohedja gave birth to several children there. They interacted there with the families of Mohedja's brothers. By 1975 the family spent the full year in Lombeni, as Tumbu had been able to purchase some agricultural land only an hour away on foot. They lived in the village rather than the new fields because Mohedja's mother and her mother's sister had become very old. The older sister suffered from

Figure 2.2 Harvesting rice, 1976. The rice was cut with a snail shell. Harvesting was done by parties composed mainly of women with men doing the transport. Note the mixture of corn and manioc interspersed with the rice.

mild dementia, and Mohedja felt responsible. Mohedja worried about her mother during the day and almost never stayed away from the village overnight while the two old women were alive.

Cultivating dry rice is not as labour intensive (or as productive) as cultivating wet rice, but it is still a lot of work.[9] Land is cleared of excess vegetation by slashing and burning and then seeded by hand. The more years a field is used, the smaller the crop. Fields were weeded twice during the growing season. The rice was harvested by reciprocal work parties that had to be harnessed quickly and all around the same time, as everyone was anxious to bring the harvest in before the rains began (*figure 2.2*). Rice stalks were transported in baskets, overland or by canoe, and threshed in the village. Rice was stored in raised granaries that each household built. Rice preparation entailed

Figure 2.3 Husking rice, 1975. Husking rice in wooden mortars was hard work, usually done by women, singly or in pairs, but with some help from boys. After husking it was winnowed in shallow round baskets, cleaned by hand, and cooked daily.

spreading it to dry on mats and protecting it from chickens, husking in large wooden mortars with a pestle, then winnowing in shallow baskets and cleaning by hand (*figure 2.3*). The work of cultivation was done by both sexes, with men carrying out the heavier tasks or working longer hours, while rice preparation from threshing onwards was the work of women (*figure 2.4*), with unmarried boys sometimes helping with husking.

People cooked rice once daily for the evening meal and ate leftovers for breakfast. The noon meal was manioc and unsweet banana, generally boiled but sometimes fried or cooked in coconut cream. The boiled version was dipped in a mixture of crushed tomatoes, chili pepper, and salt, served with fish when available. At dinner rice is served with sauces containing fish, meat, chicken, or leafy

Figure 2.4 Threshing rice for a member of an age group, 1985. The members of an age group (*shikao*) of adult women are threshing rice for one of their number who will be holding a ceremony at which many guests will be fed (*shungu*). The threshing is carried out here in festive fashion with singing and joking. The woman in the background is cleaning husked rice. Photo courtesy of Jacqueline Solway.

vegetables cooked in either a water-based broth or coconut cream. Dishes are nicely flavoured with onion, garlic, pickled lemon, tamarind, tomato, fresh pepper, turmeric, and ginger. A common dish, one I love, is pounded manioc leaves cooked with coconut cream and a bit of meat or fish. Legumes, taro leaves, unripe papaya, eggplant, or pumpkin cooked in coconut cream are also delicious. Yam and sesame were less common and have since dropped out of the cuisine. Fruits include pineapple, jackfruit, oranges, sweet bananas, papaya, and mango.

In 1975 protein came largely from fish. Fish were caught mainly by hook and line from canoes. The fishermen spent the night in the lagoon with lamps to attract the fish and sold their catch on the beach in the morning. Fish in the lagoon have become scarcer, and a decade or so later, as boats were supplied with outboard motors and generally went farther out, the price of fish soared. During the season when the wind blew away from shore there was often no night fishing and few fish to be had. Only certain families were active in fishing, which was always an accompaniment to cultivation never an alternative to it. Other families were dependent on purchasing fish. In addition, women from all families went out with nets in receding tides or harvested small shellfish and octopus at low tide. There were some small freshwater shrimp, and for a short season, grubs. People kept small numbers of cattle and goats. Cattle were tethered in the countryside and fed or watered daily by men; a man or woman might own one or two head, at a maximum ten to twelve. If the herdsman was not the owner he could receive every second calf. Cattle were mainly a form of savings or for festive occasions, at which the sex of the slaughtered animal was irrelevant. Chicken and goat were consumed somewhat more frequently. There was also protein from a delicious legume (*ambatry*; French *ambrevades*, *Cajanus cajan*). Sour milk was served over rice, especially at feasts.

Coconuts were an important element in the diet. Fresh coconuts were drunk occasionally for refreshment, but more important was the flesh, which was grated and rinsed and the liquid passed through a sieve. The ensuing coconut milk is used to enrich dishes. On festive occasions rice too is cooked in the milk, and it can be boiled down to create cooking oil. Oil production was labour intensive but a critical part of planning feasts. It has been replaced by bottled vegetable oil.

In 1975 a good deal of effort went into the cultivation of cash crops, notably coffee, vanilla, and especially ylang ylang, whose flowers are distilled to a dense pungent oil that is a staple of the French perfume industry. During the 1970s the price of ylang ylang oil was high, and many people produced it despite its being very labour intensive. Cash crops were a major source of income. Originally men worked on the French-owned plantations, but as these closed, people purchased land and grew the cash crops themselves. Cash cropping led to both increased purchase of land and the privatization of use. Whereas it had been very easy to borrow land for rice cultivation, and even more so for manioc or bananas, and hence land use rotated informally within and among families, cash crops required more investment of time and labour and took several years to mature. Thus they alienated land from the production cycle of subsistence crops and from relatively informal and flexible access. Moreover, whereas coffee and vanilla could be produced by individual households, ylang ylang had periods when more labour was required, for picking the flowers and for keeping the fires going in the stills. Men brought in their sons or sons-in-law or shared with brothers or cousins, dividing either the flowers, the oil, or the profits. Profits enabled further land purchase and became a means by which, by the late 1970s, some villagers were able to employ others part-time to pick the flowers or distil the oil.[10] But the heyday was short lived. The market was unreliable – sometimes the oil was purchased by middlemen and sometimes not – and vulnerable to global conditions. As production expanded elsewhere, prices fell.

I anticipate briefly what came after. As education increased, children were partially withdrawn from field labour. Upon leaving school, they found office employment, which was considered better than work in the fields. Rice yields declined because of tired soil, and within a short period cultivation was replaced by the use of imported white rice (mainly from Thailand). By 1992, people were saying "money (*vola*) is everything now." They explained that the size of the harvest was not worth the effort and "might be so small your children would starve. Whereas, if you work for a wage, you will be able to buy rice." Imported rice is less tasty and presumably less nutritious, but the only work it involves is transport and cleaning. The fields are left to manioc and bananas. They provide subsistence, but the need for cash escalated rapidly for the purchase of rice, protein, clothing, houses, appliances, and a heavy consumption of bottled soft drinks such as Coca-Cola. Concomitantly, people began to pay for water, electricity, taxes, and permits of various kinds.

By the 1990s people talked endlessly about money and began to leave Mayotte, temporarily or part-time, for Réunion to acquire unemployment and child benefits or to find work (see chapter 10). Divisions between white-collar and manual workers and between those formally and informally employed have grown. For the underemployed, the central question has been how to acquire cash. Older men combine various activities – working as night watchmen, fishing, keeping cattle, producing cash crops, collecting benefits, and engaging informally in the ever-active construction trade. Constructing and enlarging houses have become lifetime preoccupations for everyone. These houses have been mainly for one's daughters and subsequently for oneself. By the 1980s some men and women started working as contractors, managing small construction companies (*entreprises*) for building houses or bidding for municipal projects like paving sidewalks, digging drainage channels, or cutting stairs in the hillsides. In recent years a major source of investment is building and then renting out houses to the ever-increasing numbers of Europeans working in Mayotte. These houses have tile floors, indoor plumbing, well-equipped kitchens, terraces, and large windows.

Citizenship and Community

The literature on the Swahili coast often speaks of civility but also contrasts the cosmopolitanism characteristic of the "stone towns" with the villages (Swartz 1991, J. Middleton 1992). Yet civic life is also a critical feature of villages, a civility formed with respect to the size and scale of the community but that transcends the considerations of kinship and economy just described. This civic sociality is a matter of explicit membership and participation in active communities – whose well-being is understood by their members to be based on their actions. People are members of their communities as participating citizens, not as mere residents and not directly on the basis of kinship – though most people are kin with one another and in multiple ways – but through and by means of the responsibilities of living together in a named place and taking an active interest in it.

Citizenship has meant both participating in life internal to the community and helping represent the community in its relations with other communities. When Jon Breslar arrived in Mayotte shortly after me and began fieldwork in villages of Shimaore speakers, I began to see how different communities could be from one another, and I often heard people say how divisions of labour or consumption patterns differed from place to place. This is partly a product of their diverse origins and histories. But at the same time, and with the partial exception of the part of the island that became increasingly urbanized, the communities were and are commensurable units within Mayotte as a whole and understood themselves that way in the patterns of reciprocal hospitality among them.

When I write "village" or "community" these are rough translations of the Kibushy word *tanana*, which means at once a residential and social unity and a *Gemeinschaft* rather than a *Gesellschaft*. *Tanana* applies equally to the largest city of Madagascar, Antananarivo, which translates as "at the community of thousands," and to a village of twenty people. *Tanana* contrasts with *añala*, meaning the bush or countryside, where the fields are located, although the term means literally "in the forest."

A *tanana* is more than the sum of its inhabitants and certainly more than those who can consider themselves "owners" (*tompin*; see next chapter) there. It has a name and an identity, whether recognized in the administrative structure of Mayotte or in relations of exchange with other *tanana* (as Lombeni Kely and Lombeni Be are to one another). In 1975–6 villages were still relatively self-governing. They could regulate the behaviour of their members, set fines or the price of freshly caught fish, attempt to resolve internal disputes, eject people for bad behaviour, and readmit them after a suitable apology. On one occasion in 1975 the *tanana* of Lombeni Be threw out one of their own daughters because she refused to leave a violent husband whom the village would have none of. (She was welcome back any time she disassociated herself from him.) On another occasion, they expelled a relatively wealthy middle-aged man who was married to one of the *tompin* and who had insulted the village by chaining his canoe to a tree. He was thereby not merely refusing to share or implying theft but claiming to stand outside the moral community, rendering his canoe unavailable should messengers be needed to urgently travel to inform people of a death. Funerals were an occasion at which the moral community unfailingly came together, and members were reflected to themselves as such a community. It was the responsibility of the entire village to provide everyone who died there with a decent funeral. When I said I came from a city of two million inhabitants, the first response I inevitably received was the astonished query, "How do ever get any work done; you must be spending all your time at funerals!"

The village is more than a simple place of residence and more than a moral community. It is also an organization in which the main activity is ceremonial production and exchange. Youth "entered the village" (*miditry an tanana*) as they matured, joining a sex-specific age group (*shikao*) that coalesced in adolescence. From this point on they participated in communal labour and became enmeshed in a complex series of exchanges. They began attending the weddings of older members as invited guests, thereby engaging the obligation to marry and to invite them in turn. The rare people who declined to join (whether they grew up in the village or arrived in adulthood) could not expect village participation at their own celebrations or to be included as a participant in events organized by and for the village and its members as a whole.

People who married outside their village could decide whether to participate as full members of the ceremonial exchange in either or both
villages. These options and opportunities held equally for men and for
women, but, as noted, women were more likely to reside in their home
village than were men. These matters will be described more fully in
subsequent chapters.

In the mid-1970s each village was also understood to be a cell within
the political parties that had formed for or against remaining with
France. Each village had both men's and women's representatives, also
divided between youth and elders. The successful Sordat party expected unanimity, and villages had to fine members who had been part
of the opposing Serre la Main party and who had to ask forgiveness to
return to the fold. In practice there was much embarrassment over carrying this out, but it pointed to a sense of each community as politically
homogeneous and responsible to other communities for maintaining
solidarity. However, once the French were permanently installed and
people were able to vote in French elections, including for the officials
to run their newly constituted *commune* (municipality, comprising several villages), party politics returned with a vengeance, including a
sense of betrayal when people did not vote for the party in which their
kin were running for office. Women ran for and held office, but in lesser
numbers than men.

By 1990 the island was administratively reorganized such that Lombeni was part of a larger *commune* of nearly 5,000 inhabitants. In 1991 the
municipality had an annual budget of 4 million francs which it used
to build infrastructure (roads, water treatment facilities, schools, etc.).
Some expenses, like teachers' salaries, were covered by the state, and
others, like social assistance, were shared with the state. In 1991 some
thirty-seven residents were employed by the *commune* in a variety of
white- and blue-collar jobs, while rotational sanitation work for the unemployed (*asa chomage*), was covered by the state.[11]

The result of the referendum in 1976 was celebrated in the village
with dancing by the women, as an older man stood by holding a large
French flag. This strong support for renewed French rule might seem
surprising given what I described as the role of the *chef de village* and
people's initial reactions to me. While villagers operated with an ideal
of social self-reliance they had no illusions in the economic sphere, frequently remarking that Mayotte had no industry, "not even so much as
a match factory." Villagers also had a rather pessimistic view of the cor-
ruption that power brings. Since they had fewer demanding kinsmen,

French officials were assumed to have less temptation to graft and bribery than Mahorais. When comparing locals with Europeans (*vazaha*), it was often said, "We have more *fady* (moral prohibitions) than they do, but they are better able to observe the ones that they have." This was, of course, a somewhat left-handed compliment. While people were certain they wanted to remain French and, in the early years, to have the French serve as leaders, they were also deeply committed to Islam and certain of its values.

People marry by Muslim rite and they prepare and bury the dead in Muslim fashion. Many adults pray daily and observe the Muslim calendar, fasting and feasting accordingly. They refrain from pork (some less so from alcohol), and they wash before prayer and after sex. Women loosely cover their hair in public. In recent years, many people have made the *hajj*. Muslim recitation is essential to all kinds of activities – intimate, legal, interpersonal, and pleasurable – and I will show in chapter 6 how it is inextricable from the enactment of kinship and community. Islam has been a source and foundation of knowledge, and all children pass though Qur'anic classes, many aspiring to higher degrees of learning (Lambek 1993). Islam in Mayotte is what has been referred to elsewhere in Africa as Sufi, as opposed to Salafi, meaning that it recognizes historical and local tradition rather than returning to an ostensibly pure and original form of Muslim practice. It is open and integrative of practices such as feasting, cycles of exchange, and the joyous performance of musical works uttering the names of God or honouring the Prophet. There are people who have come from abroad to preach a return to a supposedly purer form of Islam that repudiates music and feasting and asks men to grow beards and women to cover themselves more closely, but despite some enthusiasts, this movement (*jaula*) has had little success.

Islam is a deeply significant part of personal identity, but the village is also a moral unit with respect to religion. Any village of a certain size must have a mosque for daily prayer, and larger villages are expected to run a Friday mosque service. Mosques have secluded sections along the west side for women. Religious affairs such as daily and holiday prayers, the upkeep of the mosque, and the assignment of various offices are a matter of responsibility for the village as a whole. Villages were proud of their most educated citizens and sometimes tried to attract a learned man to improve everyone's Islamic education. Adult men who marry elsewhere return home for Friday prayer and participate in the upkeep of the mosque.

Collective blessings over the village as a whole were held periodically, notably at the annual solar New Year (*mwaka*), for which the count, and hence the precise date at which it was celebrated, was maintained separately in each village. Throughout the 1980s a small group of men circumambulated the village at the New Year, reciting a prayer to protect it from harmful external forces. A goat was sacrificed of which everyone partook. Collective prayers were recited at times of crisis, in response to dreams, and on the occasion of an eclipse. Each village held a collective accountability to God and a consequent vulnerability to God's displeasure.

The main mosque in Lombeni Be was built in 1958 with a financial contribution from each adult and labour contributions from each age group in turn. When it was completed the village killed a cow and made cakes to celebrate and bless it. The mosque (originally nine metres long) was subsequently considerably enlarged, and an additional mosque was built in an expanding quarter of the village. Lombeni Kely had an old stone mosque, which was later rebuilt. In 1975–6 there was heated debate as to whether to start regular Friday prayers in Lombeni Be. Some were hesitant, worrying that it would not be sufficiently attended. A leading scholar on the island intervened, warning the elders that if they didn't proceed the village would be ostracized from all inter-village events. So the village instituted Friday prayers – and threatened to monitor attendance and issue fines to absentees. In the event, it has flourished, and is regularly attended by people from Lombeni Kely as well. The man who delivers the Friday sermon (*hutuba*; Ar. *khutba*) serves as the symbolic representative of village morality; it is of utmost importance to the well-being of the community that he not commit adultery. If he should falter, and especially if he should stumble or fall from the *minbar* (pulpit), it would signify his – and hence the entire village's – state of impurity.[12]

Villages hold regular pious musical recitations. They educate their children in the versions of the Muslim texts and dance forms, send teams to perform at island-wide or more local events, and invite teams from other villages to perform in Lombeni.[13] Performances are also held at life-crisis rites, on which I will have more to say later.

In sum, internally, relations in the village can be categorized by three broad overlapping and intersecting principles or fields of organization I refer to as citizenship, kinship, and Islam. A fourth principle, ownership, will be described in the next chapter. While they are each clearly highly salient means of linking and distinguishing people, neither kinship nor property relations determine the village as a community – that is, as a group of people with common interests and identity, a community of worship, and one understood as engaged in the reproduction of its members and with respect to its relations of exchange with other communities. The village has been much more than an agglomeration of households, units of production or subsistence.

Relations ascribed or described as kinship were and are of great salience, but kinship did not serve as a means to form fixed or bounded social groups. Kinship was a matter of daily action, concerning such things as eating together, building houses for daughters, caring for children and the sick, respecting parents and cross-sex siblings, joking with grandparents and affines, and planning and producing life-cycle ceremonies. Kinship elaborated multiple vertical and lateral relations; the emphasis was not on static units or bounded and opposed groups but on dynamic process, on acts and expectations, rather than on objects, categories, or ideals.

Islam was a matter of self-conscious attention, especially with respect to the Friday midday prayers. While both kinship and Islam afforded important fields of action and strong means of integration they were not independent of each other, nor were they the only means by which the community organized, expressed, and understood itself. The ceremonies of social reproduction exemplify dynamic aspects of kinship but are also deeply embedded within the broader community, such that the community itself was a dynamic, continuously reproduced social whole. Relations between communities were reproduced in similar fashion. Citizenship entails participation in these ceremonies, as will be explored in the chapters to follow.

In 1975 I counted 290 adults spread over some 157 households resident in the two communities; by adults I mean people who were or had been married (irrespective of an elaborate wedding ceremony). In the next chapter I will describe how the communities began and grew to that size.

3   Founding the Villages, before 1975

Mayotte is a rugged, volcanically formed (but inactive) island, once heavily forested, and almost fully encircled by a coral reef. When people first came to Mayotte and who the first residents were are the subject of a few obscure stories but not of great interest in Lombeni.[1] The villages however do have a clear and recognized beginning. Having introduced general features of village life as I first encountered them in the previous chapter, in this one I go back in time to their founding. This history, drawn from notes taken at various periods, and written up in 2016, sets the stage for the specific social dynamics to be found within and between the two communities.

I begin by briefly setting the historical context in which the villages emerged. Here, of necessity, I enter the story in midstream. I start with a brief mention of the precolonial context followed by the establishment of the French colony. In the second half of the chapter I turn to the actors who founded the villages in which I lived and worked and the consequences of their actions for the generation of people I knew.

Mayotte in the Indian Ocean World to 1975

For well over a millennium, travellers have proceeded along the coast of East Africa and across the Mozambique Channel, creating what can loosely be called Swahili maritime civilization, building stone towns, practising Islam, developing a civic sociality, interacting with hinterlands, and trading, among other things, in slaves. Mayotte was on the fringes of this world, reached by both Swahili dhows and Malagasy outrigger sailing canoes. Travellers arrived and settled from as far away as southern Arabia and the Persian Gulf. Islam has a long history, with the first Muslim grave dated to the ninth century and the oldest standing mosque on Mayotte dated to 944 H/1538 (Allibert 2015). This maritime world was increasingly disrupted by Europeans once Vasco da Gama rounded the Cape in 1498.[2] European ships took on food for the voyage to the Indies and sometimes pilots. But their interventions in the regional economy – which had become transregional – were soon much more consequential. The presence of European and American vessels eager for slaves and willing to offer guns in return fuelled the rise of the Sakalava monarchies on the west coast of Madagascar. In the nineteenth century purely mercantile interests shifted to colonial ones, and the Europeans attempted to replace the economy based on trading slaves from open ports with one of plantation agriculture in exclusively ruled colonies. However, this did not mean the end of servile labour; indeed, French planters settling in Mayotte needed to import workers and were willing to do so by any means.

The French appropriated Mayotte in 1841, ostensibly purchasing it from the Sakalava prince Andriantsoly, who had himself fled there from fighting in Madagascar and formed an alliance with the last Mahorais Sultan. I say "ostensibly" because it is unlikely that anyone on Mayotte at the time either had the authority or grasped the nature of the action as the French described it. The French built a port on the well-fortified islet of Dzaoudzi, which from the mid-twentieth century has also housed an outpost of the French Foreign Legion.

When the French took possession of Mayotte, they found a stratified society of free Muslim citizens and their slaves. Most residents of Mayotte were and are speakers of Shimaore, the language indigenous to Mayotte and closely related to the languages spoken on the other islands in the Comoros and to Swahili. Shimaore is a Bantu language with many Arabic loan words. However, interspersed with villages of Shimaore speakers were those of people who had moved back and forth from Madagascar and who spoke one or more dialects of Malagasy, an Austronesian language with roots in southeast Asia that coalesced into a dialect particular to Mayotte known as Kibushy. Some of the Malagasy speakers were relatively recent converts to Islam, and most were probably relatively uninvested in the local social hierarchy, being neither slave owners nor slaves. Malagasy had been raiding Mayotte in the beginning of the nineteenth century but then began to settle, some fleeing Merina conquest, some indentured labourers, others simply adventurers.[3]

The population was small but diverse. A census taken shortly after appropriation in 1841 reveals 600 Sakalava, 700 Arabs, 500 Mahorais, and 1,500 slaves for a total of 3,300 people (Martin 1976: 226, n10). Both the numbers and the labels were somewhat fluid. A decade later the census jumps to a population of 6,888, of whom the largest number are listed as Mozambiques (Makua) at 2,193, followed by Mahorais (2,171), as well as Antalaotes (715), Betsimi Saraka (sic, 493), Grands-Comoriens (1,045), Sakalava (464), Anjouanais (544), Zanzibarites (67), Mohéliens (39), Swahili (39), Indiens (9), plus 3 people from Pemba, 1 from Mombasa, and 5 Réunionnais, a figure that did not include the Europeans or the "assimilated" (Martin 1976: 231, n63). The category of "slaves" has been transformed to "Mozambiques" and the ethnonym "Arab" is no longer used. The census says there are 133 villages, thus the average population of a village was 51.8 persons.[4] In 1866 Gevrey (1870) recorded 11,731 inhabitants, whom he divided among Malagasy (1,682), Mahorais (4,673), Africans (3,716), Comorans from the other three islands (1,261), Creoles (84), Indians (64), Europeans (53), and Arabs (13). Among all groups save the first two the proportion of men was much higher than of women.

Of the people listed, the Betsimisaraka came from northeast Madagascar and the Antalaotes and Sakalava from the northwest, but many people counted under the other categories might have travelled from or resided in Madagascar as well. Given high rates of intermarriage and hence diversity of any individual's ancestry, a better index of distinction is language. In 1975 there were three villages with Kiantalaotsy speakers and several more of Kibushy speakers, including the ones I selected. In fact, the difference between Kiantalaotsy and Kibushy was hardly greater than dialectical variation between any two villages of Kibushy speakers. To this day there is a difference in accent and tone between the inhabitants of Lombeni and those in the adjacent village, indicative of origins in different parts of northern Madagascar. Kibushy was for some time the primary language of approximately 30 per cent of people born in Mayotte. Most Kibushy speakers are fluent in Shimaore as well, and the language contains many loan words, including from Arabic. There are much smaller proportions of Malagasy speakers on the other Comoro islands.

Mayotte is culturally a part of the Comoro Archipelago, but each island has its own history and pattern of social organization. In 1992 Sophie Blanchy had this to say about Mayotte in contrast to the other three islands: "L'origine non noble ou esclave de la population, l'hétérogénéité de sa composition, la chute dramatique de la démographie au début du XIXe siècle à cause des guerres locales, ont abouti à faire de Mayotte une île qui a oublié son passé et ses traditions anciennes et qui a choisi l'avenir" (1992: 46).[5]

Elsewhere Blanchy (1997) discusses some of these abandoned ancient traditions. She describes an early, possibly pre-Islamic political order in Mayotte, in which an ostensibly external king married local women. Although she posits a connection with Sakalava (and one can also note parallels with the "stranger king" described by Hocart and Sahlins for the Pacific), this would likely have been a regime of Shimaore speakers. While it has little connection to the villages I studied, a few traces of this order did remain. In late 1975 the villagers heard that Shehu Addinan, the most distinguished Muslim scholar on the island, had a dream reminding people that it was taboo (fady) to cultivate on Wednesdays and that those who ignored it would fall sick and die. The former Sultan, Mawana Madi, appeared in his dream to remind people to return to the practice of an abandoned prohibition. It appeared remarkable to me that the precolonial ruler should appear to the contemporary Muslim scholar concerning a non-Islamic prohibition and one that pertained to the island as whole. It was not coincidental that Shehu Addinan lived in the ancient capital, Tsingoni. In fact, most people I knew disregarded the instruction.[6]

While Islam has a long presence in Mayotte, this does not mean either that all inhabitants have been Muslim for many generations or that the practice of Islam remains unchanging. In particular, this is because Muslims are always keen to further educate each other. Residents of Lombeni remember that some time in the late 1940s a man said to be a Sharif (descendant of the Prophet) came from a village of the Shimaore-speaking elite and pledged people in large numbers to the Shathuly Sufi brotherhood. At the time, few people in Lombeni knew how to recite passages from the Qur'an or the Maulida, a popular ode to the Prophet; when they needed them performed, they would call in someone from a bigger and older village. By 1975 there was virtually no one in Lombeni who could not recite or follow the Maulida. By then, too, the Qadiry brotherhood had become equally popular, and it seemed to me that affiliation to one or another brotherhood was based largely on aesthetic preference for either the vigorous Shathuly Daira dance or the slower and more graceful Qadiry Mulidy. I found them both beautiful, and performances of each attracted many participants and observers. These performances ground people in the deep history of Islam.

During the colonial period through the 1960s there was a matrimonial exchange among five villages of elite Shimaore speakers whose members claimed connection to the former Sultans. This was articulated patrilineally, with the wife givers inferior to the wife takers. Although the last of these marriage rites took place in 1965, Blanchy reports that in 1993 and again in 1995 members of the royal line tried to have the groom and his party carried during the wedding procession; when the brothers-in-law refused to do so, the former carried the groom themselves (Blanchy 1997: 125).[7] Jon Breslar (1979, 1981) offers a striking portrait of one of these five villages that had through 1976 retained a strong distinction and antipathy between members of the class of free citizens and descendants of former slaves, a distinction reproduced in endogamous marriages, residential segregation, and ubiquitous competition and conflict. The Kibushy-speaking villages I studied are quite different in composition and history, and in them, as I will describe in later chapters, the performance of weddings displayed a strong ideology of equality in contrast to (and perhaps protest against) the ideology of inequality that Blanchy and Breslar describe.

Historian Jean Martin offers a picture of the early colonial period from the French perspective. While some colonial officials dreamed of turning Mayotte into a large military port and commercial centre comparable to Hong Kong or Singapore (Martin 1976: 208), this unlikely plan rapidly gave way to the appropriation of land and the establishment of sugar plantations. The French freed the local slaves, not only in response to the growing feeling in Europe that emancipation was legally and morally necessary, but also to provide a pool of labour available for exploitation by the French and Réunionnais planters as well as to "impoverish the Arab aristocracy" (ibid. 224). French officials were startled when many of the former slaves cast their lot with their former masters, preferring the *"régime tempéré et paternaliste"* (ibid. 216) of their Muslim owners (a "temperate and paternalist regime" of domestic slavery) to the gruelling contract labour on the plantations. Many fled with their owners to neighbouring islands. For the most part, these owners were either Mahorais or Muslim Antalaotes from northwest Madagascar, most of whom returned there. Only about a third of the slaves stayed; once emancipated, they opted either to work for the administration or to found their own small villages and live by subsistence cultivation and fishing (ibid. 220).

The planters engaged labour from the Grande Comore, the majority brought there in doubtful circumstances from East Africa, but were frustrated by absenteeism and flight. Workers were forced to submit to harsh conditions and often went unpaid. In 1856 there was an insurrection led by a Sakalava former slave owner, now in solidarity with the workers, and in 1868 workers at one plantation declared they preferred prison to returning to work (Martin 1976: 223). The plantations proved unworkable, and Martin concludes with the remark – ironic today – that Mayotte was a "useless colony" (*colonie inutile*) (ibid. 225).

Nevertheless, the French continued to import people from East Africa, men and women whose original capture was transformed into the category of indentured labour by the time they reached Mayotte. By 1870 the population had grown to 12,000. Many workers fled the plantations, whose viability also sank. Repression continued, in one instance following the murder of a plantation guard in 1913. One year earlier, a British traveller to Mayotte recorded an "impression of unspeakable desolation" (Marcuse 1914: 12) but "soil fertile beyond description [supporting] a vegetation of bewildering luxuriance and uncomparable beauty" (ibid. 25). He noted sugar factories and plantations abandoned and in ruins, but assumed, no doubt mistakenly, that the beautiful Sakalava women with gold in their hair "belonged to wealthy, French vanilla planters" (ibid. 26).

In fact, by then the majority of the population had set up autonomous villages for the practice of subsistence cultivation, taking advantage of the fact that increasingly abandoned plantation land became available for purchase. Small groups of people formed associations (*sociés*) to buy plots of a few hectares on which they and their families settled and were gradually joined by others. Land for planting (usufruct) was readily available, and people grew dry rice, supplemented by bananas and manioc and, to a lesser extent, taro, breadfruit, maize, and sesame, as well as tomatoes, onions, pumpkins, various greens, yams, pineapples, mangoes, papayas, avocados, jack fruit, oranges, chilies, turmeric, and ginger. They kept small numbers of cattle, goats, and chickens. Along the coasts people fished and also foraged at low tide. Most men worked part-time on the remaining plantations or for the government in order to acquire the cash needed to pay the head tax, buy clothing, kerosene, and soap, and eventually purchase plots of land themselves. Villagers also produced and sold their own cash crops.

This pattern continued through 1975. Over the years the original plots of land were increasingly subdivided, and certain portions became unsuitable for cultivating dry rice. Usufruct rights, apportioned annually, were less freely given, and the increasing production of cash crops in the 1970s took some land out of circulation. Usufruct rights did not extend to cash crops, and collectively inherited rights seemed threatened when someone planted them. Land ownership became a priority in order to cultivate cash crops without alienating kin and to have viable rice land. Enterprising families sought and purchased land in more remote places and often spent the planting and harvesting seasons living dispersed, returning to the villages in the dry post-harvest season when most ceremonial activity took place. Occasionally the fields became the core of new villages that grew up around a couple and their offspring.

Despite Mayotte's having been a French colony for some 134 years, in 1975 villages were still without running water and electricity. There were no latrines, and people defecated on the beach or in the bush. The town had no marketplace and nowhere to purchase fresh produce. The hospital was grossly inadequate, with no plumbing and only a couple of doctors, with racist attitudes. In the 1960s and 1970s the large majority of children did not attend school, and indeed there was no school in Lombeni itself.

Founding Lombeni Kely

Villages were constructed either on land originally purchased by private owners or on government land. Both Lombeni Be and Lombeni Kely, like the majority of villages of Kibushy speakers, were of the former type. Around the turn of the twentieth century the Frenchman who owned the entire area gave up on his plantation and began selling his land piece by piece until it was all gone and he left Mayotte. As Tumbu Vita explained, he began by selling the fringes to outsiders until some of his workers spoke up and asked whether they might purchase as well. Many of the original founders of the two villages appear to have worked on his plantation.

A large portion was purchased by Dimasy Addinan, a man from the creolized island of Ste Marie off the east coast of Madagascar. As a present-day owner of Lombeni Kely explained, Dimasy worked as an overseer on a large plantation (elsewhere on the island) and knew a little French. At the time, everyone was scared of those who knew French and didn't want their children to learn it, because they considered such people to be thieves. Dimasy himself didn't like manual labour, and so he sold off portions in turn. He sold one portion to the founders of Lombeni Kely, who were then residing in an adjacent village that has since disappeared. Some of Dimasy's own descendants are among the owners of Lombeni Be. They are fortunate to be able to cultivate on inherited land immediately adjacent to the village.

One of Dimasy's descendants told me about the practices his Malagasy ancestors once followed. As he explained, when they moved to Mayotte and became Muslim they had to forego the royal custom of burying the dead with silver. They requested permission of their ancestors to change from ancestral practices (*fomban'drazaña*) to local ones (*fomban'tany*), explaining that they were in a "different country, a Muslim country" (*tany hafa, tany silam*). "Your practices will stay with you and our practices with us" (*Fombanareo tavela aminareo, fombanay tavela aminay*), they told their predecessors. Had they not asked and received permission, heavy rain would have fallen at each burial. This account illustrates one of the main themes of this book – namely, that people acknowledge the past and are active and knowing participants in their own history and in their historical understanding.

The land on which Lombeni Kely emerged was purchased from Dimasy in 1902 by an association of three people, two men and a woman, each of whom was the child or grandchild of people from Mrima (East Africa). They held the land jointly, but their children quarrelled and divided it. One of the original men had no descendants and subsequently sold his portion to people who did not reside locally. The residents of Lombeni Kely are for the most part descended from the other two original owners, living adjacent to one another but forming a single community. The male ancestor, Seleman Juma, had one daughter with a wife of Malagasy background and a daughter and four sons with a second wife, Amina, whom he brought from another village together with the children she had from two previous marriages with other men of African origin (*figure 3.1*). The majority of the villagers are descended from Amina, who was not herself an owner. Amina had ten children in all; only those who were also children of Seleman inherited rights of place. When Seleman grew ill, Amina looked after him for some time, but as he was disabled and she had young children to see to, she left him and moved to an adjacent village where she remarried. As that village shrank as a result of disease, her children and grandchildren, and finally she herself, moved back to Lombeni Kely.

People remembered Amina as being very dark, tall, and strong. Her grandson Tumbu said, "She raised all her children herself and married them off, without parents or older siblings to help her. She was alone

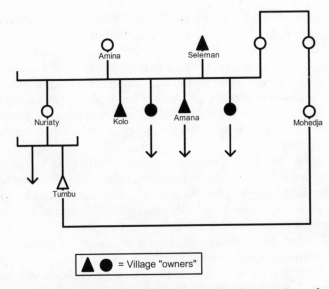

Figure 3.1 **A simplified genealogy, Lombeni Kely.** The genealogy shows the relations of kinship between owners and non-owners. Tumbu is descended from a half-sibling of owners while Mohedja is descended through affinal kin of owners. Tumbu and Mohedja have a marriage of "kin of mutual kin."

and raised them alone, with a little help from the stepfathers. Everyone was afraid of Dady (Grandmother) Amina; she was a woman, but she acted like a man, and she herself wasn't afraid of anyone. She was born in Mayotte, but her father came from Africa at the time of the *engagements*. She worked very hard; could that old lady ever cultivate! She wielded a machete (*shombu*) like a man, and she was ready to say anything to anyone, even to her husbands, when they did something she didn't like."

Amina believed in hard work, and she had a temper. All the children under her care were afraid of her. Tumbu told me how she made him cook, fetch water, and work "like a girl," such that the old men who married her in turn were pleased with him.[8] Tumbu left home as soon as he could, to avoid the humiliation of being hit and shouted at. He paid off his Qur'an teacher, headed to town, and spent a few years there working as a servant (*boy*) and then as a pedlar in Anjouan, after which he never saw her again.

Tumbu's uncle, Kolo, only a few years older than Tumbu, lived with Amina as well. One day Kolo ran off to his father's in Lombeni Kely leaving Tumbu to husk the rice for cooking. They ate dinner and went to sleep. Kolo was used to Amina leaving leftovers in the cooking pots in her kitchen shed. He slipped in at midnight, reached into the pots – and discovered raw ingredients. Amina had replaced the food with un-husked rice and uncooked greens! In the morning when he complained that he was hungry she hit him with a stick. After that he pounded rice when he was told.

Tumbu reflected that he received food and clothing and so didn't suf-fer in that sense. But in order to get along with Amina you had to work hard; she didn't like to play. As a result, he became used to working hard and has done so ever since. By contrast, Kolo went off to Madagas-car, where he learned to drink. He returned to Lombeni as an old man, a genial talker, but without children or means. As a child, Kolo had *marantudy* (mites that buried in the flesh and laid eggs, leaving holes in your feet), and so he limped. Many older people had deformed feet as a result of *marantudy*. Tumbu had the eggs too, but he was careful to cut them out.[9]

Amina died around 1950 (and Seleman before that), but through the 1990s she continued to be remembered by an annual Muslim prayer and meal put on by her descendants, who make up perhaps two-thirds of Lombeni Kely, with a few resident in Lombeni Be and elsewhere.

Hamada, one of the husbands of the original female purchaser of the village, is also remembered in prayers, as he was the Islamic teacher of the first generations of children born in the village. Hamada was a local man, the son of African parents, and said to be very intelligent. He spoke some French, picked up when he worked in the port of Dza-oudzi before marriage, and he later served as the local liaison with the government. He left five children from three different wives, who form the other side of Lombeni Kely from that of the descendants of Seleman Juma and of Amina. Hamada himself was not an owner. Either his wife purchased the land before she married him or he simply chose not to participate. As a result, only their two joint children (sons) are full own-ers. Hamada's children with other women (daughters) were granted residential rights for their lifetime by their half-siblings but cannot pass them on directly to their children. Unlike most women, the original owner herself moved villages several times, following her successive husbands, and returned home only once she married Hamada.

Seleman was an astrologer and hence must have been able to read some Arabic. Both Seleman and Amina are remembered as also knowing an African language (Kimrima, possibly Makua) in addition to Kibushy. One of Amina's daughters, Dady Nuriaty ("Grandmother" Nuriaty, Tumbu's mother), who was still alive in 1975, knew some phrases and also on occasion prepared dishes said to be of African origin.[10] Dady Nuriaty's younger half-brother, Amana Seleman, oldest surviving son of the original owner, was considered the main owner (*tompin*) and authority in the village. I had to receive his permission to reside there and was told to gain his permission before making a sketch map. However, most decisions were made collectively and through consultation.

Amana Seleman explained to me that at the time of the original purchase not many people wanted to buy land, and it was acquired without plans being drawn. Seleman first sent a letter to the government requesting official division of the land in 1919 and another letter of complaint in 1928, but the official survey was not carried out until 1932, with the three portions recorded at approximately seven hectares each. The plans are kept at the house of Amana's full sister; plans are always kept with women, he explained, as men are more likely to sell property or give it away to younger wives. Someone else told me that Seleman became embroiled in a conflict with the man who had purchased the portion from the third original owner, disagreeing on how the property lines were drawn and who had access to which coconut palms they had previously planted. Because both men were astrologers they fought by means of their "knowledge" (*hilim*) rather than with their fists; it ended with the other man dying and Seleman becoming crippled. Some time later the children from one of Seleman's wives tried legal means to increase their share at the expense of the daughter from his other wife (so the daughter's son told me), but Seleman himself put a stop to it.

Seleman's portion remained in principle a *shirika*, that is, an undivided piece of land equally accessible in all its parts to each of his descendants. In practice, however, his son Amana retained the greatest control. Amana's authority stemmed also from the fact that, like his father, he was a highly reputed astrologer, with the means to harm others' health and well-being should they cross him. First the father, and later the son, attracted many clients from across Mayotte. The inherited land extended to a hillside onto which the neighbouring village of Lombeni

Be expanded over the years, and Amana made a good deal of money and a proportional number of enemies in selling rather than simply giving individual house plots to his neighbours when it became necessary to register them individually.

Amana was alive and bedridden in 2015, cared for by his son. He and his children had always kept to themselves and now, apart from his immediate descendants and his clients from other villages, people avoided him. His status as a village owner no longer held much social or political significance, as village and house plot land were now government regulated.

Seleman and his descendants were all *tompin*, rightful and virtually inalienable residents. *Tompin* is a complex word meaning owner, master, but also agent, perpetrator, principal, or sponsor of an action or activity, indicating who is responsible or has responsibility. In this case the *tompin*, or more explicitly, *tompin tanana*, village owners, were all those who had a legitimate claim to the village land, whether through purchase, inheritance, or gift.

Marriages in Lombeni Kely have been unstable, and this was particularly the case with the first generation. People had successive spouses, and that meant that many people of a single generation were half-siblings to each other or, if not, had half-siblings in common with people who were linked through a different parent. Thus, Amana Seleman had a paternal half-sister who was also an owner (*tompin*) and numerous maternal half-siblings who were not.

Although Tumbu was surrounded by kin in Lombeni Kely, as a son of a maternal half-sister of Amana, for a long time he did not own land there himself and hence was not a *tompin*. Tumbu's wife, Mohedja, was related to Amana's half-sister on the other side (*figure 3.1*). This half-sister was an owner through her father, but as Mohedja was related to her through her mother (as the daughter of this woman's mother's sister), Mohedja was not an owner either. Indeed, having been born and raised in another village, Mohedja did not fully consider Lombeni Kely "home" until she was well into middle age. Mohedja and Tumbu were not kin to one another, yet they had kin in common. Everyone in the village was linked directly by cross-cutting kin ties or indirectly by sequential marriages, but some residents were owners while others were resident on the basis of the owners' forbearance.

People like Tumbu considered the village their home and yet were sometimes made to feel they were not first-class citizens. Tumbu's mother's brother was a powerful and difficult man, and his grown children were quarrelsome. Tumbu felt rather insecure until around 1980 when the owners of the parcel originally owned by the third member of the *socié* that purchased Lombeni Kely, located on the hillside directly abutting Amana and his family's land, put it up for sale. Together with seven other kin from Lombeni Kely, Tumbu formed a new *socié* and collected enough money to make a joint purchase, thereby expanding the village by some eight hectares. The members of the *socié* then informally divided the land among themselves, and Tumbu could finally rest easy at becoming an owner at his own home.

Tumbu and Mohedja's house had been on a nice piece of flat land, but he immediately set about digging into the steep hillside no more than fifty metres away and building a new house on what was now securely his own land. He subsequently built houses for four of their daughters around him. This is a longstanding residential pattern – adult daughters receiving houses from their fathers and settling around their parents. Most often this is land inherited by their mothers.

People have since offered to buy Tumbu's land for much more than he paid for it, but it is land for his children and grandchildren and he would "never ever" sell it. No one could any longer challenge his right to speak or say "*Anao bok' aiza*?" ("Where do you think you come from?"). This is equivalent to English, "Who do you think you are?" or "What gives you the right to speak?"

Founding Lombeni Be

Lombeni Be was larger than Lombeni Kely and of more diverse composition insofar as it was purchased by a group of five unrelated men who formed an association for the purpose, several of whom left descendants. Whereas the ascendants of Lombeni Kely were mostly people of East African origin, those of Lombeni Be had more direct connections with Madagascar and with other villages of Malagasy speakers. The purchasers bought from the same French planter who had sold to Dimasy Addinan. They worked on his land – at least one of them as a foreman (*caporal*) – and then purchased a stretch of it from him, dividing it among themselves so that each had five to six hectares.[11] Some of the purchasers may have been descendants of those people who accompanied the Sakalava prince Andriantsoly when he took up residence in Mayotte in the 1820s. According to a grandson of one of the purchasers, these Malagasy lived first on the islet of Dzaoudzi (home also to Sultan Mawana Madi) and then in a village on the main island (Hagnundru) before seeking work on European plantations, including the one at Lombeni. He said they were "used to working hard" (*zatra miasa*). The French landowner had a house on the hill above the beach.

My informant on these points was one of the very few people in Lombeni (quasi-)fluent in French in 1975, as a result of a childhood spent in town. He had learned the history from his father, a son of one of the purchasers, who had even shown him the plan, since destroyed in a cyclone. He said that one hectare of land had sold for one franc fifty centimes, the price of a large cow at the time.

Four of the original purchasers left descendants in Lombeni Be. As one resident explained to me, "The village has no trunk, only branches, and so we are people of equal status who must get together in order to make decisions." In fact, the branches have become densely intertwined through marriage. One branch has proved somewhat dominant both in number of descendants and in achievement, many of its members being highly intelligent and forceful people. The ancestor of this branch, Mze Mdery, left an Arab sabre (*jambiya*) that became a cherished heirloom and that indexes an earlier period of maritime movement and battle. It is of steel with a wooden sheath covered in leather. Mze Mdery is remembered in various stories told by his descendants that connect him to the old Mahorais elite and that afford his descendants a broad network of kin in Mayotte and northwest Madagascar. In one account, Mze Mdery's father was an Arab, possibly from Yemen, while his mother had been abducted by Malagasy raiders or Arab slavers from an elite Shimaore village. She was sold in Madagascar, where each of her owners, "whose feet she washed," would die shortly after. Finally, an old woman recognized her nobility and took her home with her. The young woman was very beautiful. A visiting Arab trader asked to marry her, and they had Mze Mdery. When their son was grown, his mother gave him a written genealogy (*salua*) and told him to return to Mayotte to seek his kin. On his arrival, the villagers were surprised, thinking that his mother had died long before, but they believed him when they saw the genealogy. However, they didn't want to share the land that was rightfully his (and perhaps considered him lowered in status as a result of his mother's enslavement), so he left by canoe, arriving in Lombeni, where he purchased land.[12]

Mze Mdery had a son who in turn had two sons and a daughter (*figure 3.2*). One of the grandsons returned to Madagascar, and his descendants remain there, while the other two grandchildren each left many descendants in Lombeni Be. The grandson who stayed, also called Mdery, married a particularly clever and charismatic woman whom I encountered in 1975 (Mdery was already deceased) and whose brother also married into the family. She claimed connection to Antankaraña and Sakalava royalty, and had the luxuriant hair and superior attitude to demonstrate it. Like Amana and his father in Lombeni Kely, the younger Mdery was also an astrologer, remembered for going out on the promontory at night at low tide to communicate with spirits in their homes in the rocks. Studying the books of cosmology appears to have been an avenue for intellectually inclined men, and they were widely respected – and feared – for their knowledge.

Mdery and his wife had a number of children; two of their sons became the leading Islamic scholars in Lombeni and one of the daughters a recognized healer. A grandson of Mdery's sister had a Grande Comoran father and was sent there for schooling, later becoming an administrator on a remaining plantation in Mayotte and eventually a wealthy retailer. Of a different social class than everyone else, he maintained one wife in the village and another in the community where his business was located. He returned to Lombeni only for Friday prayers but played a significant role in village affairs. The children and grandchildren of these families were among the first to attend school. Some received degrees and took professional jobs, and many have married among themselves, developing a dense network of cross-cousin ties.

Because of the mixed origins of the first owners, power in Lombeni Be did not lie in the hands of any single elder or line of descent. Village affairs were managed collectively by elected officials overseen by elders. One man with exceptional leadership skills was deferred to most regularly. This man, Malidy Muthary, married to one of Mdery's daughters, initiated and chaired assemblies, articulated decisions, and took the lead in implementing them. He oversaw and mentored the younger men elected as officials.

The descendants of the original owners knew where each of their portions of village land lay, but as a result of intermarriage the distinctions grew less significant and in practice families are dispersed within the village rather than living in fully distinct quarters. There is also land

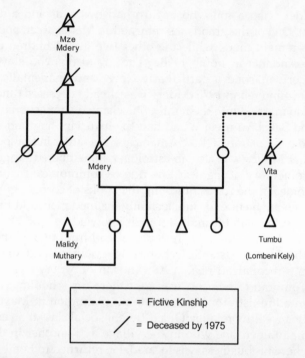

Figure 3.2 A simplified genealogy, Lombeni Be. This genealogy shows only a small portion of the live descendants (in 1975) of one of the founders of the village as well as the siblingship established by Tumbu's father with the wife of one of the owners.

held in common (*shirika*) by groups of descendants outside the village where a few crops can be grown and cattle grazed.

Owners, Residents, and Kin

In sum, the village in which Tumbu lived, Lombeni Kely, was composed of people virtually all related to one another either through descent from Amina, who had given birth with one of the original owners as well as with other men, or through descent from Hamada, who had married the other original owner. The descendants of each also intermarried within, between, and beyond their respective descent groups. The larger adjacent village, Lombeni Be, had several originally unrelated owners, but their descendants have also since intermarried. Villagers are related to one another in multiple ways; by now this applies between the two villages as well as within each of them.

The original owners and their descendants attracted others to live with them, and villages grew. In the early years, they attracted residents from a couple of nearby villages inhabited by Africans and Malagasy who had worked on the local plantation or terminated their work contracts elsewhere and where some of the original owners had once lived as well. This was land that Dimasy Addinan had purchased and included the village where Amina lived and raised Tumbu. The older villages eventually disappeared as a result of sickness. The oldest person alive in 1975 mentioned a smallpox epidemic, apparently brought to Mayotte from an early traveller on the *hajj*. He remembered this from his childhood, putting it at around 1900, while another person disputed the fact and placed the epidemic much earlier, saying that were there any living survivors they would have scars. Another person said there had been leprosy in the older village, a fact that Tumbu confirmed, as his grandmother had seen it and told him about it. Eventually the government removed the healthy young people to a village in the interior and placed the sick ones in a leper colony on a small islet.

It is evident that the original owners of the two Lombeni villages were mostly men who brought in wives. The woman owner of the first generation also attracted a husband. Subsequently, children of both sexes inherited ownership, and they either married within the community or brought in marriage partners. There was no rule of post-marital residence, but a woman who demonstrated her virginity on first marriage received a house from her father, who was likely to build it adjacent to his own, if there were room, or at least in the same village or the village in which she had been raised (likely her mother's). A house gave a woman a good deal of security; if she chose to follow a husband to his village, she could always return home. Men felt more secure living and marrying in their own village than in those of their wives so there were many intra-village unions.

The villages that emerged were situated on collectively purchased land. They were landholding corporations (*sociés*), and the village belonged to the original purchasers and their descendants. The descendants, whether through men or women, are all *tompin*, that is owners or masters, a word that carries both rights and responsibilities. Not all village residents are *tompin*, not even all those born in the village; conversely, not all *tompin* live in the village. They may live in other villages in which they are also *tompin* or in which they are not. A person could be an owner in more than one village or in none. In any case, having the status of owner in one village has no bearing on a person's status outside of it.

Whether one was *tompin* in the village in which one resided had no intrinsic connection to whether one had sufficient land to cultivate or how much land one owned elsewhere. It was possible for a village owner to have no productive land of his or her own; conversely, some-one who was not a village owner might have sufficient land elsewhere and might give annual usufruct rights to *tompin*. Distinctions of wealth cross-cut status in the village, though the privileges derived from the one did not fully make up for the disadvantages of not having the other.

On a day-to-day basis the distinction between owners and non-own-ers was largely irrelevant. However non-owners were more cautious about voicing their opinion in public. Young men who married into the village felt perhaps the most insecure, worrying about being laughed at, that their wives were having affairs behind their backs, or that they were victims of sorcery. A man who lived in his wife's village might be addressed by a nickname or find his patronym replaced by his wife's first name (e.g., "Ali *Fatima*"). But by the time people had children of their own, especially children who were owners through the other par-ent, they felt more at home and they knew their children would never expel them. Those who spent their adulthood in the community and participated in community ceremonies were de facto full members and usually chose to remain until death.

The differences in status were thus offset by relations of kinship. Such relations could be genealogical or they could be performatively instituted. When Tumbu's father, Vita, first arrived as a young man in Lombeni he instituted a sibling relationship with the woman married to Mdery (grandson of Mze Mdery, *figure 3.2*); both were outsiders and they liked one another. During Vita's lifetime, he continued to have friendly relations with his "sister"; they visited one another's house-holds informally as well as for ceremonial events. It is significant that such relationships were as likely to be constructed between people of the opposite sex as of the same sex. Constituted as kinship, they were companionate, based on mutual affinity, and they precluded sexual re-lations. Tumbu's father became a brother-in-law to Mze Mdery's grand-son, but their relationship was less significant or enduring than the one he held with the grandson's wife. It appears to have been irrelevant that the wife was light-skinned and ostensibly of Malagasy royalty whereas Vita was very dark-skinned, a migrant from the Comoros, doubtless with East African roots. This reinforces Tumbu's point (below) that denigration of those of African ancestry was a relatively recent phenomenon in 1975. Both Mdery and Vita died well before I arrived in Lombeni.

Social Differentiation

Villages in Mayotte differ from one another in composition, some containing populations more purely of Malagasy or of Shimaore origin. The villages in which I worked had core populations that were distinct in origin, yet, as the residents themselves said, they were each also quite mixed. The situation was quite unlike that in the village of Shimaore speakers in which Breslar (1979, 1981) was able to document in exquisite detail the origins of each family cluster and the way that resentments between formerly slave-owning and formerly enslaved families were maintained and continued to shape marital and residential practices as well as village politics and affiliations to the broader political movements. The villages in which I worked were ideologically opposed to inequality. People with roots in East Africa bonded to form one of the villages and people with roots in Madagascar the other. Those of East African origin had been originally indentured labourers, not slaves; those of Malagasy background were not, for the most part, descendants of indigenous slave owners and some had ancestors who were exploited as well. Some people did see themselves as better than others and for many decades were reluctant to marry with those they called "Makua," while others ignored the distinctions and did intermarry, successfully transcending differences in origin.[13] There were some cultural differences. It is likely no accident that those of Malagasy origin purchased land adjacent to the lagoon while those of African origin did not. Far more people of Lombeni Be build canoes and fish regularly; many of those in Lombeni Kely were not comfortable on the water (with many counter-examples).

One older man of Lombeni Be told me he wouldn't let his daughters marry the "descendants of slaves" in Lombeni Kely. Tumbu retorted that there is virtually no one in Mayotte who does not have some African blood in them. The mid-nineteenth-century population of Mayotte

was very small, and the French brought in African labourers who out-
numbered the prior inhabitants. He made a careful distinction between
those Africans brought on contract and the people who had been stolen
earlier from the coasts by Arab traders and sold to wealthy Mahorais
and Malagasy. The "custom" (*fomba*) of being ashamed of Makua ancestry, Tumbu averred in 1975, was recent. Everyone claims that it applies to someone else and not themselves, and yet, he suggested, no
one would tell me who were the descendants of actual slaves because
it would lead to fights. He pointed out a very dark-skinned older man
whose grandfather apparently had once purchased the grandfather of
a much lighter-skinned group of siblings. Once when a member of the
latter family insulted the dark-skinned man, his mother shamed them
by publicly reminding them of the former relationship. Not only did
Tumbu's account correspond with the written sources I drew on earlier,
but he was right that this was not a subject for conversation; convivial
relations demanded silence, and as a result the memory and status differences have largely dissipated.

No one I met appeared to have suffered abjection; on the contrary,
what this book shows repeatedly is the positive attitude people have
towards themselves and their expectation that they be treated with respect. During the period when people were travelling to Réunion to
pick up as many government benefits as they could (chapter 10), there
was absolute certainty that this was their entitlement and did not diminish them in any way. Indeed, they put the money they acquired
towards goals of positive public achievement – building houses, holding ceremonies, going on pilgrimage, or investing in education or merchandise. They were surprised and offended by the racist remarks they
encountered in La Réunion.

A more critical feature of social differentiation was whether one inherited rights to land, and this cut across distinctions based on origin.
Indeed, it cut through families themselves. Thus, for Tumbu Vita, as
noted, it was a source of anxiety that he depended on the pleasure of
his mother's brother for access to the land on which his house sat. Once
settled on his own property, he no longer needed to show the same
level of deference to his uncle or worry that the children of that uncle
might attempt to push out his own children.

Lombeni Kely and Lombeni Be were contiguous properties, on either
side of a ridge that, in 1975 was still forested. Over the years, as each
community grew, the ridge top was cleared and houses constructed on

it. The government built a road and placed schools at the juncture of the two villages, reinforcing the ways in which they were becoming a single place and part of a single municipality from the government's perspective. Intermarriage between people from the two parts has increased, but they still maintain distinct identities, and over the years they have maintained patterns of reciprocity that sustain their difference.

The communities interacted but also competed with one another. As one person put it, "the squabbling between us has gone on for so long it has become a '*fomba*' (custom)." But until the practice was stopped, they participated jointly every three years in a prayer for rain at an old tomb in the neighbourhood. And they continued to invite each other to distinct community events like annual performances of the *Maulida* as one another's guests. Moreover, as the same person pointed out, they stuck together whenever they visited a third village. The relationship thus contained some features of a classic segmentary opposition.

In the past the villages seemed spatially farther apart than they did in later times. The land between them was forested and inhabited by spirits. Even the most observant Muslims took them seriously. One of the Islamic *fundis* (experts) told the story of how as a child he determined to sleep out on his own. But he was disturbed all night by *sera nyumbe*, the "wild cattle" that trample backwards down the ravines at night. His brother, another Muslim sage, told me that you couldn't go out at night without seeing spirits (*lulu*). "There was one, known as *Dadilahy famaiky* (Grandfather axe) who carried an axe on his shoulder and would sit on a big stone on the path down to the beach. Other *lulu* lived in the mangoes on the path to the next village. The path was pitch black (*lalaña maiziky gum*)." I can attest to the latter, having walked it at night myself. He concluded, "*Mahery kabar ny taluha, mahery swuf.*" ("Things back then were tough, really tough.")

This man is speaking as much about childhood as about the past more generally. Things were perhaps especially hard for children. There were the parasites mentioned earlier and much childhood illness and mortality. One man remembered that children had only one pair of clothing and would have to put them on wet after they had washed them, which they were expected to do themselves. There was a year during the Second World War when no imported clothing arrived and even some adults dressed in sacks. After the war, conditions gradually improved.

Village Autonomy

Despite diverse origins, a common pattern developed across the first half of the twentieth century: everyone became autonomous community residents and everyone was or became Muslim, all within the Sunni Shafeite tradition, and all with aesthetic attachment to one or another Sufi brotherhood, mostly Shathuly or Qadiry, that cross-cut linguistic and residential affiliations. Villages developed models of internal governance and interaction with one another by means of norms taken from longstanding but by no means static traditions of the region. Through 1976 they were left by an uninterested colonial government to run their internal affairs mostly on their own; conversely, they were excluded from the broader structures of power and governance.

One can say that these villages were *composed*. They were neither timeless nor internally homogeneous, nor were they maintained without thought, direction, and sometimes internal conflict. They have distinct histories and particular combinations of people from diverse backgrounds. Despite the distinction between owners and non-owners, civic participation in villages like Lombeni Be and Lombeni Kely was premised on a strong ethos of egalitarianism and autonomy, in sharp response to the status differences of the precolonial period and the exploitation characteristic of the plantations. Founded as landowning settlements, they forged themselves into communities characterized by a deep sociality whose means and effects I will describe over the next chapters.

PART TWO

Exchange, Celebration, Ceremony, through 1995

A central concern of part two is what I call citizenship. During this period, the villagers were subjects of the French state, not citizens (Mamdani 1996), but they were citizens of their own communities. As citizens, a term I take from Fortes (1984), they were not simply residents of a given village understood as a geographical location or spatial unit, or members of a kin group, but active members of a self-constituting community, having a place and a voice in it. Citizenship as I describe it is not the same as kinship in the sense of descent or marriage, although it draws on processes and celebrations of reproduction (from births through mortuary events) to develop itself. Citizenship is likewise distinct from ownership as described in chapter 3. Nor is it equivalent to "ethnicity." Citizenship as formulated in Mayotte is constituted through the responsibilities and privileges of being an active member of the community, sharing one's life with others and sharing in their lives. This is established primarily by participating in ritual and ceremonial acts and exchanges of various kinds.

Chapter 4 sets out some of these acts and describes the experience of participating in the ones most salient at the time, called *shungu*. It provides a picture of social action in the mid-1970s and explores the tension around conviviality and competition with respect to the ideology and practice of equality. Chapter 4 departs from the original method of the book insofar as it describes life in the community in 1975–6 yet was composed in 2016. Like chapters 2 and 3, it was written to fill gaps in my account of the community. It draws exclusively from original field notes recorded in 1975–6 but undoubtedly is mediated by visits since. As I reread the notes, I was impressed; they are voluminous, detailed, and written very clearly, with few of the typos and shortcuts I make so often now on my laptop – better than what I can produce today.

Chapter 5 provides a formal model of the *shungu*, an elaborate system of ceremonial acts and exchanges that was central to life in the 1970s and then deliberately terminated. In chapter 5 I provide an analysis of how participation in the system constituted a mode of existence in which the person and the community became part of one another. Because the first draft of the paper was written for a panel on aging, I focus as well on how participation in the exchange system shaped the life cycle and the experience of growing older. This is, I think, a fairly original way of showing how participation in a system of ceremonial exchange unfolds over a lifetime and, conversely, what exchange means for the life cycle. The temporal dimension, however, is not only that of the space between giving and receiving or that of the life course but is also historical. The system was located at a particular historical moment, created at a certain point, and subsequently closed down in response to other changing social conditions. The first draft of the chapter was presented at a panel on aging organized by Nancy Foner at the International Union of Anthropological and Ethnological Sciences meeting in Zagreb in 1988; the next was published in *American Anthropologist* (Lambek 1990b). It overlaps in time with chapter 4 but extends from 1975 through 1985. The chapter is considerably shortened from the original publication.

Chapter 6 extends the analysis of exchange, focusing here not specifically on the *shungu* but on how all of these events form a means by which Islam became part of the social fabric and how society and sociality become intrinsically and deeply Muslim. I also show how the acts are premised on what I call, after Sherry Ortner, a reciprocity scenario. Chapter 6 extends the period of discussion through 1995. A first draft was presented at a conference on Muslim prayer at Oxford in 1998, and published (2000b) as "Localizing Islamic Performances in Mayotte" in *Islamic Prayer across the Indian Ocean: Inside and Outside the Mosque*, edited by David Parkin and Stephen Headley (Oxford: Curzon, 63–97). It also offers comparative material from adjacent northwest Madagascar where I first visited in 1987. I began serious fieldwork there, beginning in 1991 and continuing throughout the 1990s and since, that afforded me an additional perspective on Mayotte. The final section of chapter 6 is drawn from an article (Lambek 1987) first presented at a conference organized in Antsiranana by the Department of History, Université de Madagascar, in 1987 and published that year as "The Ludic Side of Islam and Its Possible Fate in Mayotte," in *Omaly sy Anio (Yesterday and Today)* 25–6: 99–122. The current version summarizes material from the revised article (Lambek 2006) published in *The Global Worlds of the Swahili: Interfaces of Islam, Identity and Space in 19th and 20th-Century East Africa*, edited by Roman Loimeier and Rüdiger Seesemann (Berlin: Lit Verlag, 161–86); several other articles in that collection provide further illustration of Muslim performances on the East Africa littoral. I discuss Muslim practice in Mayotte more extensively in my monograph *Knowledge and Practice in Mayotte* (Lambek 1993).

Over the period described in part two, the population of Lombeni grew rapidly. From 514 people (304 adults in 167 households) in 1980, by 1985 there were 868 persons, of whom 340 were adults, spread over 178 households. A government census conducted in 1996 of the much larger *commune* (administrative municipality) into which Lombeni was by then incorporated indicated a population of 6,050, of whom 3,628 were under twenty years of age and 82 were age seventy-five or over. Of 1,131 households in the *commune*, 781 were built of solid or semi-solid (*dur ou semi-dur*) materials, 735 had running water in either the house or the courtyard, 883 had electricity, and 892 remained without an indoor toilet.

4   Citizenship and Sociality: Practising Equality, 1975–1976

> Each life is thus dependent on the generative capacity of the village as a whole.
> Michael Jackson, *How Lifeworlds Work: Emotionality, Sociality,*
> *and the Ambiguity of Being* (2017: 104)

Whenever I am in the field I carry around a small notebook during the day, and at night or during slack periods I type up my scribbles, usually bringing together items from the previous twenty-four hours that seem to fit together, thus taking a first step towards abstraction. In the mid-1970s this entailed inserting sheets of onionskin and carbon paper into my manual typewriter; these days, I use a laptop.

Some of the typed notes have headings, more or less general: economy, circumcision of Bwana's boys, and so forth. Many of them are detailed descriptions of events I witnessed. By "events" I mean nothing so momentous as the conversion of St Paul or the arrival of Captain Cook but happenings that were important enough for the participants – like a funeral or a village hearing concerning who "stole" the virginity of an unmarried young woman who had become visibly pregnant – but also as ordinary as a prayer over a pregnant woman or an expedition to harvest rice. What the notes illustrate is not only my (very informal) method but what I would call the (somewhat formalized) method of life in the community, namely that social life was and is partly understood and carried out as and through a series of projects and events. Of course, the events are embedded in daily habitual practice and lubricated by particular styles and forms of interaction, by ideas and practices informed by age, gender, kinship, residence, friendship, religious knowledge, and the like. The events were – and are – composed of acts (actions) that often look simple enough on the surface, like handing someone a fried pastry, but turn out to be complex and polyvalent – the pastry being a gift, the materialization of a blessing, an acquiescence, and itself the sum of the acts and gendered division of labour that went into planning to make it, accumulating the ingredients, preparing it, and frying it.

Many of the events I describe were referred to as *asa*, "works" or "productions," or perhaps "affairs." Just as we might speak about the production of a piece of theatre, so the villagers produced performances of musical recitations such as Sufi dances, but also life-cycle events like weddings. Some affairs, like commemorations for the dead, also had embedded within them musical productions. In general, the *asa* entailed surrounding the more purely or formal ritual act with feasts and the distribution of raw and cooked food, organized by elaborate rules concerning the distribution of tasks, reciprocity, and hospitality. The sponsor(s) of an *asa* could be an individual, a married couple, a set of adult siblings, or an entire village. Throughout the dry season *asa*, interspersed with elaborate spirit possession events (not generally described as *asa* but productions of their own), were frequent events, and some were distributed across the Muslim lunar and solar years as well.

A cumulative message of this book is that the production and performance of *asa* are and have been central to the life of the community and key elements of what was once referred to by anthropologists by means of rules or models as social structure. Hence the transformation from ancient notes into a chapter is mediated as well by changes in anthropological theory and in the relatively implicit ways we understand life and social difference.

When I first went to the field my thinking was influenced by two paradigms. One paradigm – call it American – saw the world divided into social evolutionary stages and kinds of societies called bands, tribes, chiefdoms, and states, with the category of peasants tacked on alongside, as a component of states. I remember that as I was writing my dissertation one member of my committee asked me, "So, which of the categories fits Mayotte? Is it tribal?" The other paradigm was British structure-functionalism, which so well described the workings of smaller-scale non-Western societies, as exemplified by books like *The Nuer* (Evans-Pritchard 1940) that focused on kinship and the kinship idiom in organizing social and political life by means of descent ideology and descent groups. The two paradigms could be linked, and like many people, I was much impressed by Edmund Leach's *Political*

Systems of Highland Burma (Leach 1954), which charted the oscillation between two kinds of socio-political order.

As it turned out, these models did not take me very far in understanding Mayotte. The communities had no great historical depth and were not formed by centuries of adapting to a particular social and environmental niche and honing their institutions such that they functioned as an organic whole or at a consistent level of organization. They were, rather, as indicated in chapter 3, a contingent product of history, and, on the surface of things, quite recent history.

How then to categorize these communities, to describe them, and to analyse them? The paradigms available at the time (at least to me, naive as I was) did not seem to fit. They weren't quite peasants in the classic sense of inhabitants of agrarian systems; they weren't ports of trade. Economically, they were subsistence cultivators and fishers but with a partial dependence on money and on labour and land as commodities. Perhaps the closest comparison, but one itself not fully developed then, was with post-slavery communities in the Caribbean (Mintz 1989). But here, too, the differences were as large as the similarities. Dislocation had not been so great, disruption so sharp, or exploitation as violent. Many of the abductees spoke a common language and shared a cultural tradition. Most of the movement had been intraregional, and some of it had been voluntary. There was also a continuous history of habitation in Mayotte. Even among those older people whose grandparents remembered being abducted from East Africa (Mrima), there was no extant sense of violation or rebellion, and I never heard these matters discussed. By the mid-twentieth century everyone was integrated into the community of Islam and understood themselves as citizens of a wider ecumene.

These were not timeless villages or people steeped in a kind of mythical time or tradition. They were well aware of history, of movements that had brought their parents or grandparents to Mayotte and to this village. They had become Muslims and embraced the wider and transregional frame Islam provided, while at the same time being participant in and cognizant of local forms of life, receptive to the taboos and spirits "native" to Mayotte.

While the village was composed of people of interconnected families and while kinship formed the main idiom by which people expressed and understood their relations to one another, kinship was not the organizing principle of the community itself. What was most salient was not a set of rules or identifications but a set of activities. I call them rituals, ceremonies, performances, celebrations, or affairs but use the words loosely here. Their production and enactment were linked in a complex system of exchange. Performances operated at multiple levels of inclusion from that of the island as a whole down through ceremonies performed by or on behalf of individuals. But most salient was the way they were mediated through the village as a community and the way the community itself was formed and reproduced – lived and experienced – by means of the enactment of various ceremonies. Certainly, in the dry post-harvest season, rituals were very common, but they periodically interrupted the rainy agricultural season as well. Some were linked to the lunar Islamic calendar, others to the life cycle, others to circumstantial events. People seemed always to be engaging in, planning for, or resting after a ritual event. It is partly for this reason that I have found Aristotle's focus on activity critical, especially his emphasis on action, on *doing* things (alongside making and contemplating).

It seemed to me that at base the Mahorais were citizens – citizens of their communities. Being a citizen meant, as I have indicated, more than being a resident. It meant participating in the affairs of the community. What was striking was the frequency of calls for participation and the elaborate ways in which ceremonies were socially constituted and articulated with one another in various cycles of exchange. Mayotte could perhaps also be described as a society of the gift, but the "gifts" in question were largely acts rather than objects. The ceremonies were first and foremost concerned with events in the life cycle, with producing one another as persons (less with "self-fashioning" than with "other-fashioning," or with "other-fashioning" as the chief means of "self-fashioning"). The significance of the life events has changed over time, as have the rules of participation, but the fact of collective sociality remains.

More recent developments in theory that happened, or that came to my attention, well after the notes were taken included a shift from structure to practice (Bourdieu 1977, Ortner 1984) and also from society to sociality. And there was as well the strong influence (on me) before and after fieldwork of Clifford Geertz and his ability to so deftly portray the places in which he worked and their differences from one another in cultural terms (Geertz 1973a). All this meant getting at the tone and quality of life, of what it was like to be a citizen of a community in Mayotte. This returns to issues raised in the introduction. I want to describe change and how change was understood, lived, and enacted by residents – but change does not make sense in the absence of the play of figure and ground that only ethnography can offer. The historical dimension should not overshadow the ethnographic, nor overpower the depiction of the quality of life or the deep cultural conceptions that continue to shape how change takes place and how it is understood.

A way to proceed is to follow what excites people, what they focus on. In the 1970s, as the vignettes to follow show, one thing that concerned people was fulfilling their ceremonial obligations. It is implicit that another concern was livelihood, which included not only subsistence (relatively easy to acquire at the time) but also cash, which was not as easy. Cash was needed not only for household items such as clothing or kerosene but also for the production of ceremonies and to lubricate social interaction.[1]

Lombeni is characterized by a kind of contingently convivial egalitarianism, an egalitarianism that is not quietly taken for granted but in your face, comprising repeated claims to and of equality. To be treated as an equal you have to show you are an equal; conversely to be an equal, you need confirmation by the community. By comparison to what I subsequently encountered in northwest Madagascar, there is an intensity to social life in Mayotte, a drivenness to marry correctly, to build bigger and better houses, to offer larger dowries, for women to wear a new outfit in the latest pattern at each public appearance, to hold feasts as large as those of fellow citizens and in as fine a style, to become more knowledgeable about Islam and exhibit more piety. The move to stay part of France can be understood as one manifestation of this restless urgency. At the same time, it is not in everyone's character, or to the same degree, and it quietens in old age, when one's obligations are done. Moreover, alongside this frenetic activity and what, by comparison with northwest Madagascar, seems a hard edge, there is a graceful side to life – attention and responsibility towards kin, community and religion and the pleasure taken in them, easy laughter, courteous visiting, joyous music making, and both the deep sensitivity and comedic exuberance of spirit possession.

If there is a paradox it is that the celebration of equal achievement is also competitive. Everyone wants to show that they are good enough, that they are or have become social adults. Achievement and responsibility are displayed primarily through the enactment of the life-cycle rituals and in the quality of housing. Conditions have been such that achievement was available to virtually everyone, and most people could and did do what was necessary to *be* someone, to fulfil the requirements of the adult life course, and to be able at last to draw a breath of satisfaction. But there has been, after the time about which this chapter is written, increasingly a pull to do *more* – build more and bigger houses, of more solid and expensive materials, hold more and larger ceremonies, and answer more requests to assist at other people's ceremonies. This is understood as both competition and simply what any self-respecting person should do.

Age Groups in Exchange

During the 1970s the main thing was to complete one's *shungu* obligations. The *shungu* was a system in which every member of a specified group of participants had to provide a feast of a set amount to all the other members. The contents and quantity were carefully monitored so that no one could claim they had given more than their fellows, but nor could they give less. The group could also decide to add another requirement that each member would have to fulfil. So any inflation was collective and in that sense maintained equality among the members. *Shungu* feasts were held – and *shungu* obligations fulfilled – on the occasion of life-cycle rituals, namely at one's own first wedding, the circumcision of sons, the wedding of a virgin daughter, and the commemoration of deceased parents.

Shungu groups were constituted both by same-sex age mates and by the entire village that encompassed them. A man had to satisfy the demands of his age group and a woman of hers. But in addition, he or she had to feed the members of the other age groups that made up the totality of the *shungu* system, a group that closely approximates but is not identical with the adult residents of the village. This chapter describes primarily the obligation to the age group.

In order for collective activities to be performed smoothly each village was divided into women's and men's age groups (*shikao*). Each *shikao* had leaders, and the village as a whole had chiefs (*chef tanana*), men and women whose jobs were to oversee the correct management and enactment of the affairs. The *shikao* were established independently by each village, coalescing in adolescence and closing on an ad hoc basis as the next began.[2]

The number of age groups in existence and the age range within them vary from village to village. In 1976 there were six men's and six women's age groups active (plus a few surviving members of retired groups and younger groups in formation) in Lombeni Be.[3] Lombeni Kely had three active men's groups and five women's groups (plus retired groups and one group in formation). The various groups in both villages ranged in size from about ten to twenty-five members. A larger village had thirteen male age groups with more than fifty members in the youngest group.

Groups name themselves. From oldest to youngest, the women's groups in Lombeni Be were called Mahadubu ("having the last word"), Aeroplany, Pelaka ("lightning," because they worked fast), Angeky (spoiled grains of rice, because they felt unappreciated), Kararoku ("Chatterboxes," the name of a noisy bird), Algérie, and a group in formation as yet unnamed. Aeroplany and Algérie point to historical horizons extending beyond Mayotte.

Tasks for village affairs were divided by age group and so were working groups conducting the same activity (e.g., cooking).[4] Contributions to an event were sometimes collected by age group, and the distribution and consumption of cooked food was often by age group as well. While the age groups were involved in ceremonial exchange that concerned the village as a whole, some of them also had internal ceremonial exchanges, such that each member of a given *shikao* would offer a feast to the other members. It is the enactment of two of these exchanges that I describe in this chapter, one concerning a group of middle-aged women in Lombeni Kely and the other an age group of young men from Lombeni Be. These exchanges were expected to take place in the context of the fulfilment of larger, village-based ceremonial obligations. In the first case, Kala produced the commemorative ceremony for her deceased mother and used the occasion to also fulfil her obligation to her age group. In the second case, Moussa fulfilled an obligation to his age group that should have occurred during his wedding to a virgin bride.

In 1975 these events occurred in the context of a largely subsistence-based economy, one in which cash was scarce and most of the food was produced by those holding the ceremony. In principle, they drew on their rice harvests and on cattle they raised themselves. However, Kala's husband had to slaughter a cow and sell the meat in order to purchase sufficient rice. In Moussa's case the reverse happened; he used proceeds from the sale of his harvest (including cash crops) to purchase the beast that he slaughtered for the ceremony.

The structure of the exchange system is the subject of the next chapter. In this one I focus on the feel of it, on sociality not structure. I illustrate two sides to the sociality or structure of feeling that characterizes the exchange system and daily life. These might be called conviviality and care, on the one side, and agonism and anxiety, on the other. They were and are in Mayotte two sides of the same coin. Thus, people might get together to host a musical performance; they would invite a neighbouring village to dance, and they would enjoy the performance and the interchange and yet worry that the affair proceed well lest they lose face.

In sum, I illustrate a kind of intense sociality. This sociality has both a positive, optimistic face, characterized by vitality, solidarity, achievement, and cooperation, and a more cautious or anxious face, characterized by competition and the risk of failure or lack of support. The account also illustrates how leadership worked.

Kala Hamada's *Shungu* Payment

End of August, 1975. It is the late post-harvest season and Kala Hamada announces she wants to hold a ceremonial prayer (*mandeving*) for her mother, who had died the previous year.[5] The *mandeving* is an event that every adult should hold once in their lifetime on behalf of deceased parents. It consists of calling on male guests to recite in large numbers short verses of prayers (*tahalil*) in the mosque and supplying them with honoraria of cash and a very good meal. During the night before the prayers a religious musical event is sponsored, at which people gather to sing, dance, or simply watch and enjoy. Kala's mother had had only one other child, but he predeceased her, so Kala has to produce the event as the sole principal (*tompin*).

However, Kala wants to do more than this. She wants the *mandeving* to satisfy completion of a formal *shungu* payment that she owes the entire village. For this she needs one head of cattle and ten *mshia* of rice. The *mshia* is a wooden box used to measure rice; it is 25 by 24 by 22.5 centimetres in size and holds approximately 12 kilos of husked rice; thus the expectation is 120 kilos of rice. Every family will contribute a little rice and cash, but the majority must come from Kala herself.

Kala faces one further obligation. Uniquely, the members of Kala's age group have set up the requirement that at the first *shungu* of every member the principal must give a full leg of meat directly to the age group. This takes precedence over all other calls for meat. Despite the fact that Kala is already in her sixties, this is her first *shungu*; hence from the perspective of her age mates the leg of meat is long overdue.

Kala's announcement causes some consternation. Kala's husband had sold one of their two cows in order to acquire the money to buy sugar, rice, flour, and salt for the feast and to have the cash needed to offer the reciters. But he subsequently spent most of the money on palm wine, gifts of perfume to spirits, and other frivolous activities. Kala now expects her family to step in, but it is a bad year, a year of poor harvest. Moreover, Kala has no rice herself. As someone said, if a person had at least ten baskets of raw rice from their own harvest, the family would then help out with the rest, perhaps up to as many as fifty baskets. But Kala has only the second cow, a little rice, and no money.

One of her female cousins explains to me that Kala is somewhat simple-minded and "does not understand the way things work." Chanfi Abudu, a senior man who acts as Kala's father, is to speak to Kala about it. Chanfi is in fact the maternal half-brother of Kala's deceased father, Hamada; in local terms, he is Kala's *baba hely* ("small father"), and, in that light, has taken on paternal responsibility (*figure 4.1*). The cousin predicts that people will help Kala hold the *mandeving* but that completing the *shungu* is out of the question.

10 October 1975. Riziky Hamada, the chief of women, is tired, and with old age her knees have begun to ache; the thought of having full responsibility for organizing the public work for her paternal half-sister Kala's forthcoming affair does not please her. Moreover, although they maintain houses and return for village affairs, neither of the two women from the age group below her who hitherto served as her assistants currently lives in Lombeni full time, and they are never around when work needs to be done. So Riziky lets the senior men know it is time to appoint two additional village chiefs (women's chiefs) to support her. As her juniors, they will do most of the work, eventually succeeding in turn to her position.

Amana Seleman, as senior man of the village (chapter 3), calls the women together and proposes the names of two middle-aged women. When these are greeted with silence, he adds two more names; all four are from the age group (*shikao*) directly below Riziky's. Again there is silence. A "vote," as they call it, is then taken. Amana writes the names of the four candidates on several slips of folded paper, which he places on the ground. A child is called over and asked to pick them up one by one. Once a name appears three times the person is selected. The two women who come in first and second each demur, saying they couldn't handle the job, but the assembly refuses to accept this, saying it is not they but God who has selected them.

Mohedja, who came in second, tells me later in private that actually another woman badly wanted the office, though she could not say so out loud or campaign for it. In this respect, the selection process is radically different from the politics, pressure, and propaganda

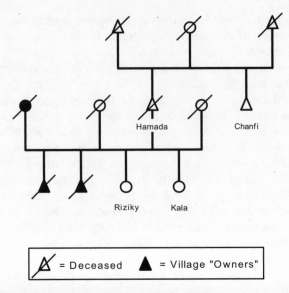

Figure 4.1 A simplified genealogy of Kala's *shungu*. Kala has no full siblings and is the sole child of her deceased mother for whom she is holding a *mandeving* (mortuary prayers). Her half-sister, Riziky, is chief of the women and her *baba kely* ("little father"), Chanfi, is looking out for her.

surrounding the referendum concerning independence from France. And it forms the baseline for the steep learning curve people will subsequently face concerning loyalty and autonomy in voting people for political office along party lines in the new government. Indeed, the local method of selection is designed to obviate such matters. As Amana explains to me, he was afraid of showing favourites and did not even propose his own wife, who was in the same age group as the others. God likes people to vote this way, he says. He did, however, ensure that each of the names he put forward were competent.

Mohedja is rueful about her own selection and, as the most junior, anticipates that the bulk of the work will fall on her. Being village chief is a hard job, involving organizing all the ingredients, cooking equipment, and people needed for every village affair. The chief oversees women's activities that concern the village (*tanana*) as a whole. Women fully "enter the village" on the third year of marriage, only then taking a public role in village "affairs." This means gathering with other members of their age group to assist in collective food preparation. Within the household young unmarried daughters are expected to carry out many of the chores, but it is only married women who can do so at public events. The village in this sense is not simply a residential community, nor a land-holding corporation, nor a kin group, but an organization that people enter and in which they are assigned specific roles by age group. The village as such is stratified by age but otherwise egalitarian. When the names for chief are proposed, the question of whether they are village owners (*tompin*) should not enter into it.[6]

Riziky times the new appointments just before Kala's affair takes place. The following day Amana calls on Riziky, who then calls on her new assistants, to bring all the women together at her compound to plan the affair. Riziky says they have to settle the date and proposes the following Wednesday, to which the group acquiesces. They will collect rice and set it to soak the day before, pounding it into flour and preparing pastries the following day. Riziky announces that they will hold a *Maulida* that night and cook the meal the following morning. Presumably these plans were agreed on beforehand with Kala and her close kin (of whom Riziky herself is one).

As noted, Kala is using the occasion of the *mandeving* to fulfil the additional obligation to her age group. This age group has some time ago voluntarily instituted an additional exchange among its members. The obligation is called a *mkungu,* and Kala's is the only age group in Lombeni Kely to have one. It consists of presenting a hind thigh of a cow to the other members of the age group. Each member has, when her time comes, to give the equivalent of what others have given. The women guard this jealously as their due.

The members in turn each bring Kala 2.5 kilos of raw rice, fifty francs,[7] two coconuts, salt, and onions to help in the production of the feast she will serve the village in completion of the larger affair. In effect, while the obligation can appear onerous to the sponsor, the person paying her *mkungu* receives more than she gives. After the event is over Kala will have to present her age group with a large plate of pastries to acknowledge the fact.

As Kala's parents are both deceased, it is her father's brother, Chanfi Abudu, who oversees the *mandeving* on her behalf (despite the fact that he is no relation to the dead woman for whom it is performed). Chanfi and Riziky have complementary responsibilities in ensuring that the performance is successful; these include ascertaining that the goods are sufficient and that they are distributed appropriately. Chanfi decides that one portion of rice will be put aside to feed the reciters of the prayers, four portions will be divided among the villagers by age group, and the rest will be used to feed outside guests. The portions in question are counted in *mshia*, the amount of rice that fills the wooden box (*figure 4.2*). But when the women measure the rice that Kala has put aside from her harvest, there are only 4.5 *mshia*, far less than the 10 *mshia* people said would be necessary. Riziky calls in the male elders to inform them and to ask how much should be turned into flour. Amana replies that the women will know this based on the amount of sugar they have to prepare pastries.

Kala's husband has given Chanfi what remains of the money he received from selling the first cow. The male elders gather at Chanfi's to count the cash, which comes to 3,800 francs. Amana suggests a budget to which the others agree: 1,000 francs to buy more rice, 300 francs for

Figure 4.2 The *chef tanana* measuring rice. Rice for the *shungu* is waiting to be publicly measured by the women's "village chief." She will ascertain how many boxes (*mshia*) it fills to know whether it is sufficient and to decide how much to apportion for cooking and for processing into flour for baking. The drying banana leaves will be used to cover the baking.

salt, onions, and spices, 2,000 francs to give the reciters of the prayers (*tahalil*), and the remainder as a reserve. The *tahalil* is estimated at 100 francs per participant.

The contributions from the women of Kala's age group are gathered at the house of the assistant chief. The money is counted, placed on a white saucer, and wrapped in a cloth. The raw rice is divided into three baskets, and these plus the other ingredients and the money are carried on the heads of the women of the age group. They march in procession, Kala in the lead with a scarf on her head and companions on either side. They walk in measured steps holding straws in front of their faces. The materials are deposited on a mat in front of Riziky's house, and the women sing. One says, "*Kamgwavenzi* – God willing – each one of us will have the opportunity to pay our own ceremonial debt!" Kala enters the house, takes the money, and returns the plate and scarf. The procession takes place in the midst of the food preparation activities. No single woman is visibly in charge; rather, there is a kind of collective initiative and busyness. Women of the *shikao* who live elsewhere have arrived, and women from the other age groups are also put to work.

During the night people recite, sing, drum, and enjoy a beautiful intense *Maulida shengy* (ode to the Prophet).[8] In the morning men recite the prayers in the mosque. Chanfi takes some of the senior men over to Riziky's to re-measure the rice. An eloquent speaker, Chanfi reminds everyone that this is Kala's affair (*asa*) and that the meat of the cow must be stretched to go around. Riziky replies that if the thigh is not big enough they will have to give the *shikao* additional meat. Although Riziky is Kala's half-sister, she is speaking as chief of the women and is mindful of the requirements of Kala's age group. Chanfi, on the other hand, is speaking on behalf of Kala's interests and replies that he wants to call over the members of the age group to explain the situation to them. Kala, he says, is not rich and they should not undermine her *asa* (i.e., by being too exigent or too liberal dispensing the food).

When the members arrive Chanfi takes up his speech again, telling the women not to complain about the size of their portion of meat. He says that today Kala will be fulfilling her exchange obligations and that because she is poor they should consider all her obligations completed and ask no more of her. No one dares speak up, although Tumbu tells me later that they would not accept this for anyone else. There has never been a case like this before. But everyone agrees to consider Kala's obligations closed, especially because she is poor and will never be able to fulfil the remainder. She has no children and no parents alive to help her.

Tumbu and another man pour the husked rice into the box. There are now five *mshia* and a bit, somewhat over sixty kilos. The age group and village elders look on as the rice is separated into three *mshia* for the village feast and two *mshia* to feed the reciters (different from what Chanfi originally proposed). The women divide the village rice proportionally according to the number of women in each age group. Kala's age group does not get extra rice to go along with their extra meat; indeed, their offering of rice has gone into the collective pot.

Kala's husband has provided a rather small steer. It is sacrificed and butchered by the men. Women are never present for these activities, but Amana calls women from the *shikao* to come and choose their piece. They look over the meat carefully and choose one thigh plus a piece of another. They carry this over to the other women in front of Riziky's house, and there is some singing. The women then form a procession to take Kala and the meat to the compound where the *shikao* is cooking their portion of the village feast. In so doing they move in the opposite direction from yesterday's procession when they brought raw rice on Kala's behalf. They place a small branch over Kala's forehead. One woman carries the meat in a platter on her head. On arrival, they stand in a semicircle, Kala in the middle, and sing in celebration of her gift and achievement. Someone gives Kala a 100-franc bill, and she dances with it in her mouth (*figure 4.3*). A woman gives a humorous speech over the meat, and someone dabs everyone with perfume. Her age-mates each shake Kala's hand and congratulate her.

At public events men usually receive a larger portion of meat than do women since it is argued that the prayers they send from the mosque are more effective if the reciters are well fed. The male hosts take what they think they need to cook and serve to the reciters, with enough left over for themselves. As a result, the portion that is divided and cooked by the women's age groups is sometimes insufficient to feed the women and children. The situation is exacerbated as villages and guest lists grow in size, as is the case today, given the inadequate size of Kala's steer. The women in the youngest *shikao* mischievously give me an empty bowl to fill from the men's pot, telling me that if anyone asks to say it is for myself (although I am already stuffed); they cannot request this themselves, and if they tried they would not receive any.

Figure 4.3 Celebrating Kala. Kala stands in the middle with a bank note
she has received in her mouth as the women in her age group celebrate
her achievement.

The women's request demonstrates their disregard for strictly gendered hierarchies, although my naive response in calling for more
meat for the women remained a joke for years. The gender hierarchy
is partly transcended in other ways. Not only is there cooperation between the women and men in planning and carrying out the affair,
but when the men couldn't find thirty male reciters of the *tahalil* they
invited four women to participate. These women received the same
rich food as the men.

In addition, one of the consequences of staging a *mkungu* is evidently
that the women of the age group acquire priority in the apportionment
of meat and ensure for themselves a significant quantity. I heard that
in the past the thigh was cooked communally and the women ate together. But on this occasion Kala's age group cooks and eats only their
share of the village meat and divides the raw meat from the haunch
to take home and cook with their respective families. The same occurs
with the intestines, which are normally eaten together by the women

as they work. Once the meat reaches the household it is shared with children and with family members of different ages.

The overall tenor of the event was more a celebration of Kala in completing her ceremonial obligations than of mourning her late mother. The *mandeving* itself is described as a gift (*zawad*) from Kala to God on behalf of her mother, and she is happy to be able to provide it. Her mother will be pleased to receive what God gives her, thanks to Kala's request to ease her condition in the afterlife. No one knows if God honours your request, but the chances are good. And with respect to the living, sponsorship of the *mandeving* fulfils Kala's status in the community, and God too is pleased with her. But if the gift on behalf of her mother is conceived as voluntary, Kala's offerings to the community and her age group are obligatory. The event is thus a rite of passage indicating both that she has accomplished the *mandeving* for her mother and that she has completed her *shungu* obligations to the community and age group.

People overlook the fact that the feast is insufficient in size (three *mshias* of rice rather than the required four and a very small animal). The reason they acquiesce in Chanfi's request not to demand the full amount is not simply because Kala is poor; they all are. Nor is it that she has no children or full siblings. Rather it is because they recognize that Kala has a disability. She is of unusually low intelligence and has been so since infancy. Indeed, they say, she was born under a very difficult astrological destiny (*nyora*), and if the cosmologer had not worked mightily at the time to counter it, she would have died. She survived, but in somewhat damaged condition. In Chanfi's and the community's support of her affair and accepting what she could offer them, they are asserting her equality as a person and citizen.[9] In fact, it is Kala's own age group who are most insistent on receiving their due, while being also the ones to most honour Kala.[10] Despite some uncertainty along the way, and in the face of Kala's evidently insufficient means, the community comes through for her. In effect, they violate the very principle of the *shungu* to ensure a felicitous performance. But this is also to ensure the principle of equality that lies behind the *shungu* itself. Kala is able to take pride in the achievement that is everyone's right.

This is a special case. Not everyone who is unable to live up to expectations is treated gently. Indeed, most people of ordinary means find that producing the obligatory gifts is neither easy nor carried out without anxiety. The next vignette illustrates the other side of thick sociality.

Moussa Madi's *Shungu* Payment

The following account shifts perspective in several ways. It is about the *shungu* payment of a young man and is told somewhat from his point of view. And it shows the more agonistic face of *shungu* exchange. It is recounted in the ethnographic present of 1975–6.

Moussa Madi is around thirty years old. He married a virgin bride[11] nine years ago and paid off his ceremonial obligations, with the exception of a portion, called the *shavua*, that he owed his age group. His wife died a year later, and he subsequently married a young divorcée in another village, where he went to live.[12] They have two children together. He was planning to marry another virgin in Lombeni Be, at which occasion he would complete the obligation to his age group. But when it was discovered that his new fiancée was pregnant by someone else (and therefore neither a virgin nor interested in Moussa), he decided to simply stay with his current wife.[13] However, he still owed his age group their feast, and so he decided to hold it in the absence of a wedding.

Moussa's age group of twelve men have given themselves the name La Marine, although they rarely use it. The men are roughly between the ages of twenty-eight and thirty-four. Men's age groups form roughly every three to five years, and a given young man could join a group where he is among the youngest or wait to join one where he would be among the oldest. The age group has two chiefs, who are in charge of organizing events and ensuring fair redistribution, and two "elders" (*ulu be*), who settle disputes and hear cases arising within the age group. Moussa is one of the adjudicators, but that gives him no advantage with respect to his own payment.

7 May 1976. A few months after breaking off the engagement, Moussa Madi feasts his age group. Early in the morning the cow is slaughtered under the close observation of his age mates. All but two are present; one of the missing, who is ill, sends his younger brother to represent him, while the other's portion is put aside, to be picked up by his father. Moussa stands to one side and watches as the chiefs of the age group supervise the butchering and distribution of the meat. The liver, heart, and lungs are Moussa's and are sent to his parents.[14] The head goes to the man who herded the cow and sold it to Moussa. The thighs, forelegs, and other portions are piled on the mat, and the members of the *shikao* stand looking at the meat. Do they recognize it as sufficient?

After a few moments, they move out of earshot of Moussa to discuss it. (I am the only outsider present.) They tell me later that they want to ensure the decision is unanimous, so that no one can make a remark later and claim that Moussa has not given enough or that the claimant isn't satisfied with the size of his portion. They are about to agree that the meat is sufficient when one of them goes over to the carcass and takes another large section to add to their pile. They now have everything, with the exception of the spine, a few ribs, and the pelvis, which they leave for Moussa, who takes it back to his father's house.

The men weigh portions as they are cut smaller, starting with three kilos a person, which they lay in twelve separate piles on the mat. They are careful to divide the hump (*tungua*), considered the tastiest portion, equally. The fat is also valued, and it too is distributed. They check that each portion has approximately the same ratio of flesh to bone. In contrast to many scenes of butchering I have observed, this one is carried out calmly, and any outsiders hoping to snatch a bit of meat are severely warned off. Once they distribute three kilos to each pile they are able to add another two kilos, and then another, and finally a quarter of a kilo, until all the meat is accounted for and they have ensured that each pile is equivalent to the others. The chiefs warn their fellows not to quarrel or grab, and each man quietly takes one of the piles, putting it in a simple palm leaf basket he wove for the occasion. Each member of the *shikao*, including Moussa himself, receives 6.25 kilos. Two additional kilos of meat are sent to Moussa's father, a portion that is reserved for the parents of the sponsor. This comes specifically from the age group's portion rather than from the remains of the carcass.

Meanwhile, at the compound of Moussa's parents, things are busy. Moussa's sisters and other female kin fry pastries. Moussa and his father carefully divide the remains of the carcass into nine piles for those who have helped prepare the food and call each woman to select one. They do the same with the stomach and intestines. I am given a piece of the liver, also a delicacy. Moussa sells a portion of the stomach, and his father also sells a kilo of the remaining meat.

The men of the age group return to Moussa's parents after taking their meat home. They call impatiently, asking when the cakes will be ready. Moussa owes his age mates a total of three *mshia* of raw rice. This is measured out by the women; then one of the male chiefs carefully hands three kilos to each member, along with a heaping spoonful of salt (Moussa owes them one kilo of salt in total), and a coconut. Everyone makes sure they get their due, down to the salt, and they joke over the coconuts, accusing some people of taking two. Each man receives eight pastries. The men drink their tea on the spot. The father of the absent age mate drinks his son's tea. As he takes his leave he remarks that while his son will see his share of the meat and rice, he doesn't believe any of the pastries will be left. Everyone laughs at this.

Moussa provided ten kilos of flour, five kilos of sugar, and six kilos of rice for the pastries. The men say that if Moussa were paying in the context of an actual wedding there would be more than 1,000 pastries; the cakes and tea today are the equivalent of what the age group would consume only on the last day of the wedding. The men give no food today to the community or to the age group of the deceased wife, who received their portions during the actual wedding. Moussa purchased the cow for 40,000 francs and estimates he spent 5,000 francs on the rest. He did not use an animal he raised himself because they were all too young and he was anxious to get the payment over with. He declares himself very satisfied with the cow, remarking how much fat it had.

One thing that is evident in both Kala's and Moussa's events is that despite the fact that this is a gift exchange it includes features more often associated with commodities. Equivalence is measured in units of food rather than price, but measurement and precision are important. Money enters the picture insofar as food items can be purchased on the market and others, notably the meat from a slaughtered cow, can be sold. The ultimate source of the item was not relevant; Moussa sold rice and cash crops in order to purchase his cow, whereas Kala used proceeds from the sale of her cow in order to purchase rice.

As the men leave the compound they give a rousing shout, and the women trill. Moussa says he feels extremely happy and relieved. He is no longer in debt to others. No one can claim anything from him anymore; his "rope has been removed."

Like Kala, Moussa has discharged an obligation rather than freely given a gift, and so it is appropriate that he is congratulated, not thanked. The equality of the *shungu* is achieved rather than ascribed. It is both a demonstration and an assertion of equality, in the face of whatever inequalities exist. The *tompin* is congratulated not for doing more than others, for standing out, but for doing his or her share and demonstrating equivalence. The complementarity is marked also in the fact that both the principals (Kala and Moussa) also receive their portion as members of their age group.

People make fun of the one member of Moussa's age group whose payment is still outstanding, and he has to take it with good grace.

There is more rivalry with the age group directly above them where fewer than half the twenty members have paid. Members of the preceding *shikao* were ashamed at lagging behind, and La Marine jokingly refer to them with the dismissive epithet "Goat's Leg" (*vity ny bengy*).[15]

In fact, members of La Marine were lucky to reach maturity during a period of relative prosperity in which there was a good deal of money available from cash crops. Yet one of them explained the discrepancy with the age group above by saying their seniors had simply been too "lazy" or lacked the foresight to raise cattle. Thus, if the *shungu* celebrates equality, it is also marked by competition. And in speaking to relative achievement, it may conceal sources of inequality.

Moussa's mother explains that the reason the meat and rice are divided raw rather than cooked is because it is the middle of the agricultural season and many families are camped in their fields. The men say they will give significant portions of their meat to their mothers. As one man says, his mother worked very hard when she married him off, and now he wants to give her something in return. This is informal reciprocity, a matter of gratitude rather than a formal prestation. Some men also give meat to their mothers-in-law or say the latter will eat out of the same pot as their wives. My friend Darwesh, who is particularly conscientious, divides his 6.25 kilos of meat into seven unequal parts. He gives the largest to his mother, while worrying it is too small. He gives portions to his mother-in-law, his older sister, and his younger unmarried brothers who are working on his fields. He also gives a portion to his mother's older sister, who counts as a mother, and regrets that he does not have a distinct portion for his grandmother. He will share his own noon meal with his father and father-in-law. The meat stretches less far than he had hoped, and he is visibly relieved when I am able to graciously turn down his offer of a portion by indicating that Moussa has already given me some.

A few months earlier we celebrated Darwesh's marriage to a virgin from the village. The marriage was delayed, first because the bride took some time to reach menarche and then because her new house was not ready. The walls were hung with cloth and the beds covered with newly embroidered sheets and pillows. Houses are rectangular with two internally connecting rooms, referred to respectively as the women's and men's halves, the former facing the courtyard and the latter the street. Bride and groom receive guests together in the women's room, at the beginning often from the marriage bed itself. The bloody cloth from the defloration is displayed over the bed. The groom's age group must be the first to open the outer door of the men's room and sit on the beds within it. On the morning after the defloration two members of the age group came to do so. Until the age group returned from the fields in the afternoon no one was permitted to sit on the beds. Had someone done so, the age group would have fined Darwesh. When the members returned to feast, they invited one member from each of the other men's age groups to join them. They crammed into the front room and gave a collective yell before consuming the meat and rice set before them. The men enjoyed their food, pleased to be getting their due and to see the age group progress one step further to the completion of all dues.

Darwesh sat to the side and silently watched his age mates eat. The men gave another yell when they were finished and applied oil and mascara and combed their hair before making a quick exit. Darwesh then invited a few older men and me to join him in a meal. He explained that whereas he had invited the age group to this first meal, on the following days it would be the age group itself who invited each of the other age groups in turn to come to a meal at the new house to celebrate the wedding. Again, note how the individual and the cohort are merged. The food itself is produced by the parents of Darwesh's bride but by means of a payment agreed upon with Darwesh when the marriage was negotiated.[16] They are also responsible for feeding Darwesh's parents for a week. The latter asked them to carry the food to different members of their close kin in turn, thereby passing on the gift, until they took a turn to eat the food themselves.

The circulation of food and the distribution of the roles of donor and recipient is obviously quite complex (and I have merely skimmed the surface). Rather in the way that Goffman distinguishes among the principal, the author, and the animator in the "'production format' of an utterance" (Goffman 1981: 145), so the discharging of the ceremonial obligation is not a simple division between two parties. In particular, the "donor" here is distributed such that the functions of animator, author, and principal shift in complex ways between Darwesh, his in-laws, and his age group. One effect is that they become part of one another, distinguishable but also intrinsically interconnected.

I have been translating *shikao* as age group, but strictly speaking this is not correct. Darwesh says it means *équipe*, in the sense of team, crew, or squad. In the ordinary course of events one enters a team composed of one's age mates, or if there are none, then those closest in age. But someone who marries into the village can enter any *shikao* he wishes (any that will have him, that is). Moreover, *shikao* with insufficient members can merge with one another. The voluntary element means that in unusual cases a person of one sex might join the team of the other. People laughed incredulously when I raised this, but in fact there was a man in Lombeni Kely who joined both a men's and a women's *shikao*. This was not based on any noticeable gender dysphoria but, as he explained, so that he could host events in his home village even though he was married out of it.[17]

To return to Moussa: he says happily that his obligations are entirely over. Having married into another village and living there, he does not plan to pay the *shungu* (ceremonial obligation) of Lombeni, expected when a man marries off his daughters or circumcises his sons. The village he married into has disbanded these obligations. At the division of the meat that took place today he did not have to call in kin from outside Lombeni; it is considered an *asa an tanana*, an affair of and for the village.

Moussa wanders around the village in the evening, unwinding, and says he will sleep very well. He repeats how relieved he is to have completed his obligation and to have done so in a respectable manner. Moussa says he bought the cow rather than waiting for his own to grow because he was very embarrassed at not having settled his obligation and afraid about what the other members of his age group might do to publicly shame him, perhaps taking their due by force.[18] He says that for people who are capable of feeling embarrassment (*mahay heñatra*), being among the few members of a group who haven't paid is painful. The other members can and do insult you; what I observed earlier as joking with the man who has still to pay was real.

The pressure on Moussa was particularly acute because his age mates knew he could afford it. He overheard them talking about how they would open the granaries of those who hadn't paid by the end of the harvest season and take their due. He did not consider it an idle threat. Not only would it be humiliating in itself, it would deny him the opportunity to perform an act that brings respect. He predicts the age group will go to the father of the remaining member whose debt is outstanding and demand a cow – and he is now ready himself to engage in such an escapade.

I ask Tumbu whether these threats are serious, and he recounts some actual events. In one case a man who hadn't paid was slaughtering a cow in order to sell the meat and buy his wife jewellery. The age group simply appropriated forty-five kilos, leaving him the head, hooves, skin, and remaining bits. He was furious but could do nothing. Another day his age mates brought him the rice, coconuts, and bit of cash that were his due in return in this particular exchange (different in kind from Moussa's in that it was due at the wedding of one's daughter rather than at one's own wedding).

On another occasion, the men of an older age group were enjoying their communal feast. One of them grabbed the arm of a man who had yet to pay and said, "What are we eating?"

"It's meat," he replied.

"Why are we eating it?" persisted the first man.

"It is payment of the *shungu*."

"Yes, and we want you to pay yours too!"

The man was ashamed; he and his wife left and he cried on his way home. Embarrassed on his behalf, his stepson gave him a cow to complete his payment. In each of these cases, the men had completed the weddings, the occasions when payment is normally given, and the members of the age group felt this was the only way to get their due.

Another man told me that a person who has not paid his part does not have the right to speak in public gatherings, particularly in front of other members of the age group. Thus those with political ambitions are more likely to complete their obligations relatively early.

It is evident that while completion of the payment solidifies a person's standing in the age group, during the payment itself the member is set apart, vulnerable to the other members' appraisal and almost their servant. But as each individual passes through the rite of passage, so the age group as a whole moves forward, anticipating full completion. The group depends on every individual to meet his or her obligations in order for the group as a whole to achieve its standing in the community. Upon Moussa's discharge of his debt the group was, if anything, even more eager to reach completion and had no hesitation in scaring its last member.

As for Moussa, having fully discharged his obligations, he is both fully identified with the age group and free of it.

Leadership and Dispute Resolution

This chapter has focused on the equality among members of a *shungu* group, yet I have also pointed to the role of appointed officials. In closing I say a bit more about leadership and authority as they were apparent in 1975–6.

Chanfi Abudu was the oldest and most respected man in Lombeni Kely. He was a garrulous but genial figure, well-disposed to others and with a jovial and slightly ironic disposition. I liked him very much. He looked out for his "daughter" Kala, and he took a similar interest in the village as a whole. But he could also feel unreciprocated.

The previous year the village had purchased a cow at 45,000 francs for the annual performance of the *Maulida*. They collected 25,000 by head, and Chanfi made up the rest.[19] When the cow was butchered and every household was allotted its fair share, there was meat left over. This was sold, and Chanfi was returned his investment. But there were additional profits, and these were divided equally among all the villagers. Chanfi thought they should have been his, but the village was adamant that he was wrong and they would not give in. At a meeting of the senior men they acknowledged that they owed him 2,000 francs for a debt he had paid off on the village's behalf for a different communal feast. They decided to return him the 2,000 francs from their own pockets, but Chanfi, still furious about the other matter, threatened to refuse the offer.

The most respected elder, the man who leads blessings over the village and from whom others seek advice to resolve conflicts, here found that people would not listen to him. In fact, they laughed about it behind his back. The dignified elder was reduced to rage. It is worth noting that when Chanfi failed to maintain the qualities of leadership expected of him, the next younger men stepped in, taking the responsibility both to pay off the debt and to resolve the conflict and make peace.

The authority of a given elder is always contingent on his actions. Everyone is subject to criticism. And yet, people take the initiative to ensure that matters are resolved and don't fester. Chanfi took the responsibility befitting his status to bail out the village, and the other men then bailed him out in turn.

Amana Seleman received somewhat less respect than Chanfi but had more power. He was the landowner on whose indulgence those kin not directly descended from his father depended for their house plots. He had final say over whether to accept new inhabitants (including the temporary residence of the ethnographer). Moreover, he was an expert (*fundi*) of cosmology, whose ability and, some said, disposition to commit sorcery (i.e., to harm others by means of his esoteric knowledge) were much feared. During the mid-1970s Amana spent most of his time living in the distant village of his wife. She was a *tompin* of her own village and had no inclination to leave it. So Amana found his time divided; he declined the position of chief in Lombeni Kely and did not mediate most internal disputes, but he still expected to be consulted on major decisions. In the end Amana took a second wife in Lombeni Kely and gradually spent more of his time there, although he remained rather aloof.

In 1975 the villagers tried to handle disputes internally, with as little recourse as possible to government authorities. Thus when Amana exiled a man who had married in, other villagers arranged a mediation. In Lombeni Be, village opinion led to the temporary exclusion of a man who had married in but had deeply offended the community (as described in chapter 2). This decision was made by the senior authority figure, Malidy Muthary, but he drew on an assembly that was called to discuss the matter.

Malidy was a charismatic, decisive, and well-spoken figure and, as a result of an astute investment in ylang ylang, was then perhaps the richest resident in Lombeni Be. He himself had married in (but a long time earlier) to the daughter of a prominent family, and he was already many times a grandfather. He was in his fifties, an age between the very senior men who were consulted on important matters and the younger chiefs who were delegated responsibilities. People generally listened to Malidy and respected him, though he had some rivals who disliked him intensely. One reason he had authority was that he was not one to stand aside but jumped in to address what he considered important issues.

Malidy stepped in to address a quarrel over land. A large parcel near the village was under dispute. The original owners, a brother and sister, had died long before. The woman, who was childless, left a portion to the child she had raised. The rest was left to the man's three sons, one of whom moved away while another died young. The third brother held the deceased brother's part in trust for the latter's children, but when they grew up he refused to give them their share. In the meantime, he had sold portions to his wife and her children from a previous marriage. In frustration, a nephew took the case to the Cathi (Muslim judge) and the ruling came to divide the land into three. So Malidy led some fifteen men, including the chief disputants, on an excursion to the fields in order to do so. Malidy tried to get the uncle to indicate where he would like the division to be, and thereby acknowledge the court's decision, but the uncle refused to do so. Malidy explained that they were there for the village to witness his acquiescence and threatened that if he refused they would write to the government on behalf of the nephews and nieces. The man finally seemed to accept their view in principle but would not indicate where the lines should be drawn.

The village members were unanimous in their opinion but could not force the man to do the right thing, nor did any one of them want to stand out and execute a decision, thereby making himself the direct object of the uncle's wrath. Malidy spoke diplomatically but forthrightly and the next day returned to measure the land in thirds. But he had no power to make it stick. The issue was resolved when the remaining brother, who had decided to give his share to his nephews, showed up in the village and, together with one of the nephews, simply made the decision as to which piece would go to whom.

Leaders and elders confer informally with each other. After the institution of Friday prayers described in chapter 2, Chanfi Abudu told Tumbu and me that he had gone to Malidy Muthary to ask why it was only young people (*zaza madiniky*, lit. "little children") rather than adults (*ulu be*) who were appointed imams at the mosque and to say he didn't think this was appropriate. Malidy acknowledged the complaint and explained frankly that the elders of Lombeni Be were afraid of the young people who were eager for change, worrying that if the young men were unsatisfied they might not attend the mosque at all. Conversely, it was the young men who decided that people who missed Friday prayers should be fined. Malidy said the elders would let them have their way but step in if they did something wrong. Chanfi observed that it looks bad to see the entire service conducted by the young. The sermon reader has to be a young person because only they have good enough eyesight, but the imam should be someone older.

These incidents say much about authority and its limits and the consultative way in which decisions are made. They show as well that people (some, at least) took an active interest in the affairs of the community and in instituting change. The system was actually quite democratic; as someone told me, they instituted the position of chief largely so that everyone wouldn't talk at once.

The most contentious issue in 1975–6 had to do with party politics concerning the referendum for independence and the expectation that the members of a given village would throw unanimous support to a given party. In both parts of Lombeni, as in most villages, this meant supporting Sordat (*Soldat*, "Soldier"), the party favouring incorporation in France. Men and women, but especially women, attended the party congresses that rotated from village to village. During the height of the tension over the vote, a congress determined that villages were to fine members of the opposing party, SLM (*Serre la Main*, "Shake Hands") as a means to bring them back into the fold. A meeting was convened in Lombeni Be concerning the size of the fine to impose on a daughter of the village who had married into a village of Grande Comorans and had become SLM along with her husband.

People gathered slowly and reluctantly, seemingly embarrassed by the whole affair. The woman herself stood towards the back, arms folded, looking nervous and sad. After a long silence, the president of the women's branch said the women were waiting for the men to say something. Finally, two men in their thirties, the local *chefs des jeunes* of the party, urged people to speak and went back and forth between the women and men. The women's president repeatedly asked the women to speak. Malidy Muthary stared at the sky and didn't utter a word. After a long period, the women collectively proposed a fine of a cow and three sacks of rice. The men said it was too much, and suggested a cow and one sack rice. None of this was uttered out loud but whispered to the go-betweens. People were urged to speak up and get things off their chests but no one did. Finally, it was left at a cow and one sack of rice. The woman's brother thanked people and asked for a *fatiha* prayer in closure.

People explained that the woman was related to most of them, a "child of the village," and that she had not harmed any of them personally. The cow was to be killed on *Idy* (the closure of Ramadan), but people felt that eating her food would be *haram* (forbidden by Islam) and were sad about it. In fact, the fine was quietly rescinded.

Things went less well for a man who had married late in life into Lombeni Kely. Riziky Hamada, as chief of the women, went to his home village to confirm the rumour that he was SLM. She and a male elder then informed him that he wasn't welcome in Lombeni Kely until he switched and made peace. He returned to his home village to publicly apologize and was fined 10,000 francs. Having paid, he was able to return to Lombeni Kely. The priority of the home village is evident; party membership is established there, and villagers are more sympathetic to their own members than to in-marriers.

These vignettes provide a feel for life in the community in the mid-1970s. I have addressed only some aspects of life, but in them one can see how the individual and group are mutually constituted; how gender is differentiated, but women's status is not wildly disparate from men's; how achievement is linked to the production of life-cycle rituals; and how money and land qua commodity encroach on forms of sharing and reciprocity. I have shown how the principles are implicit in action and practice rather than attempting to abstract a particular set of cultural concepts, symbols, or rules. People are caught up in life projects, ethical in the sense of what makes living significant and in the way that means and ends are identified. Life projects conjoin promoting the self and giving due respect to others; this is evident in both the formal procedures of the ceremonial system and the informal and circumstantial aspects that come into play. Neither Kala's nor Moussa's prestations were standard but were shaped by the articulation of contingent circumstances with the model and also by their respective persons and character.

In the next chapter I lay out more directly the principles on which the ceremonial system was based, the social consequences, and the actions taken to transform it. What I have done in this chapter is examine local interpretations of that system – interpretations first in the sense of two distinct enactments or performances (as a stage production interprets a play and a dramatic actor a role), and second in the ways people talked about them. The interpretations illustrate how the system develops. Kala's age group added a specific prestation, the *mkungu*, that preceding age groups did not have and that successive age groups rejected. One of the striking features is that while virtually everyone felt compelled to complete their obligations in the system and was committed and found it meaningful and satisfying to do so, they also reflected critically on it. The structure is fully in history and is reproduced always and only in relation to and by means of enactment qua interpretation.

5 Exchange, Time, and Person in Mayotte: The Structure and Destructuring of a Cultural System, 1975–1985

This chapter develops the analysis of the *shungu* described in the previous chapter in three ways. I render explicit the structure underlying the system of ceremonial exchange; explore how the person as citizen, the experience of aging (traversing the life course), and ultimately the community itself were constituted through it; and demonstrate how and why the *shungu* was terminated. The chapter portrays the holistic social world and experience created through participation in the exchange system, providing an implicit contrast with the more fragmented world that follows. Yet what I describe is not a breakdown or abandonment but a deliberate, reflective, and orderly closure, true to the principles of the *shungu* itself.

Systems of exchange are not timeless; they are both historically shaped and situated, and they in turn shape the experience of time in which exchange takes place. I link the temporal dimension and formal properties of the exchange system to the construction of the social persons who participate in it and elucidate how participation shapes the experience of aging and the life course. While most discussions of aging focus on the individual or family, my analysis supports Meyer Fortes's discussion of the role of age systems in "incorporating the individual into the order of society as a citizen" (1984: 118; cf Eisenstadt 1956), thereby ultimately addressing the question of how society itself is constituted. In Mayotte, this process is equivalent for women and men. I also consider how a balance of reciprocity was regulated over time, why it could no longer be, and what happened when it could not be. Finally, I document the transformation of the civic arena as the "anti-politics" of the age system (Maybury-Lewis 1984) is eroded, giving way to competition among kin groups. However, what is of considerable interest is that the exchange system is dismantled systematically, according to local principles of order and equity. Indeed, it was only through observing the dismantling process that I became aware of certain principles that underlay the system.

I begin with a set of interlinked notions: first, following Geertz (1973b; cf Östör 1984), that experience is mediated through cultural forms and that the cultural conceptions of person and time are interlinked; and second, following Mauss (1974), Lévi-Strauss (1969), and Bourdieu (1977), that persons, relations, and time emerge in part as products of a system of exchange.[1]

During the 1970s and 1980s the *shungu* was one of the chief cultural forms through which the plot of the adult life course was constructed and hence through which aging was experienced, as persons were increasingly embedded within the social whole. Because exchange has a temporal dimension (especially the interval between receiving and giving, or prestation and counter-prestation), and because of the specific manner in which exchange cycles were defined and in which moments of giving were linked to acts of social reproduction, the *shungu* system formed a *measure* of the life cycle. Equally it formed a *means* of the life cycle, that is, of the constitution of full adult citizens, as well as a *model* for goals and action over the course of the life cycle.

In focusing on exchange and personhood I am alert to three kinds of connections. First, as is well known, exchange *links* donor and recipient in a social relationship. Second, exchange serves to *distinguish* donor and recipient from one another and to mark the space between them. Third, the donor has an intrinsic relationship to the offering. One of the characteristics of a gift as opposed to a commodity is that it is essentially inalienable (Gregory 1982; cf Parry 1986). An aspect of the self, albeit the public persona, is offered and, in Mayotte, consumed by the collective other. This consumption, which in the long run is reciprocal, is constitutive rather than destructive. Following "Marx's conception of consumption as the production of human beings" (Gregory 1982: 33), the exchange system can be seen as a means of collective social reproduction (cf Weiner 1980). As Fortes suggests,

> nothing so concretely dramatizes acceptance – that is, incorporation in the self – be it of a proffered relationship, of a personal condition, or of a conferred role or status, as taking into one's body the item of food or drink chosen to objectify the occasion [or, I would add, to index the donor]; and

sharing or abstaining from the same food, means uniting in common commitment. The intangible is thus made tangible. (1987: 139)

As a result of population growth, inflation, and the increasing penetration of a cash economy, the exchange system has experienced a series of contradictions. In response, it is being dismantled in a manner that participants experience as fair and orderly. Younger age cohorts participate in a simplified and transformed system; this provides them with a less unified experience in which growing older is more individualized and in which the elderly are less deeply embedded within the community and have less access to the source of social value. Although the elderly are gaining greater access to governmental social benefits and medical assistance, the social experience of aging declines in quality.

The *Shungu* System

There are four essential features to the *shungu*: (1) rotational redistribution and (2) rigidly balanced reciprocity within (3) closed, sex-specific age groups and bounded but generationally renewed villages on the occasion of (4) personally scheduled rituals of social reproduction.

The first two of these features refer to the transactions that Sahlins distinguishes as redistribution and reciprocity (1972: 188). The *shungu* is redistributive in the sense that goods are amassed by one person or household and then given to all the others. It differs from Sahlins's primary examples in being acephalous and egalitarian (i.e., without a chief at the top or centre) and in the fact that it is rotational. There is no predetermined order in which participants hold their feasts, but each member of a *shungu* group, that is, everyone who eats the feasts held by other members, is expected sooner or later to pay (*magnefa*). The structure is not segmentary, and the *shungu* expresses relationships primarily within rather than between groups.

Sahlins emphasizes that, viewed abstractly, "pooling is ... a system of reciprocities" (1972: 188). Reciprocity is clear in the *shungu*, where collection is not anonymous (as in a system of taxation) but an explicit relation between specific parties. Moreover, the number, size, and content of feasts expected of members is strictly regulated by the group and remains constant within it (though variable between groups). Most saliently, the food distributed at a *shungu* feast must be identical to what has been offered at previous feasts within the cycle, hence precisely balanced in Sahlins's terms. Food offerings are carefully measured, not only meat and rice, but the numbers of pastries and even the spoons of salt and spices. A *shungu* offering will be rejected by the group if it is too small but also if it is excessive. Hence, within the *shungu* cycle inflation is prohibited. This means that largesse and generosity cannot be used to distinguish oneself from one's peers in order to gain prestige.

The logic of the *shungu* is thus the inverse of the potlatch, designed to establish equivalence and equality rather than hierarchy.[2] Moreover, the strict prescriptive rules of balance and timing preclude most of the strategizing, ambiguity, and effort to conceal self-interest often attributed to exchange (e.g., Bourdieu 1977: 171ff, Adams 1973).

Payment of *shungu* provides a major means for establishing personal value. The payment of each stage and the completion of the entire set of obligations mark major achievements in the life course. As described in chapter 4, these occasions are anticipated with anxiety and concluded with relief by the principals, and the ceremonies include episodes to fête and congratulate the donor. The *shungu* thus affords an assertion of equality, establishes a group of social equals, and celebrates equality. This is equality that is not simply given but demonstrated through the achievement of potential – the ability to plan, produce, and amass sufficient food, and progress through the stages of social reproduction. The marked concern with balance and the evident greed with which guests claim, snatch, or pretend to fight over their portions are playful expressions of such equality. Fulfilment of an individual's *shungu* obligations provides the necessary and sufficient basis of civic status, establishing what Chris Gregory (1982: 65) captures in the felicitous term "mutual superiority."

A third feature of the system is the composition of the *shungu* groups. Kibushy speakers belong to two kinds of groups that establish *shungus* for their members: sex-specific age groups and entire villages. An individual makes separate payments to each, although the two units are not fully independent of one another and each has a formal interest in the payments made to the other. The *shungu* complex thus articulates the autonomy of a village and the interdependence of its members linked through various loops of exchange, primarily those within and between age groups.[3] Participation is based first on membership in an age group (*shikao*) and expresses an egalitarian ethos and presentist orientation of which age groups form an obvious manifestation.

Both *shikao* and *shungu* exchanges are formed independently within particular villages and operate entirely within the context of their village, although, because of residential mobility, not all participants in an exchange group reside within the same village at any given point in time. Exchange groups are not coterminous with villages for an additional reason – namely, that not all village residents need join – but they draw their sense from and address residential community.

The fourth main feature of the *shungu* is that the feasts are provided to celebrate events in the reproductive cycle: to the age group upon one's own marriage, and to the village at the circumcision of a son, wedding of a daughter, or prayers some time after the death of a parent. Thus, the scheduling of *shungu* payments is not based on an abstract calendrical system, nor is it intrinsically linked to the time elapsed since last receipt. Instead, it depends on events in the personal and domestic domains.[4]

Reproduction is understood in social terms; people who have not had children of their own sponsor the circumcision or marriage of closely related junior kin to fulfil the *shungu* obligation and the responsibility for reproduction. Like Moussa, a man happily married to a previously married woman will engage in an additional marriage to a virgin in order to complete his *shungu*. However, while celebrations of reproductive achievement are considered the necessary occasion for *shungu* payment, the reverse does not hold. A couple who are marrying off a second daughter or circumcising younger sons will call kin and neighbours for festive meals but without following the high and highly particular requirements of *shungu* again.

In Maussian terms *shungu* events are total social phenomena, and they present a complex intertwining of religious and social elements, not to mention economic demands. I note three ways in which the system provides a measure for aging and the passage of time. First, the age groups break up the flow of time into stable, socially defined units (cf Baxter and Almagor 1978: 24). Second, as described in the previous chapter, the *shungu* distinguishes the place of individuals in the payment of their obligations, relative to other members of the age group and village, and absolutely with regard to the overall requirements of the village. And third, the *shungu* marks off the accomplishment of various contributions to social reproduction (sponsorship of a circumcision, etc.) that are also key events in the life course. In linking these processes, and in combining significant transformations in the lives of members of adjacent generations (e.g., parents' *shungu* payment is simultaneously daughter's marriage), the *shungu* provides the basis for a unified experience of aging, bridging the corporeal and social aspects of reproduction and granting collective relevance to personal events and personal relevance to public ones. Indeed, the point at issue is the way in which persons are constituted by their substantive contributions to one another and to the collectivity.

Shungu Obligations and Entailments

Before addressing the factors that led to the closure of the system, I review the entire sequence of obligations as they presented themselves within a given village at a given period. This overview is brief, but it indicates the complexity of the system and approaches the question of temporality in greater depth.

In Lombeni Be in the mid-1970s, age groups of the middle range had the following *shungu* obligations. First, upon marriage (as a virgin for a woman and to a virgin bride for a man), groom and bride faced an elaborate set of requirements set up and overseen by their respective age groups. Thus, a man had to provide a cow large enough to lav-ishly feast his age mates. At Moussa Madi's payment in 1976 where, un-usually, most of the food was distributed raw, we saw that each *shikao* member, including the sponsor, received six-and-one-quarter kilos of beef, plus other foods, new spoons, a comb, and cosmetics. A groom also had to produce sufficient meat, rice, tea, and pastries to enable his age group to feed every other male age group in the village three meals successively for one day each over a week (the *fukatry*). In return, mem-bers of his age group danced to celebrate his (and their) achievement of a major stage of social reproduction (marriage to a virgin), the produc-tivity it entailed, and the reproductive potential it implied.[5]

In addition to establishing the groom's position within his age group, the *shungu* was a significant element in affinal exchange. If the groom provided the means – cash and beast – by which his *shungu* could be fulfilled, it was up to his parents-in-law to actualize it, that is, to pre-pare the food, and feed the guests. (Thus, the bride's family performs the wife's future domestic role of hostess and cook.) While the obli-gations of the groom to his age group were precisely defined, down to the last teaspoon of salt, the reciprocity between affines was not. At the engagement, the *shungu* requirements of the groom were dis-cussed and the size of his payment to his parents-in-law set accord-ingly. But it was by no means clear whether the bride's parents would be able to produce their son-in-law's *shungu* for less money than had been given, or whether, as was more likely the case, they would have to go to some expense of their own (for which no explicit recognition was made) to produce the *shungu* on his behalf.

The groom was dependent on his in-laws in two ways. First, they had to provide the virgin daughter. Without her, the legitimate occasion for a *shungu* payment might be lost and the months and years of saving and preparation be in vain. Of course, the bride's parents were also anxious concerning their daughter's condition, especially if they were using the occasion to pay a *shungu* of their own.[6] Second, the groom relied upon his affines to prepare the *shungu*. They relied on him to have estimated his needs correctly at the engagement, but, whether he did or not, their reputation depended upon acting correctly as hosts. The outcome of the wedding was thus that groom and affines saw themselves bound together by diffuse reciprocity which approximated that of "kinship" – in contrast to the precise, direct, and highly contractual nature of the *shungu* exchange within the age group.

In turn, the bride's *shungu* requirements to her age group were usually provided by taking portions of meat presented originally by the groom to his father-in-law. Brides fed the members of their age group as well as each of the other women's age groups in turn, in a fashion similar to that of grooms, though perhaps in somewhat smaller portions. The cooking and serving was again managed by the bride's parents. Expressed here is the fact that a wife is dependent on her husband's capacity to produce, much as he is dependent on her ability to transform and redistribute the product. In addition, both bride and groom contribute to each other's social transformation – the bride's virginity providing the occasion for the groom's *shungu*, the groom's enterprise providing the occasion for the bride's emergence into adulthood. These are acts of reproduction and, because they are reciprocal, of "alliance" (Lambek 1983).[7]

In subsequent *shungu* payments the age groups continued to play a role as units of labour and consumption. However, the group to which the individual was accountable was no longer the *shikao* but the village, conceptualized as the members of all age groups who participated in *shungu* exchange. The *shungu* was offered to, and accepted by, the community at large.

A married couple generally paid their village *shungus* jointly. This was appropriate since each partner in effect paid only the members of their own sex. Women and men relied on the assistance of their respective spouses, but each was accorded recognition of payment in their own right. Men who engaged in village-exogamous uxorilocal marriages often found themselves contributing to *shungus* in two locations.

During the years of greatest interest in the *shungu*, members of Lombeni Be undertook three major *shungu* feasts for the community – on the occasion of a son's circumcision, a daughter's wedding, and a prayer for deceased parents. Although the precise requirements and patterns of distribution and consumption varied according to the kind of event, each required at least one large ox or cow, some 72 kilos of rice, and large amounts of flour, sugar, and oil.[8] The *mshia* (c. 12 kilos, chapter 4) is heaped to overflowing six times by the village chief in front of witnesses, and I have seen virtually the entire contents of two 50-kilo sacks of rice included. When considerations of rice flour for cakes, food to feed guests and helpers who are not part of the *shungu*, and feasts that are part of the celebration but not specifically part of the *shungu* are taken into account, the amount of rice rises much higher. At one circumcision *shungu* I recorded in 1985, the sponsor's husband purchased 250 kilos of rice and 50 kilos each of flour and sugar. Six *mshias* of rice were distributed to the women's age groups, two *mshias* used to prepare cakes, one and a half *mshias* cooked for the men who performed prayers, and one *mshia* cooked for guests who were not members of the village age-group organization.

In addition, some individual age groups exert specific demands on their members on the occasion of their payment of the village *shungu*. As described in chapter 4, this not only asserted the value of the women's age group but redressed the typical bias towards male consumption of meat at feasts.

Continuity and Contradiction in the History of the *Shungu*

In 1985, *shungu* feasts were still performed in the manner described, but no new *shungu* obligations were engaged. With the acquiescence of their elders, the younger age groups had decreased the number of *shungu* payments expected of them. The youngest refused to set *shungu* requirements for themselves or join the village *shungu* feasts still performed by older people in order not to become indebted to them. What food they received on such occasions was granted on an informal basis, as individual kin of the host or the official recipients. They received no fixed amount of food, no explicitly reserved portion.

The large *shungu*s characteristic of the 1970s were not part of a static tradition but had a history. At the beginning of the century, when villages were smaller, goats were used. As prosperity increased, cattle became a requisite feature, and the number of *shungu* payments to the village increased to three in Lombeni. These *shungu*s, which are still being completed, represent tremendous expense. They are the product of several years of planning and saving. And, despite the formal expression of rigidly balanced reciprocity in public events at which the beast is examined (and possibly rejected as too small) and the rice is measured, they depend on informal assistance from kin as well and small contributions in cash, kind, and labour from the age group.

The subsequent abandonment of the *shungu* is paradigmatic of the relative shift from a gift-based to a commodity-based society. The *shungu* already bears the seeds of this transformation in its insistence on reciprocity that is absolutely balanced. In Sahlins's model, balanced reciprocity is located in an intermediate spot on the continuum between generalized reciprocity, characteristic of kinship, and negative reciprocity, at least partially characteristic of capitalism. Balance introduces the sort of precision and calculation characteristic of a money economy, yet the emphasis on the identity of what is exchanged, not just the quantity but especially its quality (i.e., the fact that it must be food, and food of specified types, and that it must be presented at specific occasions), locates the *shungu* firmly in the sphere of gift exchange (Gregory 1982: 46–7). The *shungu* has foundered on the fact that the main items needed for payment, namely cattle and rice, have become increasingly commoditized and hence no longer universally accessible, yet at the same time saleable on the market to pursue a variety of other ends. Moreover, by 1985 access to rice land was no longer automatic, rice yields per unit of land were much lower than a generation earlier, and the price of beef had skyrocketed.

The rising cost of goods created a contradiction within the *shungu* system because exchanges are supposed to be equal and measured by the quantity and quality of ingredients rather than by monetary cost. Hence, as prices rise, the interval between an offering and its return renders the exchange unbalanced. If a kilo of beef or rice costs "x" amount one year and double that five years later, so the actual cost of the exchange of exactly the same amount of food doubles. In other words, the inflation that occurred in the commodity economy could not be adequately assimilated in the gift economy.

Figure 5.1 A portion of a larger village, 1975–6. This is only one flank of a large village of Kibushy speakers. Stone terracing supports the houses ranged up the hillsides. Here already some houses have metal roofs.

A second contradiction, one that bears more on the experience of recipients than of donors, is that as the population of a village grows, so does the number of recipients. Since the total amount of material given by each participant remains constant, the amount received by each guest declines. In some large villages, this amount was reduced by 1975 to a mere handful of rice per person. The size of individual portions trivialized the feasts and ensuing conflicts made them unpleasant. Hence, larger villages began to terminate the *shungu* system some years ahead of Lombeni.[9]

These contradictions emerged only because the *shungu* principle of balance was itself retained. Partial adjustments, such as decreasing the number of occasions at which the *shungu* was paid or dividing the village into wards with separate *shungu* circuits, were tried in various communities (*figure 5.1*). The changes were regulated primarily by the age groups, which form approximations of the historical cohorts who experience the changing economic, political, and demographic circumstances that led to pressure on the *shungu* system.

Newly formed age groups still require their members to perform virgin marriages. But they have abandoned the feast formerly required of their members at this occasion, maintaining only such tokens as the distribution of a packet of cigarettes to communicate the event. This does not mean that there are no longer feasts at weddings or circumcisions, but rather that neither the quantity and kind of food nor the guest lists are formally stipulated. Hosts provide what they can and choose their guests according to personal (ego-focused) factors, such as kinship and residential proximity. The ceremonies continue to have domestic and affinal importance but less civic importance. They are less firmly embedded in the social whole. The end of the *shungu* may create less a simple overall decline in the size or number of feasts than a disparity among them, with implications of inequality, calculation, and exclusion.

Even at a first marriage, the wedding celebration is no longer a *shungu*. Yet, for the moment, the *shungu* principle remains both in the ways marriages are acknowledged and in the manner through which the exchange system is being discontinued, namely by disarticulating the age groups from one another so as to leave no debts outstanding.

Balanced Reciprocity, Closure, and the Constitution of Experience

To understand the process of disarticulation and its repercussions it is necessary to distinguish the *shungu* cycles within individual age groups and entire villages.

Each age group has a finite and precise number of members, and the number remains constant once the exchange cycle begins. On the occasion of any payment it is always clear who is included as recipients. As shown in chapter 4, members gather to receive their due, affirming their unity and identity. If a member is absent, a stand-in, often a junior sibling or adult offspring of the same sex, takes their place, so that precise balance, the main theme of *shungu* exchange, is maintained. The age group records all payments; each member is acutely aware of whether they still owe the group or which members still owe them; and the members collectively experience the sequence of payments until everyone has paid and the *shungu* is declared "closed." As Moussa experienced, pressure is put on the slower members. These are ways in which social value and time are measured.

The male age groups are more salient in youth than in later adult-hood. Once all members of the age group have paid their internal *shungu*, the group begins to lose its relevance, though adult members do continue to consume their portions of village feasts collectively and take the *shikao* as a reference group. They also use performances of village *shungu* as occasions for a playful kind of collective regression (gluttony, sexual joking, and reminiscence).

In general women exhibited greater exigence than men and received the greater focus of attention and satisfaction at the payment of vil-lage *shungu*s. The enthusiastic participation of women runs counter to most writing on exchange systems (with notable exceptions, such as Weiner 1976), which stresses the role of men. Their attachment to their age groups also challenges Bernardi's conclusion that women's age systems afford "no more than a bland form of parallelism to the male system" (1985: 137), and Baxter and Almagor's flat assertion that "there are no age systems for women" (1978: 11).

The village forms a more complex *shungu* group than does the age group. As long as the *shungu* is fully functioning, the village, unlike the age group, never closes. New members enter regularly through generational reproduction and the formation of new age groups; hence, the village never arrives at the stage where all its members have paid up and exchange stops. It is a system in motion. Moreover, it exhibits centricity in the sense of being enclosed, internally focused, and self-referential. I never heard villages comparing rates of *shungu* payment the way age groups do.[10] Payment is recognized only within the village; completing the *shungu* brings prestige and may be a pre-requisite for holding certain village offices, but it carries no weight between villages.

Although in principle the village as a whole never "closes," every individual does arrive in principle at a balanced completion of his or her exchanges when they have offered a feast to everyone at whose *shungu* they have eaten and when they have eaten at the *shungu* of ev-eryone who has eaten at theirs. This became evident to me only once I observed people trying to handle the termination of the *shungu* system in an equitable manner. It was then made clear that although people stated that they were paying "the community," and although payment was channelled via the age groups, in fact everyone was aware of their individual position in the system of obligations vis-à-vis every other individual member of the community. People who had still to pay the *shungu* had to ensure that everyone at whose *shungu* they had partaken would receive a share. People who were no longer planning to hold *shungu* avoided partaking of *shungu* from those whom they had not already fed.

Thus, one woman's request to hold a second village *shungu* was turned down by her age group. She would have been the first member of the group to have paid a second time; most members were still struggling to meet their first *shungu*.[11] The woman argued that she did not want anyone to be able to say subsequently that she had circumcised her sons without paying *shungu*, but she was satisfied when the age group decided formally that it would require only one *shungu* of its members. In the end, she fed only the women in the age groups above hers from whom she had consumed two *shungu* meals.[12] Thus, the balanced reciprocity extended outside the age group, to the material exclusion of its own members. In effect, the system was winding down, step by measured step, towards a precise final closure when the last outstanding debt would be paid.

Even when there was full replacement of new generations of *shungu* "players," adults recognized both the extent of their own individual obligations and the moment when they had accepted back from younger or tardier members of the community everything the latter had once received from them. At that point they ceased to participate in the feasts given to their age groups. I observed a feast where some women did not join the remaining members of their age group at the *shungu* of a donor from a junior group because the latter woman had entered the system after they had paid their own *shungu*. The food offered to the age group was divided among a subset of the women who belonged to it. Far from withdrawing from social life, the elderly simply arrive at a point in the cycle when the total sum of their exchanges with the entire membership of the community reaches a precise balance.[13] To keep playing would mean to start over.

Exchange Cycles, Identity, and Temporal Passage

The system afforded a personalized yet precise measure of the adult life cycle, from the first *shungu* at which one participated as a guest and consumer and began one's indebtedness, through one's own series of payments, to the last feast at which one participated as a guest and received a final due return. In the civic domain, an adult life course could be defined as the period from ego's first payment of *shungu* (to the age group) to the last return feast given by a recipient of any of ego's *shungu* feasts (to the village). Civic age is ego's position within this exchange process.

The progression of an individual's adulthood depended on the scheduling of the *shungu*s, whether they occurred relatively early or late in life. If relatively late, a person remained indebted for longer, but assuming continuous entry of new age groups into the system, they invited more and younger people than did their peers and so had more return feasts they could expect to enjoy. Some people continued to be repaid after death, their portions accepted and consumed by junior kin.[14]

The *shungu* created a series of interlocking cycles whose arcs were paths of irreversible time, individual achievement within loops of exchange, and phases of social replacement in the community as a whole (cf Weiner 1980). For the community, the cycles were continuous and infinite, whereas for the individual, they were discrete and finite. In fact, the life of the community can be viewed as closely overlapping cycles of interpersonal exchange where each member engaged in reciprocity with everyone else in their own age group and about two or more age groups up and down.

The overlapping of the individual cycles had the effect of blunting the impact of the irreversible process. The system transformed generations into relative age groups and emphasized the progression of the age group over the individual, rendering the passage circular rather than fully unidirectional. Although *shungu* distributions were occasions where age groups were distinguished from one another and at which ritualized competition and joking between old and young took place, ultimately the *shungu* expanded the ideal of equality characteristic of members of a single age group to include the entire community of *shungu* players, regardless of generation or relative age. Through balanced reciprocity, all *shungu* players were rendered equivalent. Thus, the *shungu* created a gigantic peer group.

This was equality not of abstract individualism but of shared identity. The collapsing of the age differential through the *shungu* payment was predicated on the prior embeddedness of the age groups in the community. The equality can also be conceptualized as the end point in the process of reproductive incorporation. Payment of the *shungu* was not simply a cancellation of debt with equivalent parties in a system of reciprocity that was ultimately reversible or synchronic in nature; it was also the irreversible insertion of the self into the social whole via the system of redistribution. Those who completed the *shungu* can be said to have been absorbed by, and in turn to have reabsorbed, the other community members such that their individual persons could not be fully distinguished from the totality of the group. Thus, the *shungu* expressed and constituted simultaneously both a part-whole relationship and the shared identity and equality of the parts. The completion and unification of these processes was reached in old age – not at the fulfilment of a person's own *shungu* obligations but when the last debts owed one by others had been repaid.

Conclusion: Exchange and the Temporal Construction of Valued Persons

The full citizen of the community emerged through the temporal process of *shungu* exchange. As a form of redistribution, the *shungu* was, to quote Sahlins, "a within relation, the collective action of a group ... the complement of social unity and, in Polanyi's term, 'centricity'" (Sahlins 1972: 188). Centricity is evident in people sitting around a common dish to eat together. The course of each life constituted a link in the ongoing reproduction of the community as a whole. On the other hand, as a form of reciprocity, the *shungu* created between each individual member and every other member what Sahlins calls "social duality and symmetry" (1972: 188–9). People became implicated in one another's reproduction and well-being, an argument I develop in subsequent chapters (cf Lambek 2015a).

Shungu payment was both a collective and an individual achievement, and the *shungu* thus constructed a social identity based both on unity, such that aging was a collective phenomenon, and on relations with specific others through which the individual's social career was both constituted and explicitly or implicitly compared according to a mutually accepted system of value. People who paid the *shungu* became equals, an equality that was not taken for granted but was achieved and legitimated through receipt of the *shungu* by their peers and regularly reasserted in the *shungu* gifts they were offered and accepted and, in the end, rejected. Nor could a person lose this equality; since the size of payments could not be increased, a younger donor could not retroactively diminish the value of payments made by previous donors.

The ideology expressed through the *shungu* is relevant. In its adoption by communities of Kibushy speakers, the *shungu* distinguished villages formed (in part by ex-slaves or ex-indentured labourers) on a principle of equality. This principle inverted the older system found among Shimaore speakers that linked elite families and established alliances between certain villages (cf Breslar 1979). Elite *shungu* celebrated status-endogamous (but often village-exogamous) marriages, expressing exclusion and privilege through the display and restricted circulation of food. In the villages of Kibushy speakers, the meaning of the *shungu* changed from hierarchy to equality, and the principle of exclusiveness shifted from descent to locality.

The *shungu* expands the equality characteristic of age mates cross-culturally (Baxter and Almagor 1978, Bernardi 1985) to incorporate adult citizens of all ages. Yet, if age, time, and person are socially constituted, they cannot be identical for everyone. Equality is largely an ideological assertion, a matter of principle. The *shungu* did have substantive social effects, but, other factors (descent, wealth, competence, etc.) being unequal, these effects were only partial; payment of *shungu* could not fully compensate for not having inherited rights to village ownership. Moreover, there was a small minority who never managed to produce their feasts and hence failed to demonstrate their equality as citizens.

While the principle of balance remains significant for the dismantling of the *shungu*, what is potentially destructive of the *shungu* is the decline of the ideology of equality in favour of a more competitive market-based individualism. In 1985 I often heard the expression *ulun' belu tsy meriña* ("people are not identical") accompanied by the lifting of the hand to show that the fingers are not all of the same size. This is precisely the reverse of what the *shungu* payments continually attempted to demonstrate. The collapse of the *shungu* is also both indicative and productive of the decline in importance of centricity, the village as a bounded social whole, in favour of trans-village and individual networks, many of whose members participate more fully in the French educational system and the commoditized workforce.

The disappearance of the *shungu* changes the nature of the community, aging, and personhood. With the *shungu*, the individual life course was marked by an orderly oscillation between receiving and giving. Individuals accepted hospitality and gradually became beholden to more and more fellow citizens until, through a series of large payments, they turned the tables and became even with those who had paid earlier and owed by all those who had yet to pay. As the latter provided their feasts, one by one, the debts gradually closed until, at the end of life, ideally, relationships of equality with everyone in the community had been re-established and no further social movement in the civic arena was either necessary or possible. Old age could thus be conceptualized as a period of social quiescence in which all commitments in the exchange cycle had run their course. It was not that the aged were excluded or no longer socially valued, but rather that they were replete with value; their value had been completely established and hence they had no further need to participate. In a sense, the individual was most fully incorporated by the group at the same moment as he or she was released from its obligations.

The *shungu* was deliberately instituted by individual villages, and collective decisions were made within the village first to augment the *shungu* and then to reduce it. I have documented the structure and orderly winding down of the *shungu* and have attempted to portray the autonomy of the civic domain and the experience of centricity and wholeness which the system constituted and which are being dissipated with its passing. It is this transition, repeated in many ways and in all parts of the world, that anthropology has had the mixed privilege to observe and the simple obligation to report.

6 Localizing Islamic Performances in Mayotte, 1975–1995

Politics and social ethics are *intrinsic* to the psychocultural reality of conversion, informing an agent's commitment to an identity and the moral authority that commitment implies.

> Robert Hefner, "World Building and the
> Rationality of Conversion" (1993: 28)

The activities described in the previous chapters are also deeply Muslim. In this chapter I explore the Islamic dimension. The argument unfolds with respect to debates about relations between the local and the global and discussions of religious conversion that were prominent in the 1990s. The earlier spread of Islam lies like a palimpsest beneath the global encroachment on Mayotte as it became a *collectivité territoriale* of France. Islam has been present in Mayotte for centuries (chapter 3). However, given population movement in the region, some of the older Kibushy-speaking villagers have been Muslim only for about three or four generations.

I will argue that the performance of prayer (and other Muslim forms of recitation) has been the critical means by which Islam was localized – rendered central to the conduct and understanding of social relations in Mayotte – and conversely, the critical means by which social relations have been Islamicized. I begin, however, via a detour that provides two additional threads to the argument, an analytical one that refers to the question of conversion, especially as set forth in an excellent overview by Robert Hefner (1993), and an ethnographic one from the neighbouring, closely related, and yet in some respects strikingly different context in northwest Madagascar.[1] In Madagascar the Antalaotra have been

Muslim for centuries, while the Antankaraña have been partly Muslim, and the northern Sakalava have included a significant Muslim minority since at least the mid-nineteenth century. However, whereas during the 1970s and 1980s the population of Mayotte was virtually exclusively Muslim (repeated journalistic reports of numerous Christians notwithstanding), Muslims form a minority in Madagascar, and the situation in the northwest is one of lively religious pluralism and polyphony.

Conversion as Acceptance

I prefer to speak about "active participation in" or "acceptance of" Islam rather than about "conversion to" it. The word "conversion" is problematic insofar as it implies converting "from" as well as "to" and insofar as it privileges an immediate, virtually instantaneous, unidirectional, and distinct shift in self-identification over a gradual change. It is also problematic insofar as it privileges private, subjective experience over collective and public process and rationalized "beliefs" over ritual orders.[2] In all these respects the term "conversion" expresses a Christian (especially Protestant) ideology. Moreover, whereas Hefner describes conversion to Christianity or Islam as a kind of societal transformation with the effects that Weber ascribes to modernization, hence an entry into the global order, what I address here is the converse, namely the *localization* of Islam within Mayotte. "Conversion" understood as societal transformation underplays the complexities inherent in the local reception of a new order. Indeed, it may overlook some of the very dimensions of moral practice that both Hefner and I consider central.

While it is easy enough to depict Islam as the religion *to* which people converted, it is a good deal more difficult to describe that *"from"* which they converted, or indeed whether people in this region deliberately repudiated or left something behind. Contemporary inhabitants of religiously plural northwest Madagascar distinguish Muslims, Protestants, and Catholics from those they describe simply as *tsy mivavaka*, those who do not congregate in prayer. It is noteworthy that people who are neither Christian nor Muslim are described, as I am doing in English, in terms of *not* following a certain practice rather than in terms of a specific, named, religious practice or identity. While such identification by means of negation is common in Malagasy thought (Lambek 1992), nevertheless it is clear that "ancestral practices" (to take the positive label sometimes applied by Malagasy intellectuals) form an unmarked category in this context, not least because people would hesitate to reduce complex social facts to the objectified abstraction of "religion."[3] Moreover, what is described with reference to Muslims and Christians is a generic *practice* – congregating in prayer – rather than an object – a specific belief, body of thought, or cosmology in the way that Western scholars have typically thought of "a" religion.

Of course, the Malagasy distinction does not imply that anthropologists could not classify the invocations that Malagasy make to their ancestors as forms of "prayer" more broadly conceived. Indeed, Muslims in Mayotte refer to Islamic recitation by the same word, *jôro [dzoru]*, that northwestern Malagasy use to describe invocation of ancestors. Many Malagasy would say it is all the same God and the manner in which you address God is secondary, merely a cultural form. Thus Malagasy do not consider *mivavaka* to be an enormous leap from ancestral practices. Hence for Malagasy "acceptance" might be a more appropriate construct than "conversion."

I prefaced discussion of Mayotte, which was uniformly Muslim, with this detour to northwest Madagascar in the assumption that there is something regional that has shaped the reception of Islam in both places. I cannot claim that the argument holds in the same way for those inhabitants of Mayotte whose antecedents hailed originally from East Africa, but I think there are other reasons, stemming both from within Islam itself (Lambek 1990a, 1993, ch. 5) and from arguments within the anthropology of religion (Rappaport 1979, 1999), to suggest that "acceptance" is a more suitable term than "conversion," the latter term being perhaps of particular relevance to internal movement between the various sects and denominations that constitute Christianity.

The Reception and Performance of Islam

If I de-emphasize "conversion," how best to describe the reception of Islam? Without for a moment wishing to cast aspersions on the subjective commitment of adherents to Islam and without wishing to deny what we might call more purely "religious" interests and motivations that shape individual experience (illustrated in Lambek 1993), I turn to outward practice and collective process.

The spread of Islam is characterized most obviously and fundamentally by the transmission of texts. The most sacred texts exist virtually unchanged over time and from one part of the Islamic world to another, and thus may be understood as the "global" dimension of Islam; their acceptance renders all Sunni Muslims recognizable to each other. Central to the texts are a set of sacred postulates (the term is Rappaport's, 1999) and a number of explicit injunctions regarding proper goals and comportment. These begin with the five pillars and, via the legal traditions (Shafeite in Mayotte), diffuse into various domains of life from social relations to bodily hexis (disposition).

The question, then, is how these global texts are locally received – how the texts and their postulates and injunctions are put into practice. How does Islam come rapidly to engage the interests, energies, and imaginations of people living in diverse regions and specific communities? How does it come to seem right and natural? And how is it that communities retain their distinctiveness even while committing themselves to the global tenets of Islam?

Starting with these questions is a way to avoid two problematic approaches to the comparative localization of Islam, one through the relationship between ostensibly pure or universal Islamic social injunctions in relation to an equivalent corpus of local "customary law" (adat), and the other posing the question: "One Islam or many?"[4] The implication is either penetration of Islamic law such that local practices are transformed, subordinated, or rationalized in its light, or that custom shapes Islam into distinct and diverse formations. Neither seems to do justice to Muslim life in Mayotte.

I address the localization of Islam in another way. Returning to the Islamic texts, I take their significance to have lain, at least during the 1970s in Mayotte, less in their semantic or referential content (what they assert or describe) than in their performability.[5] Following Tambiah (1985), I distinguish three dimensions of performance, none of which implies something in any way less serious or consequential ("mere performance") than other forms of action. Quite the contrary. First and most obvious is the fact that the texts are enunciated (recited), that is, performed through speech. Second, there is their performative quality in the sense of illocutionary force, namely in respect of the states of affairs they bring into being through their felicitous utterance. Irrespective of the semantic content of specific verses, their utterance sanctifies, blesses, affirms, protects, appeals, commits, opens, closes, and so on. Third, one can speak of the aesthetic and sensorial qualities of performance – for example, the beautiful alliterative qualities of the recited Qur'an.

While these dimensions of performance are obviously closely interconnected, I argue that *performance in the first sense provides a primary means through which Islam was localized in Mayotte, while performance in the second sense provides a primary means by which, conversely, the social order was Islamicized.*[6] While at first glance it may appear that I am suggesting that the reception of Islam has been superficial, the thrust of my argument is the reverse, namely to demonstrate how profoundly Islamic Mayotte became.[7]

Whereas the semantic or referential content of texts might be assumed to subsist in some relatively abstract and timeless realm, performance (enunciation) is a social activity, and a temporal one, located in irreversible, historical time.[8] It requires attention to such matters as recruiting suitable and knowledgeable performers, scheduling and locating particular performance events, and acknowledging the social and moral consequences of particular acts of recitation conducted by some people on behalf of themselves or others. It thus attends to practice, much in the manner Bourdieu (1977) has argued regarding exchange, and a shift from systems of belief or cosmologies viewed in the abstract to orders of (ritual) practice, as was argued long ago with respect to witchcraft by Evans-Pritchard (1937) and more recently with respect to religion more generally by Rappaport (1979, 1999).[9]

In moving in this direction I take my cue from the reception of Islam in Mayotte. During the 1970s and subsequently, commitment has been expressed in textual performances of all kinds. These include daily prayers (*swala*), the weekly cycle of Friday prayers and sermons, and the annual cycle of recitations at Ramadan. They include as well recitation of Islamic text at critical moments of the life cycle, including birth, circumcision, marriage, and – most important – death and burial. Recitations of *dua* to bless and protect individuals, families, and communities, turn away evildoers, and support the dead are pervasive, as are spontaneous exclamations of pious utterance. Most spectacular are performances that include recitation, song, music, and dance. These occur at a large range of occasions – death and funerals, fulfilment of a vow, expressions of pleasure. The largest are sponsored by a village at festivities to which everyone on Mayotte is invited. Such events can last all night and well into the next morning, bringing together teams of performers from several villages, including hundreds of dancers and spectators. Of the three most popular genres, *Daira* and *Mulidy* are performed by men and *Maulida shengy* by women (with male drummers and leaders). By the 1980s the young women's *Deba* became equally popular. People of both sexes form appreciative audiences and engage in the provisioning of performers and spectators. During the dry, post-harvest season, performances are frequent.

The point is that the scheduling and enactment of these "global" texts (no doubt with local stylistic differences and some local composition) are *local* activities. Performances are linked to the projects, interests, and intentions of specific individuals, kin groups, and communities; moreover, scheduling and participation follow local scenarios of appropriate moral action and rhythms of reciprocity. Senior kinsmen gather to bless their juniors, neighbours are called upon to address God on each other's behalf, and whole villages turn out to host or perform for each other. As significant forms of moral action these performances are an integral part of what it means to be a parent, offspring, neighbour, and community member – in sum, to be a moral person. They are among the most significant activities to index the qualities of persons and relationships, demonstrate who one is, and establish the fact of one's commitment to others. And if to be Muslim means to look out for one's fellows, similarly, to be a kinsman or kinswoman or a community member means to participate in performances of the Muslim texts. Hence Islam is embedded in kinship and community, and kinship and community are embedded in Islam, in a very profound way. Local forms of kinship and social action are thoroughly Islamicized; simultaneously, Islam is thoroughly "socialized." Islamic performances are total social facts, and the position of Islam, following Hefner (1993), is "organic."

This embeddedness of Islam belies the contrasts with other Muslim societies that are apparent if one simply compares "beliefs" or "customs" or even "practices." The fact that certain supposedly Islamic injunctions concerning marriage, inheritance, or the seclusion of women are not advocated or followed in Mayotte is far less significant than the fact that people pray together and on each other's behalf in socially appropriate ways. It is in this sense, admittedly one in harmony with Durkheim, that one can say that Islam has been highly localized in Mayotte. People simply cannot imagine acting as parents, neighbours, or members of a community in the absence of Islamic performance. Similarly, I think, they cannot imagine Islam that is not in part about fulfilling one's obligations and responsibilities to others – not according to an abstract ethics or code of law but through the immediacy of habitual practice and according to the ways people expect to give and receive from and care for one another on a daily and long-term basis.[10]

To say this is to say both that Mahorais are as committed Muslims as Muslims anywhere and that Islam is highly localized in Mayotte, and to do so without any sense of contradiction between the two statements.[11]

Acts of Prayer

A common way that Islam is socialized in Mayotte is through prayers or recitations that people perform for one another, exchanging acts of blessing. Performances known as *shijabu* are frequently held by or on behalf of an individual, a family, a descent line, or the entire community to provide strength and well-being, to ward off danger, or to celebrate change. *Shijabu* are performed at times in calendrical and personal cycles (at the solar New Year, for an expectant mother, upon leaving Qur'anic school) and at unique events (following an ominous dream, to express general satisfaction). Whether held on community or family occasions, *shijabu* delineate and intensify social ties and reaffirm people's commitment to one another.

The *shijabu* is composed of a selection of *dua*, each recited a fixed number of times. Each performer recites part of the total simultaneously with other performers' recitation of other parts. Thus the whole is recited collectively; individual voices are not distinguished but are mixed together. Moreover, the simultaneous recital of several *dua* means that the words of each are not readily distinguishable by those prayed over or by onlookers. The subjects of the prayer sit clustered together on a mat, facing towards Mecca. The performers stand in an arc behind them, reciting in low voices, blowing into their hands, and tossing the grains of rice held there onto the heads of those prayed over (*figure 6.1*). Afterwards performers are served a good meal prepared by women of the sponsoring household.

The *shijabu* marks out those who are prayed over – the subjects – from those who are not, thereby specifying individuals who are vulnerable or in need of blessing, and distinguishing kin from non-kin. In a vertical dimension, the *shijabu* also distinguishes those who are prayed over, most frequently but by no means exclusively children and women, from those who do the praying, who are men. The men stand above and behind the women, their posture indicating their greater strength; the whole tableau is iconic of protection. In turn, at the end of the prayer it is the men who sit in a circle on the mats and the women who sustain them from the outside, this time with a good meal. The subjects of the blessing are also served, separately from the reciters. Who is called to pray and eat, who supplies the food, and who cooperates in the labour of cooking follow patterns of kinship, neighbourliness, and community.

Such demarcations can be found at virtually every level of society. But performances are no mere reflections or aesthetic embroidery on

Figure 6.1 *Shijabu* **prayer at the solar New Year, 1985.** Women and children are gathered outside the mosque facing towards Mecca while men encircle them from behind and lightly toss grains of rice that they are praying over onto the seated people, who also hold their hands cupped in prayer. No one seems unduly concerned by the curious young anthropologist standing in front of them.

more fundamental relations. It is practices such as the *shijabu* that help *constitute* social relations through their functions of focusing, separating, complementing, incorporating, reciprocating, acknowledging, and uniting. For the ordinary person the practice of religion is not fully distinguishable from the duties, constraints, and interests of kinship, friendship, and citizenship. Conversely, for the anthropologist, social structure is not fully distinguishable from acts of praying with and over others, being subject to prayer, and sharing in the production or consumption of sacrificial meals.

The dead are also attended by means of textual recitation. Depending on the circumstance they are conceptualized as the subjects of prayer, in a manner analogous to the subjects of the *shijabu*, as co-sponsors of the prayer, or possibly, and more ambiguously, as its provisional addressees whose help is asked to help transmit the prayer to God. These positions are not always clearly distinguished from one another.

Annual events are held for certain locally significant individuals who form the apices of "ancestor-focused" kin groups. Thus the people who form the core of the senior adult cohort in the village of Lombeni Kely hold an annual *fatiha* for their deceased mother and grandmother Dady Amina (chapter 2). While I originally assumed that she was simply its subject, in fact the *fatiha* continues an annual tradition practised by Amina herself when she was alive. Her kin stopped the practice after her death until she emerged (*niboka*) in a dream to one of them, instructing them to continue. A number of years later they left off again. One of her sons became sick, and again someone dreamt that the abandoned *fatiha* was the reason. Since then, they continue the practice yearly. The family invites the whole village to participate. In 1975 non-resident members of the *mraba* ("family") were among the active sponsors, but they were so no longer a decade later, by which time the size of the expected contribution had tripled. Resident members of the great-grandchild generation, who have no memory of the ancestress, complain about contributing the fifteen French francs and two kilos of rice requested in 1985 of each adult descendant. One local great-granddaughter, who did in the end participate, argues, "she is no kin of mine, maybe only kin of my kin." The case shows the manner in which the commitments that kin have to one another are enacted, confirmed, or disconfirmed by means of such performances.

It is unclear whether the great-granddaughter's statement indicates the limits of relevant social distance that have been characteristic for much of the twentieth century or whether it indicates an alternative strategy of saving versus disbursing cash and hence of evaluating social capital in a context of emerging class differentiation (cf Solway 1990). Nevertheless, the Islamic idiom is evidently capable of comprehending a range of changing social practices and commitments.

Annual recitations are held also for deceased local Islamic scholars and Qur'anic teachers. The descendants and former pupils of Halidy, a male contemporary of Amina, hold an annual performance of the *Maulida* in his memory. They chose the *Maulida* because that was his favourite text and what he taught. More famous deceased religious figures in other villages are subjects of much larger annual performances that attract visitors from across Mayotte. Commemorations are also held on behalf of people lacking a high social profile. For example, one woman produces a biannual *Maulida* on the anniversary of the death of an adult daughter. Of course, this event provides an occasion for her kin to demonstrate solidarity with the elderly sponsor.

In addition, the deceased are collectively remembered in the annual prayers of *kuitimia*. Moreover, everyone is the subject of a major performance (*mandeving*) held some time after their death, as Kala held for her mother (chapter 4). *Mandeving*s are distinct from funerals. As Gueunier (1988) has noted regarding the *arbain* (marking the fortieth day after a death), such celebration enables the kinds of exchanges previously associated with non-Islamic funerals. Indeed, much like the *shungu*, it was said that cakes are served on the third and fortieth day after death because when the deceased were alive they ate the cakes of others; this was a means to finish off their debts and quit their accounts. The separation from the funeral is significant because funerals are among the most invariant of Muslim rituals, a point to which I will return.

The time spans of these rituals are not very deep, and the kin groups that organize them are correspondingly generationally quite shallow; in every kin-based commemoration I observed, at least one child of the apical ancestor was still alive. Yet the social production of prayer can be understood as a vehicle for the reproduction and articulation of the kin group and of kin relations. This is so both in the intentional sense that through prayers people wish each other health, fertility, and prosperity and in the sense that in coming together in performances of prayer people do recommit to each other.

In the preparations and enactment of a recitation we see both the articulation of a particular family grouping or village at a significant moment of its history and the expression of more general principles and values, notably the egalitarian, bilateral, and non-segmentary nature of the kin group in contrast to the hierarchical and patrilineal models characteristic of the pre-colonial and colonial periods, like those Shimaore speakers who claim descent from the Prophet and thereby closer connection to sources of Islamic authority.

The organization of Amina's *fatiha* is different from what one would expect in a lineage-based society in which a senior kinsman might preside over the event, which would also serve to underline the dependency of members of junior generations or lines. Likewise, the responsibility of adult children to hold a *mandeving* on behalf of their deceased parents is not thereby an authority over their own children; they are not mediating an ongoing process of descent (Kopytoff 1971) so much as acknowledging and reciprocating their parents.

A degree of sexual complementarity is also evident; although the sexual division of labour is marked, both women and men have the autonomy – and bear the responsibility – to act as sponsors, and both gain the respect, including self-respect, and social maturity that accompanies it. Female kin have the same financial obligation as male kin, except that those who are temporarily unmarried are exempt from payment. Their money cannot be used towards prayers because it is assumed to derive from extramarital sexual activity, something within the bounds of local morality but regarded as impure by Islam. This is an instance where Islamic rule and local practice are in contradiction. Women's general obligation shows the cognatic basis of kinship and its relative sexual egalitarianism. If Islam forbids women from publicly performing the *fatiha* on behalf of others, it does not preclude them from the dignity or prestige inherent in sponsoring prayers.

One notable distinction between men and women is their respective roles as reciters or cooks (though there were events at which men cooked or women recited). This in turn is linked to the ways they participate as guests. There are recitations that men attend simply on the basis of their public Muslim persona; any man with a modicum of knowledge of the requisite *dua* is welcome and, indeed, co-villagers are expected. Women, however, are often invited individually by women of the sponsoring household, kin group, or neighbourhood, and their attendance is based on specific kinship or friendship links with the hosts. Thus, in one sense, women are more closely linked to the local and the particular, and men to the global and the universal. Men can pray at a mosque anywhere.

The Reciprocity Scenario

Egalitarianism and complementarity are articulated by means of balanced reciprocity. Although the expression of reciprocity differs from ritual to ritual, the principle is so ubiquitous in Mayotte that I speak of a "reciprocity scenario" (cf Ortner 1973, 1978, 1989; Schieffelin 1976) characteristic of performances of recitation. This scenario is evident in the localization of performances of the *Maulida*.

The *Maulida* is a lengthy poem about the life of the Prophet, popular throughout East Africa as a vehicle of joyful participation in Islam (Ahmed 1999). It is not the most sacred text, and it is subject to local textual and musical embellishments; hence it exists in a number of variants.[12] In Mayotte the most popular forms are the *Maulida al-Barzanji*, taught to all children and frequently recited; the *Sharaf al anam*, put to music in the *Maulida shengy*, sung and danced by women; and the Qadiry *Mulidy*, sung and danced by men. Devotion to the text is more significant than attention to the facts of the Prophet's life that the poem recounts. Many people spend years studying, copying, and reciting the text, listening to performances, and themselves performing. It is a treasured aesthetic form; musical performances are highly evocative, and for some people the performances are so charged that participants experience a kind of religious ecstasy.

Without discounting the more purely religious meanings or numinous and aesthetic experiences produced by performances of the text (Lambek 1993), I wish to trace its significance at a more mundane level. Among the many performances of a *Maulida* are those during the lunar month of the Prophet's birth. Anyone born in this month of *Maulida* is supposed to hold a *Maulida*. These are the only people for whom the month of birth or the passing of another year is marked. The performance is sponsored for children by their parents and for adults by themselves. It entails inviting a few kinsmen and neighbours to recite the text and then serving them a good meal. During the month there are certain days on which men go from house to house to participate in performances.

In addition, every local community holds a collective *Maulida* during the month. Villages (or sections of large villages) pair off with one another. Village A sponsors a *Maulida* to which village B is invited, and later in the month the invitation is reciprocated. But the exchange is more complex than this implies. For village A to host village B means that the men of village B come and perform the *Maulida* on behalf of village A in village A's mosque. Village A then serves the reciters a good meal. Each household in the host village provides an equal amount of cooked food towards the feast; the meal is served collectively to the visiting men and boys. In addition, women of individual households invite kinswomen and friends from village B to assist them with the cooking and divide the remaining portion with them.[13] Visitors of both sexes return home to village B with fried cakes that are distributed to family members who did not attend. To eat the cake is to partake of the positive state generated by the performance.

Performance distinguishes between two villages, between women and men, and between the domestic and public sites of production and celebration, while articulating the unity of each village and the equivalence of each household within it. But the event is more than an occasion for articulating social affiliation. Members of village A perform a pious activity in sponsoring the *Maulida* and are likewise the main beneficiaries of the blessing conferred by its performance. Members of village B receive approbation in God's eyes and social respect for reciting. Thus, after the first performance, members of villages A and B are mutually indebted to each other. Village A is indebted to village B for performing the recitation while village B is indebted for having received the opportunity to do so. Balance is reached and reciprocity redoubled when later in the month the roles of the two villages are reversed and village B invites village A to come to recite a *Maulida* on its behalf and receive a good meal.

Here we have a general model of relatively direct reciprocity that interlinks two parties performing reciprocal services on one another's behalf. This reciprocity scenario is common in Mayotte.[14] As depicted here, prayers are sent to God by intermediaries. In effect, each party serves as intermediary for the other; moreover, each party enables the performance of religious duties by the other. Intermediaries are shown respect by those on whose behalf they perform; those saying the prayer are temporarily shown deference by those for whom they say it. Yet an egalitarian ethic prevails in that the inter-mediation and hence the deference are reciprocated.[15]

Although the stated purpose of the *Maulida* is to honour Mohammed and glorify God, the social functions of the ritual are apparent. The annual *Maulida* provides an occasion for the articulation of community membership and the reaffirmation and regeneration of community sentiment and solidarity. The *Maulida* performance is also a vehicle for direct reciprocity between neighbouring communities, articulating their boundaries as well as their connection and mutual indebtedness: *each community is implicated in the production of well-being for the other*. Just as with the *shungu*, each assists in the reproduction of the other; thus, they are not fully separate after all. The recitations do not merely express or signify the inter-community relationship but are its substance.

The exchange does not necessarily produce harmony between communities. Indeed, annual performances in Lombeni were fraught with tension, as each side was attentive to slights in the degree of hospitality offered by the other. The ideal of equality is offset by the fact that Lombeni Be is a good deal larger than Lombeni Kely; hence the resources to feed one village by the other are subject to greater strain than the reverse. But it is precisely performances like the *Maulida* that articulate the nature of what community means in Mayotte and how neighbouring communities ought to, and in fact do, relate to one another. Conversely, performance of the *Maulida* (and by metonymic extension, Islam as a whole) is rendered meaningful in part by the ways in which it satisfies fulfilment of the reciprocity scenarios. Put another way, Islam does not merely impose moral standards but is harnessed to meet local moral concerns according to a local logic of moral practice.

Recitations outside the mosque are referred to as *dzoru,* whereas the five daily prayers in the mosque are *swala. Dzoru* is the word used in Madagascar to address the ancestors, whereas *swala* comes from Arabic.[16] *Swala* is formal prayer sent directly to God, on one's own behalf, whereas *dzoru* is the recitation of sacred text, frequently on behalf of others. *Swala* is an act of submission in which members of the congregation stand and prostrate themselves before God equally.[17] *Dzoru* is an act of address and supplication and one that entails the invocation of intermediaries, located in a hierarchical chain from subject to performer and from living humans possibly through ancestors or saints to God. Finally, if *mikoswaly* means praying largely for oneself and in regularly scheduled and recurring convocations at arm's length from the give and take and the pleasures and tribulations of daily life, then it may be seen that in devoting so much attention to occasions and acts of *dzoru,* Mahorais have radically socialized Islam. *Swala* is less amenable to localization than *dzoru,* though not immune to it either.[18]

I do not mean in this way to radically distinguish Islamic practice in Mayotte from elsewhere; *swala* of course remains important in Mayotte, and conversely, Islamic recitations performed outside the mosque are found in every Muslim society. The local contrast between *dzoru* and *swala* may point to something general about the distribution of Islamic prayer that productively articulates local/global tensions wherever Islam is found.

The Islamicization of Sociality

I have argued that Islam was localized in Mayotte by having the performance of its texts inserted into the give and take of daily life, according to reciprocity scenarios of kinship and community. This might be a primary form of localization found everywhere and true of any religion that has been successful at spreading widely. If so, this suggests one of the reasons for the relative success of the "world religions" insofar as they contain practices that can be readily deployed in local social scenarios as well as practices like *swala* that stand at arm's length from them.

What then in this process of localization is specific to Islam, and in what respects is the local social order specifically Islamicized as Islam is socialized? Does the advent of Islam also change the nature of social groups or interaction scenarios? Topan (n.d.) has remarked how Swahili matrilineality gradually changed under the influence of Islam to patrilineality. Likewise among Malagasy the practice of virgin marriage is specific to Muslims, albeit shaped in local ways.

The influences do not lie exclusively in the jural domain. Indeed, as the Islamicization of Mayotte is virtually total, I can only make a few suggestive remarks. To begin with (and bracketing the question of gender), it may be that there is an affinity between Islam and egalitarian forms of reciprocity. While, to be sure, Islam is also associated with diverse forms of hierarchy across the world, the *swala* exhibits a fundamental equality, or to be more precise, an equivalence of submission before God. While relative position within the mosque at Friday prayer in Lombeni was subject to manoeuvring such that to pray in the front was a sign that one had, or thought one had, prestige, and some people even went so far as to suggest that they did not want to prostrate themselves behind people of lower status, such gamesmanship paled – and was made to look as trivial as it was – before the stark fact that everyone prostrates themselves. The *swala* is indexical of submission and vividly iconic of a fundamental equivalence among male worshippers (and, in the women's chamber appended to mosques in Mayotte, among female worshippers). It further evokes a sense of personal dignity among all worshippers. Moreover, the mosque has no formal leader and Sunni Islam no hierarchy. In Lombeni any man can aspire to take a turn leading the prayer or reciting the sermon. Claims to descent from the Prophet aside (and in Lombeni these were discounted), the hierarchy within local Islam is one of achievement (learning and comportment) not ascription, and it is at once supported and subverted by the universal prescription to transmit religious knowledge to others.

Swala imposes its routines upon life, requiring a daily and weekly work rhythm that enables breaks for prayer. The shift to a diversified wage economy and a capitalist time clock in the 1980s has undermined this (cf Thompson 1967). A further material impediment evident during the 1970s was having the means to purchase and keep clean appropriate dress for the mosque.

Social life is thoroughly Islamicized insofar as each situated recitation of *dua* establishes commitments and moral states that are legitimated by means of Islam and indeed sanctified by it. If, as Rappaport argues (1999), performance of the canon establishes the performer's acceptance of it, then all performers are continuously re-establishing their acceptance of Islam. Moreover, if, as he further establishes, a ritual performance brings into being a new state of affairs, and if this state of affairs can best be described as a moral state, then people are repeatedly creating Islamically constituted states of blessing, protection, identification, and sociality. Much as the relationship between spouses is constituted as one of marriage and the marriage itself is sanctified through pronunciation of the correct vows in the correct manner before legitimate authorities or witnesses (in this case by means of *dua* and the transmission of the *mahary* [*mahr*]), so too are all significant social relations constituted, sanctified by, and consequent to the appropriate recitation of *dua* at *shijabu*, birth rituals, *Maulida*, and the like. Islamic recitations are deemed necessary at regular and critical moments; their utterance produces moral persons, relations, and conditions. These are specifically Islamic forms of relationality, commitment, and moral space, that is to say, sanctified by, given meaning through, and infused with Islam.

Islamic ethical ideals pervade social relations; among these, the idea that utterance of prayer is necessary for redemption is central. Most critical is the final prayer – the utterance of the *shahada* by the deceased when requested by the angels of death. The funeral and burial are directed to ensuring this outcome – hence the final prompting at the graveside; the funeral, in turn, has been the most critical ritual, the pivot of the life cycle. Because it anchors life and, in effect, renders meaningful all that is enacted before, the funeral is, I venture, among the Muslim rituals least subject to change, that is, least subject to diverse forms of localization. The most critical part of the funeral, which again, I suspect, is the most invariant, concerns the nature of the interment and the prompting of the deceased.

The situation is illuminated by Rappaport's argument concerning the hierarchy of sanctity which is simultaneously a hierarchy of invariance. I grossly compress this here. Rappaport (1999) distinguishes within liturgical orders levels that run from ultimate sacred postulates to cosmological axioms to rules of conduct. The sacred postulates (here notably the *shahada*) sanctify or certify the cosmological axioms and other lower order understandings, the cosmological axioms logically underpin the rules, and the rules transform cosmology into conduct. This hierarchy of contingency is simultaneously a continuum of increasing concreteness, social specificity, and mutability, and (going in the opposite direction) of longevity, unquestionableness, and invariance. In Mayotte, the upper levels of this hierarchy, and the most invariant, provide meta-performatives and performatives, and determine the social order as a Muslim one.

Durkheim and Weber

In the respects described here, Islam is as fully a part of Mayotte as the religion of any small-scale society is of the society which it constitutes and is constituted by. One is inconceivable without the other. In this Durkheimian respect Islam in Mayotte (when and as I saw it) perhaps does not achieve the full shift in context that Hefner (1993), following a Weberian line, would ascribe to conversion to a world religion. But of course, just as Durkheimian and Weberian perspectives do not form mutually exclusive alternatives, that is not the complete story of the experience in Mayotte. Islam is a global religion and is prevalent throughout the region. Adherence to Islam does enable people to identify themselves with co-religionists elsewhere and to see their relations with the wider world accordingly. Such identity was particularly affirmed for those able to make the pilgrimage to Mecca.[19] Increased mobility also left Mayotte further open to Islamic reformers from elsewhere. Whereas debates over religious reform in the 1970s concerned details regarding the correct methods and conditions for conducting prayer, by the 1990s Muslim reformers from South Asia were bringing ideas that were quite foreign and that started to create a wedge among the faithful.

The larger point of my argument is that there are two poles in the apprehension or affirmation of morality. One emphasizes its universal qualities and does so in an intellectualizing and abstracting manner. The other sees morality as intrinsic to practical consciousness. Thus, on the one hand, we can emphasize the abstract universals of the Qur'anic and legal texts, their translocal and transhistorical qualities. On the other hand, we can emphasize the kind of practical know-how and effects that inhere in the performance of the texts in concrete, historically localized circumstances and changing contexts. I have emphasized the latter. To leave this as an abstract contrast is itself to make a choice. In reality I imagine that religion always contains a tension between the two (one that the tension between the respective theoretical inclinations reproduces). This is a tension equivalent to the one between adherence to rule or precedent in legal decisions or between rule and case-oriented approaches in legal anthropology (cf Comaroff and Roberts 1981), and it is to be found in debates among Muslims that take place in Mayotte or anywhere else in the Islamic world. Indeed, one and the same person can shift his or her stance on these issues according to the way his or her attention is drawn to the circumstances immediately at hand.

It should be clear that to suggest that Islam is organically rooted in Mayotte is not to suggest that adherence is in any way mechanical or that people simply follow rules unthinkingly. Indeed the reverse is the case. Each time people perform a *dua* for one another they have to think about what they are doing, what the performance means, and what sort of commitment their own action entails. People have to decide when to schedule performances and how to direct to them their time, interest, skill, money, and labour. At times they have to select between competing social obligations, educational investments (whether to learn the *Daira* or the *Mulidy*, or whether to partially put aside both for spirit possession, French schooling, or wage work), and competing arguments about correct Islamic practice.

The point in seeing Islam socialized, then, is to emphasize that social practice is itself moral practice. And it is moral practice not in the strict following of rules or obligation as a narrowly Durkheimian view might have it, but, in an approach that has more affinity with Weber, in the continuous exercise of moral *judgment*. Particular recitations of *dua*, that I have referred to as prayers, are moral acts, enjoined, initiated, or participated in on the basis of moral judgment and carrying moral consequences.

In sum, I have maintained three assumptions about practice here. First, it is always to be understood in some kind of relationship to structure. In this case the structure is social, as revealed in the reciprocity scenario, and also liturgical, as revealed in the hierarchy of sanctification and invariance characteristic of Islam. Second, practice is to be understood not as abstract individuals deploying a kind of automatic and unconscious habitus but as the deliberate acts of concrete persons, albeit socially and structurally located, caught up with particular interests, obligations, projects, and problems. Third, power is not necessarily always the most critical dimension of practice, nor is prestige always the primary goal or consequence. I share completely with Hefner and the Weberian tradition the insight that moral reasoning is a central dimension of practice.

Aesthetics and Pleasure

Performances of Muslim music and dance elicit tremendous interest and appreciation; they provide a significant vehicle for social and religious identity and relations at several levels of inclusion, and a means by which people experience, conceptualize, and interpret Islam. Above all, performances are significant for the quality of experience they provide, at once deeply religious and extremely pleasurable.

The musical genres are identified with specific Sufi brotherhoods, notably the Shathuly (Shadhiliyya) and the Qadiry (Qadiriyya) for the *Daira* and *Mulidy*, respectively, but also the Rifa'i (Rifa'iyya). While older people had pledged in their youth to one or another brotherhood, the point is less commitment to a specific order, doctrines, or sheikh, or adherence to a disciplined or mystic life, than an expression of religious enthusiasm through the music itself (cf Gilsenan 1973: 157). Individuals are generally devoted to one musical form, but families and communities rotate performances of each genre, including the *Maulida shengy* sung and danced by women and, increasingly, the *Deba*, performed by young women. Boys are trained in both the vigorous *Daira* and the slower *Mulidy* and, as they grow, they express an aesthetic preference for one or the other. Girls are taught both the *Maulida shengy* and the *Deba*, and everyone learns the *Maulida al-Barzanji* that serves as the root of all but the *Daira*. While each group has its village teachers and officials, the scheduling of island-wide performances is coordinated by Shehu Addinan of Tsingoni, who had authority over Muslim practice more generally.

If performances are socially located, their internal references are entirely religious and oriented to divine communion. Performances draw on enduring sacred values and yet have a tremendous immediacy, bringing people an experience of the beauty and power of their own and the collective faith. They are intense, vivid, exhilarating, total experiences, syntheses of sacred words, music, and movement. Gilsenan speaks of the "feeling of freedom, luxury, and expansiveness" that comparable Egyptian performances induce (1973: 130). In Mayotte participants often reach a state of euphoria, and occasionally some enter trance. In the *Daira*, dancers form a circle, holding hands, bouncing up and down, swaying, and chanting the *tahlil* or simply *Allah*, faster and faster. A large *Daira* might have some 300 people, led by a conductor who regulates the pace, building up to great intensity and then releasing it. By contrast, the *Mulidy* has alternating teams of dancers in a row opposite the singers and drummers (*figure 6.2*). The movements of the arms, hands, and upper body are coordinated, precise, refined, graceful, and polished. The *Maulida shengy* combines beautiful singing with similar graceful body movements. Each genre provokes both joy and sadness, sometimes moving people to tears. There is a compression

Figure 6.2 A performance of the *Mulidy*, 1975–6. This *Mulidy* brought together performers from several villages. The photo was taken just after sunrise. The dancers are on their knees, facing the seated drummers and singers, while an adept bangs a gong. Among the spectators are women seated on a verandah. A *Mulidy* drum, open on one side, is visible in the foreground. Dance teams are age- and village-based and take turns performing, swaying their bodies and making hand and arm gestures in unison to the refrain of the sung ode and the beat of the drums.

of historical time through the archaic language and reference to past saintly figures and an experience of flow or pure duration induced by the rhythmical music, breathing, and coordinated movements. Communion and submission merge participants with the divine words and hence with divinity itself.

Objectification of Performance

The various forms can all be seen as "cultural performances" in the full sense of the term as employed by Singer (1972) and elaborated by

Geertz, ceremonies "in which a broad range of moods and motivations on the one hand and metaphysical conceptions on the other are caught up [and] shape the spiritual consciousness of a people" (Geertz 1973a: 113). People can barely imagine a world without them. "Don't you have them at home?" they would ask me with astonishment. Appreciation is universal in Mayotte, linking people of all degrees of Islamic knowledge and commitment, from the most learned and pious scholars to those who attend for sheer enjoyment. Islam is sometimes described as difficult and rule bound, but these performances can be referred to as "*jeux musulmans.*"

In 1980 they were also by far the most popular items broadcast on the new radio station. Recording and broadcasting produce subtle changes. When the radio production crew came to Lombeni the women dressed in their best clothes, but they performed the *Maulida shengy* in broad daylight, unseparated from the male drummers, and under the direction of the young producers rather than the learned *fundis*. Afterwards, it was said that the singing had not been up to par, and the women from one section of the village complained that those of the other section had deliberately failed to chorus well during the verses in which singers from the first section were highlighted. Competition rather than collective affirmation came to the fore. As the broadcasts enabled the members of each village to critically evaluate performances of other villages, quality of technique became a significant issue; religion was transformed to art.

This kind of change has been brilliantly analysed by Walter Benjamin, who wrote of the way in which mechanical reproduction creates a "decay of the aura" (1969b: 222), that is, a distortion of the real distance between both performers and audience and the acts or objects of production. The uniqueness of the event is lost, and "substantive duration ceases to matter" (ibid. 221). As the work of art is reproduced, so the context of human production in religious ritual is lost. The work's fitness for exhibition comes to determine its value; "separated from its basis in cult, the semblance of autonomy disappeared forever" (ibid. 226).

By 1980, the radio broadcasts could be heard at any time, while one was performing the most mundane activities, and they could be switched off at will. Although listeners treated the broadcasts with respect, they took place in ordinary space and durational time. Live performances continue, but people know they are no longer unique events. Performances became objectified and compartmentalized. It was striking that on the occasion of the recording the women provided a festive meal only for the radio crew; they themselves as performers did not partake, as if their own acts were no longer of particular value.

Cultural objectification has continued apace. Nevertheless, live performances are attended with great enthusiasm. In four months of fieldwork in the dry season of 1985 I counted sixteen inter-village performances at which members of Lombeni participated, an average of one major musical performance a week. In Lombeni itself, a large *Maulida shengy* was performed with approximately 200 visiting women from some fourteen communities. In addition, the boys invited two teams of *Mulidy* dancers from neighbouring villages one evening, a small impromptu *Mulidy* was held on *Eid al-Adha*, and another was held to welcome back a pilgrim from the *hajj*. Five local events (two *Mulidy*, two *Maulida shengy*, one *Daira*) were held in memory of deceased kin. During this same period one of the largest and most prosperous communities in Mayotte held four large public ceremonies attended by at least some people from Lombeni.[20]

By 1985 large events were scheduled almost exclusively on weekends, announced over the radio, and reached by taxi. One of the biggest changes was the rise in popularity of the *Deba*, in which profane and sacred elements combine. Young women dress beautifully, sing, and perform graceful hand movements in unison. Men attend largely to admire the women. Performances end in high spirits with women ululating on their way home in bush taxis decorated with flowers. The *Deba* is Rifa'i in origin but largely a product of local women's culture; it draws on the Muslim repertoire and local reciprocity scenario but expresses a "modern" identity and the vitality of Mahorais women. It was subject to controversy over whether it was proper, but it has persevered and prospered.[21]

If performances of *Maulida* form a means for the reproduction of particular social relations according to a local reciprocity scenario, they can also be used to forge new obligations and create new links. The women of the Mouvement Populaire Mahorais used *Maulida* as a means for political organizing. Musical performances were occasions to attract people from across the island to party congresses. The *Maulida* also became a sanction: any village that did not send women to congresses or demonstrations was threatened with having to host the next *Maulida* itself, and out of turn; violation of the obligation to accept an invitation was made the basis of having to issue one. The *Maulida* also provided a degree of sanctification of the political deliberations to which they were contiguous. And yet the Mouvement Mahorais was attempting to intensify relations with France and encourage French investment in such things as education, thereby supporting a means by which Islamic practice has since been undermined.

PART THREE

Dancing to the Music of Time, through 2001

The chapters in part three place the community in the full flow of history as Mayotte became increasingly embedded in France and as Mahorais shifted from being colonial subjects towards French citizenship and from subsistence cultivation towards wage labour. The emphasis is on how people understand their place in the world and grasp changing circumstances, both losses and opportunities.

The title of this part is borrowed from Anthony Powell's *A Dance to the Music of Time*, a twelve-volume sequence of novels published between 1951 and 1975 and in turn inspired by Nicolas Poussin's painting of the same name. Dancing is more than a borrowed metaphor because it is a frequent activity in Mayotte. Chapter 7 opens with an incident from a spirit possession dance and with a women's dance celebrating the referendum. Dancing returns in another fashion in the wedding described in chapter 9. And Muslim dances, the *Maulida shengy* and the *Mulidy*, appear throughout the book, notably in chapters 6 and 11.

In chapter 7 I address the question of whether "culture" in Mayotte constitutes either a consistent or a bounded whole in order to respond to the question of why its citizens readily voted to stay part of France and also as a means for thinking about the relation of the local to the global, a topic that was live in anthropology at the time I wrote. The chapter is drawn from a paper originally delivered at a panel on religious certainties organized by Wendy James in the context of a broader conference theme on the global and local at the Association of Social Anthropologists (ASA) of the Commonwealth fourth Decennial Conference in Oxford in 1993 and published in 1995 as "Choking on the Qur'an and Other Consuming Parables from the Western Indian Ocean Front," in Wendy James (Ed.), *The Pursuit of Certainty: Religions and Cultural Formations*

(ASA Monographs, London: Routledge, 252–75 [see Lambek 1995]). I am no longer happy with the tone and relevance of the first portion of that version and have deleted it here. Although I have severely cut and reorganized the remainder, and added some material, the text remains based on fieldwork conducted through 1992 and writing from the same period. I addressed the question of the local in Mayotte from a different angle in "Catching the Local" (Lambek 2011a).

Chapter 8 focuses on the thoughts and acts of a spirit medium whom I call Nuriaty Tumbu. It illustrates the perception of social change that permeated Lombeni during the 1990s, active engagement in change, and reasoned reflection on it. Nuriaty appears as a historical actor, responsive to circumstances and offering her voice and agency to address them. As the title suggests, I argue that she is both subjective virtuoso and virtuous subject. Ray Kelly first pushed me to consider succession to spirit mediumship, a topic I pursue with respect to Nuriaty and other members of her family more fully in a number of other publications. Some years after the events described here, Nuriaty terminated her mediumship of the Sultan, and her reputation suffered a precipitous decline as a result of conflict within the family that I describe in "Kinship as Gift and Theft" (Lambek 2011b). For an entry into the subject of possession in Mayotte, see Lambek 1981.

Chapter 8 was written originally for a panel organized by Richard Werbner at the Manchester '99 Visions and Voices Conference and published in 2000 in *Anthropology Today* (16 [2]: 7–12) and later in revised form in *Postcolonial Subjectivities in Africa*, edited by Werbner (London: Zed Books [see Lambek 2002b]). Portions also appeared in a commemorative lecture for Roy Rappaport at the University of Michigan in 1998, and were delivered also at Trent University and the Divinity School, University of Chicago. It is considerably shortened here.

Chapter 9 is substantially cut back from a paper that was originally delivered as the Hawthorne Lecture at the annual meeting of the Canadian Anthropology Society (CASCA) 2003 in Halifax and published in 2004 as "The Saint, the Sea Monster, and an Invitation to a *Dîner-dansant*: Ethnographic Reflections on the Edgy Passage – and the Double Edge – of Modernity, Mayotte 1975–2001," *Anthropologica* 46 (1): 57–68 (see Lambek 2004). I spoke and wrote to the meeting's theme: "On Edge: Anthropology in Troubling Times." The chapter continues the themes of the previous one, here moving from a single virtuous subject to the responses of the broader community. If Nuriaty found herself on the wrong end of the cluster of papayas (in her metaphor of the papaya tree as the inverted social world), this chapter looks at the wedding celebration of young people who were at the top of the cluster. The chapter also follows an alternative version to Nuriaty's of what happened to the saint whose tomb was violated, in order to catch the temper of the times and people's unease at letting the past go unacknowledged.

Chapter 10 traces the movement of citizens of Lombeni off the island, for trade, travel, pilgrimage, and especially for temporary residence in La Réunion in order to collect higher state benefits than were available in Mayotte. For more than two decades many of Lombeni's citizens had double residence in both Mayotte and either La Réunion or metropolitan France; some have stayed in those places, but more have since returned. The chapter draws on fieldwork conducted in Mayotte but also in La Réunion in the summers of 2000 and 2001. It was originally written for the International Conference on Cultural Exchange and Transformation in the Indian Ocean World, organized by Ned Alpers and Allen Roberts at UCLA in 2002 and was revised in 2015 for eventual publication in *African Islands: Leading Edges of Empire and Globalization*, edited by Toyin Falola, Danielle Porter Sanchez, and Joe Parrott. I thank Danielle for editing a penultimate draft. It differs from the preceding chapters insofar as, although it was mostly written in 2002 and largely about the period 2000 to 2001, it also acknowledges some developments since.

By 2000 the official census indicated that the population of Lombeni had reached 1,600, almost doubling in the fifteen years since 1985, while that of the island as a whole rose at roughly the same rate, to 147,000, with a density of 352 inhabitants per square kilometre; that has nearly doubled again by 2017 to an estimated 254,000 in mid-August (http://countrymeters.info/en/Mayotte, United Nations Department of Economic and Social Affairs: Population Division). All these figures (including the previous ones) raise questions of accuracy. This is partly because the criteria used for residence are not always consistent. In particular, there is ambiguity over whether the count includes those people residing temporarily in La Réunion or metropolitan France and, conversely, the undocumented migrants from neighbouring islands. In Lombeni in 2000 there were 107 registrations for the *école maternelle* that accepted children born between 1995 and 1997. The director saw the main task as getting the children acquainted with reading and writing and especially with the fact of writing from left to right. Many of the same children were simultaneously beginning Qur'anic classes and learning to write from right to left.

7 Choking on the Qur'an and Other Consuming Parables, 1975–1992

The questions this chapter addresses are two: how to depict Mayotte in a way that does not falsify it as an internally homogeneous, externally bounded "culture," and how to make sense of the political decision to stay part of France, how to "swallow" it? The answer to the former helps make sense of the latter.

In much contemporary thinking, local is to global as traditional is to modern, singularity to plurality, or homogeneity to heterogeneity. Hence the common assumption that, relative to "ourselves," the members of "traditional" societies enjoyed the (mixed) privileges of insularity, historical stasis, and full certainty about their identity and world. This assumption is wrong. Not only does it falsely homogenize a category of "traditional societies," but it denies the kind of historical consciousness and self-reflexivity that characterize the human condition. I provide several anecdotes from life in Mayotte that challenge this stereotype. I question both the quality of the certainty ostensibly found at the heart of the local and the quality of boundedness ostensibly found at its margins. The answers to these questions turn out to be two sides of the same coin.

Each of my anecdotes turns on an alimentary idiom. As Mary Douglas (1966) powerfully observed, food consumption serves as a key to social boundaries, and it can form a ground for legitimating certainty as well (Lambek 1992). Hence another theme of the chapter lies in the interplay between objectified and embodied practices in localizing knowledge and establishing certainties.

Bodies and Texts

While Mahorais society is deeply Muslim, as I showed in the last chapter, that is not the full picture. For one thing, Muslims debate one another. For another, Muslim ideas and practices have been jostling other traditions within the region for centuries. In an earlier book (Lambek 1993) I depicted the situation by means of what I called a political economy of knowledge. Knowledge came from three traditions that were intertwined in practice and engaged in a kind of polyphonous conversation among themselves. I argued that these traditions – Islam, cosmology (astrology), and spirit possession – are not in direct contradiction so much as they speak past, over, and around each other. Thus, while one line of thinking within Islam would like to exclude spirit possession, and possibly cosmology, from the realm of discursive practice, another compromises with it; possession itself responds by slyly incorporating Islam, including Islam's own ambivalence towards it.

The cover of my book *Knowledge and Practice in Mayotte* (1993) showed two men in conversation: one an ordinary villager dressed for morning prayer, the other a spirit in possession of the body of a male medium, wearing a royal cloth and staff, but equally dressed as a Muslim, albeit in the fashion of the last century, with a red fez perched atop his head. The spirit is a manifestation of Andriantsoly, a Sakalava ruler who converted to Islam and moved to Mayotte in the early nineteenth century.

In the Sakalava politico-religious system, deceased royal ancestors return in the form of *trumba* (spirits) who are treated with great respect by the living. *Trumba* are not an alternative species of being, as Islam acknowledges to be the case for *djinn*, but rather the dead returned to the living. This violates fundamental Muslim conceptions; not only do Sakalava posit something impossible in view of Islamic ideas of the afterlife, but they produce *trumba* out of deceased monarchs by treating their corpses in a way offensive to Islam. Hence there must have been controversy at the death of Andriantsoly. He was buried in Mayotte, where his tomb forms a Sakalava burial shrine (*mahabu*), and his *trumba*, known as Ndramañavakarivu, is very much in evidence. Indeed, despite being Muslim, he is recognized as the leading figure among the *trumba* who possess people.

Each royal spirit is a representation of the time at which he or she lived (Lambek 1998b); Ndramañavakarivu (as Andriantsoly is posthumously known) condenses in his person both Sakalava royal ancestral power and its encapsulation by Islam. Yet if he converted to Islam, this conversion is itself subsumed within the system of spirit possession that is capable of representing a Muslim spirit. This is polyphony in which people speak in several voices and with several shades of meaning.

The context is one in which people navigate the various claims Islam and possession place upon them, in which they are rarely in a position to make final and exclusive decisions in favour of one or the other. The acknowledgment of each by the other and the problematic relationship between them are reproduced in minute practices such as the following (as edited from my field notes):

> *5 August 1985, 4 a.m.* In the midst of a large spirit possession ceremony the spirit who was then in active possession of a young woman named Athimary suddenly attracted a lot of attention when he began gagging and choking uncontrollably. I was worried that something was seriously wrong but people explained the problem. Athimary had been sick for a long time. They had applied medicine to accommodate the *trumba*, but the spirit would never speak when it rose, so Athimary's mother decided to change the direction of the treatment, had an amulet made for her daughter, and gave her many doses of *singa* medicine (liquid Qur'anic verses) to ingest. This might be good medicine for a human being but it made the *trumba* very angry. Although the spirit had not yet spoken, the adepts could see what the trouble was. Indeed, the experience of having something stuck in the throat could not have been rendered more vividly.

Athimary's predicament is one of double commitment. Like virtually everyone in Mayotte, she is a good Muslim; like some, she is also on the road to becoming a spirit medium. In order to avert the sort of trauma that befell Athimary, and so as not to expose their bodies to contestations between the various forms of knowledge and power, people remove their Muslim amulets before attending a spirit ceremony. At the same time, spirit curers often prescribe such amulets for their clients.

What is "local" here is the conjunction of two distinct traditions, each widespread in the region and each expanding in its own particular way. Before the imposition of colonialism there was a flourishing regional social network embedded in an extensive mercantile system that joined the East African coast to Madagascar. Islam is a "great transcontinental sodality" linked through a common sacred language (Anderson 1991: 36); it has neither a single centre nor specific boundaries. Islam is also text-based; its practice is "textually mediated," and texts are trans-local in their scope. Islam brings literacy, albeit of a restricted sort; and it also brought to Mayotte (if indeed it did not follow) a compendium of materials written in Arabic but not part of Islam per se (Lewis 1986). These materials include elements of astrology that can be traced back to Chaldean times; "magical" practices reputed to have elements of ancient Egyptian and Hebrew derivation (Blanchy and Said 1990); and humoral medicine, which, as the result of both Islamic and Iberian mercantile activity and colonialism, has been a truly global, albeit premodern, phenomenon. It is simply ethnocentric and historically naive ("chronocentric") to assume that trans-local phenomena only become significant in the contemporary period.[1]

The spread of Islam and astrology may be compared with practices stemming from the Sakalava polities of Madagascar. *Trumba* possession is what remains in Mayotte of the Sakalava cult of royal ancestors. Living royalty and the explicit political ideas and forces of which the spirits continue to be a manifestation in Madagascar have largely disappeared from Mayotte, but the "otherness" of possession, its explicit location outside the bounds of Islam, remains. Individual spirits develop relationships with people; a person who has a long-term relationship with a spirit periodically enters a state of trance as the spirit enters and speaks through her.[2]

Possession provides a position from which Mahorais have been able to interpret and contextualize Islam. In a sense, they have been fortunate to partake of two originally independent and hegemonic forms of knowledge and power, each with its own grounds of certainty and each able to put the other in perspective and slightly off balance.[3] And by means of both Islam and possession, Mahorais are able to imagine others at great distance from themselves enacting similar performances (compare Anderson 1991).

The truth of the Qur'an is indubitable and so is the presence of spirits. Both are rendered evident through local performance, but the factors conducive to certainty have a different weight in each case. What the *trumba* refused to swallow is a text; but the act of choking is not textually mediated. Both the objectified written word and embodied acts can be powerful means of ensuring legitimacy, but they operate according to different principles and exhibit different kinds of strains. The text of the Qur'an is an "authoritative discourse" that is originally imposed from without (Bakhtin 1981: 341ff) and is available in identical form, simultaneously across space and over time, to everyone who is able to study it. This consistency, and at the same time exclusivity, is a central facet of a text's authority, its truth value. It is particularly evident with respect to the Qur'an where uniformity is preserved to the degree that translations into vernaculars have not been acceptable (see Anderson 1991: 12ff).

The act of choking brings this privileged yet diffuse trans-historical and trans-local presence to a precise moment in space and time. If the text asserts eternal truths, possession is context-bound; its existence is legitimated by the brute fact of having the body invaded by a foreign spirit. Any larger concerns are overshadowed by the immediacy of the experience, the unqualified here-and-now of the spirit within one's body or standing opposite one, taking over the body of a host one knows well. Full possession is dependent upon an "internally persuasive discourse" (Bakhtin 1981)[4] that becomes a matter of *being* as much as *knowing*. Possession gains its persuasiveness from acts of displacement, public and discrete during moments of trance, but also more private, temporally durable, and diffuse in such things as responses to tabooed substances and dream life. Active possession is vigorously embodied, presenting a striking image to onlookers and a radical shift of experience for the host. Its legitimacy is manifest in bodily responses that appear distinct from conscious will (Lambek 1988a, 1992, 1998a). Who can argue with the fact that one is choking?

Muslims read and recite texts, objectified knowledge handed down through a chain of scribes and voices. Spirits must (re-)establish their own voices in each host, a process not yet complete in Athimary's case; they inaugurate their public careers by enunciating their names. Texts detach meaning from local sites of production and interpretation; they uncouple words from the ordinary constraints of speech, action, and historicity (Ricoeur 1971). Possession is anchored in local acts; the legitimacy of each appearance of a spirit must always be established anew. Spirits speak and must be answered. The immediate context is always relevant.

It is easy to paint this in binary terms. Yet Islam has embodied, practical, and disputational qualities, and possession has objectified ones. To take the latter first, performing as a spirit does share features associated with texts (Lambek 1981), and the identities of spirits (their formal properties such as name, dress, etc.) remain relatively stable across diverse settings. The *trumba* continuously signify the power and continuity of the Sakalava royal dynasty. Like written texts, spirits "externalize social consciousness" (Smith 1990: 211).

Conversely, one of the most significant features of the Qur'an is that it is actively recited, not passively read. If spirits sometimes choke on the Qur'an, it would be fairer to talk about how often it is swallowed. The text is copied, taught, memorized, enunciated, listened to, performed as prayer and oath – and on occasion dissolved in water and literally ingested. Each of these acts is unique and immediate. Yet at the same time, each is mediated by the identical text. Swallowing the Qur'an is wholesale penetration, an act that immediately and intimately connects the recipient to the vast world and sanctified truth of Islam. It is both an embodiment of the text and a textualization of the body. This is what makes it a powerful medicine.

While Athimary's act can be understood as a form of resistance[5] and while resistance to the power of writing and the authority of the written word can be found in a number of other contexts in Mayotte, it is important to understand the contours and limits of this resistance. The act of choking is abrupt and forceful, a concise drama of rejection, yet it does not deny the validity of Islam. Indeed, the Qur'anic verses are said to be "like fire" to the spirits; the spirits quickly pull away from them. And it is the spirit who objects to the verses, not Athimary herself. Moreover, as a spirit curer explained it, some spirits, like some people, know how to recite liturgy (*midzor*). It is precisely these spirits who won't accept the verses as a means of settling them down; they know what is written, how powerful it is, and what the effects are likely to be. The most knowledgeable spirits are also the most dangerous, since they are the least susceptible to the ordinary techniques of containment and since they know how to subvert Islamic strategies.

This play between the texts and spirits provides a space in which the strengths of each are recognized, in which the power of Islam is respected even as it is subverted. Moreover, a challenge that is entirely embodied in nature must be highly context-dependent rather than absolute or universal in scope; it holds only within a limited frame. The message is not that Islam is false or that the spirits are actively opposed to Islam but that some of them sometimes stand outside it. If most spirits are not Muslims, the point is made that humans are.

This contrast between the text and the act of choking can stand as an image for relations between global and local, the enduring and the immediate, the objectified and the embodied, the discursive and the non-discursive, the essence and the act. What Athimary's performance provides is a *contextualization* of Islam. It is an acknowledgment of the incorporation of Islam within local society and at the same time a demonstration that internalization has its limits. Moreover, it is a framed performance, partial in its claims. And far from illustrating mystification or irrationality, possession has an ironic side that the earnest practice of Islam (or any of the textually mediated missionizing religions) precisely lacks.

In sum, what is lived through here is the locally informed conjunction of two different forms of knowledge and practice stemming from two powerful systems of a quite different order. The local repertoire comprises *both* Islam and possession. Each is productive of a particular form of global-local relations and its own form of certainty. While they do not often appear at the same moment or compete for the same act of commitment, as they do for Athimary, the certainty of each is compromised or at least contextualized by the presence of the other. Islam is explicitly harder on possession than the reverse, readier to pronounce exclusionary statements, and it is the dominant of the two. But if Islam comprehensively informs the practice and identity of every villager, possession makes up for this by its immediacy, its insidiousness, and its recourse to irony.

While some *trumba* choke on the Qur'an or enjoy flouting Muslim convention, others practise it, notably in performances of the *Maulida*. Perhaps this is the subtlest form of subversion. These performances are not only joyous manifestations of Islam, but they also document the history of the relationship between possession and Islam.

Ndramañavakarivu configures in his person the conjunction of Sakalava ancestral practices and Islam. He is a *trumba*, yet a Muslim one. He dresses in Muslim garb and, unlike other *trumba*, who drink rum and dance to traditional Malagasy rhythms, he prefers the *Maulida*. Every year in the month of the Prophet's birth, Ndramañavakarivu calls *trumba* from across the island to a *Maulida shengy*, performed on his behalf at his tomb. This is like other performances during the month and is comparable to the commemorations of deceased Islamic scholars indicated in the previous chapter. Yet at the same time it evokes the non-Islamic rituals (*fanompoa*) held annually for deceased Sakalava sovereigns in Madagascar. Indeed, *Maulida* are held for Ndramañavakarivu in Madagascar as well.

Ndramañavakarivu and many of his brethren rise to watch the *Maulida* performed by local women. As they dance, some performers become possessed by another kind of spirit, known as the *lulu ny Maulida* (spirits of the *Maulida*) or *lulu kimahore* (spirits of Mayotte) who join in. These spirits are also Muslim; they manifest Shimaore-speaking figures from the history of Mayotte – most saliently, the Muslim rulers of the Sultanate who welcomed Andriantsoly and his cohort of Malagasy speakers on their arrival and settlement in Mayotte. We will meet one in chapter 8.

The celebration includes human performers, spectators, and hosts of the spirits. All these people are Muslim, and the performers are adepts of the *Maulida shengy*. The performance is piously and joyfully Islamic – except that the sponsors and some of the performers and audience are spirits. Muslim participants must especially overlook the fact that Islam rejects the identification of *trumba* as deceased human beings.

If the *trumba* are in the position of "sponsors" on whose behalf the ceremony is performed, as mostly non-Muslims themselves they cannot reciprocate by performing the same ceremony on behalf of the spirits of the *Maulida*. Unlike the scenario described in previous chapters, the reciprocity is not redoubled. Indeed, the relationship between the two kinds of spirits replays the complex power relations of the late precolonial period. Shortly after Andriantsoly arrived in Mayotte he declared himself overlord; at least, it was with him that the French conducted the treaty in 1841 that in their eyes turned the island over to them. The performance indicates that the balance between Islam and Sakalava spirit possession remains a delicate one – that it is, quite literally, a dance of power (Tehindrazanarivelo 1997).

In sum, the performance is characterized by some irony. It indexes the Muslim conversion of those Sakalava who immigrated to Mayotte and equally the incorporation of Sakalava elements in a Muslim society. And yet clearly this incorporation was incomplete; the presence of the *trumba* announces that there was something left over. Moreover, the existence of spirits of the *Maulida* suggests a transmission in the other direction. The performance thus subverts the very transformation it records. In the end, the message of the performance is inconclusive. It is not clear whether either tradition has incorporated, converted, or subverted the other.[6] In a sense this summarizes the uniqueness and specificity (the "local") of Mayotte – a world constituted by the continued conversation between incommensurable discourses, each trying to comprehend the other.

The performance also opens up the tight connection between "society" and "religion" described in the last chapter, providing a partially external foothold through which it can be viewed. This is the foothold neither of the rationalizing, intellectualizing observer nor of the devout follower of a "world" religion, modernizing victors of the great transformation, but an opening for reflexivity produced by local poiesis. In other words, the performance is both a kind of recording or representation of history and a reflection upon it.[7]

If neither possession nor Islam gains conclusive purchase over the other, they both lie at the heart of things. Culture in Mayotte is not then constituted as the manifestation of an inner essence, the elaboration of a single central truth, a uniform cosmos, system, or structure, not even when conceptualized in terms of contradiction. Rather it is the conjunction of incommensurable ideas or discourses – that is, those not "able to be brought under a set of rules which will tell us how rational agreement can be reached ... where statements seem to conflict" (Rorty 1980: 316). This is not a matter of logical contradiction, since there is no neutral language or framework in terms of which the two discourses could be fully expressed; invocation of one does not logically entail the other, but nor does it rule it out. Each conceptualizes the world and the sense of problem somewhat differently.

The differences between the distinct regimes of knowledge of Islam and spirit possession are not resolvable through logic because they cannot be put in the same language. Yet their very incommensurability demands a mutual hermeneutics (Rorty 1980: 347; Lambek 1993); they can only meaningfully coexist in such a way that each attempts to interpret the other, or rather, that their respective and mutual practitioners address their conjunction. The act of expelling the Qur'an is but one (unsubtle) move in what has become a very long, subtle conversation.[8] This may at times take the form of argument but never of a full refutation or full subsumption of one by the other. Indeed, even to speak of it as a conversation may be placing too great an emphasis on the discursive quality of the process.

Even representations of history are subject to history. In performances of the women's *Maulida shengy* in Lombeni I have noticed an increasing appearance of spirits of the *Maulida*, tellingly referred to as "Mahorais spirits." These spirits speak not in Malagasy as do the *trumba*, but in Shimaore, the Comoran language spoken by the majority of the inhabitants of Mayotte. As former sultans of Mayotte, their appearance among Kibushy speakers enacts a new sense of internal unity, as all inhabitants are bound by a common history and identity in their special relationship with France. In this context, the distinction between speakers of the two languages, and perhaps even between the two discourses, Islam and possession, is recontextualized with respect to something that has become increasingly more salient, namely local proto-national identity vis-à-vis the all-powerful Other and chief local instigator of the new global order that is France.

Boundary Politics

Recipes of the Global and the Local

If the spirit's refusal to swallow the Qur'an takes us to the centre of local culture, the next anecdote reflects on the constitution of its boundaries. In 1975 a dish commonly served in Mayotte was manioc and plantain cooked in coconut cream. I recorded and started to use the name I heard it called: *gorbaly*. I don't recall exactly when I was enlightened that the term was the local pronunciation of *"globale,"* an explicit reference to the political situation. Perhaps it was when I heard a dish of rice referred to as *île par île* ("island by island") and queried the association. I had arrived in Mayotte a short time after the referendum in the Comoros that was to decide its future. When the votes were tabulated it was clear that the majority of people from each of the other three islands in the archipelago wanted their independence from France, whereas the majority from Mayotte opted to stay part of France. Debate raged as to whether Mayotte could go its own way with France or remain with the emerging new nation of the Comoros ("Comores" in French) – whether acknowledging the vote island by island could supersede the global count.

Full of moral certainty and the political sentiments that were then sweeping anthropology, I assured people that I too hated colonialism and shared their desire for independence. I was disconcerted to be told that such views would not be tolerated; unless I was able to remain silent on the subject I would be ejected from the community forthwith. Independence from France along with the rest of the archipelago – based on the global tabulation of the vote (*gorbaly*) – was, they said, a recipe for economic disaster. From the point of view of the majority of small cultivators, the immediate power to be feared and resisted was the exploitative elite on the neighbouring islands who would seize their land. People would be left with nothing to eat but bananas, manioc, and coconut – *gorbaly*. The culinary dish was an explicit metonym of the political recipe and its expected outcome. Should the vote be disaggregated *île par île* and local sentiment succeed in keeping the French in place, then there was a good chance the French would develop Mayotte. They might set up factories and build roads. And there would be rice on the mat every night.

Here we have, in local idiom, alternative visions of the global periphery; modernization through benevolent dependence versus independent "nationhood." Proponents of both positions selected their respective narratives in the spirit of hope for the future. However, while I saw this as a moral or ideological issue, most Mahorais voted on a pragmatic basis. People were willing to swallow dependency, whose negative features they well recognized, in wagering for economic security and "development."[9]

So much for my first lesson in the politics of the global and local. But the moral of the story here has to do with the tremendous ambiguity of these concepts seen as exclusive alternatives. The *gorbaly* story poses the questions: which is the global and which is the local, for whom, and where are we positioned to know the difference? A global outcome – union with the other islands of the archipelago, independence like every other African state – it was foreseen, would run down the local economy, such as it then was, forcing people to rely on the most local of their products, and subject inhabitants to the predation of elites and the larger populations on the adjacent islands. Yet the explicitly "local" alternative, *île par île*, Mayotte for itself, anticipated more obvious globalizing consequences: a rapidly increasing integration into the French political and economic system and an ostensible bypassing of the regional one.

In what must be ranked as a major political victory, although it was contested by the emergent République Féderale Islamique des Comores and received bad press throughout Africa, it is the latter scenario that largely came to pass. Some eighteen years after the referendum (i.e., in 1994), Mayotte remained a notorious political anomaly. In the discourse of postcolonial nationalism, France shamefully failed to live up to its commitment to withdraw and allow Mayotte to join the Comoros. Instead, the French responded to a greater or lesser degree to many of the demands of the party that advocated the *île par île* solution. Increased dependency and development went hand in hand. Roads, schools, and clinics were finally constructed. The economy came to be based virtually entirely on wage labour and state benefits and subsidies. While I have no wish to defend the honour of France in this matter (and while developments led to new forms of nationalist sentiment, especially on the part of educated youths who realized that they had received both more and less than their parents bargained for), a French pull-out (in 1994) would have radically disoriented and impoverished the vast majority of the population and considerably undermined their hopes and projects.

How could all this be? Did the Mahorais simply march on their stomachs? Were they cynical or pragmatic to such a shameful degree as to sell their birthright for a mess of rice pottage? Were they naive enough to let themselves be co-opted by a few Creole leaders of the pro-French movement? Or is it that local constructions of identity operate according to a logic with which Western readers are less familiar? Is it not perhaps food – the incorporative activities of cooking, serving, eating, and digesting – rather than the individuated products of reproduction that serves most strongly to articulate the nature of identity?[10] Is collective identity not perhaps grounded more in acts than in states, in collective existence more than national essence?

Possessive Individualism versus Object Relations

Collective identity in the western Indian Ocean has not corresponded to the model of reified, distinct, autonomous, but equivalent "cultures" so widely appropriated to articulate, legitimate, and control ethnic and national units – so many distinct entries in a "multicultural" festival or seats at the United Nations. This model of bounded cultures or nations is one that Richard Handler (1988) has compellingly analysed as a form of possessive individualism. In contrast, I think of identities in the region as "object-relational."

Handler writes that, "Nationalism is an ideology about individuated being. It is an ideology concerned with boundedness, continuity and homogeneity encompassing diversity" (1988: 6). In this ideology,

> Individuals demonstrate their being, their individuality, through choice; choice is the creative manifestation of self, the imposition of self onto the external world. Property is what results from choices – products that exist in the external world yet remain linked through proprietorship to the self that created them. Thus the nation and its members "have" a culture, the existence of which both follows from and proves the existence of the nation itself. (ibid. 51)

This model, raised from the biological individual to the nation, bears not a little similarity to Freudian drive theory. While the latter is still

salient in popular culture, it has largely been replaced in psychoanalytic theory by a model summarized as "object-relational."[11] It is this
model rather than possessive individualism that makes better sense of
collective identity in Mayotte.

I use the term "object-relational" rather than simply "relational" to
emphasize that the conceptual shift is not simply from entities to relationships (as in structuralism) but rather to the problematic nature
of boundedness and to the ways "betweenness" is brought "within."
In an object-relational view of identity it is the internalizing of
others – other people – that takes precedence over the building of rigid
boundaries around an individuated self. Identity formation flows in
both directions. The flux of projections and introjections ensures that
some aspects of the developing self are likely to have originally been
perceived or experienced as aspects of the primary other or others,
and aspects of the other may have originally been felt as aspects of the
self. On a psychological level, then, even the corporeal boundaries of
the individual do not separate him or her in any simple way from the
rest of the world. Identity is defined not in terms of distinct or exclusive features – distinct property or properties – but in terms of relative
internalizations and projections of others. An object-relational identity emphasizes sharing over difference, connection over separation,
commonalities over boundaries, and mutual dependency over self-
sufficiency (J. Benjamin 1988: 76). It is also dynamic; "insistent separ-
ateness" is viewed as a defence rather than a fact of nature (Chodorow
1989: 148–9). This model clearly fits both spirit possession and possession's relationship with Islam. It also makes better sense of collective
identity in Mayotte than does possessive individualism.[12]

Alliance as Incorporation

The political strategy found in Mayotte during the 1970s bears more
than a little similarity to long-standing techniques in which polities in
the region, attempting either to impose domination upon or to escape
from each other, roped in more distant allies – the French, the English,
and the Omanis – who were, of course, all too ready to exploit the situation. In the 1840s the Antankaraña of northern Madagascar made a
pact with the French in order to regain territory seized from them by
the expanding Merina state based in the central highlands of Madagascar. To this day the Antankaraña explicitly identify themselves as allies
of the French. A key artefact of the kingdom is the dagger said to have
been given to the monarch by French king Louis-Philippe in the 1840s;

Antankaraña insignia combine an Islamic moon and star (conversion to Islam in the nineteenth century having been the fulfilment of a vow subsequent to a miraculous escape from the Merina) with the *tricolore*. The very name of the Antankaraña monarch, Isa Alexandre Tsimanamboholahy, indexes the same cultural *métissage* that forms the basis of the ideology of his kingdom. The Antankaraña regularly invite French diplomats to their rituals; they call upon the consul for funds to renovate the royal residence; and they readily assimilate European tourists and embarrassed anthropologists to their French allies as well (Lambek and Walsh 1997).

"Strategy" is a concept insufficient to portray these developments if it implies historical agency in a kind of moral vacuum. Strategies are rendered acceptable and reasonable, are selected and gain popular support, according to broader understandings of the world, implicit truths. Nor is strategy sufficient to account for the disinclination towards dogmatic positions. In northern Madagascar, where Muslims, Catholics, Protestants, and non-practitioners live side by side, there is a kind of openness and tolerance of heterogeneity. Groups partially incorporate others and are often willing to be partially incorporated such that boundaries between them are ambiguous.

In voting as they did, people in Mayotte were not hampered by the sort of nationalist identity politics described by Handler (1988) that has become so common we tend to naturalize it.[13] They looked forward rather than back. There was no nostalgia for a golden past but a hard-headed realism about the possibility of an impoverished future eating nothing but *gorbaly*. For a time, party membership became the most salient basis of identity: families and villages were split in hurtful ways over the vote (Lambek and Breslar 1986) and subsequently reunited by the payment of fines and the ceremonies of reconciliation (chapter 4). It is noteworthy that these divisions did not fall along ethnic or linguistic lines.[14] Rice and bananas in coconut cream were each foods enjoyed equally by all sides. Transcending party affiliation, people identified themselves in inclusive terms as human beings (*ulun belu*) or as Muslims (*silamu*), Black people (*ulu mainting*), or simply the poor (*ulu maskin*). More narrowly, they identified by locality of origin or current residence (both island and village). Loyalty to and activity in the place of residence were generally as significant as any prejudice attributed to origins.

Nor was the political division along explicitly religious lines. Indeed, while the Comoran elites claimed to have more direct links to sources of Islamic authority than did villagers, vernacular Islam also formed a major vehicle for pro-French activism. The fight for Mayotte was engaged largely by women. It was they who organized resistance to the Comoran regime, expressly challenged the French to stay, and eventually celebrated victory.[15] Their main means of organizing was an elaboration of the ceremonial exchange system in which villages invited each other to Islamic recitals (chapter 6). Political congresses were articulated on this basis, as were more militant activities. So, on one memorable occasion women from around Mayotte gathered to protect a piece of road-building equipment from being removed to the Grande Comore and passed the time singing the *Maulida*.

In sum, what is striking is the relative inattendance to boundaries and clear-cut social divisions. Mayotte provides an illustration of a society based on incorporative principles in which residence and achievement have been far more significant than descent or ascription. There were no discrete, named, descent groups, and marriage was conceptualized more as the incorporation of new adults within the community than as an exchange or alliance between distinct kin groups.[16] People were not xenophobic, nor did they have a highly developed consciousness of themselves as distinct; boundaries were not strongly marked. The political crisis of the 1970s did enhance the development of a Mahorais identity, yet it was one based less on autonomy than on merger with France.

When the referendum was won by the pro-French party and the government acceded to the results, the women planted a French flag on the plaza and danced around it (*figure 7.1*), then crowded into bush taxis and drove across the island singing. The mode of celebration at becoming "French," the dances and songs performed by massed women, were "local" or "traditional" in kind, with no sense of anomaly or incongruity, and no sense of inauthenticity or betrayal of origins. This is an expression of cultural integrity rather than inferiority, cynicism, or breakdown. As one young man put it to me in 1975 (my paraphrase and emphasis),

> People here have lots of customs (*fomba*) and concerns (*kabar*), far more than those of Europeans (*vazaha*). After all, we take on all their customs and interests *in addition* to those proper to Islam. Many of us go on to study European practices in order to get good-paying jobs. But the French (*vazaha*) don't interest themselves in our customs. If the French know more things than we do, such as how to produce medicines, they should teach us. Once we learn, we will know more than they do, because we have Islam too.

Figure 7.1 Celebrating the referendum, 1976. Women dance to celebrate victory of the pro-French party (*"Sordat nahazu,* Sordat has won!"). They step out two by two from the line of women, singing and beating a rhythm with bamboo sticks.

The French viewed the political developments with bemusement. How could the Mahorais – who did not look or act French and who, for the majority, did not even speak French, or therefore think like the French – ever take their association with France so seriously, so literally? Nevertheless, their response too was quite literal, beginning with the infusion of universal primary education in French and the development of a more elaborate educational system. In 1992 it was with somewhat more justification (though still received with a great deal of ambivalence by the metropolitans) that the villagers sometimes responded to the question of their identity, *"Zahay fahavazaha"* ("We have become Europeans").

An Act of Consumption

The *gorbaly* story is about regional politics, in which the region is rejected for a local/global solution. Global means, in a sense, the circumvention of the immediately inter-local. Whereas in western Europe there has been a recent movement towards the transcending of national boundaries in favour of regions, in Mayotte "global" has meant the transcending of the region in favour of direct links to a metropole.[17]

In the years following the referendum, the French greatly intensified their investment in Mayotte, producing radical cultural and economic transformation. Much could be said regarding this brave new heterotopia.[18] For some there has been unprecedented opportunity. Others have been stuck in poorly paid manual labour. Ironically, given that the original pro-French vote had been partly impelled by concern for rice land, one of the most striking changes is that by 1992 rice cultivation had been entirely abandoned. A great deal of rice is consumed, but it is all imported. And for sale along with it is a large array of foreign foods.

The final anecdote comes full circle, juxtaposing the increased penetration of capital and global commodities with the act of a spirit medium. In the household where I stayed we were served tender pieces of fried chicken, quite different from the local poultry, whose toughness had always been offset by a delicious sauce. The chicken was imported frozen from South Africa and sold in the new supermarket (with video monitors and automatic checkout) in town, as well as by local merchants newly equipped with freezers. Knowing that his wife had long been tabooed chicken by her *trumba* and was even now submitting to a relatively recent taboo against goat meat, I asked my host what she was eating.

"The same as we are," he replied.

"What happened to her taboo against chicken?" I asked with astonishment.

"She is still tabooed chicken (*akohu*)."

"But this *is* chicken," I said, naive as ever, assuming some misunderstanding and worrying that if she were not warned it would have the same unpleasant effects on his wife as did the local variety.

"Of course it is," he whispered back, winking. "But we call it *vorung* (bird)!"

What are we to make of the woman's act? Is it a wholehearted embracing, a swallowing whole, of the new global capitalist relations of consumption and an expression of freedom from past constraints? Is it a dismissal of the new products as being of too little value even to merit a taboo? Is it an appropriation of the global product on one's own terms, exhibiting, in true Malagasy fashion, the power to maintain relevance by marking an absence (here the absence of the taboo)? Is it but a form of "experimental practice," "the realm of partial recognition, of inchoate awareness, of ambiguous perception" (Comaroff and Comaroff 1991: 31, 29), one whose implications are still as open to the actors themselves as they remain interpretively opaque to me? In hushing me perhaps my host is warning me not to prejudge the issue.[19]

At the least we can say that if chicken is now a foreign product, the decision to eat it is a local act, couched in a Mahorais idiom of acceptance and rejection of potent, polluting, or neutral substances. So too are the indubitable results, whether satisfaction or nausea.

Conclusion

Whereas many discourses and practices have become globalized, the conjunction of any particular set of discourses is precisely a local phenomenon. Rethinking cultures as the marked intersections and incorporations of multiple discourses and the successive attempts to make local sense of such contingencies may be appropriate. "Local culture" here is less an a priori than the complex sedimentary product of the spread of various discourses; perhaps it always was (compare James 1988). So questions to ask include how diverse discourses circulate and incorporate one another. To borrow a Marxist language, how do we talk about the articulation of modes of discursive and embodied production and consumption? And, given the fact that the circulation of discursive practices is not a new phenomenon, how have modes of articulation changed with new forms of objectification?

Mayotte was a geographic locus, long part of a region characterized by spreads of diverse practices and by weakly articulated boundaries. The constitution of identity in Mayotte did not fit the dominant global view of cultures as bounded, essentialized entities in a universe of like objects or as the discrete contents of packages so bounded. I suggest that it may be described as object-relational. I do not mean that identity in Mayotte was predicated on an explicit ideology of object relations, as Handler (1988) argues that nationalism is based on possessive individualism, but rather that object relations provides a useful model for understanding local practices of identification.

If I were not acutely aware of the ironies of generalizing the local practice I have described here, I might go on to suggest that an object-relational model makes better analytic sense of cultural processes in many places, even where it is manifestly not the model of agents themselves. This could provide an avenue for replacing the bounded and ultimately essentialist uses of culture that were a part of the anthropological tool kit and that reappear in vulgar form in the rhetoric of both nationalism and multiculturalism.

In Handler's (1988) depiction of the ideology of nationhood the claim to internal homogeneity is a central feature. The first anecdote was presented precisely in order to illustrate heterogeneity in Mayotte. The final anecdote directs attention to the way global commodities and practices are likewise articulated with ones of longer standing in Mayotte. Association with France does not violate a sense of local integrity.

Local perceptions do not rest on the bedrock of a single, deep, fully coherent or stable structure but rather are the product of ongoing conversations, acts, and shifts of attention. Culture is in motion, set in "internal" dialogue with itself and in incorporative relations with others.

Perhaps one way to avoid the negative repercussions of analytic elegance is to change our conceptual apparatus from nouns to verbs, a procedure that Schafer (1976) has urged upon psychoanalysis and a distinction that harks back in anthropology to Whorf's contrast of Hopi with Indo-European languages (Carroll 1956). It is to resurrect Leslie White's (1949) memorable dictum that "culture is culturing." When culture is reconstructed as verb rather than noun, it is active and hence cannot be objectified or fenced in.

Consistent with an object-relational perspective and with a shift from nouns to verbs, difference from others, to the extent that it becomes an issue, might be phrased in terms of negation or refusal – not being, having, or participating in specific features that are characteristic of the outside world or particular outsiders – refusing or spitting them out – rather than in terms of unique, positive, essential attributes (possessions) that belong exclusively to the inside. Taboos actively articulate identity by establishing that openness and internalization have their limits; conversely, their supersession renews openness.[20] Although the scale of such negations or refusals ranges from the personal through the community, to the local and the global, negations need not mark natural essences or firm boundaries; Malagasy readily adopt taboos associated with the community or polity in which they choose to live.

It is not surprising that ingestion forms the connecting thread between these anecdotes since it is a kind of "naturally symbolic act" by
which to express and carry out internalization, localizing that which
was global or outside. Conversely, alimentary rejection, choking, or
expulsion, is an act of boundary marking. My analysis has only pig-
gybacked on the indigenous mode of expression, providing a more abstract, disembodied account. Eating and choking are not only symbolic
expressions but indexical acts, and this adds to their persuasive force;
they naturalize acceptance and rejection in the sense that embodied responses appear beyond their agents' conscious control.

Postscript

A comment from a Mahorais friend in 2000 reinforces some of the
points made in this chapter, emphasizing both the centrality of Islam as
established in the previous chapter and its association with incorporation. As he explained to me, "Mayotte is a *tany vavy*, a female place. Just
as a mother nurtures her children, so Mayotte looks after all comers.
The Anjouanais get fed, everyone eats. If a stranger were to land in a
different country and didn't have money to buy food they would die.
In Mayotte, kin or no kin, we look after them, because we have *imany*
(faith, compassion). That is *Silam* (Islam)."

8 Nuriaty, the Saint, and the Sultan: Virtuous Subject and Subjective Virtuoso of the Postmodern Colony, to 1995

This chapter about the actions of a spirit medium responds to a call to address postcolonial subjectivity. Subjectivity is a complex term that may be construed as simultaneously about subjection to power, moral agency, and being the subject of one's own experience.[1] This is a space where a number of ostensibly competing theories might be made to meet; I approach it by focusing on moral practice and the conditions of and for acting with dignity and self-respect and making situated judgments. I draw from an Aristotelian perspective in which practical knowledge is understood not as detached from being or becoming but as a constitutive of them (Bernstein 1983: 146), yet I seek to understand the way ambivalent subjects are able to make existential choices with respect to power. My subject is a woman who, subjected to power and history, nevertheless manages to constitute herself as a subject in her own right.

With respect to the postcolonial, the locus is an anomalous one; Mayotte remains one of the few previously colonized places that is not exactly postcolonial, or rather, that has defined coloniality in an original, even postmodern way. At the time of writing Mayotte held the status of *Collectivité Territoriale*, an ambiguous designation that in practice includes government by a French prefect alongside an elected local assembly and deputies to the French legislature. This is not the place to go into the complexities of the legal status or the lively politics. Suffice it to say that the Mahorais understood themselves to know what they were doing. And, despite the inevitable continuation of colonial attitudes on the part of the French, the Mahorais have been quite successful at getting what they thought they wanted. Perhaps inevitably, they now want more and more.

When neighbouring Madagascar marks its Independence Day by means of French custom (military parades, flags, *bises*), the Malagasy are celebrating not only independence from France but independence to be *like* France, to be another commensurable nation-state within the international order of nation-states. In this aspiration perhaps they are out of date. Mayotte is not *like* France but *a part of* France – a place that reinvented postcoloniality and grasped its potential in the new global order for enhanced forms of connection and mobility.

Originally despised for its political dependency and subsequently envied for its economic success (albeit relative and artificial), and certainly less subject to World Bank policy and less politically unstable than its neighbours, Mayotte has experienced rapid transformation since 1976. Mayotte has become a society in which subsistence cultivation has been largely abandoned in favour of wage work and welfare benefits; a whole generation has been introduced to French schooling, some proceeding all the way through the *baccalauréat*; some people achieve social mobility and white-collar jobs; and many inhabitants relocate temporarily to La Réunion and even metropolitan France. Conversely, Mayotte has become a desirable destination for outsiders: for metropolitan French seeking romantic escape on a tropical island that has an ever-increasing tourist infrastructure, a supply of European amenities, and the security of the known; for poor Comorans, especially Anjouanais, who land on the beaches at night and are willing to take employment on any terms; and for Malagasy eagerly seeking work papers and drawing on old kinship connections to acquire French citizenship. Mayotte has become a local hub of movement and a whir of activity and opportunity. But in the background remain all those people who did not achieve the mobility, education, white-collar jobs, and consumer items, or the respect that accompanies them.

It is to this transformation that Nuriaty, the woman at the centre of this chapter, stands as moral witness.

Situated Judgment and Practical Wisdom

In the last chapter we saw how participation by spirits in performances of the *Maulida* manifests a kind of historical consciousness. In this chapter I turn to the thoughts and actions of an individual spirit medium, Nuriaty Tumbu.

The moral practice of spirit mediums in Mayotte and Madagascar, that is to say, their exercise of situated yet imaginative judgment, is evident in at least three respects. The most obvious is the way that mediums demonstrate flexible role shifting, empathy, and disinterestedness in their interactions with clients, each other, and their general public, both from within and outside states of active possession and their timing for moving between them (Lambek 1993: 371ff). The second is the way mediums come to be possessed by particular named spirits rather than others, thereby reproducing or initiating specific social relations and emphasizing certain social connections over others (Lambek 1988b, 1993: 320ff). The third is the way that some mediums come to assume a kind of consciousness – and conscience – of history (Lambek 1998b, 2002c, 2003). Their virtuosity is evident in the skill with which they can shift between historically distinct subject positions, their virtue in their combination of social advocate and social critic, of exemplary monarch (since most spirits are former rulers) and exemplary political subject (evident in the submission of mediums to their spirits).

When I began to trace generational continuity among mediums and spirits in Mayotte I discovered a logic of practice inherent in succession to mediumship. Asking who comes to be possessed by which spirit turned out to be much more interesting than simply asking why some people rather than others become possessed.[2] One of the central figures in my description of the dynamics of succession was Nuriaty, the eldest daughter of Tumbu and Mohedja, both active spirit mediums. Nuriaty began to acquire spirits in her mid-twenties. The first was a junior male carouser who differentiated Nuriaty from her parents, but he faded in significance as Nuriaty became possessed by the main senior spirit who also possessed her father. This occurred with her father's tacit acquiescence and then his encouragement. Tumbu passed on his knowledge of curing and sorcery extraction, and eventually Nuriaty took up his therapeutic practice as Tumbu, in his sixties, began to gradually withdraw from it. Within Nuriaty the senior spirit continued to look out for the welfare of the extended family. Nuriaty also began to be possessed by two of the spirits who possessed her mother.[3] Nuriaty's actions fitted my model of succession to mediumship very well, exemplifying a process that includes mutual identification, introjection, displacement, growth, and reproduction which resonate deeply on both psychological and social levels (Lambek 2002a).

Succession implies success, and I expected that Nuriaty would continue to expand her role as host to the main spirit who possessed her father. However, Nuriaty's career has not developed as either I or her parents anticipated. I was disconcerted to find on a visit in 1995 (when Nuriaty was around forty-six) that she was no longer an active medium of any of the family spirits. Social change had destroyed the whole pattern, I assumed, and indeed the changes in Mayotte were enormous. But not quite so. What had happened was that Nuriaty's moral horizons had shifted.

Nuriaty is a warm, jovial, and slightly aggressive woman whom I have known since 1975 when, as a mother of three sons, she seemed much older than I, although in reality she is approximately my age. She likes to eat well, pays relatively little attention to her appearance, and unlike most people in Lombeni in 1995, still lived in a wattle-and-daub thatch-roofed house. She has been married six times, but over the course of time her investment in relations with her spirits has come to supersede those with living male partners. One of her sons died in childhood, and since then, to her great sadness, she has had no full-term pregnancies. She has also raised a sister's daughter, a younger brother, and now the former's daughter.

It was her infertility that broke up the marriage that was otherwise the happiest. Her husband at the time had never been previously married and had no children of his own. After several years during which Nuriaty sought to get pregnant, he listened to his mother's advice to have children elsewhere and took the opportunity to follow the socially approved scenario, which until then he had avoided, namely to marry a virgin. This was an expensive proposition; moreover, the requirements had inflated enormously since Nuriaty herself had married as a virgin. Thus, while she lived in great simplicity, she knew her husband was putting aside most of his earnings towards gifts for the new bride. The husband decided that polygyny would be too difficult and so, when the time was ripe, he left Nuriaty.[4] She understood the reasons and even attended the wedding, which included a lavish display of gifts – a sewing machine, seventy cloth wrappers, a watch, and several pieces of gold. Nuriaty herself contributed an item to add to the gifts he brought.[5]

The new wife, more than a decade younger than Nuriaty, was a school graduate with a clerical job. She had enough money to build a fashionable house of durable materials, something which was still beyond Nuriaty's grasp (she is counting on her grown sons to help her build). There had been no comparable opportunities for schooling when Nuriaty was young. Living in relative poverty, or at least materially simpler conditions, she watched younger cousins and nieces gain white-collar jobs and incomes and display the associated signs of material prosperity and physical ease.

When I arrived in 1995 Nuriaty began to tell me about a series of dreams in which she witnessed how a saint had left his tomb, which was located on the adjacent beach. Sharif Bakar was from *Àrabie*; according to legend his burial took place well before the founding of the village, possibly several centuries earlier. His tomb had been the site of community sacrifices until a few years past. Recently the beach had become the destination of Sunday visitors from town, young people in large numbers who arrived in cars and on motorcycles and who drank, played ball, caroused, and possibly urinated on the tomb. In Nuriaty's dreams, the saint and his wife (the first I heard of her) withdrew in anger from the pollution.[6]

This is not the only account of abandonment or flight on the part of earlier inhabitants of Mayotte. Some years earlier there had been an incident in which spirits fleeing from the bush in which they had lived (which was being cleared in order to make a paved road) angrily invaded people's houses at night. However, in Nuriaty's dream, the saint did not simply quit his tomb. Nuriaty saw Mawana Madi, the Sultan of Mayotte prior to the French takeover in 1841, arrive in a boat to fetch him, in effect to rescue him.

Here is a paraphrase of her account:

The day they cleared the bush near the tomb [in order to create a football field] I first had the dream. Sharif Bakar and his wife got up and left angrily. Mawana Madi came and said to me, "Let's fetch Sharif Bakar, he can't stay there." Mawana Madi asked me to help; I am his helper. He spoke to me in Shimaore. I saw both Mawana Madi and Ndramañavakarivu [chapter 7] invite Sharif Bakar to join them. A *vedette* [motorized launch] came, filled with beautifully dressed people. They performed the *Maulida shengy*, then took the Saint and his wife away with them in the launch. They are good / beautiful people, *ulu tsara*. Their smell is very sweet, *mañitry*. They left on a golden armchair, *fauteuil dahabu*, with gold clothes on the chair.[7] After they left I woke up. I have had the dream three times.

The Saint has left for good. You can still do a *fatiha* [Muslim prayer] at the tomb, but it is now empty. He and all the elders, *ulu be*, were angry at how the tomb was treated, used as the site of ball games, etc.[8] The elders couldn't put up with drunken picnics. Sharif Bakar was angry to see his house used in this way, so he got up and left. [As she speaks we hear trucks full of noisy people leaving the beach.]

Nuriaty thus undertook to serve as a modest witness to the changes taking place in Mayotte and the violation of respect to elders and predecessors. But the fact that the Sultan included her in this scene had greater significance. The second thing that happened to Nuriaty (and was partly realized through the first) was that Sultan Mawana Madi now possessed her. Not only that, but she was apparently the only recognized medium of Mawana Madi in Mayotte, the previous medium, a woman who had lived in town and whom Nuriaty had never met, having died some years before.

This is astonishing on several grounds. First, Mawana Madi – and hence Nuriaty as his only medium – is a figure of "national" importance. A ritual of island-wide import is held at his shrine on an annual basis. Mawana Madi signifies the unity and pre-colonial autonomy of Mayotte. He is recognized throughout the island and is granted greater honour than Ndramañavakarivu, the Sakalava monarch with whom he interacts, replaying by means of spirit possession in the late twentieth century their alliance in the early nineteenth century. In effect, the relationship between Mawana Madi and his *trumba* counterpart stands for the social composition of Mayotte as a union of (a majority of) Shimaore speakers with (a significant minority of) Kibushy (Malagasy) speakers. In the present, Mawana Madi is sought by important, sophisticated clients, including, Nuriaty said, leaders of the dominant party, the Mouvement Populaire Mahorais (MPM) that engineered Mayotte's present political status. Certain clients have urged Nuriaty to move to town, a request that she has so far forthrightly declined, despite the fact that they have offered to buy her a house. Ironically, some of these clients she classifies as European, *vazaha*.

That Nuriaty has become the sole legitimate medium of Mawana Madi is also surprising because she was raised in a village of Kibushy speakers, in modest circumstances. Her family roots are Malagasy, Comoran, and East African – everywhere but among the Shimaore elite who are identified as the indigenous inhabitants of Mayotte with the longest-standing rights in the island.[9] She has, moreover, had no connection with the political elite. Nuriaty is a Kibushy speaker, but when she is in trance Mawana Madi speaks an old version of Shimaore.

Perhaps most astonishing, once Mawana Madi had risen in Nuriaty and his identity was confirmed during the annual ritual at the central shrine, the Sultan announced that he found the presence of Nuriaty's other spirits polluting and he wished for them to leave her. Someone of his stature – and there is no one higher in Mayotte – should not have to put up with their company. These spirits, the cumulative result of Nuriaty's possession activities to that date, who had formed the substantive connection with her parents, looked after her family, and served as the carefully cultivated basis of her career, agreed not to rise in her any longer.[10] Nuriaty still performed as a curer but only by means of Mawana Madi. That meant she entirely gave up participating in the possession ceremonies of other villagers. Once a devoted carouser, she now merely observed from the sidelines. Moreover, at the urging of the Sultan, Nuriaty took up regular Muslim prayer.[11]

It was an act of some courage for Nuriaty to shift from the spirits of her parents, who provided her with a stable, highly connected identity and a modest means for earning a living as a curer, to a spirit whose significance is island-wide and whose appearance transformed her into a player in the public arena, opening up a whole new set of clients and demands, sources of respect but also pitfalls. No one in her family or her community had this spirit; no one expected her to get it. Her mother, an accomplished spirit medium, was as astonished and bemused as I was. Moreover, it was the spirit himself, speaking through Nuriaty, who took the definitive step of asking all the other spirits Nuriaty had acquired over the past twenty years to move aside.

In effect, Nuriaty executed a radical shift from gradual self-fashioning to making history, plunging from a highly connected position on the family and village scene to a central yet precarious position on the island stage.[12] Why did this happen? In conversation and daily action Nuriaty had come to express a degree of resentment that I had not noticed when she was younger.[13] One can speak of personal setbacks, of relative deprivation. However, her acts cannot be described as mainly selfish or instrumental. In part, she may be declaring the decline of a kin- and village-based mode of solidarity and mutual support, yet she also gave up practices that had afforded her a good deal of pleasure and security. She had devoted much energy to developing mature relationships with her previous spirits and had been comfortably established with them. In abandoning them in her mid-forties she made a leap into the unknown, taking a tremendous risk.

Despite its edge of grandiosity, Nuriaty's act was not a direct expression of envy or an attack upon those more fortunate than herself. Instead, she viewed her situation as a product of "the times," and it was to historical forces that she turned for meaning and redress. It is clear from the dreams and the identity of her new spirit that her concerns were not merely personal. They addressed the disturbing effects of rapid social change on the entire community, the withdrawal of previous icons of authority and their displacement by new sources of knowledge, wealth, power, prestige, and pleasure, a process that left behind not only Nuriaty but many villagers, especially women of her age. People of this last cohort not to receive French schooling experienced acutely the way that those a few years younger displaced and rendered them marginal. Nuriaty's personal situation, made more poignant by her ex-husband's new marriage, was by no means unusual; her experience indexed that of a whole generational cohort. It had become, as Nuriaty's next younger sister put it, a "papaya world" (*dunia papay*) in which, as on a papaya tree, the smaller, younger fruit rest above the larger ones.

More than this, community sentiment once expressed in reverence to the saint was dissipating as the village was increasingly permeated and fragmented by external forces and eroded by internal divisions of wealth, consumption, and class.[14] By 1995 a large number of village residents worked elsewhere during the week. And on weekends their beach was invaded by privileged and disrespectful picnickers. Moreover, because the sacrifice at the saint's tomb had been to pray for rain, it was, as another villager pointed out, no longer necessary since the rice-growing community I had observed in 1975 had, twenty years later, not a single family who still cultivated rice.

If the saint withdrew from his tomb, Nuriaty was there as a witness. And if the saint was abetted by Mawana Madi, who was justifiably outraged at the treatment of his comrade, so too was it Mawana Madi who brought Nuriaty as witness. Despite the retreat of the saint, the Sultan has shown his determination to persevere, as manifested by his appearance in Nuriaty. While her acts are ostensibly passive, drawing on strong forces of identification, desire, and fantasy, most evident are moral imagination, will, and commitment. The Sultan is concerned with the dignity of the saint, and Nuriaty is concerned about respect not only for the saint and the Sultan, but about dignity for herself and her peers. Nuriaty likewise acknowledges that the locus of significant political action has shifted definitively from the village to the island-wide scene.

Nuriaty's Historical Consciousness and Conscientious Intervention

What Nuriaty offers is not just a representation or unmediated expression of problems but a consciousness of the historical process and a conscientious intervention in that process. To serve as a witness is not to be passive. The saint's tomb did not simply sink into oblivion; its passing was marked and articulated in a meaningful scenario as the saint and his wife withdrew in dignity, accompanied by the celebratory strains of the *Maulida*. As Mawana Madi, Nuriaty goes further. The Sultan escorts the saint from his polluted environs, and thereby acquiesces in change, but knowingly and on his own terms. And while the saint abandons the community, acknowledging, in effect, its abandonment of him, the Sultan does the reverse, moving into the community and into Nuriaty herself. The particularity of the village is thus transcended by "national" (island) identification, but this time on terms that Nuriaty sets.

It is important to note that the dream does not polarize Europeans and Muslims or "modernity" and "tradition." The vessel is motorized, referred to as a *vedette*, and the sailors are said to be European although they act like Arabs. The image is one of affluent gentility. The opposition governing Nuriaty's thought is not that characteristic of so much contemporary social scientific discourse, between ancestral and colonial, or local and global, resistance and power, but rather between responsible and irresponsible practice, right and wrong action. Nuriaty's position is not one of simple conservatism. She is not averse to change per se so much as to the way in which the past has been forgotten and, in effect, violated.

Dressed in his glistening white Muslim garb,[15] the Sultan himself quietly pointed out to me how he had long served (in his previous medium) the interests of the Mouvement Mahorais, guiding the leaders in their (ostensibly secular) campaign to intensify French presence on the island. MPM party leaders continued to consult with the Sultan before (hotly contested) elections and major decisions and to inform him of the arrival of political leaders from the Metropole. "The country (*tany*) has changed," pronounced the Sultan, "so we all change. We all agree now to follow France. But before any major political event the leaders have to inform the rightful masters of the land, *tompin tany*. It is right that the politicians come here when they need something, as they did before the last election, yet they remain ungrateful for their victories." He was angry, but admitted, "What can [we] elders, *ulu be* do? Elders are treated like garbage, *pringa* [literally the weeds edging the village where garbage is dumped and children defecate]." Some visitors do bring small gifts,[16] and the Sultan insists that he continue to be informed of political needs: "They [the living political leaders, the people of Mayotte] are my responsibility, *re' tarimiku*." He added that he did not discriminate between political parties and would assist all comers so long as they did not advocate union with the other Comoro Islands.

The spirit's viewpoint is composed of several intertwined strands. It is a nationalist stance, one that plays up the internal unity of Mayotte and its opposition to the neighbouring islands. Yet while the sentiment is modern in this respect and by no means opposed to increased integration into the French state, it remains at arm's length from that policy, evincing a deep suspicion on moral grounds of the permeation of Mayotte by French values. It also evokes competition and warfare among the pre-colonial sultans and fear of the rulers of the larger and more powerful islands. Nuriaty emphasizes Islam as the basis for the unity and continuity of Mayotte, albeit by means of an idiom, spirit possession, that has often been opposed by Islam. Hers is a traditionalist Islam, unlike the more recently arrived reformist and transnational strains that could develop another kind of political response to French influence.

These ideological strands are condensed in the authoritative figure of the Sultan and his place in history. The Sultan insists on his continuing relevance, on the importance, characteristic of Malagasy societies more generally, of seeking ancestral authorization for present-day actions and choices (Bloch 1971, 1986; Edkvist 1997; Feeley-Harnik 1991; Lambek 2002c; Middleton 1999), of recognizing what I call the sanctification of the present by the past. It is here that there is increasing disjuncture with the modernist leadership.

Poiesis and Virtuous Practice

Most anthropological readings of Nuriaty's practice would divide along theoretical interests in psychological motivation – desire or resentment – and political action – power or resistance. Both arguments rest ultimately on some idea of perceived self-interest and in that sense are similar to each other rather than real alternatives, though they appear to be grounded in opposed theoretical positions. I do not dispute them, but alone neither captures what I find of greatest significance. Drawing conceptually from Aristotle,[17] I emphasize the following. First, with respect to her dream narrative and her performances as the Sultan, Nuriaty engages in a virtuoso poiesis (crafting) of history, complete with plot, character, scene, and so on. Second, with respect to her judicious, situated interventions with and as the Sultan, including having and recounting her dreams, her practice is a virtuous one. Hers are acts of dignity and indignation, of courage, imagination, concern, and respect for herself and for others, of recognizing the indebtedness of the present to the past, of integrity. She speaks for collective values, for what, in her understanding, makes life meaningful and fruitful. Her means are traditional; her end is human flourishing (*eudaimonia*). Her acts are an expression of who she is, not a calculation or manipulation of external knowledge. And while clearly her practice is embodied, embodiment as a paradigm does not cover the case.

Were we restricted to the terms of Plato's opposition between poetry and philosophy, between mimetic engagement and detached contemplation, Nuriaty's practice would incline to the mimetic pole. Yet clearly this is insufficient; Nuriaty exhibits a consciousness of her historical situation and skilfully addresses it – acting within the traditional terms of spirit possession, yet saying something of relevance to the present by its means. Moreover, she is making a practical intervention – in both her personal circumstances and in the history of her society. She is exercising judgment in the situation; addressing the contingent by means of values which transcend it; articulating a vision of historical action; and acting with reason for the good. All this falls within the scope of what Aristotle terms *phronesis* (Aristotle 1976).

What Nuriaty shows is neither detached contemplative reason nor fully impassioned identification alone but practical wisdom, that is, the understanding of how to make sense of the particular, including the judgment involved in timing, in the specific incarnation, in the articulation of the dreams, and so on. Her judgment is confirmed to the degree that her actions are acknowledged by others as fitting and to the degree that it brings her a degree of equanimity or happiness and her fellow subjects an increased consciousness of history and the place of their own agency within it. We can speak of what she has done not as rational or irrational, accurate or inaccurate, clear or mystified, critically radical or blindly conservative, but (in Aristotelian terms) as elegant or clumsy, wise or foolish, courageous or cowardly, dignified or undignified, virtuous or incontinent.

I do not mean to idealize Nuriaty or suggest that she or anyone else does not act out of mixed emotions or harbour internal conflict. I worry that she is over her head.[18] But to argue that people are political, desirous, or ambivalent subjects does not preclude them from being ethical subjects, living virtuously or seeking the means by which they may do so.[19] As Max Gluckman (1963) observed, most societies hold an image of persons as reasonable and upright. Moreover, as Marcel Mauss (1974) recognized, that people act from self-interest does not preclude them from acting simultaneously with disinterest. Similarly for Aristotle, virtuous action straddles the mean between self-interest and self-abnegation. Nuriaty herself put it this way: "The senior spirits, *lulu maventy*, are angry that all the sacred places (places of pilgrimage, *ziara*) are being destroyed. [As a result,] people with spirits suffer. The spirits come and cry in our sleep."

What may remain troubling for such an analysis is the fact that Nuriaty did not claim her choices; they claimed her. The spirits came and cried in her sleep. Her knowledge stemmed from dreams, and her acts were carried out via the dissociation of spirit possession. But the act of entering a dissociated state is not itself a dissociated act. The question is, what were her relations to her possession and her dreams, to the Sultan and the saint? Was she simply their blind servant; or conversely, was she their instrumental manipulator? It should be obvious that I reject both alternatives, seeing rather the expression of her cultivated subjective disposition by means of an available cultural idiom and scenarios. Spirit possession entails the disavowal of agency; but that should not prevent us from understanding it as neither more nor less spontaneous or calculated than any other act. It is a complex intertwining of action and passion.

The knowledge Nuriaty brings to possession is composed of a *techne*, the skill of knowing how to speak in possession or as a Sultan, and of *phronesis*, knowing how to make significant and timely interventions. She is able to distribute, deploy, and subsume agency. Although Nuriaty could stand back and talk wryly in a commonsense and fairly objective way about her circumstances and the changes she had witnessed, the Sultan gave her an additional and more powerful vehicle with which to realize her concerns, to both embody and objectify them, to render them available to herself and others, and to dignify and authorize them. Mediumship expanded both her agency and her moral horizons.

Agency is a tricky concept. Leave it out and you have a determinist or abstract model; put it in and you risk instrumentalism, the bourgeois subject, the idealized idealistic individual, and so on.[20] Moral agents are always partly constituted through their acts – of acknowledgment, witness, engagement, commitment, refusal, and consent. In assuming responsibility and rendering themselves subject to specific liturgical, political, and discursive regimes and orders, people simultaneously lay claim to and accept the terms through which their subsequent acts will be judged (Rappaport 1999). People are agents insofar as they choose to subject themselves, to perform and conform accordingly, to accept responsibility, and to acknowledge their commitments. Agency here transcends the idea of a lone, heroic individual ostensibly independent of her acts and conscious of them as objects.

In their combination of action and passion and in their explicit denial of tacit agency in choosing or permitting themselves to be chosen by particular spirits, and then in following out the consequences of possession, spirit mediums like Nuriaty speak to universal aspects of moral practice. Nuriaty's practice may be clarified by, and perhaps help illuminate, Slavoj Žižek's argument (drawing on Jon Elster's *Sour Grapes*) that respect and dignity cannot be successfully "planned in advance or assumed by means of a conscious decision" (1991: 76). "If I consciously try to appear dignified or to arouse respect, the result is ridiculous; the impression I make, instead, is that of a miserable impersonator. The basic paradox of these states is that although they are what matters most, they elude us as soon as we make them the immediate aim of our activity. The only way to bring them about is not to center our activity on them but to pursue other goals and hope that they will come about 'by themselves.' Although they do pertain to our activity, they are ultimately perceived as something that belongs to us on account of what we are and not on account of what we do" (1991: 77).

I do not deny that Nuriaty's history was largely imagined. Imagined, however, is not to be confused with imaginary, nor, if it can be rendered public and socially meaningful, with private fantasy (Obeyesekere 1981). Nuriaty did not invent an idiosyncratic response to circumstance; rather she deployed the means to address circumstance imaginatively, in a way that made sense to those around her. She took up the ball that had been dropped with the death of the former medium. The nature of moral practice has been compared to producing narrative (Harpham 1995: 403; cf Steedly 1993), and we can see that Nuriaty's practice was simultaneously a self-poiesis and a poiesis – a crafting – of history. At the same time, as Žižek points out, the subject can never determine the way she appears or provokes transference in others (Žižek 1991: 77).[21]

Nuriaty is not a prophet; she is not extraordinary. She is a good citizen and a *mensch*, an exemplary political subject, engaged with the past and future of her society. She lacks the self-confidence to be an *übermensch*, but then *übermenschen* are not always the best citizens. Nuriaty is doing what she can. It is the ends and means at her disposal, the unity of means and ends in her practice, and in people like her, that ought to be among the central topics of a postcolonial anthropology.

Conclusion

I have characterized Nuriaty's practice in terms of historical consciousness. But it is clear that in taking on the burden of history, in witnessing
the heroes of the past crying in her sleep and withdrawing in anger
from their tombs, and in carrying on despite her material circumstances
and despite insufficient recognition from contemporary political leaders, Nuriaty does more than display a heightened consciousness of history; she embodies a historical conscience. This is precisely the space
where the political, moral, and personal threads of subjectivity are
intertwined.

The portrait I have painted and the mood I have evoked are very
different from the frantic sense of loss visible elsewhere in facets of the
African memory crisis (Werbner 1998), witchcraft epidemics in South
Africa (Comaroff and Comaroff 1999) or Kinshasa (de Boeck and Plissart 2006), or, for that matter, the epidemic of accusations of Satan-
ism and recovered memories of sexual abuse in North America and
northern Europe (Jean Comaroff 1997, Lambek 1997, Antze and Lambek 1996, La Fontaine 1997) in which ancestral and parental figures are
violently rejected, in response, perhaps, to what is understood as their
absence, impotence, or withdrawal of protection. By contrast, spirit mediums like Nuriaty capture a particular moment in history, seen from
a particular angle: the internalization of an ancestor (here, a historical
precursor) in the very act of withdrawal and thereby a kind of transfer
of the ancestor from the public, external scene to the internal one. In so
doing, the medium allows herself to be subjected to the ancestor, but
equally to be empowered and enlightened, to become a historical subject. It is the obverse of projection, and of witchcraft.[22] There are flashes
of bravado; a rustle of anger at the inverted and inequitable papaya
world in which dignity for some is hard to come by; and an undertone
of knowing sadness.

In that same slow, deliberate way, Nuriaty's elegy to the receding
past comes to possess my ethnography of Mayotte.

9 The Saint, the Sea Monster, and an Invitation to a *Dîner-dansant*, to 2001

A Quarter Century of Change

As I've described in chapter 7, in 1975 political sentiments were running high. The Mouvement Populaire Mahorais (MPM) urged France to maintain and intensify its presence on Mayotte. When the MPM won the agreement of the government to hold a second referendum, the women – who had been the main mobilizers and enthusiasts of the movement, who had spent a week surrounding a bulldozer in order to prevent its removal to another island (singing odes to the Prophet all the while), and who had even supplied the movement's only martyr – celebrated in an impromptu fashion. Among their dances was the energetic *wadaha* that involves passing a heavy wooden pestle from hand to hand so that it creates a steady rhythm as it is pounded into the mortar by one dancer and retrieved by the next. The performance beautifully indexes both collective interdependence and unalienated labour. The women dance in the dusty red earth plaza to a backdrop of palm trees and wattle-and-daub thatch-roofed houses (see chapter 7, *figure 7.1*). A large French flag flutters incongruously, brighter than the women's faded work clothing. In another of my photographs, an elderly man approaches to pay his respects to the women for their political efforts.

Twenty-five years later, the fruits, both sweet and bitter, of this strategy have been achieved. Some, like Nuriaty and her sister, compare these fruits of progress specifically to the papaya; they depict a "papaya world," *dunia papay*, in which, as the fruit hang on a papaya tree, the young rest above their elders (chapter 8). That is to say, in the course of rapid transition, during the specific historical period of the 1990s, younger siblings moved far ahead of older siblings, and children ahead of their parents, in wealth and privilege, and partly in respect and authority, producing a world turned upside down.

More broadly, Mayotte shifted from sleepy backwater to economic hub of the region. The French really did invest. A network of paved roads was established along with new forms of housing, water supply, and electricity and greatly improved education, health care, and personal benefits. The rigorous daily labour of husking rice with mortar and pestle is gone (see chapter 2, *figure 2.3*), along with the locally constructed wooden implements and the taste, nutrition, and availability of non-commodified field rice (*vary shombu*). Houses of brick or cement facing, with tin roofs and electric lights that are left on all night push up the hillsides.

Men of my age cohort have lived their adult working lives since the mid-1980s engaged in menial and manual labour – road work, construction, jobs as janitors and guards – combined with some independent activities such as fishing or raising livestock, or else they have followed their wives, increasingly since the mid-1990s and ostensibly temporarily, to La Réunion or metropolitan France for better unemployment and family benefits (chapter 10). But their children and younger siblings have now been through an entire cycle of decent French schooling.[1] The successful ones earn professional degrees overseas or continue to live in the village while commuting each morning, in their private cars and through traffic jams, to white-collar jobs across the island. In brief, there has been a vast and rapid expansion of infrastructure; increased commoditization; significant internal class, income, and age differentiation; and increased migration, unemployment, and opportunity. Indeed, a papaya world.

Mayotte has become what I have described as a "postmodern colony" or a post*colony*, in which the emphasis rests on the second morpheme not the first. The economy is entirely transformed. Politics are oriented towards fuller integration with France and therefore towards the same level of social benefits that are available to all citizens of the Republic. In June 2001 Mayotte shifted in status from a *Collectivité Territoriale* (initiated in December 1976) to a *Collectivité Départmentale*, in the process of what is referred to as an *évolution statuaire* (to be re-evaluated in ten years) en route to full integration in the French state. The French made huge inroads in governmentality, transforming public and private life. The currency is the euro, and enterprising young people know how to apply to the European Community for local development grants. The village contains a modern *foyer des jeunes* (youth centre) with a decent library. Moreover, despite initial disconcertion at each innovation, people are generally satisfied by the direction things have gone and feel somewhat empowered by their role in instigating the process. The situation is certainly different from that in the neighbouring islands of the Comoros, since 2002 re-formed as L'Union des Comores, many of whose inhabitants make dangerous nocturnal crossings to Mayotte in search of livelihood and citizenship.

Change does not take place behind people's backs or occur without a remainder. As they look to new horizons, what villagers say they regret is not the speed but the slowness of change, and the unfairness in the distribution of its effects, notably the way it has left some people relatively impoverished and marginalized.

Festivities

However "French" they become, people remain devout Muslims and committed to the intense sociality of village life. The dry southern winter is a time of festivity. In 1975 this was the post-harvest season; it is now conceived as the period of school vacation, when even those employed in France or on Réunion are able to take their *vacances* and, in some years, return home. As in the past, performances of all kinds succeed each other: weddings, spirit possession ceremonies, mortuary ceremonies, circumcisions, *Maulida,* and other Sufi-inspired dances. Each of these includes the preparation, distribution, and consumption of large amounts of food and other expenditures of time, money, and energy. I have long thought of the village communities of Mayotte as existing and reproducing through the almost continuous production of such feasts. It is to facets of this collective sociality that I return in order to indicate both decisive changes in practice and their collective acknowledgment and representation.

Intensive festivities continue, but their social significance has altered as communities have become less autonomous and their internal constitution has changed. In particular, centricity is weakened as villages shift from social wholes constituted through the totality and density of relationships among their inhabitants to administrative units comprising individuated parts – households, families, and individuals – in ways that festive performance indexes.[2]

The festivities of the 1970s were of roughly four social orders. First, were ceremonies conducted for, by, and on behalf of the villages as whole communities. These included the annual New Year festival (*mwaka*) in July, the date varying slightly from village to village and year to year depending on how local officials kept track, and the triennial sacrifice at the saint's tomb whose demise Nuriaty marked. Second, were rituals held on behalf of families but conducted by the entire village, notably funerals and those life-cycle rituals performed as *shungu*. Third, were rituals conducted for and by families to which kin, friends, and neighbours were selectively invited. Finally, were spirit possession ceremonies held on behalf of individuals but at which all adepts participated. This picture is oversimplified in several ways, one being that a given event might have components that would engage people through various of these forms of connection. In any case, there was a complex and quite specific way in which labour was organized, raw materials were collected, and food was distributed and consumed for each festivity.

Of these four ideal types, some, but not all, of the events of the village-based order had disappeared by 2001, while possession ceremonies have continued apace. Those of the second, that articulated families to the whole community, had mostly transformed into the third, more individual, and optative kind.

I turn to weddings.[3] The celebration of a woman's first marriage continues to be a central feature of social life and subject to a great deal of expense and interest. The main theme of weddings has been the celebration and transformation of young women, as well as their husbands and their parents. Marriage has been a critical moment in the moral life narrative in Mayotte, understood as the event that starts an adult career and leads on to the most important tasks of adulthood, namely circumcising boys and marrying off girls of the *next* generation and holding memorials for deceased parents – that is, further acts and ceremonies of social reproduction. While biological parenthood was much desired by people of both sexes it was less critical for adult status than sponsoring life-cycle rituals. Thus, a childless man or woman would sponsor a nephew's circumcision and a niece's wedding.[4] Sponsorships marked people as full social adults. The bride's virginity was critical for sponsored weddings.

During the 1970s and earlier, the major public life-cycle rituals were the occasions for the enactment of *shungu*. As described in chapter 5, the *shungu* was intricately beautiful in its structure and effects. Fulfilment established "mutual superiority" (Gregory 1982: 65) and produced, in the end, the mutual embeddedness of all members of the community as part of one another through the logic of the gift.

By 1985 the *shungu* system had closed insofar as young people no longer continued to enter it. However, *shungu* feasts still occurred from time to time until the last participant had completed their obligations. That the *shungu* was not simply abandoned in mid-cycle but wound down slowly and systematically, feast by feast, until every obligation of giving and receiving was met, is a remarkable testament to cultural integrity. The irony is that what replaces the obligatory *shungu* is a more inflationary, less regulated sequence of competitive feasting that discriminates between relatively wealthy and poorer sponsors, invites and excludes participants on an individual basis, and no longer distributes prestige even-handedly. Rites of passage are no longer the business of the whole community (*tanana*) – whose members in witnessing each other's events helped produce them and became part of them and of each other. Nevertheless, migrants still do return to the village to hold their celebrations.

The *Invitation*

At weddings, *shungu* feasts have been replaced by the aptly named *invitations* (in French). Consider two weddings that took place in 2001. In both, as in the past, the couple stayed in the bride's new house for a week after the consummation, receiving congratulations and entertaining visitors, mostly young people who danced at night to the CD player. In one house, belonging to her sister, since a new house had not yet been built, the bride was only fifteen, a fact for which her mother was criticized. The mother had wanted to ensure that her daughter was still a virgin. The groom was an unemployed man from the Grande Comore, much older than his bride. The wedding was modest, including a small festivity at which traditional cakes were served.

Across the road, the bride was twenty-two, had left school after completing the troisième, and was looking for work.[5] Her husband was thirty-six, a cross-cousin and a schoolteacher. The house was new and well equipped and the festivities elaborate. The teacher had three children from a former wife (who herself had been previously married) and told me he planned another three children in this marriage. The new wife demurred and said she would have only two; she would use the pill. The groom affirmed he wouldn't practise polygyny, that men were starting to reject it. His own (wealthy) father had three wives simultaneously, and the groom said he didn't know the exact number of his own siblings, but thought it close to twenty.

The young people's positions are partly realized as the result of decisions taken in past generations, notably successive cross-cousin marriages in the more prosperous case. Yet the class differences expressed in the two weddings derive less from the parents than, in the second house, from the young people themselves – their education, employment opportunities, and outlook.

In the new house the couple and close friends were excitedly folding invitations. They had two computer-printed versions, each including images of distinctly white couples in romantic poses. In one, bride and groom were kissing on the lips, something never seen or practised in Lombeni. On the cover was written *"Monsieur Said Abdourahim et Mademoiselle Kaisati Aboudou vous invitent à leur mariage."* Inside, the parents of groom and bride were listed and, in very formal French, *"ont l'honneur et le plaisir de faire part du mariage de leurs enfants… et vous prient de bien vouloir honorer de votre présence."*[6]

The invitation listed a Friday evening *dîner-dansant*, followed on Saturday morning by a *walima*, a *cortège* at noon, a *sirop d'honneur* at 3 p.m., and on Wednesday at noon a *mbiwi avec Viking*. These events take their names from four languages, none directly Kibushy. The *walima*, an Arabic term for a wedding feast, is a meal offered to the community by the bride's family, and requiring a large cow. The *cortège* is a procession by motor vehicle through the village and its neighbours, displaying the groom's *valise*, a "suitcase" that includes not only 1,000 to 3,000 euros worth of gold jewellery and clothing but a TV, a freezer, and frequently a VCR, a microwave, and a washing machine. *Mbiwi* is the Shimaore word for what Kibushy speakers call "beating sticks" (*mamangu ambiu*), the dance performed by women in which they sexily flex and shake their buttocks while rhythmically clacking short pieces of bamboo. Nowadays the women dress elegantly and come in large numbers to celebrate the transformation of a "daughter" into a sexual woman and the munificence of male spending on new wives.[7] *Mbiwi* is performed to a live, amplified band; the Vikings (pronounced *Vingkingy*) are preferred, if expensive at 400 euros, a cost sometimes shared between the bride and groom's kin. The *dîner-dansant* and the *sirop d'honneur*, practices begun a decade or so ago, are primarily for young people. The groom pays for them, but the bride's family helps with labour. The various elements are not intrinsic to a wedding; the number of discrete components depends in part on what people can afford. Total costs for an elaborate wedding can reach as high as 12,000 euros (C$15,000) on the groom's side alone.

People arrived at the *dîner-dansant* dressed in elegant European clothing – I was chastised for not wearing a tie – greeting each other with kisses on the cheek (French *bises*) and handshakes. A master of ceremonies took the microphone and asked everyone to acknowledge the entry of the new couple. The bride wore a white wedding dress. The couple stood and blushed as photos were taken and speeches were made, and people clapped. Everyone sat at tables, self-consciously making small talk. They drank soft drinks and ate popcorn and samosas followed by grated *crudités* (raw vegetables) with mustard vinaigrette, platters of rice with chicken or beef, and finally a multi-tiered cake topped with cherries. Couples danced under strobe lights to slow love songs played by a DJ and soon replaced by loud, amplified Western (or world) popular music, in a party known as a *boum*.[8]

All this suggests a naive appropriation of Western forms, images, and values. But when I mentioned to the young man on whose wedding video I first saw a *dîner-dansant* that people seemed to be acting like *vazaha* – Europeans – he replied that that was precisely the point. He explained that indeed they were *acting* – imitating (*mikeding*), or playing at being European. It was done knowingly, in a spirit of pleasure or play, not out of some unmediated acceptance of Western comportment and consumption. But, he added, they were also preparing one day to *be* European.

The *dîner-dansant* is a matter of seeing and being seen as European. The mimesis is a deliberate reflexive and consciously creative process, seeing oneself as another, catching oneself in the future, maintaining the distance of the spectator even as one is acting the part.[9] As another young man put it, "We imitate Europeans, want to become Europeans, indeed are already practising as Europeans" (*Mikeding vazaha; famila vazaha; famañanu kamwe*). "But," he emphasized, "acting like Europeans doesn't hurt Islam; it is play (*soma*)."[10]

In a compelling account of the way in which weddings in contemporary Lithuania address the relationship of participants to conceptions of modernity and the West, Gediminas Lankauskas (2015) draws on Victor Turner's (1985) discussion of the subjunctive "as if." Such subjunctivity is no doubt characteristic of wedding performances in many places and stems from their function in articulating the beginnings of responsible adulthood and thereby projecting hopes for a future that can be only partially known and articulated. Such performances also contain an "edge of irony" (Hutcheon 1994) and perhaps claims of entitlement.

In Mayotte, the *invitation* is at once a performance of Frenchness and a rehearsal for it, with all the entailments these terms imply. It is half wish, half realization; half serious, half gentle self-mockery.[11] The confidence of youth is in contrast to the older generation, who hold themselves back and sit awkwardly in European clothes, leave the dinner early if they attend at all, and who are certainly not seen on *this* dance floor. If people are imitating French culture, they know this full well and do so deliberately. Some participants also indicate their intention not to undermine Islam. The performance is a live metaphor, not yet congealed into artifice or dead metaphor – into a ritual carried out for reasons its enactors have long since forgotten. If the *invitation* entails implicitly a very different sociality, temporality, and personhood from the *shungu*, it nevertheless expresses quite explicitly a certain kind of historical consciousness.

The Saint and the Sea Monster

At the time these weddings took place, many older villagers were preoccupied with a troubling issue, namely several recent deaths by drowning. In each case the bodies were recovered, having been washed up on shore. They had not been eaten by sharks. The anxiety caused by the most recent death was heightened by the fact that people had just learned about the government's introduction of autopsies and were highly perturbed by and opposed to the idea.

People began to talk. They linked the deaths to the displeasure of the saint whose ancient stone tomb lies in the bush adjacent to the beach (chapter 8). The tomb had been the site of community sacrifices until they had recently been abandoned. Moreover, the beach on which the tomb sits had seen the construction of a soccer field, basketball court, and tourist facilities, and the tomb itself had been polluted by visitors seeking a place to relieve themselves. In the past, people had come from afar to the sacred and powerful spot (*ziara*) in order to utter personal prayers, bathing first and bringing incense, perfume, and rosewater; now they just held *piqueniques*, danced *boums*, and urinated there.

This saint was the same person who some years earlier had preoccupied Nuriaty and who indeed continued to do so. Nuriaty was adamant that he was gone; she had seen him leave. But now other people suggested that the saint had turned himself into a sea monster and that it was this creature who was responsible for the deaths by drowning. Angered at the loss of his sacrifice and the state of neglect and abuse of his tomb, the saint was lashing out. He had risen in a woman in a neighbouring village to announce the fact. Women organized a collection to buy a sacrificial beast to satisfy him, or rather, to pray to God to "lie him down" (*mampahandry*) and render the beach safe again. This sacrifice took place, officiated at by the leading Muslim scholar and elders of the community.

The next year Nuriaty told me that although the sacrifice had been correctly performed, the community had slaughtered only a goat rather than a cow. The saint wouldn't return, she was sure; the remains of the food were simply eaten by rats and lizards. There had been no drownings in the interim, but she knew the saint remained angry. Nuriaty, a poor, self-employed healer and former subsistence cultivator, continued to leave small offerings of perfume at the tomb, while the young man who served as the master of ceremonies at the *dîner-dansant*, a *lycée* graduate, owner of a car repair business – and son of the senior Muslim scholar – felt that the tomb should be protected as a cultural heritage site, a *monument historique*.

I see the emergence of the saint as monster as another response to the rapidity of change, this time not a self-confident grasping of the future but a regretful or anxious glance backward at what has been left behind. If people begin to ignore sacred figures, the sacred figures too can begin to abandon and even turn on them. The people most concerned were indeed those who had experienced most acutely the distortions of the papaya world in which their own juniors forged ahead and neglected them. But their concern was primarily ethical rather than forged in resentment.[12]

In addition, but looming unspoken behind the local drownings, was the loss of lives sustained by Comorans who attempted dangerous night-time crossings to Mayotte in small craft in search of livelihood. Their precarious circumstances and presence in the village, as well as the material suffering back home that pushed them to take such risks, became a further source of moral anxiety. The saint himself may have come from the next island.

Psychoanalyst Hans Loewald once wrote that "ghosts ... long to be released from their ghost life and led to rest as ancestors. As ancestors they live forth in the present generation, while as ghosts they are compelled to haunt the present generation with their shadow life"

(1980: 249). Loewald was drawing a contrast between psychic repression on one side, and identification and internalization on the other,
but the idea has broader social relevance. If Loewald says one must
transmute angry ghosts into quiescent ancestors, what the villagers
experienced was a formerly benevolent ancestor (though not a literal
one) transmuted into an angry ghost. This ghost stands for what has
been abandoned, unaddressed, unacknowledged, uncompensated; the
remainder in the narrative of progress; modernity's double edge. It is
not without irony that one boy who drowned had been attempting to
swim by clinging to a piece of foam packing discarded from someone's
new refrigerator.

The Historical *Unheimlich*

Social change isn't something that simply "happens" or that happens
"to" a community. People are caught up in change – are themselves
changed – but at the same time they can pry open moments and spaces of
distance through which to construct proto-theoretical appreciation and
appropriation of what is transpiring. Historical insight is necessarily culturally mediated, drawing on older idioms and productive of new ones.
At the same time, moments of self-recognition, of seeing "oneself as another" (Ricoeur 1992), contain a twinge of the *unheimlich*, which may be
experienced as a frisson of pleasure or shudder of unease.[13]

Let me risk a bit of *unheimlich* disruption as well. Perhaps there is
no special historical insight or consciousness, no glimpse of a literal
truth behind appearances. Perhaps this is not possible, because historical truth is not out there waiting to be discovered but is something
humanly constructed. In such a pragmatist view – Richard Rorty's –
"human history [is] the history of successive metaphors" (1989: 20); or,
as he might have said, one damn metaphor after another. However, our
understanding of what is metaphorical versus literal is entirely relative to what precedes or succeeds it, to playing one language game or
inventing a new one.

Rorty follows Donald Davidson to say, interestingly, that live metaphors are sentences that do not have fixed places in language games
and hence are neither true nor false. At the *invitation* people were predi-
cating Frenchness in a live metaphor, making a statement "which," as
Rorty says, "one cannot confirm or disconfirm, argue for or against.
One can only savor it or spit it out" (ibid. 18). (Recall the spirit choking
on the Qur'an.)

The *invitation* is significant for the audacious redescription and triumphant self-fashioning it exhibits, albeit the self-fashioning not of a single individual so much as a generational cohort. For participants, the *invitation* is *expressly* metaphorical. Conversely, for their parents and others, the sea monster is no metaphor, whether of guilt or of greedy capitalism, but is understood quite literally. The saint and the sea monster intervene and interpellate their subjects. People died, after all, and their bodies risked the degradation of autopsy rather than Muslim burial. Here it is a matter from the local perspective of discovering, explaining, or redressing something happening objectively in the world rather than speaking subjunctively. People are engaged in an old language game in which the metaphors have long since congealed to literalness; people *did* debate the truth value of the statement about the saint and the cause of the drownings.

But between the truth of the sea monster and the truth of the wedding – about that we cannot debate. They are merely successive metaphors in the non-teleological movement of history, the one possibly fading out of literalism as the other is destined to enter it. For Rorty, there is "simply the disposition to use the language of our ancestors, to worship the corpses of their metaphors" (ibid. 21).[14]

Between "Not Yet" and "No Longer"

Let me draw back from the radical modernity of Wittgenstein and Nietzsche to revisit the more temperate position represented by Aristotle's recognition of human creative and ethical activity.

People do not passively become Europeans or inadvertent poor copies; in acts of creative production (what Aristotle termed *poiesis*) they creatively fashion themselves in their image. And people do not simply forget their ancestors; in acts of practical judgment (Aristotle's *phronesis*) they witness, acknowledge, suffer, and intervene in their passing. These are each simultaneously ethical acts and creative performances, suitably framed, timed, and circumscribed.

The present is intense in Mayotte. People have acquired a strong sense of personal and collective agency; everyone is engaged in planning and building the future, and they have achieved a good deal. This is expressed in wedding celebrations. Yet some people must ground their dignity elsewhere. For them, the past cannot and does not simply vanish without trace; nor is it discarded on the trash heap to which the gaze of Walter Benjamin's angel of history is mournfully turned

(1969a). Rather, the past accompanies the present. The past leaves an insistent remainder that demands to be marked, acknowledged, addressed, and perhaps released.

The point of the saint's story is *not* that one should return to the past. No one either explicitly wants this or considers it possible. The point is rather that moving forward should be handled judiciously, ethically. For those who spoke about the saint or participated in the sacrifice, the past is not objectified as "heritage." Instead, people understand themselves to continue in some active relation *with* the past, a past that cannot therefore be thoughtlessly relinquished but must be remembered, as an old friend is. Historical figures like the saint may continue to give their blessing, or at least remain neutral, but on condition that they are not humiliated, abandoned in the rush forward. Between the wedding and the saint, we see people looking both forwards and back, poised between the "no longer" and the "not yet." Moral practice entails establishing a balance (Lambek 1996).

There is also critique here, an admission of failure. The call of the past slips in uneasily, edgily, in monsterly mutation. The saint suggests that individual consumption is not yet the full order of the day, that collective responsibility retains some weight, that people possess their past less than they are possessed by it. Yet he does so after the fact, as a monster. Much as older ways are threatened, so they have come to threaten. The threat can be mitigated only by the very historical consciousness that grasps it.

In sum, it has not been my intention to provide a definitive distinction between tradition and modernity or a definitive depiction of the transition from one to the other. It would, indeed, be ludicrous to think of modernity as an absolute break, all or nothing. Rather, I have shown "modernity" and "tradition" engaging in mutual interpellation and have evoked the edgy self-consciousness, sometimes playful and exuberant, sometimes anxious and concerned, that subsists at the horizons of history.

Postscript

It turns out that in the discussion of the literal and the metaphorical the joke was on me. In arguing that people took the monster literally, and in using the very word "monster," I myself assumed that the sea creature was a metaphor. On a later visit to Mayotte I asked more carefully about the word I had translated as "sea monster," only to discover that it refers to a species of electric stingray whose current is indeed strong enough to knock down and drown a small child. There had been such a creature lurking among the shallows at the time.

However, the fact that the stingray was "real" and present, and not the monster and metaphor I had foolishly assumed people were taking literally, does not resolve the question of why it was present just then or whether it was acting as a transformation, or on behalf, of the angry saint.

10   On the Move, through 2001

When I first arrived in Mayotte in 1975, the population was around 45,000 in an area of some 375 square kilometres. By 2001 the population had tripled. But the geographical breadth of "Mayotte" has become less clear. In this chapter, I focus on the dynamics of expansion – not of population growth within Mayotte but the expansion of the borders of citizenship, extending widely beyond its literal shores. This is another materialization of the horizon.

According to long-standing cartographic and geographic convention, the territories of islands cannot expand and contract the way those on large landmasses do. Yet the reach of states extends beyond individual landmasses, reconfiguring places and the distances between them. Over the years, the distance between Mayotte and other places has stretched and shrunk in various ways. Many of the people counted in the 2001 census resided at least part-time in La Réunion, 1,700 kilometres distant and accessible by direct flight. Changes in their political status have enabled people to readily acquire the papers to move freely between Mayotte and La Réunion (a *département d'outre mer* of long standing) and even to metropolitan France (9,000 kilometres distant) and within the EU, and to enjoy rights of citizenship in these places. By contrast, the nearest island in the Comoro Archipelago is only 70 kilometres distant but it has become another country.

In this chapter I examine aspects of geographical mobility. My attention is largely restricted to people originating in Lombeni and draws particularly on data collected on visits to both Mayotte and Réunion in the summers of 2000 and 2001, as well as during earlier stays.[1] At the time, Mayotte was in the process of what the French government referred to as an *évolution statuaire*, subject to evaluation but likely en route to full integration in the French state (as happened in 2011). Political boundaries and identities really did change. Travel between Mayotte, Réunion, and metropolitan France became "intranational" rather than international, and migrants from Mayotte formed "internal" diasporas in Réunion and the metropole. Conversely, official travel to the other islands in the Comoro Archipelago became more difficult, while travel from them to Mayotte became highly desirable. However, the focus of this chapter is not on the flooding of Mayotte by people from the other Comoro Islands seeking entry to fortress Europe via the gateway that Mayotte has become.

People travelled off Mayotte for a number of reasons, including pilgrimage, education, pleasure, and trade. Most saliently, because of the novelty, numbers involved, distance, and duration, people migrated to Réunion, and increasingly to metropolitan France, in search of economic opportunity. Those who did so were frequently originally among the poorer members of the community. They hoped to find work, but they went, in the first instance, because of the greater social benefits available. During the period under discussion, and so long as Mayotte was not yet a full *département* itself, its citizens had rights to greater benefits from the state if they resided in La Réunion or metropolitan France rather than at home. Benefits included higher allowances for children, unmarried mothers, seniors, and the unemployed, and for housing. Virtually all Mahorais from Lombeni living in La Réunion or France were taking advantage of this situation and said they planned to return permanently to Mayotte. Mayotte, they said, was where they felt "really at home" (*teña an nakahy*).

In economic travel, women have been the pioneers.[2]

Three Takes on Change

When I returned to Mayotte in 2000 after five years' absence, people had three things they wanted to tell me. One was a narrative of prosperity and growth. This was especially evident among young people who had achieved the educational qualifications to gain jobs in the white-collar sector or in skilled trades as drivers, electricians, and so on. Their wealth, prospects, and outlook were particularly displayed at weddings, celebrated by means of the elaborate *dîners-dansants* at which they rehearsed being European (*vazaha*), as described in chapter 9. But the positive narrative was also evident in the voices of older and poorer people.

When Dady Aïsha, one of the oldest women of Lombeni, looked down from her house on the hillside she expressed satisfaction at the changes in her view. "The community is clear (*mazava*) now," she said, "with no more dirty palm thatch." The houses of raffia poles and of wattle and daub that had once stood in a clearing in the secondary forest had been replaced by structures of cement and brick with metal roofs, and their number had doubled. The forest had retreated, and the village trees – coconut palms, kapok, and fruit – had fallen in storms or been cut down on government orders (ostensibly for reasons of safety). Bulldozers had cut steps for new houses into the hills, exposing gashes of red earth. The village that had been reached in 1975 only by canoe or steep forest paths now had paved roads traversed by school buses, taxis, and the cars of a large number of daily commuters.

Dady Aïsha was emphatic that the present was better than the past, and indeed everyone spoke approvingly about the changed appearance of the village. Those who had travelled appreciated the even larger and "cleaner" communities in Réunion. From her balcony above St Dénis, Dady Moussy, another older woman from Lombeni, spoke in terms similar to those of Dady Aïsha about the very different (and spectacular) view there. She waxed eloquent, not over the dramatic steep green and flower-covered hillsides, or the blue expanse of ocean, but over the urban growth, the conquest of the countryside by the city, and the increase in population it represented.

If people approved of the outward changes and the new opportunities, lingering doubts or anxieties at cultural loss were displaced elsewhere (chapters 8 and 9). The appearance of "modernity" and the expansion of houses and people were mirrored by a retreat of the spirits that had once lurked on the outskirts of the villages. It was the bush spirits, not humans, who disliked the smell of gasoline or were disturbed by the noise of machines and who moved deeper into the forest. In other words, spirits migrated in the opposite direction from humans. It was not that people stopped "believing" in spirits, but rather that the conditions for encountering spirits of this kind contracted (cf Howard 1996).[3]

The second thing people had to tell me, in some contradiction to the first, was a narrative of impoverishment, commoditization, and the final collapse of the agricultural economy. Dry rice cultivation, once the basis of subsistence, had been abandoned over a decade earlier. Ylang ylang and vanilla, cash crops that during the 1970s had created a mini-boom and constituted a substantial form of wealth for enterprising villagers, no longer had a significant market and had been largely uprooted (following the earlier histories of sugar cane, copra, and sisal). In 2000, banana plants were suffering from disease and a high rate of theft, and people said that tomatoes and chili peppers no longer flourished without fertilizer, pesticides, or irrigation; even manioc was less productive. "Farming," concluded my mentor, Tumbu Vita, "can no longer support people."

Not only did people purchase much of their food, they struggled with a host of new or growing expenses: water, electricity, and phone bills, school books, clothing, and packed lunches for their children. Many adults suffered in demeaning, low-paying jobs or unemployment, and there was a pervasive sadness among those who no longer had the means to do decent work.

Tumbu, who generally shared Dady Aïsha's appreciation of the present, summed it up: "What was better about the past was food. Everyone could eat. Now it is difficult – everyone needs money. From the moment children first open their eyes they need money. Our country is now fixed up (*taninay voadzary*). We have cars and electricity. Houses are better, there are refrigerators, and so on. But *we have become poor*. There are lots of nice objects but now one cannot eat without money." He describes a shift from primarily subsistence and cash crop cultivation to wage labour, unemployment, and welfare.

The third thing people talked about, and again in some contradiction to the first, was that the village was "empty." A large number of those born and raised there, people with rights of residence and owners or builders of village houses, were absent. For the most part they had not moved to Mamoudzou, the urban core of Mayotte, where, during earlier decades, a number of enterprising people had lived for a time. Residential dislocation for work on Mayotte had been replaced by daily commuting.

"Everyone is in La Réunion (*Larunyó*) or France (*Farantsa*)," people said. Indeed, almost every family had kin in those places, and many of those who had not yet gone were thinking about it. Although some young people left to pursue their studies, often on government scholarships, the main reason people gave for migration was linked not to the first narrative of expansive modernity but to the second one of impoverishment, namely that they could no longer survive on Mayotte. The majority of those who made the trip were people without work. In the face of the demise of both subsistence and cash crop production, they were former cultivators or the offspring of cultivators who had not been able to complete French schooling or acquire employment as skilled labour.

Although life in Réunion was more expensive and more commoditized than in Mayotte, state benefits were higher and enabled both
social reproduction and some savings. Frequently women went first,
started collecting unemployment and child benefits, and then sent their
husbands money for a ticket. Their partners followed and collected unemployment as well. Because Islamic marriages were not recognized by
the state and because the women went ahead, some households were
also able to take advantage of allowances offered to single mothers.

Empty, Growing Villages

How to account for the "emptiness" yet expansion of the villages? There
were two factors. First, social reproduction has always been marked
by the building of houses for young women on their first marriage,
and the goal of married couples has been both to provide such houses
for their daughters and, more recently, to build better houses for themselves. Paradoxically, housing is one of the things that fuels migration;
people emigrate in order to acquire the means to build houses at home
in Mayotte. Houses were often under construction or even completed
in the village while their owners continued to live in Réunion.

The move to Réunion, everyone said, was temporary. As soon as the
level of benefits was raised in Mayotte and equalized with the rest of
France, people would return; the migrants were biding their time. There
was great hope, unrealized, that the equalization of benefits would be an
outcome of the change in political status arranged in 2000. The migrants
were also ensuring that their children acquired skills that would prove
income generating upon their return. Young people did courses and ap-
prenticeships in Réunion and France as plumbers, electricians, bakers,
auto mechanics, gendarmes, and so forth.

Second, most houses were in fact occupied, but the owners had been
temporarily replaced by Anjouanais. These were economic refugees
who had crossed from Anjouan (Nzwani) at some considerable risk
to themselves in small boats during the night. Prior to 1976 Anjouan
and Mayotte formed part of a single country, and people could move
easily between the neighbouring islands. But the same political transformation that enabled people with identity papers issued by Mayotte
to travel freely to Réunion prevented people from Anjouan, Grande
Comore (Ngazidja), and Moheli (Mwali) from migrating to Mayotte.
Without papers, they were somewhat dependent on local villagers,
who hired them for odd jobs, cattle guarding, and, of course, house
construction. Salaries were neither regulated nor taxed, and the village

employers, who were poor themselves, uneasily recognized the exploitation. If discovered by the police, migrants were sent back to Anjouan.

Unlike the majority of economic migrants from Mayotte to Réunion, the Anjouanais were not already married, or at least did not travel with their families. Indeed, they sought to legitimate their new residence by means of kinship and affinity. Some linked up with kin who were the descendants of earlier generations of migrants. Many engaged in marriage (i.e., in the first instance, Islamic unions, not registered by the state) with citizens. Young women became the second (often polygynous) wives of established villagers or the first wives of those too poor to purchase a sufficiently large "suitcase," while male migrants often found divorced or widowed local women. This gave them a foothold in the community, but still left them outside citizens' rights and benefits until they had children (see chapter 12).

The picture is one of successive displacements: as people from Mayotte moved to Réunion and France, Comorans moved to Mayotte. However, the two movements are not equivalent. The first is legal and the second informal. In the first, the migrants both receive state benefits and expect them as their right, while in the second the migrants do not receive most benefits and are much more vulnerable. Moreover, while the Mahorais in Réunion expect to return home, and invest in that return, I suspect most Anjouanais had fewer such hopes or were less likely to realize them; their return home was through force. In addition, Anjouanais migrants established new roots through marriage and kinship in Mayotte in a manner that most Mahorais have not done in Réunion. Thus, the number of actual inhabitants of the village has not declined, while the number of those with claims to or interest in residence has grown.

If there were fewer spirits to fear on the path at night, villagers said it was now people who had become dangerous. Some attributed the rise in theft to migrants, but there was also a general worry that children were no longer under parental control and had become delinquent (*voyous*, note the French word). Instead of working in the fields as they once did, youth were said to hang around the village and smoke marijuana (*bangy*). Surprisingly to me, increased parental control was one reason people gave for moving to Réunion or metropolitan France.

A Brief Historical Perspective

Mayotte is a small island and was once relatively insignificant in regional exchanges. In precolonial times Anjouanais sailors were more likely than Mahorais to join European sailing vessels en route to India; Grande Comorans were more likely to travel to East Africa. Grande Comorans had a significant impact on East African Islam in the nineteenth century, and their numbers were always much larger than those of the Mahorais. At the end of the eighteenth century, Mayotte was the victim of annual raids from Madagascar, while after French appropriation in 1841 the plantation economy under the yoke of Réunionnais planters began earlier than on the other islands. It was Mayotte's relative insignificance and powerlessness that influenced the majority of its population to vote in the referenda of 1974 and in higher numbers in 1976 to stick with France rather than join the other Comoro Islands in their independence in 1975. Mayotte had more Malagasy speakers than the other islands, and in the 1970s it already included large settlements of Grande Comorans as well as some Anjouanais. There was a somewhat cosmopolitan feel to the place, a term that seems more accurate than "polyethnic."

In the 1970s people said, "How can we become independent? We have no manufacturing; we don't even produce our own soap." Now there is minor manufacturing, but Mayotte is much more dependent on imports than before. In 1975 it produced the majority of its basic foodstuffs; in 2001 virtually all food was imported, and largely by monopoly holders. A South African woman owned the supermarket, the meat-packing plant, and the soap and plastic factories. She controlled the import of beef and chicken and was setting up a chicken plant. The protein staple throughout the island was her frozen chicken wings (*mabawa*), selling wholesale for 13 francs a kilo and at 15 francs a kilo from the freezers of village shopkeepers. Local fish was more expensive: from 18 to 20 francs a kilo fresh on the beach or 23 to 25 francs from the freezer. Twenty-five-kilo sacks of rice cost 100 francs in town and 105 in the village shops. Coca-Cola was delivered weekly from the local bottling plant and had a high turnover in village shops.

The market that five years earlier had been full of Malagasy fruit, vegetables, and meat was empty of these products as the result of a government ban consequent upon a cholera epidemic in Madagascar that was long over. The ban helped the South African importers, limited access to fresh produce, and significantly reduced the means of many petty traders in and from Madagascar.

Mayotte can no longer be considered an economic periphery in any simple sense. It is a periphery as far as access to the means of production or being remote from centres of decision making are concerned. But it is not peripheral with respect to what one might call the means of consumption. It is a part of France and of the EU. The currency was the franc in this period and shortly after changed to the euro. The sources of loans, grants, and subventions are those available in Europe. The economy is entirely dependent on French government subsidies, jobs, and benefits, as well as import controls. Claude Allibert's depiction of Mayotte as a *plaque tournante* (hub) of the Indian Ocean (1984) has now become apposite. Mayotte is an economic magnet for Comorans and Malagasy and sends a good deal of money to the Sakalava temple in Mahajanga. The number of French sojourners has increased enormously – and many original inhabitants have by now spent a good deal of time in France and elsewhere. Having completed a full French education, young people are "hybrid" relative to their parents' generation and cosmopolitan with respect to a broader "culturescape." Geographic mobility is by now a taken-for-granted feature of life. Horizons are broad.

Population expansion is connected to a decline in infant mortality that preceded any "demographic transition" in birth rates by more than a generation. But it is also connected to the changing political topography of the region and inter-island movement. During the 1970s and into the 1980s, people of Mayotte were inhibited from out-migration to a degree they had not been previously. When Mayotte refused to join the emergent independent Comoran republic, inter-island travel was severely curtailed. Many in the preceding generations had gone to Madagascar, but in the mid-1970s travel to Madagascar became both difficult, because of the absence of regular transport, and unappealing, for political and economic reasons. Indeed, 1976 saw a reverse migration from Mahajanga after the massacre of Comorans there. Since the 1990s the population has been greatly enhanced by increased migration to Mayotte on the part of Malagasy and especially Comorans. The vast majority are from Nzwani (Anjouan) and are without papers. They have an incentive to have children, as this gives them rights to stay.

This is not the place to write about the huge influx of informal migrants or the measures taken against them. Instead I single out three points from this brief overview. First, the relative immobility of the population that characterized my ethnographic experience in 1975–6 was a product of that particular moment in time and not of long standing. Over the *longue durée*, population movement has been typical of the region.

Second, it is evident that population movement responds and is sensitive to microfluctuations in political and economic constraints and incentives. The world expands or contracts according to the means of transportation available and the perceived balance of opportunities at either end of the routes.

Third, the status of migrants is established by means of successive regimes of law and citizenship, and such laws, more than anything else, configure the colonial and postcolonial patterns of migration and trade.

Gendered Pioneers

In 1975 I lived for the first six weeks in town in a relatively elite household of women whose polygynous husbands travelled between the islands. Some of those women had travelled, too, but the picture was one of matrilocal households with mobile men. By contrast, in 2001 village women (who had not adopted polygyny with the enthusiasm of their urban counterparts) were more mobile than men. Postmarital residence was still largely and ideally uxorilocal. But women travelled in order to establish and support their households and to help build houses for their daughters.

The first person to leave the village of Lombeni for Réunion was Nafouanty, a newly married woman who, in fact, was taken there by her husband, a goldsmith from a larger village that had been opened to new opportunities earlier on. He went originally in 1982 in order to look after a brother who remained hospitalized after an automobile accident and brought his wife the following year. Nafouanty and her husband divorced, but both remained in St Dénis. Their daughters have grown up there and speak Creole more easily than Kibushy. When I met the girls in St Dénis in 2000, they were watching *ER* in French in their sitting room.

The second person to arrive was probably Sakina. When her husband was killed by a drunk driver in 1984 she went to Réunion at Nafouanty's suggestion, because of the benefits she could acquire there as a widowed mother of three children. Sakina was not one to sit back. She saved her monthly benefits until she had enough for trade goods and airfare and began the first of what were many trips as a long-distance trader. By 2001 she had not only moved goods between Réunion and Mayotte but had collected merchandise in East Africa, Mauritius, France, Dubai, and even farther afield. In addition, she sponsored and supported a number of relatives from Lombeni in Réunion.

As a young girl in 1975, Sandaty used to stop and stare at me as the lone white foreigner in the village. In 1980 I helped celebrate her wedding. A decade later her husband was stricken by a blinding headache and airlifted to hospital in Réunion where he died within a few days. With the help of relatives living there he was buried in the Muslim cemetery in St Dénis. Sandaty did not relocate, but she used the modest monthly payments that were by then available in Mayotte to widows of government employees with young children to start a shop, and she too began to travel in search of merchandise.

When Sandaty first told me about having visited Mumbai and Bangkok I simply didn't believe her. In fact, by 2001 she had been four times to Bangkok on wholesale shopping expeditions organized by an entrepreneur. Groups of local women travelled by air, stayed a couple of weeks in Dubai and other destinations, worked through translators, and shipped their merchandise home by container. A trip to Thailand cost Sandaty 7,000 francs. She imported children's clothing, planning the arrival for the end of Ramadan when everyone purchases gifts for their children. She left her own children with kin while she travelled. Sandaty's brother also owned a shop, and she introduced the pattern of transnational shopping to her sister-in-law. Although people on Mayotte have long referred to themselves as "poor" (*maskin*), a result of Sandaty's travels in Asia was to put this into perspective.

Sandaty never moved to Réunion, but she sponsored a school vacation for her grown son in 2000 that coincided with my own visit. We went together to the grave of his father (who had been my friend) and visited a good many other villagers who had relocated to communities in Réunion. He carried a bag full of traditional women's wrappers printed with political slogans from the recent referendum in Mayotte that he was selling in Réunion on his mother's behalf and in order to subsidize his trip. He sold the four pieces necessary for a full garment (*complet*) for 100 francs. They cost 80 francs in Mayotte where, in fact, just three pieces (thus 60 francs) suffice for a *complet*. One of the designs was a "*cameo*" portrait of Bwenzena, a woman leader of the pro-French political movement.

Of course, not all village entrepreneurs are women. Noman, a former cultivator some five years my senior, became a successful contractor, bidding for government contracts and building houses and drainage ditches. He managed some ten employees including younger kin and Anjouanais. By 2001 Noman had been to Mecca, had sent two daughters and three sons to metropolitan France to study and his wife subsequently to visit them, and had himself travelled to Kenya, Mauritius, Réunion, and Dubai for merchandise for a village shop he had established. Noman also studied both Islam (*'ilim fakihy*) and cosmology (*'ilim dunia*) and has a cabinet full of books in Arabic to prove it. He rotated as deliverer of the Friday sermon for some five years, but stopped because he "had too much on my mind." Noman showed me a home video his wife had brought back from France. One son, married to a Grande Comorienne from Mayotte whom he met in France, lived in a high-rise in Toulouse; the other siblings lived together in a high-rise in Lyon.

À La Réunion

Sakina (mentioned above) raised her children in La Réunion. One daughter, whom I met when she visited Lombeni for a family wedding, barely spoke Kibushy. A son had taken up with a Réunionnaise of South Asian descent and had a child. Sakina never stuck to a nuclear family model. Among the people she helped bring to La Réunion were her mother, Moussy, then in her seventies, and her younger brother, Abdoul.

Moussy had been coming to Réunion for about ten years, but made regular trips back to Mayotte. She was a bit defensive about her lifestyle, since her husband remained in Mayotte. She said she wouldn't travel without his acquiescence but was happy to have some autonomy. Moussy explained that she could not survive on the pension her husband received in Mayotte. She sent him a portion of her monthly benefits and also helped the offspring of a deceased son. She concluded, "I worry about them a lot and that is really why I come to Réunion. I have become a person of two places."

Having tried a number of living arrangements, Moussy looked after her daughter's subsidized apartment in St Dénis during Sakina's frequent absences. It was in a nice building, with several large rooms, but on the outskirts of town. Sakina bought her mother a monthly pass on public transportation. Moussy said the only thing that held her back was fear of *voyous*; some Mahorais, whose ethnicity is visible from their clothing, were the victim of taunts and threats by xenophobic youth. Moussy helped care for various grandchildren and other younger kin who stayed in town or passed through. She also worked informally as a healer, dispensing herbal medicine she brought from Mayotte or grew in La Réunion. In addition to trips to Mayotte, Moussy saved enough to go on the *hajj*, at a cost of around 12,000 francs, with assistance from kin. She was accompanied by her brother and his wife and by Sandaty.

While some migrants found employment in the formal sector in La Réunion and others worked in the informal economy (in both cases, most frequently in the building trades and therefore mostly men), their main source of support was state benefits. These were of varying amounts for unemployment, old age, single mothers, dependent children, and housing. To receive monthly payments one registered at the social security office and collected at a different spot. Some people collected monthly all year long, asking relatives to go in their place in months when they were back in Mayotte. Other people, making shorter trips or single sojourns in Réunion, just collected for the months they were present. During her frequent stays in Mayotte, Moussy left an identity card with her brother, who picked up her stipends on her behalf. Once she was cut off for two months but was reinstated following a complaint by Sakina. Mahorais became skilled at dealing with the bureaucracy, learning how to combine ostensible submissiveness and courtesy with strategy and persistence.

Several women from Lombeni visited Réunion in order to help daughters or daughters-in-law following childbirth. They stayed a few weeks or months and would begin collecting benefits. Their daughters and sons made return visits to Mayotte in order to have their sons circumcised, to attend weddings and mortuary rituals, or just to be "on vacation" (*en vacances*) (*figure 10.1*). But if women's kin obligations induced travel, they also constrained it. Several women said they could not leave Mayotte so long as their aged parents were alive. Those who relocated felt guilty or had sisters who remained behind to look after the parents. Moussy said that she couldn't have come to Réunion without married daughters to look after her husband in Mayotte, but many younger women felt less concern about leaving husbands. Zalia's husband worked in Mayotte, but he drank and didn't look after her well financially. So she travelled to Réunion for a few months at a time and collected sufficient benefits to cover her air fare and needs upon her return. By contrast, when Daoulaty arrived in La Réunion in order to get away from her mother-in-law, she was soon followed by her husband and, a few months after that, by the mother-in-law herself, who quickly made up with her.

Hadia, a young woman with two small children, said she came to La Réunion because she had no work at home. Her husband had work, but there was a new sense in her historical cohort that both members of a

Figure 10.1 A bilocal family on the terrace of their apartment in La Réunion, 2000. The group includes parents, brothers and sisters, a visitor from Mayotte, and two additional children.

couple should be receiving a wage. In La Réunion she had no wage employment either, as most women from Mayotte did not. However social benefits were considered equivalent to a wage for both their economic consequences and their contribution to personal dignity. It was largely women who received benefits, or who received larger amounts, handled most of the household money, and managed the savings. In both La Réunion and Mayotte, where the equivalent benefits were smaller, certain sums were paid by the state directly to women.

Married couples generally maintained separate bank accounts and had an understanding as to which spouse was responsible for what. Usually, in La Réunion as in Mayotte, the husband provided the subsistence needs for the household and could do what he liked with the remainder of his salary, while the wife accumulated and managed the savings and could spend on extras for herself and the household. Unlike the case in Mayotte, in La Réunion women did not own houses;

couples shared responsibility for finding a residence and, I think, for paying rent. Savings from both parties were directed in large part into the houses the couple was building for themselves and for their daughters back in Mayotte. Visits to Mayotte during the dry season entailed working on or monitoring house construction in Lombeni.

Some men used portions of their income to maintain polygynous unions. These could be transnational. I know one man who boasted of having wives in Mayotte, La Réunion, and Madagascar; he would alternate a few months with each of them. For people making a little money, Madagascar was a good place to invest, as life was cheaper there. In addition to men who took wives or girlfriends, an increasing number of people, mostly women, went to Madagascar to hold their spirit possession ceremonies. They also contributed money towards the annual collective ceremonies (*fanompoa*) for the ancestral spirits there.

Receiving social benefits from the state was understood neither as shameful nor as charity but rather as a right. People argued that France was responsible for Mayotte and that if there were no jobs available people still had the right to basic income. In this they were perfectly in accord with modern political philosophy and indeed with the French government's institution of the RMI, the Revenu Minimum d'Insertion, social welfare for the unemployed. With the exception of things like trips to Mecca, and the occasional polygynist, migrants lived frugally but decently. They bought nice furnishings, which they planned to take back with them to Mayotte. They ate a staple of rice served with chicken legs purchased frozen in bulk, supplemented with frozen beef or fish, and sought the best bargains. At 20 francs a kilo fish was cheaper than in Mayotte and the rice (at 200 francs for fifty kilos of broken jasmine grains) was better quality. Chicken legs (350 francs for a ten-kilo carton) were a kind of index of the standard of living in La Réunion; they replaced the frozen wings that had become the protein staple in Mayotte.

Metropolitan France

Sakina's youngest brother, Abdoul, was sent to Réunion by his older siblings at the age of ten in 1987. Because he was too old for the state school they placed him in a Catholic one and paid the fees. He left school in 1996, a year before the *bac*,[4] and participated in what was then obligatory military service for a year. Happily for him, this included a period in France studying telecommunications and computing, which he supplemented with training as a sound technician. He then acquired a series of excellent jobs in Mayotte, beginning with the phone company and later with the government. In 2001 Abdoul's monthly salary was 5,600 francs per month. He was building a six-room house for himself and his family and planning to rent out the three-room one he currently occupied, a strategy he estimated to be the best investment. Housing construction costs were indexed according to income; for him three rooms cost between 30,000 and 40,000 francs to build, payable in monthly instalments. He drove a new Peugeot that cost 80,000 francs (much more than in the metropole, he pointed out) and was paying back the bank loan at 2,000 francs per month. Abdoul owed his success not only to his own talents and enterprise but also to his sister Sakina's original move to Réunion and to her support, as well as that of other siblings.

It was not only men who were so upwardly mobile. One of Moussy's granddaughters completed a higher degree in La Réunion and was returning to Mayotte to teach special education. She married a cousin and fellow villager who had also entered the white-collar workforce. Another granddaughter passed her *bac* in Mayotte and was awarded a scholarship direct to France. She received 10,000 francs every three months (a high amount, her mother thought, because her father was deceased). While I was visiting the mother (who had struggled for years to support her children), she opened a money order from her daughter for 500 francs. This young woman (the daughter) had become engaged before she left. As the fiancé was himself about to leave for France, the mother held the contractual part of the wedding (*kufungia*) so that the couple could start living together on his arrival. She expected a letter once the marriage was consummated, with some sign of blood. The celebration of the virgin marriage (*harusy*) was postponed until their return. The ideal of the virgin bride was still in place, while the decoupling of the stages of marriage had become common.

Other women were not virgins when they left for France and went in order to marry, not study. One uneducated young woman, Amina, had a child out of wedlock in Mayotte. She responded to a marriage request from a stranger in the metropole and set off to join him. Before Amina left she built herself a small house with the money earned from doing the work given to the unemployed. (This minimally paid labour, known as *chomage*, included sweeping public buildings, collecting trash, and tidying the beach; it was given in periods of rotation to all who sought it.) Once Amina arrived in Marseille[5] and found the husband satisfactory, she sent for her child. She also sent money to her mother. Amina's mother was hoping to visit her in France once she was freed from the obligations of caring for her own young children and aging parents. She said her husband could fend for himself or take up with an Anjouanais woman during her absence. In the meantime, Amina returned to visit the village. People said, "She left with nothing, but now she has become a somebody (*ulun'belu*)."

Not all mail-order brides have such positive experiences. Sandia too had a child in Mayotte and then went off to marry a man in France whose picture she had been sent. She didn't like him, separated, and eventually found a man from Mayotte in Lyon with whom she had two more children. People said she wouldn't return to Mayotte until she had the money to put up a house. Sandia's case is interesting because she is the product of several generations of inter-island migration. Her father's father came to Mayotte from the island of Mwali and married the daughter of indentured labourers originally from East Africa. Sandia's father, Bako, left home as a young adult and settled in Antsiranana (Diego Suarez), Madagascar, where he sold bananas in the market. Diego had a thriving community of Mahorais who maintained a mosque and numerous rituals. Bako sent home money to purchase land, but never returned himself. He was once ready to do so, but his savings were stolen and he stayed on to rebuild his fortune. Bako's mother travelled to Madagascar and collected his elder daughter to raise in Mayotte. Many years later, after Bako's death, this woman went to collect her younger sister, Sandia, when Sandia was in early adolescence. So Sandia herself has lived in three very different settings.

A woman in her fifties on a visit in Mayotte said she had originally gone to France to follow her children. She married an Algerian in Marseille. "I need some way to keep warm when it's too cold and cool when it's too hot, don't I?" she said. Her husband spoke better French than she did and cooked his own food. He did not seem to have much say about her visiting home.

The husbands of these women were described as *Africains*; in most cases it was unclear to me whether they came from North or West Africa. They sought brides with citizenship papers in order to legitimate their own residence; Mayotte proved to be an ideal source. Although the men were culturally different and spoke different languages from their wives, they too were Muslim.[6]

Several women spoke to me of migrating with their children in order to acquire welfare benefits and a good education. One woman said that instead of La Réunion, she hoped to "jump ahead" to France. A woman visiting for her father's memorial (*mandeving*) lived in Marseille with her Grande Comoran husband and six children. She said her children studied better there, with less distraction and wandering about. The goal of providing children with a better education was commonly expressed by women and men.

More than one woman who considered herself the underappreciated wife in a polygynous marriage said she was saving to take the youngest children to go to live in France.[7] One woman, who spoke no French, declared herself unafraid. She would join one of the village women already in France. She had no plans to remarry and said her husband could follow if and when he wished.

Occasionally the gender positions were reversed. One man disappeared from the village, writing after a few months to ask his children and wife to join him in Marseille. The wife sent the younger children but declared she had too many interests in Mayotte to go herself. Another man, whose older sons were in France, one studying and the other in the army, planned to send their sisters to join them so that they might earn money to contribute to the houses he was building them in Mayotte.

La Réunion Again

People left Mayotte with the intention of returning, and there was a fair amount of visiting between migrants and their families, despite the cost. Those travelling between Mayotte, Réunion, and France without benefit of state subsidy acquired tickets by participating in a rotating savings circle (*shikawa*) of about ten people, selling a cow, or receiving a loan from those who had gone ahead, in a form of chain migration. Women in Lombeni participated in *shikawa* that demanded contributions of between 200 and 500 francs per month; in Réunion such contributions were between 1,000 and 1,500 francs.

If the movement is comparable to the "urban" migration characteristic of much of the African continent and the world in general over the last few decades, it has a specific twist in "small places" like Mayotte, where the move is off-island. However, there was a kind of paradox, since most migrants from Lombeni to Réunion lived not in St Dénis, but in smaller towns. The largest congregation was located in St André (San'tan'dré), in the cane-growing northeast, where certain patterns of life back home could be reproduced. Residents of St André were able to cultivate manioc and fruit, and they engaged in regular inter-household visiting. Migrants in other locations could find themselves more isolated from fellow Mahorais. There was a trade-off: the best government-subsidized housing – in modern high-rises – was often the most isolating. Television and the telephone took on a centrality they lacked back home.

Claude Dernane, the director of the Maison de Mayotte à la Réunion at the time, estimated that 95 per cent of Mahorais families on Réunion didn't work (officially) and were on government assistance (RMI). He added that approximately 90 per cent lived in unsanitary housing and that 80 per cent of the children had trouble following school programs.

While some migrants did complain of poor housing, in general they saw things differently. One woman with many children who had lived in St André since 1999 was able to pay 1,000 francs from her benefits into a monthly savings association in addition to rent. Her husband worked in the informal sector, and they practised some small-scale subsistence cultivation. "So," she concluded, "you can see that we have enough to live on." Other than being bothered by expressions of anti-Comoran prejudice on the part of some citizens, she was satisfied. She said, "The money is what 'makes us drunk on' (*mankamamu*; i.e., crazy about) Réunion."

Moussy's brother, who is considerably younger than Moussy, preceded her to Réunion. Led by his wife in 1991, he worked in the official sector as a carpenter and then a mason. The couple provided their several children with a solid education in both the French and Islamic school systems. Construction work declined with the importation of prefabricated building parts, and the work became increasingly deskilled. The brother then took odd jobs, engaged in various kinds of non-monetary exchanges (e.g., giving his mechanic a therapeutic massage), and, along with his wife, drew on social assistance. His family's monthly rent in a large, airy – indeed beautiful – apartment on a hillside adjacent to the most luxurious hotel in the city was around 4,000 francs, but after subsidies their cost was only 1,700 francs. The housing assistance was calibrated to his employment record and number of children, but the quality of the flat was also a matter of luck and time. It took several years for the family to find such a good apartment.

The quality and cost of housing inhabited by Mahorais is quite variable, from the spectacular to the "unsanitary" *bidonvilles*. Another family paid 3,500 francs for a shabby private house in a poor location in St Paul while awaiting government housing. They left a quarter of St Dénis because of ethnic harassment and were hoping for a location near a mosque. The husband earned some 6,000 francs per month officially in construction and hence was ineligible for free health care. His wife received an RMI of 1,500. Her husband supplied the family's protein (*shireo*) and also gave her 1,000 francs per month. He used a portion of his salary for building houses in Mayotte for daughters from a previous marriage.

Migrants compared the quality of life in both places. Réunion was described as "cleaner" than Mayotte. But a young man who spent seven years in Réunion and felt it had more opportunity for advancement nevertheless returned home because, he explained, there was more "breathing space" (*nafass*) in Mayotte. He illustrated this by saying that when he was ill he could spend weeks recuperating at his mother's. The point, I think, is that there was a wider field of less commoditized relations in Mayotte.

Conclusion

No one in Mayotte was afraid to travel; everyone was eager to see new places. The gendered patterns of movement exhibited the demands placed on women but also their ambition, initiative, and autonomy. People travelled for many reasons. One was to receive maximal benefits, which, as French state policy would have it, enabled people to achieve a minimally acceptable standard of living, especially when it was accompanied by various kinds of informal work and exchange. In some instances, migration was the price paid for personal and social dignity. For most people, the terms and recognition of this dignity were established back home.

There was a difference perhaps between the people who travelled in order to further "traditional" social ends back home – acquiring the means to hold weddings or build houses – and those who travelled on new agendas of education for its own sake, and so forth. But the difference should not be exaggerated, and most people's projects combined both. One man explained that he migrated to Réunion, "like everyone," in order to educate his children. Unlike Mayotte, he said, in Réunion parents received help with school supplies. "In Mayotte the rich get richer and the poor fall further behind, so we leave."

The situation began to look different the longer people stayed away and especially for the next generation. This was evident with respect to language; those educated in La Réunion spoke Creole, a language that was unknown in Mayotte (since the time of the planters) and, as people soon noticed, useless for mobility in metropolitan France.

While some people who returned to Mayotte described life in La Réunion as boring and said they had lived in front of the television, migrants did engage in a number of activities. There was informal work of various kinds, and many people studied at French or Muslim institutions. An Islamic teacher from the Grande Comore offered widely attended classes in St Dénis. Cassettes of sermons were circulated. The range of musical and dance forms of Islamic piety that were engaged in so intensely in Mayotte were also practised in Réunion. One young woman concluded that, for migrants, La Réunion "has become Mayotte" (*Eto izeo fa Maore*).

Throughout this period of geographic mobility, dual residence on the part of many, and extensive travel on the part of a significant minority, and despite the reproduction of Mahorais life in La Réunion and in various communities in the metropole, eyes were kept steadily on the horizon of economic and social success back in Mayotte.

PART FOUR

Contingent Conviviality, through 2015

The chapters in the final section are all newly written and all refer primarily to what I am tempted to call the "current" period but is actually 2015.

Chapter 11 describes a popular wedding ceremony, drawing comparisons with celebrations in 1975–6 and with the wedding of 2001 described in chapter 9. It also picks up conceptual themes articulated in the introduction. An early version was delivered at the annual conference of the Australian Anthropological Society, at which, by happy coincidence, the theme was "moral horizons." It was subsequently presented in the Anthropology Department at the University of Helsinki, the Max Planck Institute in Göttingen, and African Studies at the Humboldt University, Berlin. The chapter owes a great deal to conversations with Jacqueline Solway, drawing from our mutual research in 1985 and 1995 in Mayotte and especially her analyses of comparable changes in Botswana (Solway 1990, 2016).

Chapter 12 brings the picture of sociality in Mayotte up to 2015. Its goal is to offer an overview of people's consciousness concerning the state of the community and the changes that have taken place within it over their lifetimes, as well as their place in the wider world. In particular, it addresses perceived tensions within families (*mraba*) that have to do with uncertain solidarity between adult siblings and with differing outlooks between young adults and their parents. One manifestation is the conflict between Muslim reformers and spirit mediums. Obviously, much more could be said about these topics, and even more about Mahorais as French citizens and the immigration crisis, but those would be the subjects of new books.

Chapter 13 is what I prefer to call a summation than a conclusion. It reflects briefly on both what has transpired in Mayotte and on my recounting of it. I use as a kind of parable a dream my sister Mariam had in 1975 but only told me about in 2015, a period of elapsed time equivalent to my own in first visiting Mayotte and in writing this book. In Mariam's dream, I attempt to capture her "soul" in my mirror. That is one way to describe the practice of ethnography. But, without wishing to get myself off the hook, what her mirror makes most evident is the way that all historical reflection and action, representational and non-representational, immediate, prospective, and retrospective, are infused with ethical concern but also with ethical ambiguity.

11   Marriage and Moral Horizons, 2015

Each time I return to Mayotte I listen to what is on people's minds – what they are talking about with each other and what it is they want to tell me. In 2015 Mayotte was a full *département*, and that brought many changes. Nevertheless, a main subject of people's attention was a relatively new kind of marriage celebration, called *manzaraka*. This returns to themes recurrent throughout the book – the community's focus on celebrations of social reproduction, especially weddings, the significance of cycles of exchange, and the ways in which celebrations articulate present horizons of past and future. These celebrations, which are at once personal, kin-based, and communal, are a window on the changing nature of sociality and personhood. They are moments of social reproduction but also performances of heightened attention in which people offer explicit representations of their lives. Hence they are sites of access to those lives.[1]

Like the *shungu* described in chapters 4 and 5, or the *dîner-dansant* in chapter 9, the joyous *manzaraka* entail effort, organization, social support, and anxiety; if anything, the scale has increased. And like those celebrations, *manzaraka* manifest historical horizons as people express what is important to them, what resources in tradition they acknowledge and draw from, and what they look forward to, offering a subjunctive "as if." They articulate the moral horizon, a horizon that continuously moves ahead as people move towards it.

History as Interpretive Acts

In *The Interpretation of Cultures*, Geertz (1973a) advises anthropologists to read over the shoulders of the natives, or at any rate, describes anthropologists as doing so; however, he is less explicit concerning the work of reading that the natives are doing as opposed to what the anthropologists are doing. The way we lead our lives *as* natives, the way the members of any society lead their lives, can be understood as interpretations of local "texts" – drawn from the repertoire of relatively objectified acts, exemplary characters, roles, scripts, scenarios, projects, and modes of practice that society has on offer. Each interpretation (like each production of Hamlet, or each new performance as prime minister or professor) is a kind of *re*interpretation of the text, character, or role and has the potential for reinscription or transformation such that both revised and new texts are added to the repertoire.[2]

Such interpretations, ultimately lives *as* they are lived and *in* the living of them, correspond to the points Gadamer makes about interpretation as a kind of subordination to the cultural texts or forms – entering into them, rather than dominating or standing outside them – that I raised in chapter 1. This can also be phrased in a language of deference (Bloch 2005) or responsivity (Wentzer 2014). We more or less take this for granted when we speak of interpretations of a score by musicians. The layered succession of remembered, overlapping interpretations produces the "contemporaneity of the noncontemporaneous" (Koselleck 2004: 95) as it also constitutes the moving horizon of history as understood from within rather than outside.

Gadamer shows that the ways scholars achieve a hermeneutic understanding of texts or historians of events apply more broadly to the members of any tradition and to all of us as subject to our historical condition, and on stages ranging in scale from the personal to the global. We could think of different interpretations of being an anthropologist by successive generations who take up the subject. A community like a village, whose members all know and interact with (or avoid) one another, can be understood as moving in time by means of successive acts of interpretation that respond to one another. These include interpretations of texts (as performances of scripts or enactments of scenarios), interpretations of events (turned into narratives), and interpretations of circumstances (turned into political discourse, rumour, etc.). Interpretive acts are manifested in further texts, performances, events, and circumstances. As I have indicated, "texts" include rules, rituals, ceremonies, musical scores, key scenarios, characters, roles, and so forth. Interpretations overlap and succeed each other. Each enactment of a wedding celebration is a practical iteration and interpretation of a script, scenario, or model. But each enactment is also a *reinterpretation*, new, unique, and consequential, indexed to particular persons and a particular moment.

No interpretation is mere repetition or simply routine. Gadamer demonstrates this by addressing what he calls "the hermeneutic relevance of Aristotle" (1985: 278), drawing from Aristotle's account of ethics and practical judgment to substantiate his picture of interpretation qua application. Just as ethical judgment applies to each particular situation or conjunction of circumstances, so too, with respect to historical understanding, each new interpretation of past texts must relate to present situations (ibid. 289).[3]

The recourse to Aristotle's *Ethics* is no mere analogy; rather, we can conceive of historical horizons as moral horizons. As Gadamer suggests, "moral being, as Aristotle describes it, is clearly not objective knowledge, ie the knower is not standing over against a situation that he merely observes, but he is directly affected by what he sees. It is something that he has to do" (ibid. 280). It is not an application of universals to particular situations but seeing what is right within the situation (ibid. 287).[4]

History as it happens is, as it were, the movement of practical interpretations with respect to moral horizons. These are successive interpretations of the worlds in which people live and the circumstances in which they find themselves. People interpret the cultural texts that constitute their world through the exercise of judgment in selectively reiterating and re-enacting them in the living of their lives. As elaborated in the introduction, history as lived, as action, can be conceived as the work and intervention of successive interpretations with respect to horizons; and history as represented, as understanding, can be conceived as the articulation of horizons as perceived through enactments. In successive acts of interpretation the community constitutes its collective – but not homogeneous – history.

As the horizons of each age cohort of men and women unfold, the successive practices of each cohort, the ways they interpret their world through institutions like marriage celebrations, form overlapping steps or waves in the progression of history as it happens, that is, as it is effected, lived, experienced, and perhaps contested. Weddings are well suited for this kind of interpretation because they are marked events and ones in which parents explicitly look back to authorized ways of doing things and young people look forward, projecting themselves into the kinds of persons they want to be and rehearsing the kinds of worlds in which they want to live – and for both parents and youth, the wedding is an intense enactment, a condensation or concentration, of the present.

One day in July 2015 I visited an old friend, Hassanat Kolo, around the time she and her household were helping the sponsors prepare a *manzaraka* for a young couple, both of whom were her kin and were moving into an expansive two-story house adjacent to Hassanat's simpler dwelling. The *manzaraka* is an event (*asa*) to celebrate marriage, or more precisely, the transfer of the dowry from the groom's side to the bride, that has been present in Mayotte only for the last decade or so;[5] in 2015 it was all the rage, and *manzaraka* were held overlapping with one another over the course of a few weeks after Ramadan ended. Everyone insisted that I attend and observe them and remarked how significant and beautiful they were.

The *manzaraka* are very exciting, though the people producing or planning them are stressed about the expense and work they entail. *Manzaraka* exhibit some continuity with, but also departure from, celebrations of the past, elaborating the groom's procession as a display of Muslim identity. They require considerable accumulation of resources, great expenditure, but also the display and receipt of large amounts of money. As someone said to me, "*On joue avec l'argent içi* (We play with money here)." Needless to say, money is both alluring and disturbing, but there is much more going on.

The *manzaraka* can be taken as cultural texts, interpretations of the world of the participants, much as were the celebrations of virginity in the 1970s and the *dîner-dansants* of the early 2000s. Such texts are evidently not fixed or timeless – as enactments they occur in history, change in form and content, and speak to temporal matters. They are also interpretations that are lived rather than abstracted from life. *Manzaraka* are optional, and so one can also see people's decisions about holding them as further interpretations of their situation and of what they want to say about themselves, each other, and the world.[6] All of these interpretations are *ethical* insofar as they instantiate criteria, embody judgment, articulate values, make commitments, discern incommensurables, display virtue, and assert and acknowledge dignity and care; they are about what matters profoundly in the course of a life. They are also *horizontal* in that they draw explicitly from the past and look towards the future. The performances have an expansiveness characteristic of relatively unbounded horizons, of anticipation without precision.

I first met Hassanat shortly after her own wedding, forty years ago, when she was in her mid-teens. Her husband, Daudu, was my friend and self-appointed field assistant. He was ambitious and wanted to make something of himself, despite being from a cohort that, unlike his younger brothers, had missed the opportunity to attend school. It was a first marriage for both Daudu and Hassanat. Their respective families conducted the engagement and established the *mahary* (Ar. *mahr*), the gift of money prescribed by Islam that confirms the union and that goes from the groom to the bride's family, and in Mayotte, generally from the bride's parents to the bride herself. They later held the *kufungia*, the official Muslim performative act in front of witnesses, including transfer of the *mahary*, that initiates and sanctifies the jural union. This is the core transformative act of marriage but not the focus of my analysis, as (predictably) it is relatively unchanging.[7]

A wedding house was prepared for the couple; like all houses at the time it was a simple two-room affair, furnished with wood-framed rope beds covered with embroidered sheets and pillows. Bright new cloths decorated the walls. At a time ascertained by an astrologer, and doubtless verified by the spirits who possessed older members of the family, Daudu and Hassanat were secretly placed in the house. As they consummated the marriage in one room, their grandmothers sat in the other, ready to confirm the blood.

The bride's virginity was of enormous importance and the most critical criterion for effecting a felicitous wedding. From the birth of a daughter, parents anxiously awaited this moment. Had Hassanat not been a virgin, Daudu could have walked out, the marriage annulled, or he could have concurred in deception with chicken blood.[8] The maintenance of virginity was less a sign of patriarchy than an affirmation of a young woman's discipline and autonomy and, in particular, her respect for her mother. The gift of her virginity served as an act within an elaborate cycle of exchange in which the bride received a house built for her by her father and clothing and household implements from her husband and in which her parents reciprocated their peers.[9]

Immediately after the consummation, the grandmothers began ululating. Hassanat's mother rushed over in great excitement to congratulate her daughter and to be congratulated in turn. The bloody cloth was hung for display, and women from across the village congregated in the courtyard to dance the *lạdaimwana*, the "joy for the child," in which they shook their buttocks and mimicked sexual intercourse, celebrating an induction into the pleasures of sexual life (*figure 11.1*).

Figure 11.1 A wedding dance (*ladaimwana*), 1975–6. As a successful
defloration is announced, women gather at the bride's house to dance
their joy, shaking their buttocks and beating rhythm with bamboo sticks.
It is a scene of laughter, pleasure, and jokes at the expense of men. The
wattle-and-daub house in the background is badly decayed, revealing
its structure.

Hassanat and Daudu were very happy; they reclined in bed and
were visited by well-wishers. They stayed in the house a full week, during which various complex exchanges of food were enacted. Different
age groups were feasted daily until the whole village had consumed a
precise amount and the distinct exchange obligations of Hassanat and
Daudu and especially of Hassanat's parents, who had eaten at other
people's weddings, were satisfied (chapter 5).

At week's end, Daudu was whisked to a house across the village
where he and two supporters were dressed in Muslim gowns and led in
a stately procession to Hassanat's house. Women bore his *valises*, suitcases of clothing as well as gold jewellery and household implements
like cooking pots that he was offering to Hassanat (*figure 11.2*).[10] On this

Figure 11.2 The *valise* and procession of a groom (hidden behind sunglasses), 1975–6. A week later, the groom is discovered in another house. Women gather to escort him back to the bride's house. Here it is men who are celebrated. One of the women carries the suitcase of gifts to the bride while the groom, flanked by two friends, is hidden behind sunglasses and shaded by umbrellas.

occasion it was men who danced (the *mlelezi*), gracefully in a line, with women's scarfs draped elegantly across their shoulders (*figure 11.3*). A final feast served to the entire village ended the wedding. The series of events were for members of the community, participants in the closed formal system of mutual exchange (*shungu*). As discussed in chapter 5, the performance of each virgin wedding was thereby articulated with the social reproduction of the community as a whole.

The contemporary *manzaraka* is a development of the groom's procession to enter the bride's house. The distances traversed are longer, the procession is more elaborate, and the crowds are much larger, with guests attending from across Mayotte. Most strikingly, the procession now moves to the drumming and singing of the *Mulidy*, a version of

Figure 11.3 A men's wedding dance, 1975–6. Men escort the procession of the groom by dancing gracefully, adorned with women's headcloths as scarfs.

the East African *Maulida* associated with the Qadiry brotherhood and widely popular in Mayotte. Adepts of the *Mulidy* (including the team of village boys who study it) lead the joyous yet slow and stately procession that is explicitly Muslim. Indeed, the word *manzaraka* itself comes from a phrase in Arabic sung in the *Maulida*.[11]

In brief, the recent *manzaraka* for Hassanat's cousin took place as follows. The young man borrowed a house in a distant quarter of the village where he and his friends spent the morning chatting and dressing. Over white shirts and ties they wore Muslim gowns and long black coats embroidered in gold and purchased on the *hajj*. They wrapped turbans over their hats, the groom in a bright red one and his brother in green. They pinned on sweet-smelling corsages provided by the bride's mother. A group of young women from a distant village, with whom they had become friends when they all lived for some years as students and apprentices in the same town in metropolitan France, joined them.

The women teased the men and helped them apply eye-liner and fix their clothing. A photographer with a video camera and tripod began filming.

In the procession the groom was flanked by two "best men," and this line of three men abreast was preceded by a similar row and followed by two others – some twelve men in all, their heads shaded by pink and green parasols held by women behind them. Each row was preceded by a row of women walking backwards, facing the men, fanning them and wiping off perspiration. Lines of dancing men led the procession. The *Mulidy* is beautiful, and the men danced gracefully. The groom's male entourage (the *bweni harusy*) followed the *Mulidy* step but did not sing and kept their faces expressionless, behind dark glasses. The procession gathered momentum and grew in size to more than sixty persons, joined at the end by several European guests. Everyone walked in very slow steps to the *Mulidy* beat, surrounded by spectators along the way, men, women, and children. The groom's father briefly stepped out of the procession to be interviewed and express his pleasure in front of the camera.

At the bride's new two-story house, the groom's party had to pay a fee and utter the call to prayer in order to be let in the door. About thirty people, all men except for a few European women, were then served an elaborate meal. We sat at tables with individual dishes, napkins, and cutlery and ate more slowly than the rapid gorging by hand from shared platters laid on mats that I remembered. The meal began with a salad, samosas, and mini pizzas, followed by various forms of prepared beef, rice pilaf, spicy papaya relish (*anchary*), and vegetable dishes. The groom and one other man of his party were hand fed by young women standing behind them. We were each served bottled water and soft drinks, finishing with yoghurts and pineapple compote, and given gift bags with sodas and packaged cakes to take home.[12] A few women danced for the seated men, and the groom's brother rose and danced with them. A saucer covered by a cloth was passed around into which the guests slipped money.

The bride was not present. Veiled, heavily made up, and dressed in finery, she was seated in an armchair in a large tented field where several hundred women guests were fed, seated in clusters on mats. (Children were served at a different locale.) A wide variety of dishes were served – as someone said, "all the different kinds of food found in Mayotte." The emphasis is more on local than French recipes, yet the variety itself is an innovation. In the 1970s and 1980s the festive food was only plain and coconut rice topped with freshly slaughtered boiled beef or curdled milk. The labour-intensive preparation of the meals is the responsibility of the bride's family and especially her mother; the bride's kin serve it. The bride's father told me he slaughtered three head of cattle for the occasion. He had raised them himself, but at many such events whole animals or sides of beef are purchased, as are other food items.

As the meal drew to a close, a line of women danced up to the bride. Her mother-in-law lifted the veil and placed 3,000 euros in her mouth. As the French women pushed forward and inappropriately called the bride to look at them while they took photos, each woman in turn from the groom's side, eventually all those being fed, presented the seated bride with money, which she put in a purse by her side. Women waved poster boards to which bills of various denominations were affixed. Some danced in front of the bride for some time, clutching 100- and 50-euro notes. I was told repeatedly that a bride could receive many thousands of euros, possibly enough to build a house, or perhaps pay off the feast. But the total was unpredictable; people disagreed on whether it would cover costs and on whether the bride's or groom's side had spent more, thereby affirming the giftlike quality of the exchange. In any case, the bride is celebrated by means of exchange between women constituted as affines in the occasion.[13]

Someone said one could spend 50,000 euros on the *manzaraka* and invite 500 guests. Another person put the typical amount at 20,000 euros and 300 to 400 guests. There is no guarantee on the return from guests; it might include the gift of a new car (from the groom) or it might come well under expectations. Kin help with labour and through *côtisations* (set contributions, *mtsangu*). In one large extended family I know, each cousin contributes 20 euros to a *kufungia* and at least 50 for a *manzaraka*. In smaller families or among closer kin the amounts are higher. Hassanat worked hard cooking and serving for the bride's side and contributed money to both sides, as she was related to both parties.

The "suitcase," long a metaphor, was brought the following day. It too transfers wealth from the groom's side to the bride, here the donors being identified as largely male. The groom's older brother showed me, stored at his mother's house, boxes with every major household appliance – refrigerator, freezer, washing machine – all of which he had purchased for his brother – plus trays of clothing and household items covered in transparent gift wrap, several sets of gold jewellery, as well as costume jewellery, and more. The groom's female kin had purchased most of this on the groom's behalf and with his money.

The size and contents of the "suitcase" are an expansion from the past, indicative of how people live now and the money at their disposal, as well as honouring the bride. The procession continues to honour the groom and the activity of men. But the other parts of the *manzaraka* are new, especially the conspicuous gifting between women. A major difference is that weddings of Hassanat's day had strict limits on the size of the feasts and restricted invitations to those villagers who were part of their *shungu* exchange. The feasts were designed to represent and maintain equality and equivalence. In contrast, the *manzaraka* has open and individualized guest lists, including people from all over the island and Europeans with whom members of the wedding party now work. Conversely, village women now attend only if they are personally invited to help cook and serve or to eat and provide gifts. With no limits on spending, the *manzaraka* are inflationary and express achievement and inequality, even if sometimes the display is built on bank loans that take years to pay off.[14]

The equivalence that marked the *shungu* system was in its time a tacit rejection of the hierarchy invoked by the traditional Mahorais elite from which these villages had been excluded. Conversely, the *manzaraka* borrows directly from the older elite forms and especially from the pattern found among the Grande Comoran elite, those very people from whom the pro-French vote had been designed to separate citizens of Mayotte.[15] The *manzaraka* demonstrates Muslim self-assurance, splendour, and prestige equal to that of the old elite while simultaneously showing that education and employment have overridden older forms of inequality and expressing a new form of market-based inequality. The *shungu* was appropriate for a community that was based largely on subsistence cultivation; indeed, recall that one of the reasons the *shungu* exchange was terminated was precisely because, as subsistence cultivation declined and people began to purchase food for the feasts on the market, the equivalence of prices and expenditures could not be maintained over time. The *manzaraka* goes along not only with the market but also with a form of social identity and differentiation based on individual achievement that the market enables.

As more than one person told me, the *manzaraka* is a form of showing off (*mpwary*). Yet at the same time, it forces everyone else to show they are equally capable. The sense of reciprocal obligation is thus likened to the *shungu*; if you have been invited to a *manzaraka* you want to hold one of your own. It is inescapable, people said, although they also pointed out that, unlike the *shungu*, a return is not obligatory. In fact, people recognize that the burden has become greater; the *shungu* was held for only one child; but now each child wants a *manzaraka*. And in the *shungu* you measured quantities and could not exceed the set limits, whereas spending for the *manzaraka* is open.[16]

The scale, the Islamic music, and the money given to the bride all differentiate the *manzaraka* from weddings like Hassanat's. But the most significant divergence concerns the timing. The *manzaraka* procession did not coincide with the end of a matrimonial week. In fact, the bride and groom were already wife and husband; they had been married in 2012 by *kufungia* and they already had two children. People told me it was common and even preferable for the *manzaraka* to be held after children are born and once the couple recognize the marriage as reasonably stable.[17] From the groom's perspective, even if the bride later throws him out, he knows his children will benefit from the gifts. But the main reason for the delay is that marriages are often initiated before the full means to celebrate them are available and perhaps before the couple have found jobs, built houses, or returned to Mayotte.

This speaks to another major shift, namely that – means permitting – the primary financial sponsorship of the ceremonial events has devolved from the parents to the young couple, indicating that they are more successful economically (and able to take on the responsibility at an earlier age) than their parents. If the couple work, they pay for the events themselves, though parents help out. The parents do sponsor the *kufungia* and take the lead in organizing the *manzaraka*, but the latter indexes in the first instance less their achievement or rise in status as parents than the achievement of the young couple.[18] Phrased with respect to bride and groom, the *manzaraka* serves less to initiate something new than to recognize ongoing achievement; it is less about the initiation of the union than about the success of the household. And it is not about purity (or potential fertility), as indexed in the transition from virginity to sexuality, or about the interdependence of the generations, but about the social relations that educational, professional, and especially financial success can support and engender. It also provides the bride with both a material dowry and a large sum of money.

It is evident that wedding celebrations continue to indicate both the distinction and the reciprocity between bride and groom, wife's side and husband's side, and between women and men more generally. In some villages, forthcoming *manzaraka* are announced in the mosque; men are entitled to attend as members of the community, but for women it is by personal invitation. Moreover, the expectations of male and female guests are different. Women on the groom's side are expected to give money and would be ashamed to leave less than twenty euros. Men can simply place money in the saucer after the meal and it can be as little as five euros. The money is slipped discreetly under a napkin so no one sees the amount – exactly the reverse of the display among women.

Throughout the *manzaraka*, bride and groom – or wife and husband – are kept apart, and the various components of the celebrations are gendered with respect to participants and exchanges, albeit with some crossover. The wife does not observe the groom's procession, nor does the groom attend the bride's receipt of money, and in fact few men were present there. Nor do they eat together.[19] But the *manzaraka* is only one event among several. That night the couple sponsored a *shigoma*, a performance at which the men dance in line holding women's scarves and moving in a slow circle. This is done to a small orchestra and with the participation of a semi-professional team of dancers. The rhythm is compelling, and women enter the dance if they feel inspired to do so. The bride and groom were seated together on a sofa in the middle of the circle. They watched the proceedings and chatted with each other.

On the following day, the sexualized women's dance (*mamangu ambiu*; formerly carried out immediately after the consummation) took place. It is performed by women dancing individually or two by two as they feel moved, to an amplified band and before a large, mainly female audience and in the absence of both bride and groom. At both dances spirits sometimes rise. A few days later there was a *dîner*, a meal hosted by the groom's side and carried out in ostensibly French style. The *dîner* is by invitation on formal printed cards, and guests attend mostly as couples; recall the *dîner-dansant* I attended in 2001 (before the prominence of the *manzaraka*) with a DJ, toasts, cake-cutting, and couples'-style dancing (chapter 9). Comparing these modular events, one sees not only a range of different relations between the sexes but the expression and rehearsal of an overlapping constellation of Muslim, French, and local forms of identification and value.[20]

Any given wedding includes a selection of these events, which can be extended in different combinations over time.[21] Of course, the very word "wedding" is far from precise. The events celebrate and confirm marriage, but they are disarticulated from the formal legal and sexual transformations. In effect, as someone said, weddings are now celebrated twice, with a smaller feast initially at the *kufungia* and much bigger feasts years later.[22]

Each of these performances places the couple in a different light, oriented differentially to past, present, and future. It is evident that while the *dîner* anticipates and celebrates being French, the *manzaraka* that has partly displaced and partly subsumed it proudly affirms Muslim identity – and adherence specifically to an older regional expression rather than contemporary reform Islam. If the *dîner* was once playing at becoming French, trying it out, the *manzaraka* asserts a definitive pride in Muslim identity. And the procession is equally a dance – expansive, stately, joyous, inviting both participation and observation. It is, just as everyone told me, very beautiful. Together the ceremonies look to a range of horizons, or rather, to a broadly fused one.

I make two further remarks with respect to the *manzaraka*. First, attention on the couple should not distract from the point that a main subject of these events remains the personal transformations of bride and groom as embedded individuals. While affinal exchange may have become more important than in the past, and while there is greater attention to constituting stronger and more permanent conjugal unions (as encouraged in the civic marriage laws),[23] the emphasis remains on the way in which the groom and his party assist in the transformation of the bride and, in complementary fashion, the bride enables the transformation of the groom, and the mutual gratitude expressed for these actions.[24] In effect, the *act* of marrying (successfully holding the ceremonies) remains important in and of itself and irrespective of the state of being married, or staying married. The emphasis on weddings that I describe pertains largely to a woman's *first* marriage. As some women pointed out to me, women in Mayotte still want to get married though they may not want to stay married.

Shortly before one planned *manzaraka* in 2015 the groom – or rather husband, as they had been married for several years and had three children – absconded with another woman and refused to participate. The wife's family had all the preparations in place and decided to go ahead without him.[25] The husband's mother concurred and declared she would still oversee sending the gifts from the groom's side. Neighbours confirmed that the *manzaraka* could proceed in such circumstances but suggested it would be relatively unappealing. As it happened, the husband finally agreed to come and act his part. He shaved his recent dreadlocks, walked in the procession, and sat with his wife at the *shigoma*. The wife's father told me he didn't know or care if the husband planned to stay; the main thing was that his daughter had her *manzaraka*.

The second point has to do with the degree to which the *manzaraka* is optional and its value as a Muslim ritual. The procession is held to the performance of the *Mulidy*, a display of honour to the Prophet, joy in Islam, and confidence in Muslim and local identity. It is open to metropolitan (white, Christian) French guests, some of whom shyly entered the procession while others watched. The act of inviting these guests – friends, co-workers, fellow students – is a statement of equality with them. Conversely, their participation tacitly acknowledges Islam and the value of local custom even if some attend from mere curiosity.

Yet to Muslim reformists (*jaula*), the *Mulidy* is inappropriate: an unwarranted innovation, *bid'a*. Reformists also disapprove of excessive feasting and think celebrations should be modest. In this respect, the reformists' view corresponds with that of the most assimilated young people, who argue in favour of private saving and investing their capital more productively than in social display.

A woman of reformist bent confided that she was reluctantly planning a *manzaraka* on the occasion of her daughter's wedding. The groom's mother had threatened to cancel the engagement otherwise; this was her oldest son and she was determined to find a bride whose family would provide him a *manzaraka*. The bride's mother gave in. They would hold the *kufungia*, enter the house for seven days, and then perform a *manzaraka* immediately upon exit. But they would forgo other festivities, including the *dîner* – all of which the reformists reject. I did not speak to the young couple themselves, but here they were clearly positioned, as in older days, as secondary to the concerns and authority of their parents. And it is evident that mothers (a widow in the bride's case) rather than fathers have the clearest investment and say in weddings.

The transition from Hassanat's wedding to that of her much younger cousin took place in overlapping stages, as each historical cohort, shorter than biological generations, interpreted the circumstances, shifted their horizons, and renewed the forms by which they understood their world and the nature of marriage. During the 1980s *shungu* exchange was deliberately wound down and terminated in favour of the open *invitations* of the 1990s. The blood of defloration was no longer displayed, the salience of virginity declined (though it has not disappeared), and the week of seclusion was observed less rigorously and in some cases abandoned. The various components of transformation and celebration were disarticulated, the *dîner* was invented, the "suitcase" was expanded to a truck full of goods and trays of clothing, the groom's procession was reinvented as the *manzaraka*, and the gifting by and between women was greatly expanded and publicized.

A recent change is the addition to the celebration of the *kufungia*, the Muslim legal act of marriage, of a kind of mini *manzaraka*, with a feast sponsored by the bride's family, a procession bearing gifts from the groom's side, and money given to the seated bride. I attended an engagement that unexpectedly turned directly into a *kufungia* and *walima* (feast) held by the bride's parents the following day.[26] The family explained that since so many people showed up for the engagement they agreed to follow immediately with a marriage. The day began with a blessing over the household. Large numbers of women on the bride's side arrived to cook and set out enormous quantities of food. Guests included men from both sides who recited a blessing (*shidjabu*) over the bride, who was elaborately dressed and painted with henna. The groom's party of women, led by his mother, then arrived bearing twenty-six carefully wrapped trays of gifts, mainly clothing, on their heads. All in all, some 200 people were fed, each from their own dish.[27] After eating the women danced up to the seated bride to present the gifts and money. The bride received 1,500 euros and some pieces of gold jewellery from her in-laws. The following day she redistributed some of the clothing to female kin.

The couple were officially married at this event, albeit in the absence of the groom, who had been called up to army duty in France. He came from a neighbouring village, and the couple had met on Facebook. The consummation was postponed to his anticipated return in six months' time, another kind of disarticulation.[28]

One woman expressed a general feeling about the *manzaraka* when she said, "We have to do it. If I see someone else doing it, I want to do it too. We want to keep up and show we are as good and capable as the next person." But there are always further innovations; I heard of communities in which there are now chairs for both wife and husband at the receipt of money, and the groom too rises and dances. Yet despite the pressure and the popularity, people are divided about the *manzaraka*, and their horizons now extend beyond it; I heard the prediction that it would disappear within a few years. One man aged around thirty said it was pointless and far too expensive, costing more than he earned in a year. He would never hold one for himself, he said, but would contribute to those of his siblings. A well-to-do man, aged around forty, explained that you should build your house and educate your children first and only when you are fully established hold the *manzaraka*, which, he said, is "to give back to people."[29] He added that he didn't like the fact that you display to everyone what you are bringing; that only creates jealousy and bad feeling among those who cannot give as much.

As noted, the bride's virginity has declined in importance; it is still relevant to many older women but no longer critical. Not only is the legitimate sexual consummation of the union often separated in time and place from the celebrations, but it is also recognized that many brides are no longer virgins at the moment of *kufungia*. As adults explained, once they go to metropolitan France, who knows if the women remain virgins.[30] Indeed, the timing of ceremonial events is based on an assumption that young people have been in France. The young people phone their parents to say whom they want to marry. The parents meet each other and set up the *kufungia*. The couple are informed and can then cohabit in France, and later return to celebrate the wedding (*harusy*) in Mayotte. If they are in Mayotte to begin with, a wedding is held as in the past, with an entry and exit and food for a week,[31] but without virginity being a public issue. People say, "We have become (turned, *nivadiky*) French." In fact, the Muslim reform movement also decries the display of blood. The *manzaraka* can also be held when it is not a woman's first marriage and even for a woman who never married as a virgin. However, virginity at first marriage remains valued by mothers.

The *manzaraka* procession, the s*higoma* dancers, the *dîner* on top of the meal at the *manzaraka*, the band for the women's dance, the giving and display of so much money – why is there such excess? Each of these events has a different style and atmosphere and offers a somewhat different interpretation on the world, as well as a different articulation of bride and groom or husband and wife in their relations with each other and with kin, friends, and community. There is also the construction of ever more elaborate houses and the transmission of ever larger "suitcases." Perhaps one can discern an augmentation of social being – a social disposition towards outward display and adoption of the new and a habitus of competition.[32] And yet there are also elements of ironic and critical responses towards the world the actors inhabit.

Changes of horizon are evident not only in the ceremonies but in features of marriage itself. I illustrate with a brief look at the experiences and decisions of Hassanat's three daughters, making history and interpreting culture as they live it. The eldest daughter, Sua, now aged around forty, caused a furor in 2000 when she was the first woman in the community to marry a non-Muslim. Sua was already separated from a local man, and Jean-Marie divorced his French wife for her. But when Jean-Marie refused to participate in the *kufungia*, Sua married someone else until eventually he agreed to a Muslim wedding. The couple moved to the metropole, but after some years Sua left him because he declined to have more children than the two he had with his first (European) wife and Sua's own child from an earlier marriage. Sua is now married to a local man and lives adjacent to Hassanat. Marriages with non-Muslims are no longer uncommon, and there has even been a *manzaraka* for a couple where the husband had not converted. As one woman who was herself quite devout said, people now are pleased even if their children marry Europeans, and there is no more talk of *kafiry* (heathens).

The second daughter, Ratuya, did marry a Mahorais. The *kufungia* took place in Mayotte and the consummation in France. Two years later, with a child and the sense that the relationship was stable, Ratuya and her husband held a civil wedding in France at which she wore a white dress. They have since returned to Lombeni but live with their children a more or less French lifestyle (as described in the following chapter). They do not plan to hold a *manzaraka*, having decided that the money could be better invested elsewhere. Mother and daughter recognize that they live in somewhat different worlds.

The third daughter, aged twenty-two, has studied in France but now lives at home. She is engaged to a village man who is currently working in France, and she is impatient for the *kufungia* and consummation so that she can be more independent of her mother. She says that if her fiancé doesn't return soon she will take someone else. From her perspective, Islam grants legitimacy to intimate unions that could be relatively short-term commitments. Serious marriage might be reserved for a later phase of life.

Despite its consequentiality for the bride's person, the idea that the first union could be provisional is something I heard elsewhere as well – for example, from a father advising his son not to agree to a civil marriage right away. Although first marriages may produce children, they are rather like premarital partnerships in the West – without intrinsic commitment for the long term. A woman really has no other choice than to marry if she does not wish to offend her mother. But whereas in the past the elaborate ceremonies all went towards a woman's first marriage, now the most expensive ceremony, the *manzaraka*, can be postponed until a couple are more mature, established, and certain of each other. Of course, this does not mean there are no separations after a *manzaraka*.

Finally, there is Hassanat herself, single after several marriages, who was politely fending off suitors of her own. These were informal migrants from the Grande Comore looking for a stable and secure place in which to live and from which to begin the search for residency papers, horizons of a different sort.

I have been arguing that the conduct of weddings no less than the constructs of marriage or decisions about when and how to marry are historical. They are historical not only in the sense that they are located at a specific time but that they are part of the ongoing history of a given community or society, indeed part of the *making* of that history. While none of the individual weddings could be described as momentous in import, weddings are of broad social interest and consequence in Mayotte, highly visible events at which everyone participates and to which sponsors devote a great deal of time, money, and emotional energy. Cumulatively, marriages and their celebration constitute history as it transpires and as it is experienced. The marriage form shapes historicity – that is, the distinctive cultural shape that historical consciousness takes – and is shaped by it.

If the Geertzian anthropologist interprets culture, so part of that interpretation is constituted through understanding how the members of a given community interpret it for themselves, drawing selectively on the repertoire available to them and creatively adding to it. In the end, culture itself is constituted as and through successive acts of interpretation – and those acts are lived history. The *manzaraka* is not a timeless custom but is constituted through aesthetic innovation and recomposition within a tradition. The events at weddings exemplify and instantiate people's explicit statements of who they are and want to be, now that they want to follow both Muslim and European customs fused in forms and combined in repertoires they proudly announce as their own. The events are serious and consequential, yet people also describe what they are doing as play or celebration (*soma*) and as showing off (*mpwary*). They play in creative, beautiful, and compelling ways.

The celebrations exhibit moral horizons. Historical action is ethically oriented and informed by the things people care about. Conversely, ethical life needs to be understood as historically in motion, a product of successive acts and new criteria, dynamic rather than static, and oriented to specific horizons of past and future. It is a matter of how people take the circumstances in which they find themselves, and perhaps remake or redescribe them.

To put it another way, if the phrase "the interpretation of culture" is understood as the manner in which people live their lives – actively interpreting and selecting from among the repertoire of symbolic vehicles, ideas, and practices afforded them – then history is the enactment, accumulation, clash, and orchestration of multiple and successive interpretations – multiple iterations – among people more or less in conversation with one another, more or less sharing or oriented towards the same shifting horizons. History in one sense is the temporal dimension of these lived overlapping interpretations, as they are sequentially reiterated or revised, each time differently or responding to new and changing circumstances, including prior enunciated and lived interpretations.

Viewed in this manner, neither history nor interpretation can be directly opposed to structure or transformation. With respect to transformation, I briefly mention two ideal typical structural concepts that have perhaps been haunting this chapter. Solway (2016) has discerned in weddings in Botswana a shift towards possessive individualism in the sense of C.B. Macpherson (1962), in which people are understood or understand themselves as the proprietors of their persons, owing nothing to society. Despite the display of wealth, this is not what "playing with money" and the stately procession of the *manzaraka* demonstrate. Indeed, they continue to celebrate the fact that people are produced through the acts and acknowledgments of others as well as playing their own part. It is the nature of this part that has shifted, especially for women, and the relative part of young people vis-à-vis their parents. It may be that the decision of Hassanat's second daughter, Ratuya, not to hold a *manzaraka* does manifest a structural transformation to possessive individualism, but this remains as yet unclear.

The second ideal type is that of companionate marriage (Hirsch and Wardlow 2006). Here too I am cautious. This ideal is available, partially realized, but not fully in practice.[33] One man in his late thirties did say to me that, "Whether you hold the *manzaraka* immediately on marrying or later is irrelevant; what counts is how you and your spouse get along." While this emphasizes the primacy of the couple and the quality of married life, Hassanat's third daughter offers a different view as she seeks in marriage first of all the transition to adult autonomy rather than romantic love or conjugality. When the *manzaraka* is planned jointly by a couple, it does indicate a stable and possibly companionate marriage, but the performance itself says something quite different, and, as shown, can be contemplated even in the absence of the husband.

There is clearly an elective affinity among middle-class employment, an ideology of possessive individualism, and a goal of companionate marriage, but the connections are not necessary, and transformations to individualism and companionate marriage do not appear instantly or exclusively. They are on the moral horizon, but they do not dominate the view. The preoccupation in Lombeni with the enactment of weddings, one's own and those of others, remains a dominant social fact (a part of the habitus), and these weddings put a variety of ideas and images into play. The idea of the "happy marriage" is not something I have seen explicitly displayed.

Moreover, the "play with money" is also a *circulation* of money; the bride who receives money at her *manzaraka* hands out money at the *manzaraka* of others. The *manzaraka* functions collectively, rather like a savings group in which the pooling of money circulates. This circulation continues to presuppose and reproduce a social whole.

Manzaraka show the continuing relevance of the social. People continue to gather to produce and celebrate new adult members of the community. Their enactment is a celebration of community and sociality as well as of wealth, ease, pride, and the production of new households.

Nevertheless, the celebrations tend to mystify the increasing economic and social differences between households. *Manzaraka* are extremely costly as well as labour intensive, and many people go into debt or wonder how to display as opulently as their kin and neighbours, at whose *manzaraka* they work hard to produce and serve food, fix up the house, or provide gifts. Yet *manzaraka* are optional, and a few people simply rebel, whether directly out of practical considerations or by way of reformist Islam that frowns on excessive consumption.

I conclude with two limitations of the analysis. First, I have abstracted the celebration of marriages from a much bigger and more complex picture. As I will show in the next chapter, the moral horizons of villagers are characterized by a heterogeneous mix of sentiments, including aspiration, exultation, regret, and unease. There is something necessarily optimistic or intrinsically forward looking about weddings, yet there is tension between the model of extended families (*mraba*) in which adult siblings and their children help each other in enactments like the *manzaraka* and the envy and anxiety generated by the differential incomes and needs of individual households.

It is true that, relative to many other places, and as expressed in the *manzaraka*, Mahorais have been enjoying what one could call a run of moral luck (Williams 1981). Looking back, people can say that their political actions were justified. Just now, for most people the horizons do not seem either immensely distant and unreachable or low and closed in. Large numbers do perform the *manzaraka*; most are able to marry in a way that does not cause them embarrassment or humiliation. The conditions for dignity are present. This is evidently not the case everywhere in the world, and perhaps not for most people. Many anthropologists report shrouded horizons and temporal distortions. In Mayotte itself, life is considerably harder for unofficial migrants from neighbouring islands, who sometimes are wedding guests, sometimes able to marry citizens, and certainly oriented to moral horizons of their own, including sometimes absconding from their spouses once they obtain papers. In sum, I do not wish to equate the idea of moral horizons with naively positive outlooks or circumstances.

Second, the image of horizons needs to be juxtaposed to, or articulated with, an image of fronts. I think here more immediately of weather fronts than of battle fronts (Lambek 2013b), but the point is of moving forces (e.g., financialization, reformist Islam, *laïcité*, racism) that confront or conflict with one another, movements that are likely to lead to clashes of some sort, stormy weather that lowers rather than raises horizons and produces not a fusion of moral horizons but a break, or perhaps a haunting (Grøn n.d, Waldenfels 2011). It may be perverse to end my story of the exuberant and exultant weddings of Mayotte with such weather warnings, but then such perversity is perhaps itself what distinguishes social analysis from ethnographic description or indexes the separation of the moral horizon of the critical observer, potentially one of tragedy, from the open horizon, immediacy, intensity, hopefulness, and comedy of marriage.

12   Present Horizons, 2015

I last visited Mayotte in the summer of 2015, intending simply to collect a final round of observations in order to write a last chapter concerning the community after departmentalization. But from the start, this trip felt different. I was living directly in the home of a "sister" (when we were younger, a stronger avoidance relationship between siblings of the opposite sex was in play). From her terrace one could see across the village and even a patch of the lagoon that was not entirely hidden by an incongruous apartment building newly erected on the ridge. For the first time, I was living in a house with a tile floor, adequate lighting, and Internet service. I felt at home and comfortable, almost on holiday. But most of all, I felt my sixty-five years and the depth of acquaintance and kinship they had enabled. It was my third visit since Tumbu and Mohedja had died; their absence was a shared weight with my siblings, but none of us missed them so acutely any more. Young adults treated me warmly and with respect, unlike the teasing to which I used to be subjected. The most profound feelings I had were with my age mates, especially the men I have known since we were all young. I felt very strongly how moral luck had played a hand in each of our lives, not mine versus theirs collectively, but between each of us as individuals, distributing our respective gains and losses, plans realized and foiled, illnesses suffered or escaped. If I can compare each of these lives with my own, so can I compare them with each other.

This portrait of the community in 2015 orchestrates the voices of a number of inhabitants as they reflect on their current condition and its relation to the past. Although I continue to use pseudonyms, I see this chapter as more explicitly collaborative than preceding ones, reaching an understanding of the present situation by drawing on insights voiced in conversations with me by my peers. Needless to say, I have been selective, and many people I spoke with are not directly represented here.

A major lesson of this book is to distinguish the perspectives of different age cohorts – since their respective historical experiences are different – within a given generation and often even within a given decade. I try to carry this through here. The effect is one captured in the felicitous phrase of German historiographers, "the contemporaneity of the noncontemporaneous." Rather than subsisting independently side by side, the horizons of each age cohort articulate and overlap with those immediately preceding and succeeding them. Each of their attempts to make sense of their condition can involve challenging and implicating the others.

By 2015 social transformation was no longer something eagerly anticipated. Over the past forty years, people had been living a whole series of changes, some incremental and some implemented and then retracted as the French tried various policy measures. It has been hard to keep up with the laws concerning identity papers and marriage, as well as with respect to finance and title to house plots and land. Changes in modes of livelihood, household expenditures, education, health care, habitation, and communications technology have been continuous. These are lived and experienced differently by people of each age cohort. This means that when I asked about the past it did not have the same reference for everyone. Some people remembered living in wattle-and-daub houses or having home births; others could not imagine them.

One change is that the horizons I share with all my interlocutors have increasingly fused, that is, come to overlap, but differently with different age cohorts. Many younger adults now speak French and a few even English; many have spent time living and travelling in Europe; and a few have served in the French army in various parts of the world. Practices like limiting family size or taking out bank loans and topics like atheism or events in the Middle East are now within our common horizon. So is a language or mode of critical reflection on and analysis of historical circumstances and the quality of life in the community today. With older people I share an arc of the horizon of the past, concerning the village as it was, that younger people do not have.

In earlier chapters I described a mix of anticipation and anxiety. By 2015 much of the anticipation had levelled off – full departmentalization had been achieved in 2011 – and people of my age have less to anticipate in any case. To some degree anticipation is replaced by satisfaction. Yet I concluded the last chapter by pointing out that the exuberant performances of the *manzaraka* were insufficient to depict the mood of the community as a whole, that the picture needs to be balanced by attending to other sentiments and to forces that can lower as well as raise horizons. In this chapter I redress the balance with a more comprehensive look at the situation in 2015. Social tension is the main theme.

Despite the differences in historical perspective, what I address are common and broadly voiced concerns, shaped by the structural forces and contradictions, opportunities and obstacles that are present now. The concerns have to do with the nature of family (*mraba*), relations between adult siblings and between mothers and daughters, and relations with migrants. I close with some discussion about religious practice, the changing contextualization of Islam, and the attacks by some reformers on certain local practices, notably spirit possession. As I have shown throughout the book, from within their horizons, people respond to their historical condition in active ways. This condition is shaped in turn by what people can make of and with it.

Many people feel they do not have sufficient money to accomplish their goals of living well. Standards of living have risen; food is expensive; houses are bigger and better furnished and hence cost more to build and maintain; water, electricity, and taxes have to be paid. As in so many parts of the world, there are simply not enough decent jobs to go around. In addition, people live among a tide of unofficial residents – people seeking livelihood, health care, and most of all residence papers in Mayotte and ultimately French citizenship.

Unhappiness is generated less by direct material effects (no one I know is malnourished) than by obstacles to achieving dignity. It is still very much a papaya world, one man affirmed, with "seniors on the bottom and juniors on top" (*maventy ambany, madiniky ambony*), but the phrase is by now insufficient to describe social differentiation. I attend to the effects of differentiation along a number of planes, within both the family and the community, with respect to everyday sociality, expectations of care and mutual assistance, and debates over correct Muslim comportment. Whether or not it is true in practice, there is a discourse concerning loss of solidarity among kin, mistrust, and the rise of selfish individualism. This is partly expressed – and exacerbated – by an increase in the experience of being subject to sorcery and the equally salient experience of being subject to accusations of practising sorcery. Positive models for how to live and how to succeed are offset by a discourse of abandoning or undermining others (i.e., feeling abandoned or undermined) in the rush to get ahead.

This is certainly counterbalanced by attempts at ethical cultivation through religious practice, but Islam itself is articulated in a more individualist fashion than before. There is a critique of ostensibly excessive spending for social celebrations of life-cycle events, while at the same time some people make repeated pilgrimages to Mecca. There is also a heightened discourse about the afterlife that focuses on individual interest rather than the social good. Aspirations for the future in this world have also become more individuated, with an emphasis on moving up the economic ladder, as manifested in consumption patterns, especially the construction of ever larger houses.

Houses are expanding in size and number; many are now two stories, with tile floors, glass windows, indoor plumbing, and modern kitchens. The old two-room houses are referred to as "chicken coops." Houses consume the space that once existed between them, relocating activities that took place outdoors and in relatively public settings indoors to relatively private settings. Some villagers invest in additional houses to rent to people from the metropole, several of whom now live in the village, turning it further from an integrated and inward-focused community of citizens to a neutral residential space of commuters.[1] Streets and alleys have been given names; interestingly, they are not neutral but called after deceased members of the community.

There is a sense that everyday sociality has changed. Many people remarked on how there is less informal visiting between households. Indeed, as houses have grown in size and more activity and leisure take place within the house than in the courtyard, so people are less visible and accessible to one another. Work schedules and commuting also limit sociability. As a result, adults often feel somewhat hurt or else guilty at not spending enough time visiting their kin, not even so much as coming around to say hello in the morning.

My sister Mariam (not the sister with whom I stayed) observed how people used to just drop by and eat and talk together. Now everyone stays in their own house. Neighbours no longer ask each other for green bananas to cook. And people no longer offer each other cooked food when they do drop in. She described this as a very big change – but just then one of her adult daughters arrived from the fields with a whole stalk of bananas and instructed one of the girls to cut off a large hand for Mariam.

Mariam was expanding her own house. Although she has lived there a long time, she recently purchased the plot of fifteen square metres for

8,500 euros from the descendants of the original owner. Previously the municipality (*la mairie*) had granted her and others the space, but then descendants of Hamada (chapter 3) complained that it was their land, and the municipality decided that the residents should purchase their plots from the descendants. Ali, the male descendant, said he couldn't just throw her off, since he was afraid of God. "If you are afraid of God," Mariam retorted, "just let me have it for free" – and she went about her business. Eventually her grown children collected the money for her, sensing the risk that someone could have bought it from under her.

I asked Mariam about the *fatiha* that the *mraba* used to hold annually for Amina, the family ancestress (chapter 3). She said they had recently held a small one, which not all Amina's descendants attended. At the *fatiha* they told Amina that they could no longer continue to do so. They killed a goat and said, "Here is your *fatiha*, may you be well and we too. We cannot afford to do more." So they ended the practice. As in other instances I have described, they did not simply casually or unthinkingly abandon the *fatiha* or the ancestress, but acknowledged the fact to her and to themselves, marking its passing.

The community continues to sponsor some large-scale ceremonies. From time to time, the two parts of Lombeni join forces to invite villages across the island for performances of *Maulida* and the like. One person said this cooperation made life easier; not as much meat or money and not as many cakes are expected from each household to feed the guests. But recent annual *Maulida* exchanged between the two villages (as portrayed in chapter 6) have been poorly attended.

As I described in previous chapters, kinship ceremonies have become partly disembedded from the community as a whole. Parents continue to sponsor weddings and circumcisions for their children, and adult children are responsible for holding *mandeving* for their deceased parents. Sponsorship of the new *manzaraka* has become largely the responsibility of the married couple themselves, replacing the former obligations among members of an age group. The age groups themselves only function sporadically at village-wide events, and there are no longer village chiefs to organize them. Many people are simply not in the village to help out when ceremonies are produced. Nevertheless, most people who are abroad do return home, to the community, to sponsor their ceremonial events.

Indeed, given how many people travel and live elsewhere, it is remarkable how many return. Some say simply that they prefer to live "at home" (*an nakahy*). Others feel the obligation to look after aging parents. Most of those living abroad are saving money to build houses at home. Much of this is unquestioned. As one young woman, a great-granddaughter of Tumbu and Mohedja on vacation from her university studies in France, said, "We have to come back here – that's just the way it is." She added that there are things she appreciates in the village – notably family – and things she doesn't – namely that people mix too much in each other's business. Family is singled out from community, but even family impinges on the individual.

The ceremonies put additional weight on households and raise the question of the *mraba*, the wider kin grouping. As described in chapter 2, the *mraba* are extended families or kin, the range of people who assist each other in sponsoring various social events. In the past, close members within the *mraba* cooperated in such things as land purchase and the cultivation of cash crops; they helped one another in investing in the means of production as well as in labour at peak periods such as the rice harvest or picking ylang ylang flowers. They also participated in the life-cycle events of family members, as indeed they still do. The *mraba*, in effect, refers to the range of practical kin.

There is a widespread sense that kin solidarity is not what it used to be. Most critical is the observation that every household puts its own interests ahead of the interests of the households of siblings. This was expressed in many ways. When I asked one man in his early thirties who the head of his *mraba* was, he replied that there was no longer a head and in fact that *mraba* are a thing of the past; "It is all *la famille* now," he said. Other people did speak of *mraba* and heads, but it is interesting how the French term has been borrowed for the relatively new concept of the nuclear family. This points to the fact that to translate *mraba* as "extended" family is misleading; it is rather that "family" is now retracting to a nuclear form. The very appearance and distinction of the narrow "*famille*" indicates how much broader family was in the recent past. The retraction is frequently experienced as a kind of personal abandonment or betrayal.

This man continued with the bleak observation that there is not a single *mraba* in the village that remains "in order" (*manzary*); each is characterized by internal conflict. He noted that a central factor contributing to conflict is that adult siblings make unequal amounts of money. The richer ones don't want to share or distribute their earnings. The implication is that the poorer relatives resent it.

Two distinct families that I am close to regretted that when their parents died the oldest sister did not step up to assume the role of "mother" of the family. I don't know whether this is just happenstance related to whom I knew well at what stages of their lives,[2] but I think it speaks to a wider sense of insecurity about the fact that adults or married couples look out for themselves and that siblings and their children are now secondary. This is reinforced by the prevalence of personal bank accounts and the monthly bills that each household is faced with – for water, electricity, school supplies, permits, transport, loan repayment, and so on. Taxes for land and house plots are just around the corner as well. Benefits also are directed to individuals, and the elderly now receive state-sponsored care in the form of health visitors almost daily. The ways both the state and the economy single out the individual adult or the married couple strongly shape both the perception and the reality of a kind of individualism.

Land inheritance has become an issue because the government requires transfer of title and imposes taxes on both ownership and inheritance.[3] As Ashiraf, an educated man, explained, the people using land for raising cattle and growing some staples are usually those least able to afford the costs. Land prices have risen enormously, and the mandatory lawyers (who are European) take 20 to 30 per cent of the value at transfer. And so wealthier siblings propose buying out poorer ones. This is understood as a kind of expropriation of nephews and nieces and hence a violation of parenthood. As Salima put it explicitly, "the only father that counts now is the one that gave birth to you; the *baba kely* (father's younger brother) is no longer *baba* (father)." Hence the weakening of sibling solidarity has effects on the next generation.

As prices and taxes continue to rise, more and more land will be expropriated from the local owners, especially the poor. In the meantime, the situation produces tensions within the family. Consider the case of a plot of land purchased in the 1970s by a man, A, on behalf of his full brother, B, who was living elsewhere and sent him the money. The land was put in A's name since he was present, and A and his children made use of it, as did B's daughter. B died first. When A was dying, he reminded his children that the land belonged to B's daughter. They are willing to pass it on to her, but she lacks the money to pay for the transfer. Moreover, it is A's son who grazes both his cattle and the cattle of B's daughter on the land and pays the annual tax. Other people with the means to purchase the land are eyeing the situation.

The sharpening differences in wealth, income, and prospects among kin and between neighbours create envy but also the sense that other people are being either selfish or irresponsible. (By contrast, some young people, like Tumbu's unmarried great-granddaughter, speak of too much intervention by their kin.) In order to sponsor an event like a circumcision or wedding you need help from family, but the problem is that there are so many requests, from so many sides. People have to balance what to give siblings and siblings' children with what is needed to build houses for their own daughters and to hold the rituals of those most closely related to them, as well as what to spend or put aside for such things as automobiles, the pilgrimage to Mecca, medical and curing expenses, or even pleasure trips to Madagascar.

Moussa, in his early fifties, told me repeatedly that kin could not be trusted and only looked out for themselves. You have to have your own children, he said, because only they can be relied upon to look after you. "It's not like in the past when kin helped each other; now everyone just goes after money. Siblings no longer see after each other's children." Moussa could be accused of doing exactly what he accuses others of. He was married with several grown daughters in Lombeni whose houses he was constructing. And yet he had taken not only an Anjouanais second wife in a neighbouring village but also a third wife in Madagascar whom he visited every couple of months. He had children with all three women. His government salary as a night watchman supported this, and by now he even had frequent flyer points on Air Austral. Both his wife in Lombeni and his siblings claimed that Moussa neglected them. For his sisters, the first issue was that he did not drop by to greet them anymore. From his perspective, he probably had little time, even for sufficient sleep. After a life of hard labour, Moussa enjoyed the ability to be generous with his other wives, especially in Madagascar, where the cost of living is much lower. As several people explained, people who are "poor" in Mayotte become "rich" in Madagascar. Polygyny is also a means by which some of the wealth brought in by the French (including the wage and annual increments Moussa received as a watchman on government property) filters through to people outside the formal sector.

Moussa's structural position is that of a man who missed out on a formal French education. But not everyone in his position responded in the same way. Moussa's brother-in-law, Souf, is a few years older than Moussa and also formally uneducated. Souf makes his living in a variety of ways. He is one of the very last to still grow ylang ylang and distil the oil. Once, he wasn't paid after three months' labour on a road crew and since then he does only informal work, like house construction. He spends many hours a day walking between the various sites of labour and finds work in the sun increasingly debilitating. Moussa and Souf each also keep a few head of cattle and goats, and Souf's wife has a small shop. Souf thinks he put the wrong age on his birth certificate, which he made when he got married; he has been told he is too young to receive an old-age pension even though he sees people younger than himself receiving one.

Souf has three full siblings and five maternal half-siblings and says without qualification that he is the head of the *mraba*. When there is trouble among the siblings or any issue to be discussed, he calls them together and they take a decision. Even if they are angry with him, things soon calm down. When he holds an *asa* (ceremony) they immediately come from the next village to help out. He says his nephews and nieces are very reliable; they showed up to help him build his new house. When matters concern the family beyond the sibling set, he says it is his mother's brother (*zama*) who is *chef*. Souf's wife, Salima, adds that cooperation within the *mraba* means collective planning and producing of kinship ceremonies. She was hurt to have been excluded from the wedding planning for one of her brother Moussa's daughters. The *mraba* is also critical for the boy's side in a wedding. A prospective groom could never approach his in-laws alone; people would say, have you no family?

Souf said forcefully that kin should visit each other regularly, make sure they are okay, and help them when they are in need. What concerned him was how this form of sociality would be reproduced. Reflecting that his generation had lost control of the education and moral upbringing of their children, he said to me, "Mayotte is really broken (*rubaka swuf Maore*). Kids go down to the beach for football or music, which is fine, but now there is someone selling liquor there. They sell even to children, to whoever wants to buy. And kids today turn up their noses at food. They won't eat greens and demand meat. In the old days, you ate what was served." He concluded, "They behave like Europeans" but they aren't Europeans" (*kabar ny vazaha fo reo tsy vazaha*). Note the resonance with those young people a generation earlier explicitly performing as European at the wedding parties (chapter 9).

Souf's own children are relatively responsible and respectful. But Salima (in her late forties) reflected on their oldest son, who had moved to France and married there. His wife is not Muslim, and they did not have a Muslim marriage. "Everything she cooks would be *haram*," Salima wryly observed. Phoning between Mayotte and the metropole is cheap, and they call frequently, but when she reaches her daughter-in-law they can only somewhat stiffly ask each other, *"Comment ça va?"* Her son visited briefly with his two older children; the wife did not accompany them but called daily, worried about their welfare. Salima feels as though she has lost this son and set of grandchildren.

Salima's remaining sons spend the school vacation watching animated action shows on their laptop or playing football. It was Ramadan, and she told them how in the past people had to fast even when walking to the fields and cultivating in the hot sun. "Life in the past was tough!" The boys ask her more questions, about what their grandfather planted, and so on. He never relaxed, she said; only on Fridays could he be found in the village. One of the sons then said, "People suffered in the past; they had to live in mud houses." Salima replied, "Back then everyone was equal, everyone had food to eat. It's not like today where everyone looks at others and compares. You had food, you ate. You left for the fields early in the morning and came home late. People were strong then."

As Said, the man whose *dîner-dansant* I described in chapter 9, now in his mid-forties, told me, "The youth are lost." Surprisingly, he used the Arabic word *shabaab* for youth. They are too Westernized and watch too much TV. He says this doesn't help them identify themselves or see their own value. It used to be that a child learned discipline and respect both at home and on the street. But people no longer dare comment on a child's behaviour in public. Today kids simply retort rudely, "I'm not your child" (i.e., mind your own business), thereby illustrating the retraction of the family of which I spoke. Said has given a lot of thought to child-rearing. He says in French, *"Il faut apprendre un enfant de se prendre en charge."*[4] Said keeps his children mostly in the house; the older boy is allowed out, and I have observed him going to the mosque. He looks after his younger siblings when his parents go out. If they are stuck in traffic on the way home, they call him to start cooking dinner. I notice how calm the boy is and how ready to do what he is asked.

There are virtually no more of the bachelor houses that adolescent boys used to construct; they get rooms in their parents' houses now. "We are raising our children like Europeans," says someone. And Salima observes that since young people no longer want houses of earth and thatch, they would demand cement ones that they couldn't build for themselves. A few boys still do build bachelor houses, and parents vary with respect to how they oversee their children.

One evening during Ramadan I went to break the fast at the home of Bwanaidi, a man in his early forties whom I have known since he was a small child. He and his wife, Hidaya, some ten years his junior, are cross-cousins. They are both educated through high school. Bwanaidi is a son of the leading Muslim scholar of the community; he is relatively uninterested in religion but a very smart and enterprising person. At the meal were also his wife's sister and her children and a woman introduced as a friend (*camarade*) from Anjouan and the wife of a villager who was currently in Madagascar to visit a different wife. The "friend" is employed to look after Bwanaidi and Hidaya's children when Hidaya works and to help in household tasks. It is not exactly that kin do not help in childcare; during the meal Hidaya's mother called from France where she and her husband look after Hidaya's younger siblings who are studying there.

Bwanaidi says people are interested now in only two things – making money and building houses. In this, he could include himself. He built a nice house on a plot his father had inherited in town which he rents out for 1,000 euros per month. He has also built two apartments above his own house that he rents to Europeans at 600 and 700 euros monthly. They have hot and cold running water, an air conditioner, and small terraces with an ocean view. On the floor Bwanaidi inhabits there is no such vista. The construction cost for the two apartments was around 60,000 euros. With a contractor, he estimates, it would have been 200,000 euros, but because he worked slowly, buying the materials himself and drawing on craftsmen in the village, he did it for much less. He financed the house from his salary and bank loans.

Bwanaidi told me that many people buy their cars on credit. He recently lowered his monthly credit allowance in order to temper his spending. Hidaya and Bwanaidi have separate bank accounts. She buys what she wants from hers, and he expects her to share in household expenses, like electricity. He takes care of food purchases. He estimates that they spend 350 euros per month on shopping and, every two months, 250 euros for electricity and 100 euros for water.

Bwanaidi is one of the village intellectuals. At one time he considered writing a village history. When I ask them to reflect on changes, both Bwanaidi and Hidaya emphasize the improvement in health care. In the past women died in childbirth, and there was high infant mortality. Hidaya remembers as a child seeing her mother in a very long and painful labour; when the baby emerged, it was dead. She had been looking forward to a younger sibling. Local healing was inadequate. Bwanaidi recalled a memory of his grandmother possessed by a spirit saying a client would get well just as she died in the very next room. They did not know about several of the healing practices I recorded in the 1970s.

Hidaya adds forcefully that in the past women were little more than slaves. She acknowledges that they owned their houses but says they were dependent on men and deferred to them, afraid to criticize their husbands for fear they would leave. I don't think this view is typical of women even of her cohort, but it does show the effects of a certain kind of discursive shift. In my view she misreads women's condition or how they felt in the past, but she makes a point when she observes that, "Women are better off now because we can work [i.e., for a wage]." One factor, I think, as expressed also in the changing performances at weddings, is that women no longer have to rely on their sexuality as a major resource,

Unlike most people I spoke with, Hidaya thinks there is more equality within the community now than before. She remembers her grandfather, Malidy Muthary (chapters 3 and 4) as rich. He controlled the family money. At the end of Ramadan, he would hand out new clothing to all his children and grandchildren. He was very generous, but the money was all in his hands. He was also bossy and harsh (*mashiaka*). As village chief, he could forbid certain marriages. She remembers how when one young woman wanted to marry an outsider with a reputation for violence, Malidy Muthary banged the drum and called the village to a meeting to declare the man inadmissible. If she wanted to marry him, the young woman would have to follow him elsewhere. In the end, she didn't marry him.[5]

Bwanaidi's widowed father is bedridden in his own house. He receives daily care from a government nurse. A kinswoman lives there and prepares his meals.[6] Bwanaidi oversees the care, visits daily, finances the medical expenses, and does his father's laundry. He said that when his father first fell sick everyone crowded in to pay respects, but as the illness lingered no one offered to help. Although Bwanaidi considers the *mraba* still very important, in this instance he agrees with Moussa that people have become dependent on immediate lineal kin to the exclusion of lateral ones.

Although he jokes that he thinks about money all the time, Bwanaidi describes himself as relaxed and happy. "I have work, three houses, four sons, a daughter, and a wife; what more could I want?"

Bwanaidi's cousin (his father's sister's son) Ismail also says he feels very good about himself. But his circumstances are quite different. A few years older than Bwanaidi, Ismail had no formal education. He and his wife, who was also from Lombeni, lived for many years working and cultivating in a small town in La Réunion. He returned to Mayotte in 2006 to be close to his mother, who was then in decline. His wife said they wouldn't be able to support the kids in Lombeni and stayed with them in Réunion. Ismail got busy, planting manioc and bananas and raising cattle, and finally convinced her to join him. She said she and the children would visit, to which he replied he would pay only for one-way tickets. They came, and she approved of his efforts and agreed to stay. He paid for a container to ship her goods home. In the meantime, he got what he considered a good job, as a watchman for government buildings.

Ismail has thirteen children. He says people used to tell him he would be poor for having so many kids, but he is rich! He is rich from his children, he declares; they provide him with food and other comforts. He works as a mason on their houses but otherwise doesn't support them. A son in the army will get retirement soon, providing more financial assistance. He has ten grandchildren; they call him *shef*, especially when he brings them candy. As we talk he is fasting the extra days after Ramadan (*shteti*). He says it offsets the sins of his youth when he drank and slept around. He was going fishing that night and, for the following day, was arranging the rental of two buses to transport women from the village to the wedding of one of his sons across the island.

Interestingly, Sakina, whom we met in chapter 10 also living in Réunion and now back in Lombeni, made precisely the opposite argument to Ismail, saying she stopped at four children because she was poor. She calculated the costs of paying for her children's education. Sakina and Ismail are cousins and are approximately the same age. Sakina is undoubtedly wealthier in sheer monetary terms than Ismail, and her perception is quite different; she has wider horizons with respect to both her economic activities (as an international trader and now owner of a large shop) and the education of her children. Moreover, Sakina also helped kin who were not her biological offspring. Both are "rich in people."

While some young people like Souf and Salima's son settle in the metropole, many return. They then must readjust to village life and the expectations of their parents and peers. Most settle back quite easily, but others live lives their parents cannot fully appreciate.

Ratuya married a man from Mayotte in France but eventually returned home. I encounter Ratuya one day at her mother Hassanat's
(chapter 11) and she suggests I visit her own house, on the opposite flank of the village. She leads me through what is essentially a
"French" house, spacious and well laid out, with a bathroom off the
main bedroom and another for the children and guests. Each has a
toilet, shower, and tub, and there is a washing machine. They are
repeating the same plan on the second floor and plan to move there
and rent out the lower floor. She asks her children what they want
for dinner and prepares a *gratin* of thin slices of potato laced with
cheese and cream baked in the oven. She makes as well a local *gulu-
gulu* cake, with pumpkin and flour, using a mixer. She has a freezer
stocked with chicken nuggets and hunks of beef. She leaves her children alone when she goes to work; it is safer for the youngest to be
there than at Hassanat's, where he could run into the street, she says.
They watch TV or play Internet games.

Ratuya appears very much at ease with her children. She had two
early in the marriage and then stopped but eventually wanted and had
a third. She says she will have no more. She speaks of needing two
salaries and hopes to move up in her profession. She converses with
her children mostly in French and agrees with my observation that she
is raising them in European rather than local fashion.

Ratuya is intelligent and charming and speaks with remarkable
frankness. She is glad her house is at some distance from Hassanat's;
while they were building it, she lived at her mother's, which she found
extremely difficult. Ratuya originally returned to Mayotte at Hassanat's
insistence. It was meant to be a long vacation, but she found a job and
decided to stay. Her husband was a parachutist in the army and on assignment for the time she was to be in Mayotte. He was angry at her
decision and didn't want to return to Mayotte. He followed eventually
but took a long time to adjust; he gave up an excellent career, and they
had owned a nice house in France. But most of all he complained that
Hassanat interfered too much and that Ratuya listened to her.

The husband worked first as a truck driver but rapidly rose to become a manager at the state construction corporation, with skills that
helped him finish the house. Ratuya herself is in her last year of a
demanding nursing program after having taken some years off in
France. She told me she was inspired to become a nurse after seeing
the terrible treatment her father received as he was dying of cancer
when she was an adolescent; she thought she could do better. During

vacation she works two days on and two days off at the main hospital. Ratuya and her husband both have cars and commute to work.

Hassanat is an active spirit medium. Ratuya said that as a child she never liked the spirits and would leave the house whenever her mother was possessed. Now she acknowledges the spirits when they rise and agrees to do what they ask her – for example, to give certain herbal medicines to her children – but then she ignores their advice. Unlike her sisters, she has not inherited any spirits. To my surprise, however, she adds that her husband does have a *patros* (Mahorais spirit), passed on from his father, who was also an active healer. One day in France she found him rigid and tried to call an ambulance until he stopped her. The *patros* never rises in public to dance but does come to warn her when someone doesn't like her or is saying bad things about her. She does pay attention to this.

Ratuya is, as she says, quite distant from her mother in *mentalité*. She tries not to spend too much time at her mother's; when they disagree, she doesn't get angry but just says it is time to go back to her house. There they live the life of a French nuclear family. Nevertheless, Ratuya decided that the family should return to live in Lombeni, and she does visit her mother regularly and shows her respect and affection.[7]

Whereas in the past everyone wanted large numbers of children, there are now many women like Ratuya and Sakina who limit the number. Other women still think differently. A woman with a baby and two very young children in tow asserted without any prompting from me that someone had challenged her for having too many kids and she had replied that she wanted twenty! Men also continue to have large numbers of children, whether for reasons of support, as Moussa and Ismail assert, or simply because of the availability of Comoran and Malagasy women who want children for their own reasons. People continue to pity me for having only two children. The ideal is to have kin around for pleasure and to help look after you. Much is expected of children; as one man put it, thinking of his own responsibilities, there is no one to whom one owes more than one's parents, not even one's children.

Women today all want to marry and have children but not until after they complete the *bac* or a higher degree. They say they have fewer children because they want to work. There is a village nursery school, and some children are watched during the day by grandparents, but as with Hidaya, occasionally a care giver is hired.

While everyone marries by means of the Muslim confirmation (*kufungia*), most delay civil marriage because benefits are higher if women are classified as single mothers and also because divorce is difficult and expensive. Salima says people postpone civil marriage as late as they can. She and Souf did it only when they needed the marriage certificate in order to establish family names, necessary for passports. Children now take the same family name as their father, "like Europeans."[8]

Among people for whom the *mraba* remains strong there has been pressure to continue cross-cousin marriages. But people say that when marriages are imposed, they end up in trouble because the young people are in love with someone else or simply prefer their freedom. Pre-marital liaisons are common, but some young women remain careful to retain their virginity, and a few men who are Muslim reformers think that wedlock is the only appropriate outlet for sexual release.

Both the demographic pattern and the changing nature of marriage are heavily influenced by state policy, especially with respect to immigration. As part of France and the EU, Mayotte attracts large numbers of migrants. Most arrive without papers, and when they are caught they are sent back home. This causes great hardship on the migrants but is not very effective. One man from Anjouan whom I know returned some twenty-four hours after he was deported.[9]

There are means by which the *clandéstins* can acquire residence permits (*séjours*) and eventually apply for citizenship. The best is to marry a citizen or give birth with one. Anyone born on Mayotte has, according to the French constitution, the *droit du sol*, the right first to stay and then to apply for French nationality when they come of age. Children born in Mayotte cannot be expelled, and so their parents are not either. If parents of a child born in Mayotte are non-citizens, they get a provisional identity card (*carte d'identité provisoire*) until the child is eligible for citizenship. Once the child achieves it, the parents can apply. Non-citizens having offspring with citizens receive a *séjour* for one year, renewable; after three years, they have the right to a ten-year *séjour*, and after three more years they can apply for citizenship. Thus there is both *droit du sol* – regarding birth – and *droit du sang* for the parents. This is how people explained things to me; it is true in outline, but the details change according to government decree, especially with respect to procedures concerning civil and customary marriage and ascriptions of paternity (Blanchy and Moatty 2012).

The experience of Safy is instructive for the way changing political conditions impact local marriage. After three unsuccessful Muslim marriages with Mahorais men, Safy married someone from Ngazidja (Grande Comore) who was without papers. He convinced her, against her parents' and siblings' advice, to have a newly instituted civil marriage at the city hall. This is a marriage from which divorce is not easy, but it enabled him to acquire a residence permit. It was a happy marriage; the husband worked in town and supported the family, including Safy's children by previous husbands. They had two children together, and as a result, after some years, the husband was able to acquire French citizenship. One day Safy woke to find he had absconded with the two children to mainland France. Legally, she cannot remarry, while, people speculated, the husband is likely preparing a customary *grand mariage* to another Ngazidjan, something to which every Ngazidjan aspires and which was probably in his plans for years as he bided his time until he gained French citizenship.

Even though French law has now forbidden polygyny in principle, in Muslim practice it remains easy. What is forbidden from the local perspective is to have children outside wedlock. And so male citizens take migrant women as additional wives, whether or not they have registered their first marriages civilly. Various permutations are possible, and there is a double standard. It was something of a scandal when an older village woman married a young Malagasy man, as "Everyone knows the immigrants do this not out of love but for practical reasons." And yet when local men marry young migrant women it is sometimes described as seeking *"l'aire fraiche"* (fresh air).

For many years, migrants have established solid social relations with villagers. But as numbers increase, the resources for reciprocity become increasingly strained. I started hearing how migrants couldn't be trusted. You would hire them to look after your cattle or your fishing boat, and before you knew it, they had disappeared. Some of this was undoubtedly true, the migrants often acting out of desperation. And conversely there were residents who exploited the immigrants. But the larger point is that the growing crowding and insecurity have generated a moral crisis in which one can no longer fulfil one's obligations as host, guest, kin, citizen, or pious Muslim. One way to respond is to conclude that the other is not worthy of mutual recognition. The situation resembles what is taking place in Europe, but here it is all the more immediate and painful as, until recently, migrants and citizens have shared culturally much more with one another than members of either group shared with the metropolitan French.[10] Despite the tensions, there are also very good social relations between many migrants and people born in the village. Migrants are treated politely when they come to rent the older houses or seek work or marriage partners. I saw

Hassanat show great courtesy to a suitor whom she had no intention of marrying.

Is life in 2015 better or worse than it was forty years earlier? This is not for me to decide, and I do not want to force a teleology on history or to moralize the story. There have been some exciting developments, and many people have explored new opportunities and come to feel very good about themselves. The moral horizons are open rather than closed. But it is also true that when I asked various people to reflect on whether "the past" or "the present" was better, and bearing in mind that "the past" is a deictic term, depending on age and memory, I often heard a common refrain, namely that while material conditions have improved, social relations have deteriorated; that the quality of social life has eroded.

People say that today there is less illness and more medical care. Infant mortality has declined; some pests and diseases are gone and there are no longer seasons of hunger. But some people recognize a higher quality of material conditions in the past. One man, a bit older than me, put it this way: "Today is good for young people, they have lots of things. But the past was better for us [his generation]. We planted and harvested, carried the rice home, husked and cooked it, went to sleep. Now there are so many distractions and things to attend to – papers, identity cards, passports, tax. Everyone needs cars, new houses. When I was young, fish were sold down on the beach in piles, not by kilo. Big fish! You could grill breadfruit and eat your fish. I used to carry big fish to sell in inland villages. We would walk. *Before we were satisfied.*

The past has gone. But it was better."

As I sat with my age mate Abdallah, one of the most generous people I know, he called out to a woman passing by and gave her some fish he had caught the night before. Her deceased father, he explained, had been his good friend, and he thinks of her as a daughter. He said sarcastically, "Oh, the present is much better! Back then you had to work to eat; now you can just steal." In fact, "The past was better; you had what you earned." He said that over the last few years he has lost twenty cows to theft as well as a motorcycle. He is happy fishing and cultivating and was unhappy during the years his wife insisted they live in Réunion to collect benefits for their children.

Another older man adumbrated other concerns. "People today don't listen to each other. In the past, people would listen respectfully and reach consensus. People used to treat each other with courtesy (*ishima*); now everyone thinks he is smarter than the next. A community needs respect in order to work. The old people are dead and people don't listen to us [his generation]. There is also more theft now; if I leave my bag outside the mosque, it will be gone by the time I finish." He said all this very thoughtfully, not bitterly or resentfully. And he concluded by mentioning the violence elsewhere in the world they now hear about from the news.

Men in their forties waxed less romantic about the subsistence economy and generally contrasted material improvements with social decline. Ali, who has lived for a time in France, made an observation that I often heard – namely, that the solidarity and mutual aid that characterized the past have been replaced by *individualisme*. He added that they haven't seen the results they hoped for by sending children to study at higher levels in the metropole; they return and can't find jobs. There are simply too many of them. On the other hand, when he was young, access to food, health care, and housing was nil. Moreover, there was more jealousy in the past (here presumably the period called in chapter 8 the papaya world); now everyone can have a nice house. He concluded that, all things considered, life is better now; children have access to both French and Muslim education and there is better nutrition.

Abudu spoke in the same vein. Before, there was not much hypertension or diabetes, and people ate only "natural products." But overall, health is better now, as are housing and education. The drawbacks are that today it is *chacun pour soi*. And life takes place inside houses, in private. The custom where a group of men would go from each other's house to house to eat has disappeared.

Ashiraf said that society has become *très égoiste*, with every household thinking of its own economic well-being at the expense of its neighbours. People are caught up in social expectations, and everyone wants something bigger than the next person's.

It is notable how many European words – individualism, *chacun pour soi*, egoism – enter these remarks, as if modernity cannot be described without its own discourse.

A central theme that emerges in these conversations is that the strong expectation of kin solidarity regularly leads to disappointment. People's attention is dispersed, their needs and obligations are multiple, and they cannot care equally for everyone. In a local idiom, some of the experience of disappointment is phrased as sorcery. One successful man in his thirties who lived for a decade in France said in one breath that he did not believe in sorcery and in the next that the young people who do the best are the ones who escape the community so that they are not pulled down by the envy, meddling, and sorcery of others. "Sorcery" is more than an idiom.[11] There were intense and mutual accusations within several *mraba*, very painful to those people subject to attack but equally to those subject to accusation, and all the more painful for being so close to home. Because of their intimate nature I will not describe particular accusations here; suffice it to say that they cause a lot of damage, even to the extent that some people who consider themselves victims of sorcery move away. One of the most elaborate houses in the village stood empty because the owners had fled what they considered sorcery conducted by close kin against them.[12]

What then is the condition of Islam in the village in 2015? How has it met the challenges of French education and the changing mode of life? And how has it changed its relationship to spirit possession?

Islam remains a unifying force and in some respects a form of collective political identity. Although Christian missionaries have visited and even resided in Lombeni, no one has converted.[13] One day after Friday prayer I observed a young man sporting a Bedouin kuffiyeh (head covering). I joked that he had become Arab. He replied seriously, "We all are; we are all Muslims." I said, "But you are French now," to which he responded, *"Farantsa papier"* (France on paper).

Yet, while there was always some diversity in Muslim practice, there is now a broader range of modes of being Muslim. For one thing, there is a distinction between "belief" and practice that was not manifest in the past. The concept of "belief" implies doubt (Pouillon 1982), and it implies alternatives. People are now faced with the alternative of scientific reason on the one side and challenges to their practice from reformist Islam on the other.

Ashiraf, a scientist in his late forties who prays regularly, explained that Islam is not only or mainly a matter of belief (*kuamin*) but of practice. The reason people don't abandon Islam is that, whether or not they believe, Islam is their way of life, manifested in habits of dress, talking, eating, and so on. I imagine this was his own situation, as a religious sceptic who acknowledged that his life was shaped by such practice.[14] Moreover, he was concerned to be a good citizen, engaging in the forms of sociality which, as I argued in chapter 6, are indissociably Islamic, and to preserve the form of life.

When I asked another assimilated villager, Ratuya, whether she was Muslim, her first response was to say *"faux musulman"* (false Muslim). Her criterion was also practice; she had not prayed all week. And yet she was fasting for Ramadan and so concluded she was a Muslim after all. But she also had the criterion of belief in mind. She described her husband, who was fasting as well, as an atheist. This was the first time I heard the word used; the concept is not only expressible now but possible to consider without immediate moral condemnation.

Atheism remains a rarity; most people of intellectual disposition are fully devoted Muslims and able to rationalize the relations of science and religion. In Lombeni as a whole there is a continuous and enthusiastic interest in Islam. It is evident in the fact that the village hosts three teachers (*ustad*), two Grande Comorans and the third a village son, Abdou, aged around forty, who has returned from study in Egypt and France. It is evident also in the institution of the *majlis* (religious gathering). At the one I attended, organized by Abdou, rows of chairs were laid out one evening in the open air and invited speakers took turns giving forceful speeches that seemed to be about how to live a good Muslim life rather than about more formal matters of bodily discipline. About thirty people attended and listened seriously.

There is broad discussion about correct practice. Abdou is critical of practices endorsed by his father, formerly a leading *fundi* of the community. He contrasts what he calls (correct) *Sunnite* to local *Sufite* practice and frowns upon singing in the mosque. He left after nightly prayers to avoid the *tarawih* that is sung there during Ramadan. Nevertheless, Abdou operates in a spirit of tactful conversation and gentle correction, and he is adamant that he is not *Wahhabi*.

A somewhat different perspective comes from what is called *jaula*, a proselytizing movement of *Tablighi Jamaat* that has been present in Mayotte for several decades. A significant minority of villagers have been influenced, some simply with respect to their personal conduct while others are openly critical of kin and neighbours.[15] This movement of purification is not opposed to Sufi practices per se but does hinge on a critique of innovation (*bid'a*); in particular, adherents condemn the production of large feasts and public performances of *Maulida* and related musical forms. The ostensible return to the past is actually individualist, concerned about personal salvation and encouraging others to attend to their personal salvation. This is quite different from the joyous communion found in the *Daira* circle or the *Mulidy* dance line (*figure 12.1*).

In fact, feasting and musical performance remain very popular. Especially popular is perhaps the most innovative of the musical forms, the *Deba*, performed by young women. The television station to which most sets remain tuned has non-stop performances of all the musical

Figure 12.1 A *Mulidy*, c. 2005. The *Mulidy* is still very popular. Young men dance, gracefully extending their bodies. The musicians and singers face them while other adepts stand behind and join in. During these years striped scarfs were a popular piece of dress but not worn outside the *Mulidy*.

varieties, most often the *Deba*. And the *Deba* is being promoted as a kind of icon of "authentic" Mahorais culture.

If some people are pulled towards a more European style of life and others to an ostensibly purer form of Islam, the majority remain self-consciously committed to the mode of Islam that characterized the lives of their parents and grandparents. This is of course not static (it acknowledges innovation), and in fact people can draw on contemporary circumstances to enhance their practice. I illustrate by means of two men, the second educated in the French system and the first not, but both devoted to local forms of practice.

Sula, a man of my age, says he has gone to Mecca seven times, three times with his wife. The price of the trip has risen to 3,000 euros but he has managed it from his salary as a guard. Sula is a lively person, gregarious and full of jokes. He emphasizes that he is not among the reformists. For him it is the transcendent experience that is central to his identification with Islam.

Sula recounted some of his misadventures on *hajj*. Once he managed to get right up and touch the *Kaaba*. But he was crushed against it and thought he would die until he found himself pushed up in the air over the people crowding in. He has never again tried to get near it. Another year, together with two fellow villagers, he decided to go pray at 2:00 a.m. During prayer Sula realized he had forgotten his money belt in the toilet. Amazingly, it was still there; no one using the facility had spotted it. Sula repeats what attracts him to Mecca. "I really love it, because there are no distractions and everything is focused on the Qur'an."

Along with other men his age, Sula attends regular lessons offered by one of the Grande Comoran *fundi*s. Of the reformers, he says they are always complaining about innovations, like recital of the *Barzanji* and so forth. "But cars and airplanes are innovations too. If Mohammed were alive today he would drive a car, not ride a camel. There is nothing wrong with innovation."

Abudu, the son of a strong traditionalist and himself a school teacher, has reflected deeply on Islam and its place in contemporary society. He asserts that Islam is fundamentally tolerant. Hence it is difficult to accept the hardline positions. "After the original *jihad* (propagation), Islam becomes a matter of *jihad avec toi-même*, a struggle with yourself. You have to discipline yourself" (*être le gendarme de toi-même*.) Abudu is aware of international events. He says violence is not Islamic, nor is the drug money that extremists pay for weapons with. No one in the village would disagree.

We discuss the pull between being French on the one side and *musulman* on the other. He illustrates by placing three glasses on the table. On one side is religion, Islam, fundamentalists; on the other side is *laïcité*, the constitution, the laws of the republic. Between these poles is *le Mahorais*, the person, with his/her traditions, life, heritage.

Abudu asserts that he is a practising Muslim and not tempted by atheism. He argues that, "We should fall into neither fundamentalism nor unbelief; that is, we should be in this respect as people were before." He explains that "*Maulida* comes from the Arabic word *walid* – *enfant, né, naissance* (child, born, birth). It is performed to celebrate Mohammed's birth. The *Barzanji* is the biography of the Prophet's life, from the womb to death. People who call it *haram* are mistaken; it is *normale* to want to understand the life of the Prophet. The point is to

read or recite it; what is forbidden is only to venerate it." As for singing, "when the Prophet arrived in Medina from Mecca he was greeted
with song. If singing were forbidden, he would have told them to stop.
And we should remember there was poetry at that time." He adds that
Sufi dances help attract people to the mosques and even provide an
alternative to drinking.

Unlike Sula, who happens to be Abudu's father-in-law, Abudu expresses
little interest in going on the *hajj*. His mode of attachment is more cerebral,
and his defence of "tradition" is expressed in a modernist idiom. He says
that only God has no beginning. Everything else has. And he thinks that
we are slowly discovering the convergence between Islam and science.

One target of the reformers is spirit possession. Along this front there
has been conflict in families where young reformers have turned against
the possession activities of their parents. It is not that they do not "believe" in spirits or can't acknowledge that their elders are possessed,
but rather that they consider possession a sinful activity for which they
will suffer after death. This entails a more vivid picture of the afterlife
than previously and it calls for intervention.

Reformers agree that sorcery and spirits exist but insist that when
present spirits be removed by means of prayer. One former spirit medium effected this by her own concerted efforts and soon was able to
sit calmly without temptation of becoming possessed even when she
heard the music of a spirit ceremony. While she minds her own business, some reformers do not.

Asmina Malidy's younger brother, Ismail, was the first to confide
that Asmina had become somewhat crazy (*sera*) and quite paranoid.
He reflected that his sister's problems may have begun when her son,
Mahamudu, threw away the clothing belonging to the spirits who possessed her. By chance, a day later Mahamudu accosted me. He had the
full beard of a serious reformer and an aggressive tone. Before I could
speak, he explained that in the past, before it was translated, people
didn't know the meaning of what was in the Qur'an. It was customary to ask help from spirits. But now, people who meddle in matters
concerning spirits or ask their help are punished by God. That is why
one of the *fundi*s in the village was lying ill and why Mahamudu's own
father had a stroke. You can be punished in this world, as these people
evidently are, and also in the next.

Mahamudu said he threw his father's amulets and copy of the *badry*
prayer book into the sea. His father wants to live with him (his parents

are long divorced) so he has to accept it; Mahamudu won't have a *badry* in his house. "The *badry* [prayer recited to turn back aggression onto perpetrators and recited especially at circumcisions] is not Islam! It mixes things from God and from *shetwan* [devils, false temptation]." God divided Islam from what is *shetwan*; things fall exclusively into one sphere or the other and "spirits" (*lulu*) are *shetwan*.

Mahamudu confirmed that Asmina threw out her spirit's accoutrements at his request but said she couldn't maintain the restrictions (*fady*) and remained attracted to the spirits – and so she was seized by them and shifts between angry outbursts and paranoid reclusion. The only way she will improve, said Mahamudu, is to undertake another Qur'anic cure – and this time stick to the restrictions.[16]

No one I talked to agreed fully with Mahamudu's interpretation or mode of approach. The Muslim scholars attributed the father's stroke to high blood pressure. Asmina's case was less clear. One man thought her condition could have been brought on by her excessive habit of taking snuff. A woman suggested that Asmina had become crazy long before Mahamudu became a reformer. Another person said that after the ritual to remove the spirits, Asmina and her husband returned to the beach, retrieved the red chicken that had been given to the spirits in compensation, and ate it themselves.

A possession healer provided more detail. Asmina's problems arose because she let her son throw out her spirit implements. These included an ebony staff (*tunguzu*) with three bands of silver that had originally belonged to her father, from whom she inherited it along with the spirit who had possessed him. (This was the first I heard that the eminent Malidy Muthary himself had been host to a spirit. The spirit never announced his name in Malidy Muthary, but his identity is clear from the specific food taboos the various hosts share.) Someone recovered the staff at low tide and brought it to a neighbour, also a medium, who cleaned it and returned it to Asmina's brother, Ismail, who is host to the spirit as well.

In another family, a young man attracted to reformist ideas found himself incapacitated with guilt when his mother, an active spirit medium, died suddenly. He said he felt terribly angry with himself for not having forced her to stop before it was too late and grieved that she would suffer in hell. In order to offset her punishment, after his mother's death he burned the spirits' clothing and some 800 euros she had received from her curing activities. The act angered the spirits, who harassed the young man in his dreams and prevented him from marrying.

More directly than Asmina's, the case illustrates how conflict is not merely intellectual but profoundly ethical. And like hers, it manifests not only abstractly, or in argument, but viscerally and emotionally. Spirits retaliate. The young man manifests in his embodied condition the very opposition between possession and reformist Islam, and with much more depth and consequence than did Athimary when the spirit possessing her choked on the Qur'an (chapter 7).

It is evident that the main challenge to possession comes not from European "modernity," at least not directly, but from changing currents within Islam. Some mediums told me they were reluctant to perform in public for fear of criticism. I cannot judge whether possession is in decline as I was present in 2015 during Ramadan, when possession is always absent, but I think it remains active.[17]

My view of Islam in 2015 is coloured by Ramadan, a time of intensified bodily discipline and heightened Muslim self-consciousness. The celebration of *Idy* (*Eid al-Fitr*) at its conclusion proved a day of collective effervescence. No one went to work and the streets were clogged with parked cars. In the morning, men and boys attended the mosque while most women professed to be too busy, sweeping, changing bedsheets, and preparing festive meals. In the afternoon, it was the turn of the girls and women to perform the *Deba* under an awning set up adjacent to the mosque. Kin visited each other and ate or received currently fashionable baked goods (samosas and filo rolls at Amina's, cake and waffles at Mariam's). People shook hands, looked each other in the eye, and wished each other well in Arabic. One woman said to her sister's daughters, "May you find good husbands and love each other."

The good feeling on this day offsets much of what I said above. Invitations among kin to share the nightly meal during Ramadan and dropping in at *Idy* indicate the continued salience of the *mraba*. The spirit of community was evident at all levels, from the prayers in the mosque, freshly painted in blue and pink, to performance of the *Deba* and the greetings people gave each other. It was a day of happiness, and a day to wish happiness to others, with a focus on children.

13 Summation: Mariam's Mirror

In 2015 my sister Mariam confessed that when I first arrived forty years earlier, she dreamt I had a mirror and was going to use it to steal her liver (*haty*; equivalent to "heart" or "soul"). She spoke to her father, but Tumbu only laughed. He said that God had brought them a new son and they accepted it.

Mariam was right in at least two respects. First, my presence, questions, and actions did serve as a mirror, provoking reflection on the part of residents of Lombeni. Often I was not even aware of it; once in the 1990s a young man came up to me and said in French, "*Monsieur, vous avez marquez ma jeunesse* (you made an impression on my youth)." Without exaggerating my significance, the point is that my presence indexed a period of historical change, and I no doubt served for some people as a kind of foil against which they could reflect on their own changing ideas, circumstances, and opportunities.

Marquer is a verb one could play with, as it also means to note, show, celebrate, score, emphasize, and perhaps most to the point, to *write down*. So maybe he was simply saying, "You recorded my youth." This is more in line with the concern that Mariam was expressing, and the second respect in which she was right. One of its results is this book. I did attempt to take something of what was their life. But what I took, as in a mirror, is only a reflection, not the substance; like an ultrasound, this is an image, not the live organ itself. Mariam and the young man have gone on to live their lives irrespective of what I was writing.

My application of the mirror raises two kinds of questions. One is ethical – are my actions theft or have I accepted and do I pass on a gift? Naturally, I like to think I have received rather than stolen and that what I pass on remains theirs. A further ethical point, and one I cannot fully resolve, is whether I have the right to circulate what I have taken or been given. How much can one disclose and when does disclosure become exposure? Is it right to use pseudonyms; conversely, perhaps I have not sufficiently disguised identities? To some degree Mariam is correct that my acts (those of any ethnographer) are a kind of betrayal.

These concerns must be balanced with consideration of the second kind of question raised by the mirror. This is epistemological – how accurately does my mirror reflect, with what degree of clarity or with what distortion? Insofar as my account is truthful, is it a truth of correspondence or coherence? I like to think that the truth the book offers is one of both reasonable correspondence (full correspondence is impossible), as correspondent or accurate as my *techne* can make it, and reasonable coherence (full coherence is an ideal), as coherent as my art and sensibility can make it. There is the matter both of doing justice to people and events and of enabling the truth to disclose itself.

Beyond the reflection or the return (parallel concepts!) stands the larger question of grace – the graciousness of Tumbu and Mohedja, and of the entire community, and whatever insight or illumination may grace this account of their life.[1]

Tumbu's response to Mariam illustrates a central message of this book. People in Mayotte were unafraid, open to new horizons. Circumstances and events are not mere givens, impositions mutely assumed, but to be evaluated, accepted, and acknowledged. People ascribe meaning to circumstances and weave them into their own projects, whether for enlarging a family or for some broader end like becoming French as well as Mahorais.

The course of history is unpredictable, but it is neither random nor blind. As I have emphasized throughout, history takes place in Lombeni with a lively consciousness on the part of each adult cohort with respect to what counts in the present, what is setting along the horizon of the past, and what is rising on the horizon of the future. This is not to say that people always operate with specific long-term goals or plans in mind but rather that they are engaged with the world, in acknowledgment of their commitments, and open to new possibilities.

When I asked people to reflect on the past and present, as described in chapter 12, perhaps the simplest response was also the wisest. "*Taluha, taluha,*" Fatima, a woman in her late seventies said in 2015, "the past is the past." ("Then was then and now is now.") Fatima is a daughter of the woman with the broken hip whose joking with me I describe in chapter 2 and someone whose devotion to Islam I have recounted elsewhere (Lambek 1993: 156–9). In 2015 she lived in quarters within her daughter's well-constructed house and was visited several times a week by a nurse practitioner who attended to her needs. Her material comforts could not have been more different from her mother's. But what Fatima meant is that each period should be understood in its own terms; the past is not to be judged by the values or conditions of the present, relative to it. That is part of the method behind this book, allowing each period to be grasped in its synchronicity, without retrospective judgment. Yet I also emphasize that any given present has historical horizons; at each period, people orient themselves with respect to past and future.

In fact, there was considerable consistency in what people said across these periods. Recall the remark I quote in chapter 7 from a young man who explained in 1975 that people did not want to trade their practices for European ones but add them together; Europeans would have only their culture, but the Mahorais would have both Islam *and* European know-how. I heard this again in 2015, and it is exemplified in the combination of the stately and joyous Muslim procession of the *manzaraka* and the display of money and consumer goods. It is exemplified as well in the conjunction of the powerful *shigoma* or the erotic shaking the buttocks dances *and* the *dîner-dansant*. The logic is one of "both/and" rather than "either/or." This logic was evident already in the long-standing articulation of Islam with spirit possession. It manifests in a confident, assertive, and open stance, attentive to equality and dignity.

All along, people have known that the rights to achieve the benefits of European citizenship and to be treated as coevals are only just. There was never any shame associated with making political demands or taking state benefits. It is evident that many of the material goods and affordances wished for have been achieved and also that villagers are now in several important senses the social equals of their former colonizers and exploiters; indeed, in some respects they have become one with them. At the same time, there is serious environmental degradation; greater anxiety concerning jobs, goods, and money than forty years earlier; and most saliently, the moral uneasiness generated by the massive influx of migrants – the privileged, occasionally racist metropolitans and especially the poor and vulnerable from neighbouring islands who closely resemble Mahorais in many respects and yet do not share the benefits of citizenship.

An ethnographic history may resemble a chronicle, but it is not a fully consistent or continuous narrative with a plot or ending. Nor is it designed to reach a conclusion. Throughout the book my intention has been *not* to prioritize a master narrative of a single "great transformation." There have been many developments since the Mahorais first voted to remain part of France, some welcome (to most people) and some unwelcome (to many people), some expected and some unexpected; but I do not want either to force a teleology on history or to moralize the story. Nor can I predict how horizons will shift next. The unique experiment in postcoloniality that Mayotte has become remains open.

What has changed in forty years? What has remained continuous? And what is the relationship of continuity to change? These are challenging questions. Like a number of anthropologists (e.g., Bloch 1986), I think the question of continuity is the more interesting and the harder to address. At the same time, some changes are slower or harder to see than others. The observation of change is also a matter of perspective; in particular, I have to be careful to distinguish my own perceptions, based on discontinuous visits, from the perceptions of those whose continuous lifetime it has been. I also need to distinguish, as I have tried to do, the perspectives of different cohorts whose pasts, presents, and futures differ from one another.

The pace of change has been uneven, moving faster for some than for others. Some people have seized new opportunities while others have felt left behind or unanchored. Older people assert that the quality of social life has been eroded. But in the course of domestic reproduction – getting married, raising children, constructing houses, marrying off children, praying for deceased parents – everyone remains embedded in relations of family (*mraba*) and community (*tanana*). Everyone participates in what I have called in chapter 6 the reciprocity scenario, in which people invite one another to pray on their and their family's or community's behalf, feed them well, and expect to be invited back to do the same. The primary gift is not one of material objects but of *acts* – of invitation, response, acceptance, prayer, hospitality, and labour, manifesting care and mutuality, above all of acts of mutual acknowledgment.[2] Insofar as these acts are conceived as symmetrical, Mayotte could be said to maintain the relational mode or integrating schema that Philippe Descola (2013: 310ff) distinguishes as "exchange."[3]

What remains continuous also includes ideals of personal dignity and what Sahlins (2013: 29) calls "the transmission of life-capacities among persons." Despite the showing off, the almost hysterical (yet ironically self-conscious) attraction to each new fashion of display, and the competitive and mildly aggressive quality of performance, the reciprocity scenario and the principle of reproduction and condition of mutuality it comprehends have nevertheless continued to underlie activity. Paradoxical as it sounds, the chief goal of competition is equality; what counts, as it were, is to finish the race, not who comes in ahead.

In Mayotte, social reproduction has been at once the central value and end of life and the chief means of its pursuit – as exemplified notably in the celebration of weddings. Social reproduction is a matter of constituting, transforming, enlarging, and renewing persons, relationships, capacities, and values through acts of acknowledgment and celebrating them in ceremony. Yet in the course of the last forty years, the nature of marriage and the enactment of weddings and other ceremonies have undergone change. In what respects are such changes transformations in the means or mode of reproduction (and hence of the subjects reproduced) and in what respects do they serve merely to continue to reproduce more fundamental interests? What is the relationship between social reproduction and societal transformation?[4]

If the mode and means of material production have largely slipped from their hands, villagers continue to claim the mode and means of social reproduction and its celebration.[5] Moreover, production (labour) takes place in the service of reproduction (insofar as these can be separated from each other) as much as in the interests of private consumption or accumulation. Put another way, resources are directed to consumption that takes place in the enactment and celebration of ceremonies. This is manifest in the displays of food, dress, household furnishings, and of money itself. As I noted in chapter 11 (note 27), many women have individually purchased literally hundreds of matching dishes, which are stored and kept ready for use at an affair. If money and material goods are fetishized, celebration is equally embodied, enacted, and enjoyed through prayer, music, and dance – in the sacred, measured, and beautiful *Mulidy* and joyous *Maulida*; the intense, pulsating, stately *shigoma*; and the sexually confident dance exclusive to women. Bodies, persons, and relations are established, maintained, transformed, reproduced – and simply enjoyed – by these means that can be considered values internal to practice, done for the doing rather than for some external alienable or alienating end.

The mode of reproduction and the values it manifests have shifted in certain ways. Here I remain in the arena of village celebrations, omitting consideration of things like school and work, which obviously bring innovations.

In *shungu* exchange people were creating the community as a kind of continuous and containing object like a pot, rising and widening with each generation, as in the hands of a potter, and like pottery making, demanding and rigorous.[6] *Shungu* exchange was a round, such that in the end no part could be distinguished from the others. The *shungu* was also commensal; members of the community shared a cooking pot and a common bowl and perched metaphorically on the rim of a shared pot or bowl, looking primarily inwards, facing one another.

In kinship, the inward orientation is evident in the depiction of the family as a *mraba* (fenced enclosure) and the conjugal unit as a house (*tranu*). But the enclosure metaphor has always been complemented by openness. The effects of bilateral kinship are such that the enclosure is never more than a model, specific to any given individual and project.[7] In practice, people participate in multiple and overlapping *mraba*. They have also long travelled within and off the island and made new friends and kin. As a young man, Tumbu worked in town and on a neighbouring island, as both a servant and a peddler. Tumbu's father had arrived on Mayotte from a different island, and Tumbu's older brother went to seek his fortune in Madagascar, where I found him selling produce in the market in Antsiranana. For her part, Mohedja moved with her mother between different villages as a child. She rejected several suitors before Tumbu came along. Early in their marriage Tumbu and Mohedja spent a number of years living at some distance from Lombeni. Tumbu once went on the *hajj*, sponsored by the wider community. Neither ever went to Réunion or metropolitan France, but some of their children have done so, and some of their grandchildren are married and live there permanently. As I began this book in 2016, one of their great-granddaughters wrote me an e-mail in perfect English, sent from France where she is a university student.

In 2016 horizons and networks extend far beyond the bowl of the village and beyond Mayotte itself. And yet people continue to use the village as a reference point, to build houses there, most often to marry a fellow villager or islander, and to return home to conduct their ceremonies of reproduction. If they are no longer subject to the formal demands of the *shungu*, people have imposed on themselves *mtsangu*, dues or contributions of fixed size taken up among all family members for reproductive events and by resident households for community events. The enactment of ceremonies of reproduction continues to mark the responsibilities and stages of successful adulthood. The ceremonies are necessary and desirable and (differences in scale not withstanding) attainable by everyone. In this sense, and irrespective of divisions of wealth and class, the phrase I drew on earlier, "mutual superiority," still holds.

A brief comparison with adjacent northwest Madagascar heightens the singularity of Mayotte. Whereas in Mayotte the ceremonies of greatest elaboration and salience are weddings, among Sakalava (more specifically, among those who are not practising Muslims), weddings are minor events, if observed at all (Lambek 2014b). Consider too the ubiquitous questions I receive in Mayotte: *"How many children do you have? What, no more? Aren't your children married yet? But you do have grandchildren, don't you?"* The questions reveal primary obsessions and what people expect of themselves. When the suspicion emerged that my wife and I might have stopped intentionally with two children, people simply could not grasp this failure in our calculative reason and, more importantly, in our moral reasoning. The telos of life is reproduction. This is not simply biological but social – and it is acts of social reproduction that preoccupy people.[8]

I rarely received similar questions in Madagascar and not only because people there are more circumspect. Sakalava emphasize less their descendants than their ascendants and are concerned with how one is interpellated by individual grandparents and ancestors. To exaggerate the difference, in Mayotte what counts is producing yourself through reproducing others, while in northwest Madagascar what counts is who are reproducing themselves through you.

In any case, the reciprocity scenario remains strong, entailing the way people call upon and respond to others. Inviting neighbours to play a role in the reproduction of close kin produces a kind of de facto dual organization, simultaneously distinguishing and tying together kin and non-kin. All this is also to say that the community (*tanana*) remains salient insofar as it provides the source for participants in the reciprocity scenario, insofar as reciprocity scenarios are produced and enacted within its scope, and insofar as it serves itself as an actor in certain enactments of the scenario between communities.

If the community continues to engage in the reproduction of its members through enacting prayer and celebration via the reciprocity scenario, change takes place in two complementary ways. The first is heightened differentiation within the community and narrower, more selective calls and responses to participation. The second is the loosening of the boundaries of the community such that diffuse external relations become as significant as internal ones.

Community and family remain of central importance, yet people now experience competing pulls – or experience them more sharply – between living in the village and moving beyond it; and between attending to immediate kin – one's parents and children – and to those slightly more distant – one's siblings and parents' siblings, and their children – or even to one's friends and colleagues. The strength and solidarity of the adult sibling bond is weakening; while a point of segmentation, no doubt, in any society and at any period, this is particularly painful just now in Mayotte. The expectation that siblings and parents' siblings will remain reliable and mutual sources of support and solidarity throughout their lives and beyond the death of their parents has declined, causing a diffuse sense of betrayal or abandonment. Kinship as actually lived is different from the ideal of "mutuality of being" (qua Sahlins 2013). More generally, the tension in the community during the 1970s and later between a norm of equality and the reality of competition (chapter 4) has become a tension between the ideals of equality and mutuality and the facts of inequality and separation.

During the 1970s people produced each other such that the community and its individual members were a part of one another. As people travel and increase their education, their experiences and professional knowledge become more diversified and they produce themselves by new means. From the equivalence and mutuality of the *shungu*, individuated being has gained greater salience. Some younger people are "lost" (*very*) to metropolitan France, though they may phone or send remittances; others return, with horizons overlapping more or less closely with those of their parents and siblings. Over all, some people feel empowered and freer, while others feel caught in the demands of daily livelihood and social expectations. There is no single or consistent narrative for what has happened to people.

One could say that the bowl has cracked or that its contents have spilled over; the focus is no longer as fully inwards as it was, and the salience of citizenship in the village is offset by citizenship in France and in the world. Nevertheless, the core remains in the pride people take in their achievements as citizens of Mayotte and of Lombeni and as members of a kin group. People call upon each other and remain concerned that kin and community respond, holding up a mirror that reflects and magnifies rather than extracts their achievement.

More than one person has remarked over the years how full Mayotte is of joyful celebrations. "We all *misoma* (play, celebrate), going from one collective event to another." The man who said this was referring to a popular musical performance that was neither Muslim nor kin-based to which he was en route, but he included in its scope all the *Maulida, Deba, manzaraka*, and, as he said in French, *fêtes* of various kinds. While these are *soma* – play or entertainment – they are equally *asa* – work or works, carefully produced, serious affairs with responsible *tompin* (principals and sponsors), whether these are constituted as individuals, households, families, descendants, or communities.

Just as Bali has been depicted as a "theatre state" (Geertz 1981), so perhaps Mayotte can be described as composed of "ceremonious or celebratory communities." The community has been constituted as and through the frequent sponsorships, productions, and enactments of *fêtes* of various kind and scope, in which the bases of participation vary according to the kind of "work" performed and the action taken. However, the community has become somewhat porous. As a brief final illustration, one elder told me in 1975 that even though a person identified as a Muslim may not go regularly to pray they will feel compelled to attend funerals; it would be unthinkable not to. In 1975 this meant that on the announcement of the death of one of its residents, everyone in the village stopped what they were doing and attended to the deceased from that moment until the completion of the interment. Messengers were sent to inform kin living elsewhere. In 2015, death was announced over the radio and by cell phone; some members of the family and community were absent abroad, others might leave work in town to return for a short period – and the village would also temporarily fill up with kin and associates of the deceased from elsewhere.

If the community has weakened, social horizons have broadened. People have become much more dependent on government and embedded in the state but also more active participants in it. The egalitarian ethos remains strong as does the practical orientation to the future that has been present throughout the past as I have recounted it here.

The story I narrate is radically different from that of Piot's (2010) influential account of Togo or de Boeck and Plissart's penetrating portrait of Kinshasa (2006), in which in the face of crushing disappointment and blockage, distinctions between the real and the imaginary appear to invert or collapse. However, the situation in Mayotte is not simply rosy either. If, during the 1970s, the salient distinction was between village residents who were owners of the land on which the village stood and those who were not, since then it has become the much bigger one between those who have papers as citizens of Mayotte, and hence of France and the EU, and those migrants from elsewhere who do not.

In sum, there is a shift from being colonial subjects to being full citizens of France. But along with that comes a weakening of what I have called citizenship of the local community. And, in addition, has come the uncomfortable juxtaposition with migrants who are very much subjects rather than citizens, an omnipresent reminder of moral and material precarity.

There is a further way to think about continuity and change that informs this book. In the last stages of writing and as mentioned in previous chapters, I have been reminded again and again of the salience of a phrase that is common in German historiography, namely *the contemporaneity of the non-contemporaneous*. This concept was developed in the 1920s by art historian Wilhelm Pinder (1926).[9] Addressing the "problem of generations" in artistic production, Pinder observed that two works of art produced in the same year might be of very different, older and newer styles, depending on when the respective artists had been trained or had come of age. The presence and experience of the contemporaneity of the non-contemporaneous grew in Mayotte with the rapidity of change as it progressed through shallow historical cohorts, separating sibling from adjacent sibling and generation from generation and moving at different rates within different families. Moreover, as I have shown repeatedly, older customs were not necessarily abandoned with the acquisition and acceptance of newer ones; hence practices of non-contemporaneous origin and derivation have been performed alongside each other. Finally, it is implicit that the elements of what we call "structure" have been deposited or created at different times; hence that even synchronic description and analysis must recognize the non-contemporaneity in the contemporaneous.[10]

The contemporaneity of the non-contemporaneous also describes the method and structure of this book. My visits at different periods are simultaneously present in my memory (and no doubt somewhat confused therein) and also simultaneously present in the compilations of my field notes and articles. Each chapter attempts to describe one of these multiple sediments, based on notes or articles written at given times. The composition of the book, in setting periods side by side in distinct chapters, is itself one of rendering contemporaneous the non-contemporaneous. Yet the point is that what the chapters describe are not fully discrete periods either; rather, the material in each chapter is like a wave, overlapping with but extending a little farther up the shore than the previous one.

Insofar as this book can be considered a work of history, it combines chronicle, starting in 1975 and moving towards the present, and retrospection, starting in 2017 and returning to 1975 and before. I have tried to show history from the local perspective, not as it is represented now but as how it has been lived over the course of time, both "then" and "now," and how representations are part of the living of it. The book is as much an ethnography *of* history as it is an ethnographic history. History as it happens, as it is made, can be broadly understood as a series of acts, including recollection, recounting, and representation of the past, but also acts of anticipation, oriented towards a future. Broadly speaking, these are successive interpretations (in the sense of enactments) of roles, characters, performances, and scenarios. Each interpretation is repetitive but also original and moving along with, and in reference to, specific horizons. Action is historical not only insofar as it is consequential but as it is informed by historical consciousness, a consciousness that must be elucidated with respect to horizons of past and future.

Both horizons and the acts undertaken within them are ethically informed. The horizon of the future embraces goals and values that people work with and towards, as well as obstacles to be avoided and simple unknowns. The horizon of the past has attachments, commitments, obligations, and preceding acts that inform the present, that have put present relations under a description, and that need to be acknowledged. How, with what understanding and care, one attends to horizons, moves towards or beyond them, or strives to raise them, is critical. And if historical action and imagination are ethically informed, so too should ethical life be understood in its historical enactment and unfolding, rather than as timeless or caught in sheer immediacy. Moreover, insofar as specific ethical concerns exist within a given social field, we must consider the diverse ways that people interpret how their circumstances and horizons fit, overlap, or clash with one another – how agreement is forged and disagreement addressed. I've tried to show how ethical considerations are intrinsic to the playing out of exchange obligations and the reciprocity scenario and to the tensions between attachment and separation that each generation faces.

In one sense the ethical describes living as if it matters, being alive to life, being attentive, being aware. That means being receptive and reflective as well as being active. It means being *present*. But being present also means attending to horizons of the future – looking where we are going – and horizons of the past – acknowledging where have we come from (as each of these is culturally and historically shaped). The salience of *presence* needs to be juxtaposed to the remark of Gadamer with which I began the book (see the epigraph to the Preface), namely that, "Historical thinking has its dignity and its value as truth in the acknowledgment that there is no such thing as 'the present,' but rather constantly changing horizons of future and past" (1985: 484). There must be awareness as well that other people have other horizons and that the work of history is partly about fusing horizons. In Gadamer's felicitous phrase a fusion of horizons does not mean achieving identical horizons (reaching an identical space in relation to them) but opening a space or sight line, an arc, however small, in common together.

The concept of horizon may partially offset the dualism inherent in oppositions like structure and transformation or continuity and change. Horizons show, in effect, the continuity in change and the change in continuity as they extend and retract somewhat differently for each historical cohort. The moral horizons in Lombeni have shifted among its inhabitants as cohorts have become shallower. People of my age cohort have experienced enormous change in their lifetimes, growing up in a relatively isolated village based largely on subsistence cultivation and living now in a community well served by roads and the Internet, where most people drive to work or fly to locations where they can maximize state benefits. Mayotte has shifted from a neglected and remote colony (though it retains traces of both) to become a full part of Europe and a gateway to it. The members of this cohort have looked both forward and back, forward with political aspirations for Mayotte and social and economic aspirations for their children, back with respect to the habitus, values, and commitments acquired in childhood and youth. They have had to address issues of personal dignity in a community that demands public display of success through the sponsorship of ever-inflated life-cycle rituals and the building of ever larger and fancier houses. Many of their children, now adults, received an education in the French school system and some have gone on to successful careers. Some of their grandchildren now maintain a partially French lifestyle with respect to such things as domesticity and child-rearing. For the most part, the people of my age cohort have accepted and addressed these matters with grace and a mixture of enthusiasm, pleasure, and sadness.

Moral horizons have a broad circumference. They include acknowledgment of and deference towards the past, a past that for successive cohorts has rapidly receded; aspiration through education and economic and reproductive success; exultation in the immediate present displayed at ceremonies of social reproduction; and anxiety about economic, social, and ethical failure. There is also the moral horizon of the afterlife and the role of religious devotion in this one. Despite the growing distance from religion on the part of some young people, for the reformers matters of the afterlife have gained a greater salience than they held for their parents. For most people, Islamic practice in its local form remains vibrant and serious.

There are also the challenges produced by rapid population growth, high rates of immigration, and urbanization. These have taken an immense toll on the natural environment no less than the social one; environmental sustainability and sufficient access to land at such high population density, no less than peacefulness, security of property, and economic and social justice, are salient issues. The horizons are not as unclouded as they once were.

Forty years of observing a community give one pause. You see children growing to adulthood and giving birth themselves; mentors and old friends die, people marry and separate, become competent and incompetent, go mad, argue a lot, and sometimes make up. You see how people – individuals, a community – have led their lives, thereby also providing the ground to think more generally about what it means to lead a life and what leading a life has meant – or been – in Mayotte during this period, and even how the very idea of leading one's life, no less than the actual leading of it, changes over time.

While I have brought a number of voices into play, they are discontinuous: I decided not to write this book as the life history of one or more individuals. The focus has been less on the singular individual than on the living of life. If ethnography is "about" anything it is surely about human being-in-the world. In Heidegger's characterization of *Dasein*, it is a matter of "care," of being open to the world, of operating with the capacity to make sense of other beings as they are, of recognizing our condition, and of being receptive to possibility.[11] Despite our thrownness in the world, that is, our subjection to determining conditions of existence and the constraints of our times and circumstances, and despite our negative inclinations, as captured in the concept of fallenness, we should hold ourselves open to surprise. For ethnographers, this is a necessary part of our practice.

The human condition is a historical one. The title of this work, *Island in the Stream,* may evoke the image of the river into which you cannot step twice. Yet the idea of stepping in or out presupposes the perspective of an outsider, a view from nowhere, or from theory. By contrast, the island and its inhabitants are in the stream; theirs is a view from within, of where they are heading and where they are coming from. The stream expresses the human condition of historicity, a condition at once of location and of movement.

I close with one of the last encounters I had in 2015, at once exhilarating and poignant. As I chat with an old friend down by the beach, a young man in his late twenties approaches and inquires whether I am Michel. He affirms how important my presence has been as a witness and how he has wanted to meet me. He says he knows a little English and we shift languages. His English is excellent; not only is it my first time to fully converse in English with a Mahorais, let alone a citizen of Lombeni, but the subject matter is sophisticated. He completed a *bac* in literature and has continued to study at the newly opened university on Mayotte. He likes nineteenth-century French novels and is also a fan of Baudelaire, but his favourite author, on whom he plans to write his MA thesis, is Voltaire. Nevertheless, he is also an observant Muslim, and even a reformist, and someone who is caught up by spirits who possessed his mother and are now retaliating against him for rejecting them.

This very impressive and entangled young man epitomizes much of what I have talked about – the seizure of new opportunities along with the ethical charge of past commitments. He illustrates not just "both/ and," but "both/and" *and* "either/or." His horizon is in one respect wide open – and *and* and *and* and ... But in another respect, it is narrowed by the incommensurability inevitably raised, and that he lives.

Acknowledgments

I am immensely grateful to everyone in Lombeni and especially to those mentioned in the book. It has been a privilege to live my life in partial proximity to yours.

I spent fourteen months in Mayotte during 1975–6 and revisited for various lengths of time in 1980, 1985, 1992, 1995, 2000, 2001, 2005, 2007, 2009, and 2015. The field trips have each been generously supported throughout by the Social Sciences and Humanities Research Council of Canada, with assistance from the National Science Foundation in 1975–6 and the National Geographic Foundation in 1985.

Writing has been supported by a Canada Research Chair and the University of Toronto Scarborough. A major portion of the manuscript was completed during a fellowship from the magnificent Wissenschaftskolleg zu Berlin. Heartfelt thanks to all the staff and to the fellows who shared 2016–17 together.

I am very grateful to the Federation for the Humanities and Social Sciences for an award that makes publication of this book possible. Their Scholarly Publications Programs is an invaluable resource for Canadian authors and publishers.

Deep appreciation goes to my family: most immediately, Jackie Solway, Nadia Lambek, and Simon Lambek, who shared periods of the research with me, and Carey Demichelis, who joined later. All have added insights to this book; Jackie's have been so helpful and so merged with mine that I cannot distinguish them, except at moments of criticism (when she is almost always right).

My brothers, Larry and Bernie Lambek, have been my most faithful readers. Our late parents, Hanna Weiss and Jim Lambek, were seriously interested as well. Ruth and Zwi Guggenheim, Robin and Margaret

Weiss, and the late Laurent and Marie-Hélène Schwartz provided hospitality and insight in Zurich, London, and Paris, respectively, on European stopovers to and from Mayotte.

Among scholars of Mayotte and the Comoros, I thank especially Chanfi Ahmed, Sophie Blanchy, Jean-Michel Vidal, Henry Wright, and the late and much missed Jon Breslar. I have received insight and support from Sophie Bouffart, Bonnie Breslar, Susan Kus, Harriet and Martin Ottenheimer, Gillian Shepherd, and Iain Walker and the late Paul Ottino, and Pierre Vérin. And for Madagascar, I thank especially Rita Astuti, Maurice Bloch, Gillian Feeley-Harnik, Karen Middleton, Lesley Sharp, Emmanuel Tehindrazanarivelo, and Andrew Walsh. Cooperation with Gwyn Campbell, Sarah Fee, and Eric Jennings on our annual Madagascar workshops has also been fruitful.The acknowledgments extended in the original publications still hold; in addition, and partly overlapping with those, for intellectual friendship or particular insights, I am grateful to Paul Antze, Sandra Bamford, Joshua Barker, Janice Boddy, Fenella Cannell, Jean and John Comaroff, Filip de Boeck, Stefan Feuchtwang, Bob Hefner, Wendy James, Ray Kelly, Anne Meneley, Sherry Ortner, Michael Peletz, Rüdiger Seesemann, Jack Sidnell, Charles Stafford, Paul Stoller, Megan Vaughan, Richard Werbner, and the late Olivia Harris. I thank as well all my other colleagues at Toronto and the London School of Economics and my graduate students and postdoctoral fellows past and present, especially in this instance Sarah Gould who, among so many other things, read a draft for me and compiled the index. Big thanks to my *zuky*, Maurice Bloch, and to my late and much-missed teachers, Aram Yengoyan and Skip Rappaport.

I have benefited in recent years from exchanges with an extraordinary group of interlocutors including Giovanni da Col, Veena Das, Didier Fassin, Jane Guyer, Charles Hirschkind, Michael Jackson, James Laidlaw, Rena Lederman, Saba Mahmood (much missed), Cheryl Mattingly, Thomas Schwarz Wentzer, and others. Michael Jackson's work and work ethic are inspirational.

Chapter 10 was first written for a conference at UCLA at the invitation of Ned Alpers; another version will be published in a book on African islands edited by Toyin Falola, Joe Parrott, and Diane Porter Sanchez. A more extensive version of chapter 12 was first delivered as a keynote address to the Australian Anthropological Society in 2015, with thanks to Catie Gressier, Amanda Gilbertson, and Monica Minnegal and also to audiences in the Department of Anthropology in Helsinki, the Max Planck Institute in Göttingen, and African Studies at the

Humboldt University, Berlin. A talk on the larger project at the Wissen-schaftskolleg elicited many useful exchanges, for which I thank Luca Giuliani, Carey Harrison, Barbara Kowalzig, Katharina Volk, Thorsten Wilhelmy, and many others.

Douglas Hildebrand was an open and enabling editor and he found three remarkably responsive referees to whom I am very grateful. Jodi Lewchuk admirably took up the reins on his departure. In an editorial world where production values have declined in recent years, those at the University of Toronto Press remain very high. Margaret Allen and Janice Evans have taken great care with the manuscript. Any remaining infelicities are of my own doing.

Notes

Preface

1 During those weeks I was accompanied first by Susan Kus and then also by Henry Wright, archaeologists conducting a survey on Mayotte who then left for Madagascar.

2 Shimaore is the language of the majority of the islanders. It is a Bantu language, closely related to the languages of the other three islands of the Comoro Archipelago and to Swahili. Kibushy is a dialect of Malagasy, an Austronesian language, spoken by about a third of the population of Mayotte.

3 They are Jacqueline Solway and Nadia and Simon Lambek.

4 For further ethnographic studies conducted in Mayotte see Breslar (1979), Blanchy (1990), Vidal (1994), and Bouffart (2009). These fine works all deal predominantly with speakers of Shimaore.

5 Piers Vitebsky (2012) offers a compelling reflection, with a similar time frame but different relationships to mine. Michael Jackson's work is exemplary and, as Shirley Yeung reminds me, some of it (e.g., 2011) focuses not only on his own return to postwar Sierra Leone but on the homecoming of Kuranko as well. The champion of long-term fieldwork is undoubtedly Elizabeth Colson, who began with the Tonga in 1946 and continued until her death in the field – that had also become her home – in 2016, thus for seventy years.

6 Intriguingly, it is the reverse premise that motivates Jonathan Lear's insightful account of conquest from the perspective of the Crow (2006).

7 This is a point well addressed with respect to the identity of the self by Paul Ricoeur (1992). Thanks to Simon Lambek for the point.

8 A further practical reason for radical pruning was to reduce the percentage of previously published words such as to retain eligibility for a subsidy from the Federation for the Humanities and Social Sciences, whose Awards to Scholarly Publications Program is so critical for the health of academic publishing in Canada.

9 One referee was curious about the role of Rappaport. I attended his lectures, if I recall correctly, only after I returned from the field. His ideas on ritual and performativity were not salient for chapter 5, but were for chapter 6 and especially in later essays (see Lambek 2015a) that focus directly on action and its ethical consequentiality.

1. Introduction: The Presence of History

1 It may be more common among historians (Hunt 2011). I contrast ethnographic history with historical ethnography, a genre that comprises ethnographic-like accounts of life at a single moment in the (distant) past, drawn usually from archival sources. Anthropologist Carole McGranahan offers a different use, such that, in contrast to oral history, "ethnographic history takes history, its production, and its narration as an anthropological scope of inquiry." She distinguishes "ethnographic truths" from "a singular historical truth" (McGranahan 2012: 215).

2 One source of this view lies in Nietzsche. As Raymond Geuss puts it, "For Nietzsche, I am 'interpreting' a situation by reacting to it in a certain way ... [Nietzsche] claims that life itself is a process of evaluating and giving preference (*Beyond Good and Evil* §9)." Moreover, each interpretation takes over a pre-existing form of living and acting. Interpretation is understood as "acting, feeling, and perceiving in a certain way" (1999: 16).

3 I develop the argument concerning the relationship between performativity and practice with respect to ethical life in Lambek 2015a.

4 The phrase is associated with Reinhart Koselleck (2004) but also the work of art historian Wilhelm Pinder (1926) as well as reflections by Kierkegaard (1985, *Philosophical Fragments*, ch. 4). My thanks to Luca Giuliani and Michael Moxter for these references.

5 Keith Tribe suggests intriguingly in his blog that *Being and Time* ought now to be translated *into* German from one or more of the many languages into which it has been translated from the original German.

6 The ethnographic present is not quite the same thing as the grammatical present. In fact, within each chapter the grammatical tense often varies.

7 This might be considered a phenomenological history, but in a cultural sense; my method is one of thicker cultural contextualization rather than

reductive bracketing. For more explicitly phenomenological anthropology, see Jackson 1996 and Desjarlais and Throop 2011.

8 See also Hirsch and Stewart 2005, Palmié and Stewart 2016, and for a different perspective Peel 1993. On African historiography see Cooper 1999.

9 The poiesis of the past, as I call it, by means of spirit possession is not as elaborate in Mayotte as in northwest Madagascar (Lambek 2002c). On the history of possession itself see also Feeley-Harnik 1991 and Sharp 1996.

10 Another relevant institution is French schooling; unfortunately, this is not something I have investigated directly.

11 Gadamer notes that the concept is also found in William James, but draws from his teacher, Martin Heidegger, and directly from thinkers who influenced Heidegger. In addition to Husserl and Simmel, Gadamer follows Graf Yorck that, "Life is determined by the fact that what is alive differentiates itself from the world in which it lives and with which it remains connected, and preserves itself in this differentiation. The self-preservation of what is alive takes place through its drawing into itself everything that is outside it. Everything that is alive nourishes itself on what is alien to it. The fundamental fact of being alive is assimilation. Differentiation, then, is at the same time non-differentiation. The alien is appropriated" (Gadamer 1985: 223).

12 As Throop (2010: 269) and other writers in the phenomenological tradition note, modes of attention articulate with or are constituted through different orientations to time, whether immersion in a full present (Csikszentmihalyi 1990); in activities like dance (James 2003); or in reminiscence, boredom, anticipation (Guyer 2007), and so forth. When we lift our eyes from the ground our visual horizons expand, and as our eyes continuously shift, so too do our temporal orientations. The anthropological question concerns collective modes of and for attention and temporal experience.

13 Such interpellation is especially strong in northwest Madagascar (Baré 1977, Feeley-Harnik 1991, Lambek 2002c).

14 As Sahlins argues, "in the nature of symbolic action, diachrony and synchrony coexist in an indissoluble synthesis" (1985: 151).

15 This is, in effect, what Sahlins (1985) describes with respect to the Hawaiian interpretation of Captain Cook.

16 As Sahlins puts it, "If culture is … a meaningful order, still, in action meanings are always at risk" (1985: ix).

17 For insiders' perspectives see Bamana 2008, Kamardine 2008; on social change, Blanchy 2002a, 2002b, Blanchy and Moatty 2012, Vidal 1994, 2010; on recent cultural politics, Regnault 2011.

18 Chapter 10 does expand the location to La Réunion.

19 https://www.theguardian.com/world/2011/apr/19/mayotte-votes-modernity-france-hopquin. Last accessed 18 Sept. 2016. This is the French view and not the whole story. The remark about the passing century, clearly occidental in formulation, echoes comments made in the early modern period in Europe concerning the acceleration of time and the incommensurability of experience on the part of adjacent generations (Koselleck 2004: 269–70).

20 The *grand mariage* is comprehensively described in Blanchy 2010.

21 Many disturbing films are readily accessed on line. For an illustrated firsthand account from a child's perspective see Kamil 2014.

22 I thank Marco Motta for inspiration concerning the temporality of life. The musicality of history is recognized by many thinkers and writers, from Nietzsche to Lévi-Strauss. *A Dance to the Music of Time* is the title of Anthony Powell's twelve-volume (1951–75) series of novels. Other inspiring approaches to history not covered in the introduction include White (1973) and, from a very different angle, Wolf (1982).

2. Village Life: Kinship, Community, and Islam, 1975 and After

1 On daily life in Mayotte, compare Blanchy 1990.

2 I am not attempting to conceptualize either "marriage" or "weddings" analytically and take them only in the commonsense meanings they hold for us and for people in Mayotte. No doubt they belong to a polythetic class of phenomena with distinct if overlapping criteria among them.

3 This incident is also described in Lambek 1993 in the context of a somewhat different description of the village.

4 Not all nicknames derive from French.

5 Obviously they would not deny this in instances of marriages between genealogically related people, such as cross-cousins.

6 There were no evident *sarambavy* (gender-queer people) as reported for many places in Madagascar, and I never heard the term applied in Mayotte.

7 Hence the pattern could be described as patri-uxorilocal. Compare Blanchy 1992, Ottenheimer and Ottenheimer 1979.

8 In principle, Islamic rules of inheritance applied, but land was rarely formally divided, houses went to daughters, and little or no cash and few other material resources were available to distribute at a death.

9 Wet rice is not cultivated in Mayotte, and there is none of the terracing and irrigation characteristic of Madagascar.

10 As late as 1989, of exports of 35,530,000 francs, ylang ylang oil accounted for close to 30 per cent. Imports the same year were estimated at 338,139,000 francs.

11 In fact, there were three budgets and sources of funding, namely the state (*l'état*), the *collectivité* (now the *département*), and the *commune* as well as the possibility to apply from external sources like the EU, which subsidized the construction of a *foyer des jeunes* in Lombeni.

12 The position was not permanent but rotated among men with sufficient knowledge and good eyesight.

13 They once had wrestlers (*mrenge*) and now have football teams as well.

3. Founding the Villages, before 1975

1 Archaeologists currently date the first settlements in the Comoros from possibly the fifth to the eighth or ninth centuries CE. For a summary of views and evidence see Allibert 2015, who has discovered Chinese pottery, indicative of broad trading networks, from a large and probably pre-Islamic site at Dembeni in Mayotte. See also Vérin 1994 and compare, for Mauritius, Vaughan 2005.

2 Allibert (2015) estimates some thirty villages and a population of 10,000 in Mayotte at the time.

3 The Merina, inhabiting a kingdom in the central highlands of Madagascar with a well-organized army, attempted to conquer and incorporate the whole island in the early nineteenth century. Today they make up the dominant ethnic group in Madagascar.

4 The census is found in the *Archives nationales section Outre-Mer* MAD 220: 464.

5 "The origins of the population as neither noble nor slave, the heterogeneity of its composition, and the dramatic demographic collapse at the beginning of the nineteenth century as a result of local warfare have led Mayotte to become an island that has forgotten its past and its former traditions and that has chosen the future." (My translation.)

6 Blanchy (1997) also suggests a connection between the former political order and prayers for rain, as well as a structural link between rain and excessive crying on the death of one's parents. Her remarks resonate with collective prayers for rain at an ancient tomb adjacent to Lombeni (chapters 8 and 9) and strenuous disapproval of crying at a death that I encountered.

7 See also Allibert 1984. Gillian Shepherd notes three "ranks" in Ngazidja and Nzwani: *masherifu*, descendants of the Prophet; *waungwana*, freeborn; and slaves, *warumwa*, with de facto endogamy (1977: 145–6). In Mayotte,

waungwana refers only to certain Mahorais speakers; Malagasy speakers and others are outside the system.

8 Tumbu's parents separated before he started walking. His father was angry and said Tumbu should not be raised by Tumbu's mother, Nuriaty. As Tumbu's father had no kin in the area, he settled on Nuriaty's mother, Amina, to raise his son.

9 *Marantudy*, lice, fleas, and bedbugs were all a nuisance but have disappeared since the French began spraying with DDT in the 1980s. The prevalence of stomach worms (*hankana*), poisonous centipedes (*trambuñu*), wood rats, and many other pests has also declined as a result. An insect introduced to standing water radically reduced the incidence of mosquito-spread filariasis. Parasites and infectious diseases have been partly replaced by sharp rises in hypertension, and diabetes.

10 A niece of Dady Nuriaty's disputed the fact that Amina spoke Kimrima. She said Amina spoke Kiantalaotsy and that Nuriaty picked up Kimrima from her father. Dady Nuriaty was dead at this point, and I was not able to confirm it.

11 My informant here, a descendant of the foreman, stated that the purchasers of Lombeni Be were all foremen, whereas those of Lombeni Kely and even Dimasy Addinan had been simple workers.

12 A different version, never uttered in Lombeni (I heard it from someone in a different village), had it that Mze Mdery was unable to give birth with his wife in the elite Shimahore village and had no children until he followed the advice of a diviner to marry his slave. He then took this woman with him to Lombeni. However, that Mze Mdery's mother was a freewoman from the Shimahore village is probable; people from Lombeni continue to interact occasionally with descendants of her brother.

13 These cases are not consistent or straightforward. When Tumbu's full brother wanted to marry a woman of Lombeni Be, her father refused on account of his being Makua. But in fact, this man had been married for a time to Tumbu's mother until she rejected him. In the next generation, when a boy from the family in Lombeni Be wanted to marry the daughter of Tumbu's brother it was the latter's turn to refuse the marriage. But in the meantime, other marriages between the families had transpired.

4. Citizenship and Sociality: Practising Equality, 1975–1976

1 Cash in larger quantities was needed for the purchase of land and for investment in cash cropping – which at the time was also the major source of cash. Only a glimmer on the horizon in 1975 was long-term investment through sending children to school.

2 Age groups are officially recognized when the members announce themselves and "enter the village" (*miditry antanana*) by distributing sugar water or tea to the senior groups. As members marry, they invite one another to their wedding feasts.

3 Retired groups no longer take an active role; members are simply lumped together as "elders."

4 The age system is less formalized than many in East Africa, and the age groups are not political or military in nature but function primarily in the production and consumption of feasts.

5 Kala's father was Hamada, mentioned in the last chapter; her mother was not a village owner.

6 Complaints are sometimes voiced. Someone passed over for leading the prayer claimed that the man selected was not a full owner. Instead of removing the man selected, the elders carefully enabled the complainant to take a turn in rotation. From their point of view the relevant criteria were competence, reliability, and proper Muslim comportment, not descent or ownership.

7 In 1975–6 there were about 200 francs to a dollar.

8 In this much-loved version, the performance is initiated and drummed by men, while the singing is performed by a chorus of women.

9 When Chanfi gave me the final accounting a few days later, he estimated the expenses of Kala's affair at 12,000 francs (c. $60) plus the steer. These covered the honoraria for the prayers (5,000 fr.), rice (2,500 fr.), sugar and flour (4,000 fr.), and kerosene and matches for the mosque (500 fr.). The income included 600 francs from her mother's kin, 1,000 from her father's kin, 750 from her in-laws, and 3,000 from Kala herself. Assuming contributions from guests and members of her age group, this still left things short, and presumably Chanfi and perhaps other elders quietly made up the difference.

10 Meeting the demands of the age group's *shungu* took priority over meeting those of the village.

11 Young women are expected to marry as virgins, and it is the responsibility of men to enable them to do so by refraining from premarital sex with virgins and by marrying them. For an account of virginity's significance for women see Lambek 1983.

12 It is considered correct to marry elsewhere after the death of a spouse.

13 He told me he wanted to live in Lombeni, but, as his wife did not, he was planning polygyny. In fact, he never returned to live in Lombeni.

14 Married elsewhere, Moussa has no house of his own in Lombeni. A woman I knew who resided outside the village returned to Lombeni for a full year in order to prepare and carry out her *shungu*.

15 A decade later all but two of the men in the older group had paid.
16 Ideally, it is served by the bride's father's sister since the bride's mother must avoid her son-in-law and especially the conjugal bed.
17 This man enjoyed being idiosyncratic in many ways and was proud of it.
18 In fact, he put the cow ahead of purchase of a still for his ylang ylang. Ylang ylang sales helped pay for the cow, but he has to give a third of his product to the owner of the still he rents from.
19 Communal affairs are supported by collecting equally from each household; for some events the amounts requested are distinguished by age group

5. Exchange, Time, and Person in Mayotte: The Structure and Destructuring of a Cultural System, 1975–1985

1 Two caveats are in order. Aging as used here refers to a socially constituted progression not an unmediated biological process. Also, the *shungu* is only one social form to articulate the experience of aging. Patterns of kinship, naming, joking relations, Islamic authority and piety, and spirit possession are all relevant.
2 Even when the potlatch balances out over the course of a life cycle and is interpreted as integrative rather than competitive, it is based on a relationship between status and size of prestation (Adams 1973). Examples of balanced feasting are found elsewhere – for instance, among Malays (Fraser 1966: 36).
3 Additionally, groups of friends and acquaintances of the same sex from more than one village sometimes participated in voluntary *shungu* groups formed specifically for the pleasure of reciprocal feast giving and the challenge of meeting the payment.
4 Circumcision takes place at any time from infancy to puberty, and brothers are often circumcised together. The scheduling of a circumcision or wedding is influenced by the ability to amass the goods necessary for the *shungu*.
5 Virgin marriage is expensive for the groom not only because of the *shungu* but because of the clothing, jewellery, and other gifts he must provide to the bride.
6 Virginity is discussed in Lambek 1983. Since all concerned are generally more interested in completing their respective *shungu* payments and achieving the public recognition for a virgin marriage than in actually undertaking a defloration, consensus to simulate evidence of virginity may be easily reached, other complicating factors – such as an angry lover, overt signs of pregnancy, and so on – not intervening. People marry

virgins (or as virgins) more to formally accomplish social reproduction than because they value virginity for its own sake.

7 The description has not included mention of the pattern of food distribution to affines, which is a significant feature of weddings without being a part of the *shungu*.

8 The main *shungu* feast at weddings was the *walima*, held by the bride's parents in conjunction with the recitation of blessings (*shidjabu*); the equivalent at circumcisions was recitation of the protective *badry* prayer. Another one-time distribution was the *karam*, composed of unhusked rice distributed to every member of the village.

9 One large village maintained through 1975 a one-time-only *shungu* (whether at a wedding, circumcision, or mortuary commemoration) of 2 head of cattle, 15 large baskets of rice, 300 coconuts, 16 kilos of salt, 150 francs worth of green onions, plus turmeric and tamarind. The woman who listed this said women work hard but get very little from the feast and hence are readier than men to abolish the *shungu*.

10 When the subject of *shungu* in other villages came up, it was as a matter of curiosity concerning the contents and organization of the payments.

11 The woman was "ahead" of other members of her age group because she had raised an older sibling's child and sponsored her wedding.

12 She also put aside two *mshia* of rice as a courtesy (*ishima*) to the village, but the village refused to accept it.

13 The termination of participation at *shungu* feasts need not happen all at once for an individual. The women who stayed away from the feast mentioned above might have gone to a subsequent feast held by a woman who had entered the *shungu* system earlier than the others but who was tardier in making her own contribution.

14 I only observed this among women, and, in fact, at one feast the decision by women to put aside food on behalf of deceased age group members was hotly debated by men, who argued that death terminated all calculations of exchange.

6. Localizing Islamic Performances in Mayotte, 1975–1995

1 In this chapter "Malagasy" refers to persons or practices pertaining to Madagascar rather than specifically to Malagasy speakers in Mayotte.

2 These points are recognized by Hefner (1993).

3 All this implies that a theory of conversion ought to distinguish the shift from "traditional" to "world" religion from the shift from one "world" religion (or sect) to another. It is unclear whether one can usefully speak of conversion from one "traditional" religion to another.

4 For trenchant discussion see Asad 1986 and now Ahmad 2015. On Islam in
    East Africa see, inter alia, Ahmed 2006, Ahmed et al. 2002.
5 This is emphatically not to separate "belief" from "action" (Abu-Zahra
    1991) nor to deny that questions of referential meaning were uppermost
    for some people some of the time. The perspective adopted here is that
    of the "man [person] on the street." It needs to be supplemented by the
    perspectives Schutz calls the "well informed citizen" and the "expert"
    (cf Lambek 1993).
6 Performance in the third sense contributes simultaneously to both.
7 This is aside from the politicization of Islam, which became of global concern
    after this chapter was written and remains fairly negligible in Mayotte.
8 Reading is also a socially and historically located activity. However, insofar
    as silent reading is a solitary practice, the social implications are somewhat
    different from what is described here as performance.
9 Bourdieu emphasizes the improvisational and Rappaport the orderly
    execution of acts. Moreover, whereas Bourdieu emphasizes personal
    prestige or honour, Rappaport focuses on collective frames for moral
    evaluation (Lambek 2000b, 2001).
10 This is not to suggest that a universalistic concern for the well-being of all
    humans was absent.
11 For a similar conclusion in Acheh, see Bowen 1992.
12 Seesemann (2006: 238) notes that the musical version originates in the
    Hadramawt.
13 Whereas in a *shungu* one family supplies the food and the age groups
    divide it up for cooking, at the village *Maulida* each household supplies
    its portion of food. In 1976 Lombeni Kely shifted from collecting cooked
    food from each household to collecting raw food and cooking communally,
    thereby experimenting with the production of the event. Each village has
    its own mode of organizing these productions.
14 Compare chapters 4 and 5. The model is diagrammed on page 118 of
    Lambek 1993.
15 Contrast Lamu (el Zein 1974) where performances of the *Maulida* marked
    hierarchy. Meneley describes performances of *mawlids* among the elite of
    Zabid, Yemen, which "mediate the ever-present contradiction between
    equality of Muslims before God and the hierarchy of families so evident in
    everyday life" (1996: 178). See also Kresse (2006). Tapper and Tapper (1987)
    and Nuotio (2006) attend to women's performances.
16 *Dzoru* refers to recitation, and what are recited are verses of invocation,
    called *dua*.
17 One can also perform *swala* alone, whether in the mosque or at home.
    Indeed, women more often pray alone at home than in the mosque.

18 Questions with respect to *swala* include whether women pray in the mosque, the size of the congregation, the regularity of prayer, the conduct of the Friday sermon, and so on. Compare Bowen 1989.

19 When logistically possible, some people also participated in the pilgrimage circuit of northernmost Madagascar (Gueunier 1988, Walsh 1998).

20 Intense musical performances have continued through 2015.

21 Years later the *Deba* became iconic of "indigenous" and "authentic" Mahorais culture, suitable for performance at national holidays and international cultural and folklore festivals.

7. Choking on the Qur'an and Other Consuming Parables, 1975–1992

1 Movement within the region has been significant throughout the last millennium, but its relative importance and ease have declined in recent decades. It is now quicker to reach Paris from Mayotte than to get to Zanzibar, and easier to order goods from a French mail-order firm than to receive Islamic books or medicines from Mombasa. Within Madagascar, in the summer of 1993 people in the larger cities followed the day-to-day development of the Marseille football scandal on television, while those in many parts of the countryside waited weeks for the results of the national elections.

2 Hosts are predominantly but not exclusively women. I discuss possession extensively in two books on Mayotte (Lambek 1981, 1993) and one on Madagascar (2002c).

3 I grossly oversimplify both because there are several forms of possession, including spirits indigenous to Mayotte, and because Islam does not imply consensus. See Giles 1987 for the scope of East African possession. The question of Islamic consensus can be seen in terms of a fissure between the "certain knowledge" constituted by the sacred texts and the "contestable authority" of those who claim to speak on the texts' behalf. This is characteristic of Islam not only on the periphery (Lambek 1990a) but everywhere (e.g., Eickelman 1992, Fischer and Abedi 1990, Gilsenan 1982, Messick 1989) and, indeed, of any body of propositional knowledge (Asad 1988: 78).

4 The word "discourse" may be problematic here; certainly, spirit possession contains elements one would characterize as "non-discursive."

5 Boddy (1989) and Jean Comaroff (1985) provide outstanding ethnographic analyses of embodied practices with respect to resistance.

6 Topan (n.d.) makes a similar point and notes comparable practices among Swahili speakers, notably *ruhani* possession in which spirits mimic Sufi brothers.

7 See further Lambek (1993: chapter 2). Other dimensions of possession's contextualizing qualities are discussed in Boddy 1989, Lambek 2002c, and elsewhere.

8 Rorty himself speaks of swallowing or spitting out; see the remark quoted in chapter 9 below.

9 Events prior to the referendum certainly did not encourage people to expect much good from the French. During the nineteenth century, colonialism was highly coercive and exploitive (Martin 1983, Shepherd 1980); for much of the twentieth it meant political and economic stagnation.

10 Compare Carsten 1997 on alimentary practice in Malay kinship.

11 Object relations is an approach stemming from the work of British psychoanalysts such as Ronald Fairbairn and Donald Winnicott, with roots in Freud's theory of narcissism. It "sustains the view that we are all incorporations and extensions of – take in and provide aspects of – one another" (Chodorow 1989: 147). For an excellent synthesis see Mitchell 1988.

12 I draw on these terms metaphorically rather than to invoke psychic causality.

13 See also Nedelsky 1990 for an analysis of the pervasive discourse of boundedness in American legal and political thought.

14 Ethnic background may have played a greater role in the political affiliations of functionaries than among villagers, but this was more a matter of *de facto* political connections than recourse to primordial sentiment. The lack of conflict over linguistic issues was striking to an anthropologist hailing from Quebec but ought not to surprise readers of Vail (1991). Ranger (1991) provides a concise account of colonial interventions that led to the development of objectified linguistic boundaries in the African continent.

15 Women were also the active force on the opposing side. In general, women were more certain of what they wanted than were men, or at least felt freer to assert their wishes.

16 On incorporative societies generally see D. Turner (1979). Relevant factors in the underplaying of descent include the dislocations of the nineteenth century, the egalitarian ethos, and concealment of slave ancestry. In general, however, there is a similarity with the principle of performative identity discerned for the Vezo, another Malagasy group living on the borders of a more hierarchical society (Astuti, 1995). Such a position may be characteristic of being subject to a tributary mode of production but is also consistent with widespread features of coastal Malagasy kinship and marriage practices.

17 By 2018 there has been a retreat from region back to nation in Europe.

18 For this period see also Vidal 1994, 2010.

19 A common explanation was that store-bought wrapped chicken meat is "clean" unlike the local variety that pecks in the dirt and walks over its own shit.

20 I discuss taboos extensively in Lambek 1992 (reprinted in 2015).

8. Nuriaty, the Saint, and the Sultan: Virtuous Subject and Subjective Virtuoso of the Postmodern Colony, to 1995

1 This was the trenchant formulation of Richard Werbner in his invitation.

2 My gratitude to Ray Kelly for first posing the question to me.

3 They had not held their ceremonies or had the opportunity to announce their names before they were displaced.

4 Not all men readily handle the social and financial obligations or emotional commitment to more than one wife, and not all women are prepared to accept it.

5 Much of this was described to me by Nuriaty's ex-mother-in-law, who wished to justify her own actions and to praise Nuriaty.

6 As another medium put it, the saint was undoubtedly sad to have Islamic recitation replaced by pop music from the radio.

7 "Good people" are here described as Muslims able to indulge in outward signs of piety: elegant clothes and scent signifying the epoch of Muslim hegemony.

8 Football (soccer) was a major means by which the French reoriented and disciplined youth, promoting a civil rather than a Muslim identity.

9 Nuriaty's primary childhood caregiver, her father's mother, mentioned in chapter 3, still knew some Kimrima (an East African language, possibly Makua), indicative of indentured labour. The possession literature is replete with illustrations of identity transformation and mimesis (e.g., Boddy 1989, Kramer 1993, Sharp 1996). It is also not uncommon for people at the bottom or the margins to become spirit mediums or diviners of the elite.

10 The most important of these, the spirit whom Nuriaty shared with her father, continued occasionally to offer advice in her sleep. The others, she said, left outright. Nuriaty emphasized the Sultan's objection to the non-Islamic practices of the other spirits, especially the drink and noise; her father added that the Sultan is a king and kings rule singly.

11 This was common among older, post-menopausal women.

12 Her day-to-day life changed little. In 1995 she was still embroiled in the affairs of her parents' extended families and lived extremely modestly.

13 To my wife, who had also known her a decade earlier, she appeared harder, her warmth coloured by a streak of bitterness (Jackie Solway, personal communication).

14 In addition, the security of uneducated women had altered. With rising domestic costs, declining subsistence production, and female immigration, local women were increasingly vulnerable to abandonment by their spouses and found it harder to support their children. On difficulties faced by educated youth see Vidal 1994, 2010.

15 The Sultan sported a spotless white shirt, long waist wrap, cloth belt, lacy scarf, red fez, and staff. The items were expensive, some purchased by Nuriaty and her husband, others provided as gifts from devotees of the Sultan. The Sultan consumes rose water, betel nut, and a drink made of powdered sandalwood, all long out of fashion in Mayotte.

16 Clients should remunerate spirit mediums with gifts (*ishima*) not payment; the amount is up to the donor (Lambek 1993: 95–8, 361) and an index of respect. Nuriaty may anticipate that the Sultan will receive larger gifts from wealthy politicians than her other spirits received from village supplicants, but cannot count on this. Moreover, any indications of greed would immediately undermine her authority. Hence, while not irrelevant, material considerations are unlikely to be central to Nuriaty's shift in practice.

17 I am referring to *The Poetics* (Aristotle 1947) and *The Ethics* (Aristotle 1976). On the value of an Aristotelian perspective, see Lambek 2000a, 2015a, and Mattingly 2014; for substantiation with respect to poiesis, see Lambek 1998b. Beattie (1977) and Leiris (1958) provide more literal treatments of spirit mediumship as theatre.

18 Things are changing so fast in Mayotte that she may become unable to attract and retain the degree of social respect necessary for her own self-respect.

19 That we place so much emphasis on the political may say more about us than about our subjects. Might the aporias of our own attempts to construct a viable politics not lead us to project yet another burden upon subjects elsewhere?

20 Perhaps agency ought to remain a question rather than an answer (Richard Fardon, personal communication, 1999).

21 Žižek illustrates the point by means of the *femme fatale* of film noir, who, through no action of her own other than her presence, "brings about the moral decay of all men around her" (Žižek 1991: 77).

22 These observations draw from object relations theory (chapter 7).

9. The Saint, the Sea Monster, and an Invitation to a *Dîner-dansant*, to 2001

1 The first primary school in Lombeni was set up in 1982. Prior to that, a few intrepid children walked to schools in neighbouring villages. In 2000 there were some five *lycées* (high schools) on the island, which then had a population of around 135,000. That year, 545 students took the *bac* (high school leaving exam, at a higher level than the North American equivalent) with a pass rate of 56 per cent, though only five students received the mention of *"très bien"* (very good).

2 The differences correspond in part to the types of peasant communities famously discerned by Wolf (1957).

3 I deal only with certain aspects of the festive, public side of weddings.

4 Sometimes these were children whom they had fostered. Parents sponsored the life-cycle rituals of all children who had not been taken over by relatives, but their public responsibilities were met by the first circumcision (often of several closely related boys at once) and first virgin wedding they sponsored. Thus the weddings of sisters were often not identical in scope and elaboration.

5 Troisième is three years prior to completion of the *bac*.

6 "Mr. Said Abdourahim and Miss Kaisati Aboudou invite you to their wedding." The parents of groom and bride "have the honour and pleasure to invite you to the marriage of their children ... and request the honour of your presence." My translation; the names are pseudonyms.

7 During the 1970s the women's dance was held spontaneously immediately following the consummation, whereas the arrival of the groom's gifts, a week later, was accompanied by a men's dance. By the 1990s marriages were often enacted and consummated a year or two before the groom brought the *valise,* and the wedding was celebrated with feasting and dancing at the latter event.

8 One reader points out that *boums* were prominent in Madagascar during the mid- to late 1980s. Malagasy music videos circulated in Mayotte along with French ones.

9 It is quite different from Plato's concept of spontaneous unreflective imitation.

10 It is also, as another successful groom confessed, a form of conceit or showing off (*mpwary*). *"Vazaha"* can indicate equally a person or attribute that is French or more broadly European or "modern."

11 Some guests were already more "European" than others – that is, performing as Europeans less self-consciously and in more domains of their lives.

12 Chapter 8. See also Weber's challenge to Nietzsche's argument that religion is forged in resentment (1946: 270).

13 *Unheimlich*, a term used by Freud, is usually translated as "uncanny" but could be "uneasy," "disturbing," or "edgy" – that which makes us feel no longer "at home."

14 This is, of course, an interesting reading of Nietzsche's aphorism concerning the death of God.

10. On the Move, through 2001

1 The pattern of migration from 2001 through 2011 remained approximately the same, if considerably enhanced, especially with more travel by students to metropolitan France, than what is reported here.

2 Nevertheless, this is different from women's migration elsewhere; women travel not as factory or domestic workers and not at the expense of their families or children.

3 Spirit possession itself remains common (Bouffart 2009), and indeed by 2015 many people travelled to Madagascar for cheaper or ostensibly more authoritative spirit possession ceremonies, and possession was also flourishing among migrants to France (cf Lambek 2010).

4 Short for *baccalauréat*, the qualifying exam at the end of high school for admission to university.

5 Marseille is France's largest port city, with a highly diverse population, including many Comorans.

6 Hence the practices are quite different from those overseas marriages described by Jennifer Cole (2010).

7 Polygyny has since been declared illegal in Mayotte.

11. Marriage and Moral Horizons, 2015

1 Weddings can of course be seen as total social facts (Mauss 1974, Meneley 2016).

2 For a fuller argument and exemplification see Lambek 2014a.

3 There is a parallel here with the way Rappaport (1999) describes the performance of a ritual as simultaneously "canonical" (repeated, identical) and "indexical" (circumstantial, unique).

4 I think this fits with Wittgensteinian accounts concerning statements.

5 I first saw a *manzaraka* procession in 2009 without fully grasping its significance. Compare Blanchy 2012.

6 In addition to changes in how to celebrate marriage, there are changes in the understanding of marriage itself and in how to live as a married couple.

7 Of course the size of the *mahary* has grown considerably over time.

8 Had he walked out, the man responsible would have been sought and forced to pay a fine.

9 For a full discussion of virgin marriage see Lambek 1983.

10 This too was not a timeless custom. An elderly man told me in 1975 that in his own youth there was less of a burden on young men. Not only did the age group not require a *shungu*, but the groom brought the bride only clothing. Jewellery (then silver rather than gold) was then the responsibility of the bride's parents.

11 "« *Man zāra qabra Muhammadin/ Nāla-sh-shafā ʿata fī ghadin* » (*Celui qui effectuera une visite pieuse sur le tombeau du Prophète Muhammad [sur lui la paix et le salut] bénéficiera de l'intercession de celui-ci le Jour du Jugement dernier) (Traduction de Chamsdine Kordjee.)*" (Blanchy 2012: 2, n2). The one who makes a pious visit to the tomb of the Prophet Muhammad will benefit from his intercession on the final Day of Judgment. The word "*manzaraka*" cuts the phrase after the first syllable of the word for "tomb." My thanks to Sophie Blanchy for showing me the etymology.

12 People make far fewer of the pastries that were once ubiquitous. They are labour-intensive, and people now say they are wasteful, going bad if not eaten quickly.

13 As in former weddings, the bride's family hosts and produces the feasts requested by the groom's family and to which the latter are invited and which they help pay for. At the engagement, the groom's side clearly state the exchanges they want fulfilled in the course of the wedding. In the past, they provided the bride's side with the means to ensure the production of the requisite meals. The *manzaraka* too is discussed during engagement negotiations, but the return comes largely after the fact, in the form of gifts of money from the groom's female kin. The imprecision of the exchange is implicitly a statement about the moral relations between the parties.

14 I was told that the debt produced by the first *manzaraka* led to a move away from bank loans to formalized support from family members and even distant kin. Solway (2016) discusses the significant social consequences of a shift from public exchange to private, often secret, bank loans to support "white" weddings in Botswana.

15 The procession of the old Mahorais elite was much smaller and led the groom to the bridal chamber on the first day of the wedding.

16 One can make the *manzaraka* as big as one likes or is able. Moreover, it is not a matter of completing a limited set of obligations as the *shungu* was. Whenever a groom requests a *manzaraka*, the bride's family have to produce it.

17 The groom's older brother held his *manzaraka* when he was thirty-three, but the marriage lasted only a few more years. Some people hold a second *manzaraka* on remarriage, but he had no intention of doing so. One would have to be rich, and he thought two would be excessive boasting. Sometimes the *manzaraka* is held, following the older model, at the end of the week following consummation.

18 I asked some people of my age whether, having finished their *shungu*, didn't it appear to be starting over again to have to sponsor a *manzaraka*? They responded, "The *manzaraka* is the *shungu* of youth (*jeunes*)." One man said he was not the *tompin* (owner, sponsor, principal) of the *asa* (work, event, ceremony), his children were.

19 During the meal the groom held one of their children on his lap.

20 Some days following the *manzaraka* and after I left Mayotte, the groom's father sponsored a *majlis*, a public lecture on Islam.

21 Whereas recent developments in Mayotte extend getting married as a process over time, the turn to "white weddings" in Botswana does the reverse, condensing what was a lengthy and ambiguous process taking many years and possibly even generations to complete (John Comaroff 1980, Solway 1990) into a single, very expensive ceremony (Solway 2016).

22 A couple who are highly educated professionals and who married quite late had a *kufungia* in 2006 where they purchased 50 kilos of beef for the feast. Two years later, they held the *manzaraka* for which they took responsibility (were the *tompin*). They estimated that they contributed two-thirds of the cost, and their families covered the rest. They purchased two cows for 5,000 euros and held a catered *dîner* for which *traiteurs* (caterers) brought in food. They planned it for 600 people but only between 400 and 500 showed up. They also held a *mamangu ambiu* dance.

23 French law has shifted with respect to distinctions between *droit commun* and *droit local*, thereby making divorce more difficult. See Blanchy and Moatty (2012) for a vigorous critique of the irregular, confusing, and possibly deliberately misleading fashion in which the laws have been applied. Civil marriage need not coincide with the *manzaraka* and is not part of it.

24 Note as well that, in contrast to much alliance theory, the exchange is fundamentally of acts rather than of persons or objects; and, with respect to money, primarily between women rather than between men.

25 The wife had put aside 18,000 euros for the event. It was not enough, and her parents supplemented it.

26 Engagements (*kurmidza*) have also inflated; since the man's party started bringing gifts to the fiancée at the engagement, the parents respond with a meal.

27 Most women now individually own hundreds of matching white china plates and sets of cutlery, kept in storage for such events.

28 The bride's mother's brother affirmed his pleasure but said he would be even happier once the groom returned and the bride's virginity was confirmed. The *manzaraka*, at which the bride's family estimates receiving 11,000 to 12,000 euros, will be held after the consummation,

29 This man married while he was in France. His brother stood in for him at the *kufungia*. The bride then travelled to France, where the couple consummated the marriage. They had now been married ten years and were planning to hold the *manzaraka* once he completed a house for his parents. As the couple already owned appliances, he said he would bring his wife only clothing and personal items.

30 Moreover, the availability of contraception and abortion in Mayotte has meant that loss of virginity can be concealed.

31 If their jobs do not permit it, they do not stay in the house for the week.

32 I draw here on ideas of Bourdieu, as elaborated by Hage 2014.

33 It was de facto characteristic of some older marriages.

12. Present Horizons, 2015

1 As one reviewer noted, the irony of larger houses built back home by absent labour migrants or standing as monuments to vanished or transformed sociality is found in many parts of the world, from Ireland to India and Peru to Poland.

2 The *mraba* conflicts are partly an index of succession and fissioning, hence true for any time period, but people linked them to the exigencies of the present.

3 Land law has changed in confusing ways. According to a knowledgeable villager, in 1939 there was a law that *indigènes* did not have to purchase titles to the land they bought but outsiders did. In the 1980s the law was changed without taking the former practice into account; the untitled were considered not to have land until they registered it. Following a law of 2008, anything done since by the *cathis* – who used to register land – is no longer recognized. Transfer must be conducted through a lawyer. In sum, it is precisely local people who have had to scramble for title and who can least afford it.

4 "You have to teach children to take responsibility for themselves."

5 A grandson of Malidy Muthary remembered him quite differently, as charismatic and a real leader. He attributed his death to sorcery (manifest as diabetes) by envious people who wanted someone from their own family (*mraba*) to become *chef* in his place.

6 She is actually kin to his deceased wife and comes herself from one of the other islands.

7 She says she doesn't really have friends (*camarades*) in the village but knows a few people at work with similar experiences to her own.

8 See M'trengoueni, Mouhktar, and Gueunier, 1999.

9 At departmentalization, "Mayotte, which now counts as a French département, will retain a special status regarding illegal immigration. There are an estimated 60,000 undocumented immigrants ... making up a third of the population. Last year 26,400 people were deported, a 30% increase on the previous year. The authorities are intercepting rising numbers of *kwassa-kwassa* (small fishing boats) which generally come from Anjouan, one of the Comoros islands, packed with men, women and children. The shanty towns where the newcomers live on Mayotte are the target of repeated police raids. More is also being done to stamp out illegal employment, focusing in particular on the building trade, catering, farming and taxis" (Hopquin and Canavate 2011). See also Hachimi-Alaoui, Lemercier, and Palomares 2013, Math 2013.

10 See for example Edouard de Mareschal, http://www.lefigaro.fr/actualite-france/2017/07/12/01016-20170712ARTFIG00204-mayotte-un-departement-francais-sous-pression-migratoire-extreme.php.

11 Sorcery (*voriky*) concerns deliberate but concealed acts of harm; its reality consists in diagnoses, accusations, and suspicions. It is unlike the fantastical inversions of reality found elsewhere in Africa (e.g., Piot 2010).

12 While an index of the times, escaping sorcery is not new. Tumbu and Mohedja spent several years living in the countryside far from Lombeni during the 1960s in part to avoid what they experienced as sorcery attacks from fellow villagers.

13 A very few Mahorais in other villages have done so.

14 Both his father and grandfather were Islamic *fundis*.

15 I am unable to generalize about who is attracted to *jaula* or how strongly. It seems mainly to be a matter of personal disposition and perhaps chance educational encounter. Of those who have taken it seriously such that it has transformed their lives, I can think of only one person older than me, a woman, who gave up spirit possession for piety. A woman born in the year of my arrival has taken, anomalously, to full veiling. A variety of men in

their fifties or younger have been influenced for longer or shorter periods of time. Abdou is the only one to receive extensive training abroad, and his approach to reform is measured.

16 He did not reject out of hand my suggestion that his mother see a psychiatrist.

17 Sophie Bouffart (2009) describes intense possession activity in Mayotte during the first decade of the twenty-first century. I have encountered clients from Mayotte in Madagascar, and Sarah Gould (personal communication) notes the active participation at Sakalava shrines of women from Mayotte resident in France.

13. Summation: Mariam's Mirror

1 I draw here from Shryock and da Col (2017) on Julian Pitt-Rivers.

2 One could say that social life in Mayotte remains performative rather than prescriptive (Sahlins 1985). I elaborate on the gift as act in Lambek 2013a.

3 In addition to exchange, Descola identifies predation, gift, production, protection, and transmission (2013: 311). He is interested in describing not only the dominant mode of relations among humans but also between humans and other beings in their environment. As has been evident by its omission in the text, people in Mayotte have not elaborated their relations with other natural species, but they do conceptualize their relations with spirits as ones in which potential predation needs to be transformed into relations of exchange.

4 On the distinction and relationship between reproduction and transformation, no less than the broader questions of structure and history and of multiple historicities, see notably Sahlins 1985.

5 This is less the case with respect to birth and the welcoming of new infants or with respect to circumcision, the former almost fully medicalized by now and the latter partly so. They are described as they were through the early 1990s in Lambek 1993.

6 Put on the trail by Gillian Shepherd, I recently learned from Chanfi Ahmed that *shungu* could be a transformation of the Swahili *nyungu*, meaning cooking pot, an etymology I never heard in Mayotte. Kjersti Larsen confirmed for me that *shungu* refers to a clay pot in Zanzibar. In 1975 pottery was a local art and in partial use; older courtyards had each an enclosure containing an immense clay jar affixed to a platform under which a fire was lit to provide hot water for bathing. Both the craft and the products have since disappeared.

7 In its practical contingency, it compares with lineage segments among the Nuer (Evans-Pritchard 1940). For a society with a much stronger focus on fixed enclosure and interiority see Boddy (1989) on northern Sudan.

8 In fact, as illustrated in chapters 9 and 12, many women do limit family size.

9 I first encountered the phrase in Koselleck (2004). Pinder is largely neglected today because he subsequently became a Nazi.

10 There is an affinity here with Nietzsche's conception of genealogy in contrast to pedigree, as discussed in the introduction.

11 I draw here on the entry "Martin Heidegger" from the *Stanford Encyclopedia of Philosophy* (Wheeler 2016).

References

Abu-Zahra, Nadia. 1991. "The Comparative Study of Muslim Societies and Islamic Rituals." *Arab Historical Review for Ottoman Studies* 3–4: 7–38.

Adams, John W. 1973. *The Gitksan Potlatch*. Toronto: Holt, Rinehart and Winston.

Ahmad, Shahab. 2015. *What Is Islam?* Princeton, NJ: Princeton University Press.

Ahmed, Chanfi. 1999. "La passion pour le Prophète aux Comores et en Afrique de l'est." *Islam et Sociétés au Sud du Sahara* 13: 65–89.

– 2006. "Networks of the Shadhiliyya Yashrutiyya Sufi Order in East Africa." In *The Global Worlds of the Swahili: Interfaces of Islam, Identity and Space in 19th and 20th-Century East Africa*, ed. Roman Loimeier and Rüdiger Seesemann, 317–42. Berlin: Lit Verlag.

Ahmed, Chanfi, Françoise Le Guennec-Coppens, and Sophie Mery. 2002. "Rites de mort aux Comores et chez les Swahili entre Islam savant et culture locale." *Journal des Africanistes* 72 (2): 187–201. https://doi.org/10.3406/jafr.2002.1314.

Allibert, Claude. 1984. *Mayotte: Plaque tournante et microcosme de l'océan Indien occidental*. Paris: Editions Anthropos.

– 2015. "L'archipel des Comores et son histoire ancienne. Essai de mise en perspective des chroniques, de la tradition orale et des typologies de céramiques locales et d'importation." *Afriques. Débats, méthodes et terrains d'histoire*. Paris: Institut des mondes africains. 06 | 2015. https://journals.openedition.org/afriques/1721.

Anderson, Benedict. 1991. *Imagined Communities*. London: Verso.

Antze, Paul, and Michael Lambek, eds. 1996. *Tense Past: Cultural Essays in Trauma and Memory*. New York: Routledge.

Aristotle. 1947. "Poetics." In *Introduction to Aristotle*. Ed. Richard McKeon, 623–67. New York: Random House.

– 1976. *Ethics*. Ed. J.A.K. Thomson, trans. Rev. Hugh Tredennick. Harmondsworth, Middlesex: Penguin.

Asad, Talal. 1986. *The Idea of an Anthropology of Islam*. Occasional Paper, Washington, DC: Center for Contemporary Arab Studies, Georgetown University.

– 1988. "Towards a Genealogy of the Concept of Ritual." In *Vernacular Christianity: Essays in the Social Anthropology of Religion Presented to Godfrey Lienhardt*, ed. W. James and D.H. Johnson, 73–87. Oxford, New York: JASO/ Lilian Barber Press.

Astuti, Rita. 1995. *People of the Sea: Identity and Descent among the Vezo of Madagascar*. Cambridge: Cambridge University Press. https://doi. org/10.1017/CBO9780511521041.

Bakhtin, M.M. 1981. *The Dialogic Imagination*. Ed. M. Holquist, trans. C. Emerson and M. Holquist. Austin, TX: University of Texas Press.

Bamana, Z. 2008. *Le choix du refus: Mayotte et l'indépendance des Comores*. Mamoudzou: Meso éd.

Baré, Jean-Francois. 1977. *Pouvoir des vivants, langage des morts. Idéo-logiques Sakalava*. Paris: F. Maspero.

Baxter, P.T.W., and U. Almagor. 1978. *Age, Generation and Time: Some Features of East African Age Organizations*. New York: St Martin's Press.

Beattie, John. 1977. "Spirit Mediumship as Theatre." *Royal Anthropological Institute News* 20 (June 1977). https://doi.org/10.2307/3032484.

Benjamin, Jessica. 1988. *The Bonds of Love*. New York: Pantheon.

Benjamin, Walter. 1969a. "Theses on the Philosophy of History." In *Illuminations*, ed. Hannah Arendt, trans. Harry Zohn, 253–64. New York: Schocken.

– 1969b. "The Work of Art in the Age of Mechanical Reproduction." In *Illuminations*, ed. Hannah Arendt, trans. Harry Zohn, 217–51. New York: Schocken.

Berger, John. 1979. *Pig Earth*. London: Writers and Readers Publishing Cooperative.

Bernardi, B. 1985. *Age Class Systems: Social Institutions and Polities Based on Age*. Cambridge: Cambridge University Press. https://doi.org/10.1017/ CBO9780511557941.

Bernstein, Richard. 1983. *Beyond Objectivism and Relativism: Science, Hermeneutics, and Praxis*. Philadelphia: University of Pennsylvania Press.

– 2002. "The Constellation of Hermeneutics, Critical Theory and Deconstruction." In *The Cambridge Companion to Gadamer*. Ed. Robert J. Dostal, 267–82. Cambridge: Cambridge University Press.

Blanchy, Sophie. 1990. *La vie quotidienne à Mayotte*. Paris: l'Harmattan.

– 1992. "Famille et parenté dans l'archipel des Comores." *Journal des Africanistes* 62 (1): 7–53. https://doi.org/10.3406/jafr.1992.2333.

– 1997. "Note sur le ritual d'intronisation des souverains de Mayotte et l'ancien ordre politico-religieux." *Etudes Océan Indien* 21: 107–29.

– 2002a. "Changement social à Mayotte: Transformations, tensions, ruptures." *Etudes Océan Indien* 33–4: 165–95.

– 2002b. "Mayotte: 'Française à tout prix.'" *Ethnologie Francaise* 4: 677–87.

– 2010. *Maisons des femmes, cités des hommes: Filiation, âge et pouvoir à Ngazidja.* Nanterre: Société d'ethnologie.

– 2012. "Matrilocalité et système d'âge à Mayotte: Notes pour une étude comparative de l'organisation sociale dans l'archipel des Comores." *Taarifa, Revue des Archives départementales de Mayotte* 3: 9–21.

Blanchy, Sophie, and Yves Moatty. 2012. "Le statut civil de droit local à Mayotte: Une imposture?" *Droit Social* 80: 117–39.

Blanchy, Sophie, and Mussa Said. 1990. "Inscriptions religieuses et magico-religieuses sur les monuments historiques à Ngazidja." *Etudes Oceans* 11: 7–62.

Bloch, Maurice. 1971. *Placing the Dead: Ancestral Villages and Kinship Organization on Madagascar.* New York: Seminar Press.

– 1986. *From Blessing to Violence: History and Ideology in the Circumcision Ritual of the Merina of Madagascar.* Cambridge: Cambridge University Press.

– 2005. "On Deference." In Bloch, *Essays on Cultural Transmission*, 123–37. London: Berg.

Boddy, Janice. 1989. *Wombs and Alien Spirits: Women, Men and the Zar Cult in Northern Sudan.* Madison, WI: University of Wisconsin Press.

Bouffart, Sophie. 2009. "La possession comme lieu et mode d'expression de la complexité sociale. Le cas de Mayotte." PhD diss., Paris-Ouest Nanterre.

Bourdieu, Pierre. 1977. *Outline of a Theory of Practice.* Trans. Richard Nice. Cambridge: Cambridge University Press. https://doi.org/10.1017/CBO9780511812507.

Bowen, John [R]. 1989. "Salat in Indonesia: The Social Meanings of an Islamic Ritual." *Man* 24 (4): 600–19. https://doi.org/10.2307/2804290.

– 1992. "On Scriptural Essentialism and Ritual Variation." *American Ethnologist* 19 (4): 656–71. https://doi.org/10.1525/ae.1992.19.4.02a00020.

Breslar, Jon. 1979. *L'habitat Mahorais: Une perspective ethnologique.* Paris: Editions A.G.G.

– 1981. "An Ethnography of the Mahorais (Mayotte, Comoro Islands)." PhD diss., University of Pittsburgh.

Carroll, J.B. 1956. *Language, Thought and Reality. Selected Writings of Benjamin Lee Whorf.* New York: Wiley.

Carsten, Janet. 1997. *The Heat of the Hearth: The Process of Kinship in a Malay Fishing Community*. Oxford: Clarendon.

Chodorow, Nancy. 1989. *Feminism and Psychoanalytic Theory*. New Haven, CT: Yale University Press.

Cole, Jennifer. 2010. *Sex and Salvation: Imagining the Future in Madagascar*. Chicago: University of Chicago Press. https://doi.org/10.7208/chicago/9780226113326.001.0001.

Comaroff, Jean. 1985. *Body of Power, Spirit of Resistance*. Chicago: University of Chicago Press.

– 1997. "Consuming Passions: Child Abuse, Fetishism, and 'The New World Order.'" *Culture* (Québec) 17: 7–19.

Comaroff, Jean, and John Comaroff. 1991. *Of Revelation and Revolution*, vol. 1. Chicago: University of Chicago Press. https://doi.org/10.7208/chicago/9780226114477.001.0001.

– 1999. "Occult Economies and the Violence of Abstraction." *American Ethnologist* 26 (2): 279–303. https://doi.org/10.1525/ae.1999.26.2.279.

Comaroff, John. 1980. "Bridewealth and the Control of Ambiguity in a Tswana Chiefdom." In *The Meaning of Marriage Payments*, ed. John L. Comaroff, 161–95. London, New York: Academic Press.

Comaroff, John, and Simon Roberts. 1981. *Rules and Processes*. Chicago: University of Chicago Press.

Cooper, Frederick. 1999. "Africa's Pasts and Africa's Historians." *African Sociological Review* 3 (2): 1–29. https://doi.org/10.4314/asr.v3i2.23163.

Csikszentmihalyi, Mihalyi. 1990. *Flow: The Psychology of Optimal Experience*. New York: Harper and Row.

Das, Veena. 2015. "What Does Ordinary Ethics Look Like?" In Michael Lambek, Veena Das, Didier Fassin, and Webb Keane, *Four Lectures on Ethics*, 53–125. Chicago: HAU.

de Boeck, Filip, and Marie-Françoise Plissart. 2006. *Kinshasa: Tales of the Invisible City*. Brussels: Ludion.

Dening, Greg. n.d. "Challenges to Perform: History, Passion and the Imagination." http://www.nla.gov.au/events/history/papers/Greg_Dening.html: accessed 4 December 2016.

Descola, Philippe. 2013. *Beyond Nature and Culture*. Trans. Janet Lloyd. Chicago: University of Chicago Press.

Desjarlais, Robert, and Jason Throop. 2011. "Phenomenological Approaches in Anthropology." *Annual Review of Anthropology* 40 (1): 87–102. https://doi.org/10.1146/annurev-anthro-092010-153345.

Douglas, Mary. 1966. *Purity and Danger*. Harmondsworth, Middlesex: Penguin. https://doi.org/10.4324/9780203361832.

Edkvist, Ingela. 1997. *The Performance of Tradition*. Uppsala: Almqvist and Wiksell.

Eickelman, Dale. 1992. "Mass Higher Education and the Religious Imagination in Contemporary Arab Societies." *American Ethnologist* 19 (4): 643–55. https://doi.org/10.1525/ae.1992.19.4.02a00010.

Eisenstadt, Shmuel. 1956. *From Generation to Generation: Age Groups and Social Structure*. Glencoe, IL: Free Press.

el Zein, Abdul Hamid. 1974. *The Sacred Meadows: A Structural Analysis of Religious Symbolism in an East African Town*. Evanston, IL: Northwestern University Press.

Evans-Pritchard, E.E. 1937. *Witchcraft, Oracles and Magic among the Azande*. Oxford: Clarendon.

– 1940. *The Nuer*. Oxford: Clarendon.

Feeley-Harnik, Gillian. 1991. *A Green Estate*. Washington, DC: Smithsonian.

Fischer, Michael, and Mehdi Abedi. 1990. *Debating Muslims: Cultural Dialogues in Postmodernity and Tradition*. Madison, WI: University of Wisconsin Press.

Fortes, Meyer. 1969. *Kinship and the Moral Order*. Chicago: Aldine.

– 1984. "Age, Generation, and Social Structure." In *Age and Anthropological Theory*, ed. D. Kertzer and J. Keith, 99–122. Ithaca, NY: Cornell University Press.

– 1987 [Original work published 1966]. "Totem and Taboo." In Fortes, *Religion, Morality and the Person: Essays on Tallensi Religion*, ed. Jack Goody, 110–44. Cambridge: Cambridge University Press. https://doi.org/10.1017/CBO9780511557996.007.

Fraser, T.M., Jr. 1966. *Fishermen of South Thailand*. New York: Holt, Rinehart and Winston.

Gadamer, Hans-Georg. 1985 [Original work published 1960]. *Truth and Method (Wahrheit und Method)*. New York: Crossroad.

Geertz, Clifford. 1973a. *The Interpretation of Cultures*. New York: Basic Books.

– 1973b. "Person, Time and Conduct in Bali." In Geertz, *The Interpretation of Cultures*, 360–411. New York: Basic Books.

– 1981. *Negara: The Theatre State in 19th Century Bali*. Princeton, NJ: Princeton University Press.

Geuss, Raymond. 1999. "Nietzsche and Genealogy." In Geuss, *Morality, Culture and History: Essays on German Philosophy*, 1–28. Cambridge: Cambridge University Press.

Gevrey, A. 1870. *Essai sur les Comores*. Pondichery: A. Saligny.

Giles, Linda. 1987. "Possession Cults on the Swahili Coast." *Africa: Journal of the International Africa Institute* 57 (2): 234–58. https://doi.org/10.2307/1159823.

Gilsenan, Michael. 1973. *Saint and Sufi in Modern Egypt*. Oxford: Clarendon.
– 1982. *Recognizing Islam: An Anthropologist's Introduction*. London: Croom Helm.
Gluckman, Max. 1963. "The Reasonable Man in Barotse Law." In Gluckman, *Order and Rebellion in Tribal Africa*, 178–206. London: Cohen and West.
Goffman, Erving. 1981. "Footing." In Goffman, *Forms of Talk*, 124–59. Philadelphia: University of Pennsylvania Press.
Gregory, Chris. 1982. *Gifts and Commodities*. London: Academic Press.
Grøn, Lone. n.d. "Pitting the Possible against the Predictable." Paper presented at the American Anthropological Association conference, Denver, 2015.
Gueunier, Noel. 1988. *Les chemins de l'Islam: Documents sur l'Islam à Madagascar*. Antsiranana: Institut Supérieur de Théologie et de Philosophie de Madagascar.
Guyer, Jane. 2007. "Prophecy and the Near Future: Thoughts on Macroeconomic, Evangelical, and Punctuated Time." *American Ethnologist* 34 (3): 409–21. https://doi.org/10.1525/ae.2007.34.3.409.
Hachimi-Alaoui, Myriam, Élise Lemercier, and Élise Palomares. 2013. "Reconfigurations ethniques à Mayotte." *Hommes & Migrations* 1304: 59–65.
Hage, Ghassan. 2014. "Eavesdropping on Bourdieu's Philosophers." In *The Ground Between: Anthropologists Engage Philosophy*, ed. Veena Das, Michael Jackson, Arthur Kleinman, and Bhrigupati Singh, 138–58. Durham, NC: Duke University Press. https://doi.org/10.1215/9780822376439-007.
Handler, Richard. 1988. *Nationalism and the Politics of Culture in Quebec*. Madison: University of Wisconsin Press.
Harpham, Geoffrey. 1995. "Ethics." In *Critical Terms for Literary Study*, ed. F. Lentricchia and T. McLaughlin, 387–405. Chicago: University of Chicago Press.
Hefner, Robert. 1993. "World Building and the Rationality of Conversion." In *Conversion to Christianity: Historical and Anthropological Perspectives on a Great Transformation*, ed. R.W. Hefner, 3–44. Berkeley: University of California Press. https://doi.org/10.1525/california/9780520078352.003.0001.
Hirsch, Eric, and Charles Stewart. 2005. "Introduction: Ethnographies of Historicity." *History and Anthropology* 16 (3): 261–74. https://doi.org/10.1080/02757200500219289.
Hirsch, Jennifer, and Holly Wardlow, eds. 2006. *Modern Loves: The Anthropology of Romantic Courtship and Companionate Marriage*. Ann Arbor: University of Michigan Press. https://doi.org/10.3998/mpub.170440.

Hodges, Matt. 2015. "Reinventing 'History'?" *History and Anthropology* 26 (4): 515–27. https://doi.org/10.1080/02757206.2015.1074901.

Hopquin, Benoît, and Laurent Canavate. 2011. "Mayotte accède à son statut de département dans la confusion." *Le Monde,* 31 March. Reprinted in translation in *Guardian Weekly,* 19 April.

Howard, Alan. 1996. "Speak of the Devils: Discourse and Belief in Spirits on Rotuma." In *Spirits in Culture, History, and Mind,* ed. Jeannette Mageo and Alan Howard, 121–45. New York: Routledge.

Hunt, Nancy Rose. 2011. "African History Matters." Lecture delivered at Wisssenschaftskolleg zu Berlin, 30 May 2011.

Hutcheon, Linda. 1994. *Irony's Edge: The Theory and Politics of Irony.* London: Routledge. https://doi.org/10.4324/9780203359259.

Ingold, Tim, ed. 1996. "The Past Is a Foreign Country." In *Key Debates in Anthropology,* 199–248. London: Routledge.

Jackson, Michael, ed. 1996. *Things as They Are: New Directions in Phenomenological Anthropology.* Bloomington: Indiana University Press.

– 2011. *Life within Limits: Well-being in a World of Want.* Durham, NC: Duke University Press.

– 2017. *How Lifeworlds Work: Emotionality, Sociality, and the Ambiguity of Being.* Chicago: University of Chicago Press.

James, Wendy. 1988. *The Listening Ebony: Moral Knowledge, Religion and Power among the Uduk of Sudan.* Oxford: Clarendon.

– ed. 1995. *The Pursuit of Certainty: Religions and Cultural Formations.* ASA Monographs. London: Routledge.

– 2003. *The Ceremonial Animal.* Oxford: Oxford University Press.

Kamardine, Mansour. 2008. *J'assume.* Chevagny-sur-Guye: Editions Orphie.

Kamil, Abdou. 2014. *Mes déchirures.* Mouzillon: Histoires à Partager.

Kapferer, Bruce. 2005. "Sorcery and the Beautiful." In *Aesthetics in Performance,* ed. Angela Hobart and Bruce Kapferer, 129–60. New York: Berghahn.

Kierkegaard, Søren. 1985. *Philosophical Fragments.* Trans. Howard Hong and Edna Hong. Princeton, NJ: Princeton University Press.

Kopytoff, Igor. 1971. "Ancestors as Elders in Africa." *Africa: Journal of the International Africa Institute* 41 (2): 129–42. https://doi.org/10.2307/1159423.

Koselleck, Reinhart. 2004. *Futures Past: On the Semantics of Historical Time.* New York: Columbia University Press.

Kramer, Fritz. 1993 [1997]. *The Red Fez: Art and Spirit Possession in Africa. Verso.* Trans. Malcolm Green. London: Verso.

Kresse, Kai. 2006. "Debating *Maulidi*: Ambiguities and Transformations of Muslim Identity along the Kenyan Swahili Coast." In *The Global Worlds of the Swahili: Interfaces of Islam, Identity and Space in 19th and 20th-Century East*

Africa, ed. Roman Loimeier and Rüdiger Seesemann, 209–28.
Berlin: Lit Verlag.

La Fontaine, Jean. 1997. *Speak of the Devil: Allegations of Satanic Child Abuse in Contemporary England*. Cambridge: Cambridge University Press.

Lambek, Michael. 1981. *Human Spirits: A Cultural Account of Trance in Mayotte*. New York: Cambridge University Press.

– 1983. "Virgin Marriage and the Autonomy of Women in Mayotte." *Signs* (Chicago) 9 (2): 264–81. https://doi.org/10.1086/494047.

– 1985. "Motherhood and Other Careers in Mayotte." In *In Her Prime: The World of Middle-Aged Women*, ed. J.K. Brown and V. Kerns. South Hadley, MA: Bergin and Garvey. Revised version reprinted in *In Her Prime*, 2nd ed., 76–92. Urbana: University of Illinois Press, 1992.

– 1987. "The Ludic Side of Islam and Its Possible Fate in Mayotte." *Omaly sy Anio (Hier et Aujourd'hui)* 25–6: 99–122. Revised and reprinted as Lambek 2006.

– 1988a. "Graceful Exits: Spirit Possession as Personal Performance in Mayotte." *Culture* (Québec) 8: 59–69.

– 1988b. "Spirit Possession/Spirit Succession: Aspects of Social Continuity among Malagasy Speakers in Mayotte." *American Ethnologist* 15 (4): 710–31. https://doi.org/10.1525/ae.1988.15.4.02a00070.

– 1990a. "Certain Knowledge, Contestable Authority: Power and Practice on the Islamic Periphery." *American Ethnologist* 17 (1): 23–40. https://doi.org/10.1525/ae.1990.17.1.02a00020.

– 1990b. "Exchange, Time, and Person in Mayotte: The Structure and Destructuring of a Cultural System." *American Anthropologist* 92 (3): 647–61. https://doi.org/10.1525/aa.1990.92.3.02a00060.

– 1992. "Taboo as Cultural Practice among Malagasy Speakers." *Man* 27: 19–42.

– 1993. *Knowledge and Practice in Mayotte: Local Discourses of Islam, Sorcery and Spirit Possession*. Toronto: University of Toronto Press.

– 1995. "Choking on the Qur'an and Other Consuming Parables from the Western Indian Ocean Front." In *The Pursuit of Certainty: Religious and Cultural Formations*, ed. Wendy James, ASA Monographs, 252–75. London: Routledge.

– 1996. "The Past Imperfect: Remembering as Moral Practice." In *Tense Past: Cultural Essays in Trauma and Memory*, ed. Paul Antze and M. Lambek, 235–54. New York: Routledge.

– 1997. "Monstrous Desires and Moral Disquiet: Reflections on Jean Comaroff's 'Consuming Passions.'" *Culture* (Québec) 17: 19–25.

– 1998a. "Body and Mind in Mind, Body and Mind in Body: Some Anthropological Interventions in a Long Conversation." In *Bodies and*

Persons: Comparative Perspectives from Africa and Melanesia, ed. M. Lambek and A. Strathern, 103–23. Cambridge: Cambridge University Press.

– 1998b. "The Sakalava Poiesis of History: Realizing the Past through Spirit Possession in Madagascar." *American Ethnologist* 25 (2): 1–22.

– 2000a. "The Anthropology of Religion and the Quarrel between Poetry and Philosophy." *Current Anthropology* 41 (3): 309–20. https://doi.org/10.1086/300143.

– 2000b. "Localizing Islamic Performances in Mayotte." In *Islamic Prayer across the Indian Ocean: Inside and Outside the Mosque,* ed. David Parkin and Stephen Headley, 63–97. Oxford: Curzon.

– 2001. "Rappaport on Religion: A Social Anthropological Reading." In *Ecology and the Sacred: Engaging the Anthropology of Roy A. Rappaport,* ed. Ellen Messer and Michael Lambek, 244–73. Ann Arbor: University of Michigan Press.

– 2002a. "Fantasy in Practice: Projection and Introjection, or the Witch and the Spirit-Medium." In *Beyond Rationalism: Rethinking Magic, Witchcraft and Sorcery,* ed. Bruce Kapferer, 198–214. New York: Berghahn.

– 2002b. "Nuriaty, the Saint, and the Sultan: Virtuous Subject and Subjective Virtuoso of the Postmodern Colony." In *Postcolonial Subjectivities in Africa,* ed. Richard Werbner, 25–43. London: Zed Books.

– 2002c. *The Weight of the Past: Living with History in Mahajanga, Madagascar.* New York: Palgrave-Macmillan.

– 2003. "Memory in a Maussian Universe." In *Regimes of Memory,* ed. Susannah Radstone and Katharine Hodgkin, 202–16. London: Routledge.

– 2004. "The Saint, the Sea Monster, and an Invitation to a *Dîner-dansant*: Ethnographic Reflections on the Edgy Passage – and the Double Edge – of Modernity, Mayotte 1975–2001." *Anthropologica* 46 (1): 57–68. https://doi.org/10.2307/25606168.

– 2006. "The Playful Side of Islam and Its Possible Fate in Mayotte." In *The Global Worlds of the Swahili: Interfaces of Islam, Identity and Space in 19th and 20th-Century East Africa,* ed. Roman Loimeier and Rüdiger Seesemann, 161–86. Berlin: Lit Verlag.

– 2010. "Traveling Spirits: Unconcealment and Undisplacement." In *Traveling Spirits: Migrants, Markets, and Mobilities,* ed. Gertrud Hüwelmeier and Kristine Krause, 17–35. London, New York: Routledge.

– 2011a. "Catching the Local." *Anthropological Theory* 11 (2): 197–221.

– 2011b. "Kinship as Gift and Theft: Acts of Succession in Mayotte and Israel," *American Ethnologist* 38 (1): 1–15.

– 2012. "Ethics Out of the Ordinary." In *ASA Handbook of Social Anthropology,* Vol. 2, ed. Richard Fardon, 141–52. London: Sage.

– 2013a. "The Value of (Performative) Acts." *HAU* 3 (2): 141–60. Special issue on value, ed. Ton Otto and Rane Willerslev. Reprinted 2015 in Michael Lambek, *The Ethical Condition: Essays on Action, Person, and Value.*

– 2013b. "What Is 'Religion' for Anthropology?" Introduction to *A Companion to the Anthropology of Religion*, ed. Janice Boddy and Michael Lambek, 1–32. Boston: Wiley-Blackwell.

– 2014a. "The Interpretation of Lives or Life as Interpretation: Cohabiting with Spirits in the Malagasy World." *American Ethnologist* 41 (3): 491–503. https://doi.org/10.1111/amet.12089.

– 2014b. "Ritual as a Social Diagnostic and Lens of Comparison in Mayotte and its Neighbours." *Anthropologie Comparative des Sociétés Insulaires de l'Océan Indien Occidental*, ed. Sophie Blanchy and Laurent Berger. *Etudes Rurales* 194: 63–77.

– 2015a. *The Ethical Condition: Essays on Action, Person, and Value.* Chicago: University of Chicago Press.

– 2015b. "Living as if It Mattered." In Michael Lambek, Veena Das, Didier Fassin, and Webb Keane, *Four Lectures on Ethics*, 5–51. Chicago: HAU Books.

– 2016. "On Being Present to History: Historicity and Brigand Spirits in Madagascar." In Special section "The Anthropology of History," ed. Stephan Palmié and Charles Stewart. *HAU* 6 (1): 317–41.

– 2018. "After Death: Event, Narrative, Feeling." In *A Companion to the Anthropology of Death*, ed. Anthony Robben, 87–101. Malden, MA: Wiley Blackwell.

Lambek, M., and Jon Breslar. 1986. "Ritual and Social Change: The Case of Funerals in Mayotte." In *Madagascar: Society and History*, ed. Conrad Phillip Kottak, Jean-Aime Rakotoarisoa, and Aidan Southall, 393–410. Durham, NC: Carolina Academic Press.

Lambek, M., and Andrew Walsh. 1997. "The Imagined Community of the Antankaraña: Identity, History, and Ritual in Northern Madagascar." *Journal of Religion in Africa. Religion en Afrique* 27 (3): 308–33. https://doi.org/10.2307/1581742.

Lankauskas, Gediminas. 2015. *The Land of Weddings and Rain: Nation and Modernity in Post-Socialist Lithuania.* Toronto: University of Toronto Press.

Laugier, Sandra. 2015. "The Ethics of Care as a Politics of the Ordinary." *New Literary History* 46 (2): 217–40. https://doi.org/10.1353/nlh.2015.0016.

Leach, Edmund. 1954. *Political Systems of Highland Burma.* London: G. Bell.

Lear, Jonathan. 2006. *Radical Hope.* Cambridge, MA: Harvard University Press.

Leiris, Michel. 1958. *La possession et ses aspects théâtraux chez les Ethiopiens de Gondar.* Paris: Pion.

Lévi-Strauss, Claude. 1966. *The Savage Mind*. Chicago: University of Chicago Press.

– 1969 [Original work published 1949]. *The Elementary Structures of Kinship*. London: Eyre and Spottiswoode.

Lewis, I.M. 1986. "The Power of the Past: African 'Survivals' in Islam." In Lewis, *Religion in Context: Cults and Charisma*, 94–107. Cambridge: Cambridge University Press.

Loewald, Hans. 1980. *Papers on Psychoanalysis*. New Haven, CT: Yale University Press.

Loimeier, Roman, and Rüdiger Seesemann, eds. 2006. *The Global Worlds of the Swahili: Interfaces of Islam, Identity and Space in 19th and 20th-Century East Africa*. Berlin: Lit Verlag.

Macpherson, C.B. 1962. *The Political Theory of Possessive Individualism*. Oxford: Oxford University Press.

Mamdani, Mahmood. 1996. *Citizen and Subject*. Princeton, NJ: Princeton University Press.

Marcuse, Walter D. 1914. *Through Western Madagascar in Search of the Golden Bean*. London: Hurst and Blackett.

Martin, Jean, 1983. *Comores, quatre îles entre pirates et planteurs*. Paris: l'Harmattan.

– 1976. "L'affranchissement des esclaves de Mayotte, décembre 1846 – juillet 1847." *Cahiers d'Etudes Africaines* 16 (61–2): 207–33.

Math, A. 2013. "Mayotte, terre d'émigration massive." *Plein Droit* 96 (1): 31–4. https://doi.org/10.3917/pld.096.0031.

Mattingly, Cheryl. 2014. *Moral Laboratories: Family Peril and the Struggle for a Good Life*. Berkeley: University of California Press.

Mauss, Marcel. 1974 [Original work published 1925]. *The Gift*. London: Routledge and Kegan Paul.

Maybury-Lewis, David. 1984. "Age and Kinship: A Structural View." In *Age and Anthropological Theory*, ed. D. Kertzer and J. Keith, 123–40. Ithaca, NY: Cornell University Press.

McGranahan, Carole. 2012. "Mao in Tibetan Disguise: History, Ethnography, and Excess." *HAU: Journal of Ethnographic Theory* 2 (1): 213–45.

Meneley, Anne. 1996. *Tournaments of Value: Sociability and Hierarchy in a Yemeni Town*. Toronto: University of Toronto Press.

– 2016. "Preface to 20th Anniversary Edition." In Anne Meneley, *Tournaments of Value: Sociability and Hierarchy in a Yemeni Town*, 20th anniversary ed., xiii–xxii. Toronto: University of Toronto Press.

Messick, Brinkley. 1989. "Just Writing: Paradox and Political Economy in Yemeni Legal Documents." *Cultural Anthropology* 4 (1): 26–50. https://doi.org/10.1525/can.1989.4.1.02a00020.

Middleton, John. 1992. *The World of the Swahili: An African Mercantile Civilization*. New Haven, CT: Yale University Press.

Middleton, Karen, ed. 1999. *Ancestors, Power and History in Madagascar*. Leiden: Brill.

Mintz, Sidney. 1989. *Caribbean Transformations*. New York: Columbia University Press.

Mitchell, Stephen. 1988. *Relational Concepts in Psychoanalysis*. Cambridge, MA: Harvard University Press.

M'trengoueni, Mohamed, Soilihi Mouhktar, and Noel J. Gueunier. 1999. "Nom, prénom: Une étape vers l'uniformisation culturelle. Identité et statut juridique à Mayotte." *Revue des Sciences Sociales de la France de l'Est* 26: 45–53.

Nedelsky, Jennifer. 1990. "Law, Boundaries and the Bounded Self." *Representations* (Berkeley, CA) 30 (1): 162–89. https://doi.org/10.1525/rep.1990.30.1.99p0354u.

Nuotio, Hanni. 2006. "The Dance That Is Not Danced, the Song That Is Not Sung: Zanzibari Women in the *Maulidi* Ritual." In *The Global Worlds of the Swahili: Interfaces of Islam, Identity and Space in 19th and 20th-Century East Africa*, ed. Roman Loimeier and Rüdiger Seesemann, 187–208. Berlin: Lit Verlag.

Obeyesekere, Gananath. 1981. *Medusa's Hair: An Essay on Personal Symbols and Religious Experience*. Chicago: University of Chicago Press.

Ortner, Sherry [B.]. 1973. "On Key Symbols." *American Anthropologist* 75 (5): 1338–46. https://doi.org/10.1525/aa.1973.75.5.02a00100.

– 1978. *Sherpas through Their Rituals*. Cambridge: Cambridge University Press.

– 1984. "Theory in Anthropology since the Sixties." *Comparative Studies in Society and History* 26 (1): 126–66. https://doi.org/10.1017/S0010417500010811.

– 1989. *High Religion*. Princeton, NJ: Princeton University Press.

Östör, Akos. 1984. "Chronology, Category, and Ritual." In *Age and Anthropological Theory*, ed. D. Kertzer and J. Keith, 281–304. Ithaca, NY: Cornell University Press.

Ottenheimer, Martin, and Harriet Ottenheimer. 1979. "Matrilocal Residence and Nonsororal Polygyny: A Case from the Comoro Islands." *Journal of Anthropological Research* 35 (3): 328–35. https://doi.org/10.1086/jar.35.3.3629906.

Palmié, Stephan, and Charles Stewart. 2016. "Introduction: For an Anthropology of History." *HAU* 6 (1): 207–36. https://doi.org/10.14318/hau6.1.014.

Parry, Jonathan. 1986. "The Gift, the Indian Gift and the 'Indian Gift.'" *Man* 21 (3): 453–73. https://doi.org/10.2307/2803096.

Peel, John. 1993. "Review Essay." *History and Theory* 32 (2): 162–78. https://doi.org/10.2307/2505350.

Pinder, Wilhelm. 1926. *Das Problem der Generation in der Kunstgeschichte Europas*. Berlin: Frankfurter Verlags-Anstalt.

Piot, Charles. 2010. *Nostalgia for the Future: West Africa after the Cold War*. Chicago: University of Chicago Press. https://doi.org/10.7208/chicago/9780226669663.001.0001.

Pouillon, Jean. 1982. "Remarks on the Verb 'To Believe.'" In *Between Belief and Transgression: Structural Essays on Religion, History, and Myth*, ed. Michel Izard and Pierre Smith, 1–8. Chicago: University of Chicago Press.

Ranger, Terrence. 1991. "Missionaries, Migrants and the Manyika: The Invention of Ethnicity in Zimbabwe." In *The Creation of Tribalism*, ed. L. Vail, 118–50. Berkeley: University of California Press.

Rappaport, Roy. 1979. "The Obvious Aspects of Ritual." In Rappaport, *Ecology, Meaning and Religion*, 173–221. Richmond: North Atlantic Books.

– 1999. *Ritual and Religion in the Making of Humanity*. Cambridge: Cambridge University Press.

Regnault, Madina. 2011. *Du pouvoir de la culture à la culture du pouvoir: Analyse compare des politiques culturelles à La Réunion et à Mayotte*. Thèse du doctorat, EHESS Paris.

Ricoeur, Paul. 1971. "The Model of the Text." *Social Research* 38: 529–62.

– 1992. *Oneself as Another*. Trans. Kathleen Blamey. Chicago: University of Chicago Press.

Rorty, Richard. 1980. *Philosophy and the Mirror of Nature*. Princeton, NJ: Princeton University Press.

– 1989. *Contingency, Irony, and Solidarity*. Cambridge: Cambridge University Press.

Sahlins, Marshall. 1972. "On the Sociology of Primitive Exchange." In Sahlins, *Stone Age Economics*, 185–275. Chicago, IL: Aldine Atherton.

– 1985. *Islands of History*. Chicago: University of Chicago Press.

– 2013. *What Kinship Is – and Is Not*. Chicago: University of Chicago Press.

Schafer, Roy. 1976. *A New Language for Psychoanalysis*. New Haven, CT: Yale University Press.

Schieffelin, Edward. 1976. *The Sorrow of the Lonely and the Burning of the Dancers*. New York: St Martins.

Seesemann, Rüdiger. 2006. "African Islam or Islam in Africa? Evidence from Kenya." In *The Global Worlds of the Swahili: Interfaces of Islam, Identity and Space in 19th and 20th-Century East Africa*, ed. Roman Loimeier and Rüdiger Seesemann, 229–50. Berlin: Lit Verlag.

Sharp, Lesley. 1996. *The Possessed and the Dispossessed*. Berkeley: University of California Press.

Shepherd, Gillian. 1977. "Two Marriage Forms in the Comoro Islands: An Investigation." *Africa: Journal of the International Africa Institute* 47 (4): 344–59. https://doi.org/10.2307/1158341.

– 1980. "The Comorians and the East African Slave Trade." In *Asian and African Systems of Slavery*, ed. J.L. Watson, 73–99. Berkeley: University of California Press.

Shryock, Andrew, and Giovanni da Col. 2017. "A Perfect Host: Julian Pitt-Rivers and the Anthropology of Grace." Introduction to *From Hospitality to Grace: A Julian Pitt-Rivers Omnibus*, ed. Andrew Shryock and Giovanni da Col, xiii–xxxix. Chicago: HAU Books.

Simmel, Georg. 2010 [Original work published 1918]. "Life as Transcendence." In *The View of Life (Lebensanschauung)*, trans. John A.Y. Andrews and Donald N. Levine, 1–17. Chicago: University of Chicago Press. https://doi.org/10.7208/chicago/9780226757858.001.0001.

Singer, Milton. 1972. *When a Great Tradition Modernizes*. New York: Praeger.

Smith, Dorothy. 1990. *Texts, Facts and Femininity: Exploring the Relations of Ruling*. London: Routledge. https://doi.org/10.4324/9780203425022.

Solway, Jacqueline. 1990. "Affines and Spouses, Friends and Lovers: The Passing of Polygyny in Botswana." *Journal of Anthropological Research* 46 (1): 41–66. https://doi.org/10.1086/jar.46.1.3630393.

– 2016. "'Slow Marriage,' 'Fast *Bogadi*': Change and Continuity in Marriage in Botswana." *Anthropology Southern Africa* 39 (4): 309–22. https://doi.org/10.1080/23323256.2016.1235980.

Steedly, Mary. 1993. *Hanging without a Rope*. Princeton, NJ: Princeton University Press.

Stewart, Charles. 2012. *Dreaming and Historical Consciousness in Island Greece*. Chicago: University of Chicago Press.

Swartz, Marc. 1991. *The Way the World Is: Cultural Processes and Social Relations among the Mombasa Swahili*. Berkeley: University of California Press.

Tambiah, Stanley. 1985. "A Performative Approach to Ritual." In Tambiah, *Culture, Thought and Social Action: An Anthropological Perspective*, 123–66. Cambridge, MA: Harvard University Press. https://doi.org/10.4159/harvard.9780674433748.c6.

Tapper, Nancy, and Richard Tapper. 1987. "The Birth of the Prophet: Ritual and Gender in Turkish Islam." *Man* 22 (1): 69–92. https://doi.org/10.2307/2802964.

Tehindrazanarivelo, Emmanuel. 1997. "Fieldwork: The Dance of Power." *Anthropology and Humanism* 22 (1): 54–60. https://doi.org/10.1525/ahu.1997.22.1.54.

Thompson, E.P. 1967. "Time, Work-Discipline and Industrial Capitalism." *Past and Present* 38 (1): 56–97. https://doi.org/10.1093/past/38.1.56.

Throop, Jason. 2010. *Suffering and Sentiment*. Berkeley: University of California Press.

Topan, Farouk. n.d. "Pepo: A Fluid Dimension of Swahili Religious Culture." Lecture delivered at the SOAS Africa seminar, March 1997.

Tribe, Keith. 2004. "Translator's Introduction." In Reinhart Koselleck, *Futures Past: On the Semantics of Historical Time*, vii–xx. New York: Columbia University Press.

Tugendhat, Ernst. 2016. *Egocentricity and Mysticism: An Anthropological Study*. New York: Columbia University Press.

Turner, David. 1979. "Hunting and Gathering: Cree and Australian." In *Challenging Anthropology*, ed. D.H. Turner and G.A. Smith, 195–213. Toronto: McGraw Hill Ryerson.

Turner, Victor. 1969. *The Ritual Process*. Chicago: Aldine.

– 1985. *On the Edge of the Bush: Anthropology as Experience*. Ed. Edith Turner. Tucson, AZ: University of Arizona Press.

United Nations Department of Economic and Social Affairs: Population Division. 2017. http://countrymeters.info/en/Mayotte.

Vail, Leroy, ed. 1991. "Introduction." *The Creation of Tribalism*. Berkeley, CA: University of California Press.

Vaughan, Megan. 2005. *Creating the Creole Island*. Durham, NC: Duke University Press. https://doi.org/10.1215/9780822386919.

Vérin, Pierre. 1994. *Les Comores*. Paris: Karthala.

Vidal, Jean-Michel. 1994. "L'adolescence à Mayotte: Histoire, changements et paradoxes." PhD diss., Université de Montreal.

– 2010. *Voyage dans le monde de l'adolescence: Parcours Mahorais d'un médecin devenu anthropologue*. Paris: L'Harmattan.

Vitebsky, Piers. 2012. "Repeated Returns and Special Friends: From Mythic Encounter to Shared History." In *Returns to the Field: Multitemporal Research and Contemporary Anthropology*, ed. Signe Howell and Aud Talle, 180–202. Bloomington: Indiana University Press.

Waldenfels, Bernhard. 2011. *Phenomenology of the Alien: Basic Concepts*. Evanston, IL: Northwestern University Press.

Walsh, Andrew. 1998. *Ritual, History and Identity among the Antankaraña of Madagascar*. PhD diss., University of Toronto.

Warnke, Georgia. 2002. "Hermeneutics, Ethics, and Politics." In *The Cambridge Companion to Gadamer*, ed. Robert J. Dostal, 79–101. Cambridge: Cambridge University Press. https://doi.org/10.1017/CCOL0521801931.005.

Weber, Max. 1946 [1922–3]. "The Social Psychology of the World Religions." In *From Max Weber: Essays in Sociology*, ed. H. Gerth and C. Wright Mills, 267–301. New York: Oxford University Press.

Weiner, Annette [B.]. 1976. *Women of Value, Men of Renown*. Austin: University of Texas Press.

– 1980. "Reproduction: A Replacement for Reciprocity." *American Ethnologist* 7 (1): 71–85. https://doi.org/10.1525/ae.1980.7.1.02a00050.

Wentzer, Thomas Schwarz. 2014. "'I Have Seen Koenigsberg Burning': Philosophical Anthropology and the Responsiveness of Historical Experience." *Anthropological Theory* 14 (1): 27–48. https://doi.org/10.1177/1463499614521723.

Werbner, Richard, ed. 1998. *Memory and the Postcolony*. London: Zed Books.

Wheeler, Michael. 2016. "Martin Heidegger." In *The Stanford Encyclopedia of Philosophy*, ed. Edward N. Zalta. <https://plato.stanford.edu/archives/win2016/entries/heidegger/>.

White, Hayden. 1973. *Metahistory: The Historical Imagination in Nineteenth-Century Europe*. Baltimore, MD: The Johns Hopkins University Press.

White, Leslie. 1949. *The Science of Culture*. New York: Farrar, Straus and Giroux.

Williams, Bernard. 1981. *Moral Luck*. Cambridge: Cambridge University Press. https://doi.org/10.1017/CBO9781139165860.

Wolf, Eric. 1957. "Closed Corporate Peasant Communities in Mesoamerica and Central Java." *Southwestern Journal of Anthropology* 13 (1): 1–18. https://doi.org/10.1086/soutjanth.13.1.3629154.

– 1982. *Europe and the People without History*. Berkeley: University of California Press.

Žižek, Slavoj. 1991. *Looking Awry: An Introduction to Jacques Lacan through Popular Culture*. Cambridge, MA: MIT Press.

Credits

Chapter 5

Adapted from Michael Lambek, 1990, "Exchange, Time, and Person in Mayotte: The Structure and Destructuring of a Cultural System," *American Anthropologist* 92 (3): 647–61. https://doi.org/10.1525/aa.1990.92.3.02a00060.

Chapter 6

Content on pp. 124–41 adapted from Michael Lambek, 2000, "Localizing Islamic Performances in Mayotte," in *Islamic Prayer across the Indian Ocean: Inside and Outside the Mosque*, ed. David Parkin and Stephen Headley, 63–97, Oxford: Curzon. Content on pp. 142–6 adapted from Michael Lambek, 2006, "The Playful Side of Islam and Its Possible Fate in Mayotte," in *The Global Worlds of the Swahili: Interfaces of Islam, Identity and Space in 19th and 20th-Century East Africa*, ed. Roman Loimeier and Rüdiger Seesemann, 161–86, Berlin: Lit Verlag.

Chapter 7

Adapted from Michael Lambek, 1995, "Choking on the Qur'an and Other Consuming Parables from the Western Indian Ocean Front," in *The Pursuit of Certainty: Religions and Cultural Formations*, ed. Wendy James, ASA Monographs, 252–75, London: Routledge.

Chapter 8

Adapted from Michael Lambek, 2002b, "Nuriaty, the Saint, and the Sultan: Virtuous Subject and Subjective Virtuoso of the Postmodern Colony," in *Postcolonial Subjectivities in Africa*, ed. Richard Werbner, 25–43, London: Zed Books.

Chapter 9

Adapted from Michael Lambek, 2004, "The Saint, the Sea Monster, and an Invitation to a *Dîner-dansant*: Ethnographic Reflections on the Edgy Passage – and the Double Edge – of Modernity, Mayotte 1975–2001," *Anthropologica* 46 (1): 57–68. https://doi.org/10.2307/25606168. Reprinted with permission from University of Toronto Press (https://utpjournals.press). © 2004 Canadian Anthropology Society.

Index

virgin marriage / virginity, 39–40,
69, 79, 84–5, 95, 98–9, 111–14, 117,
138, 174, 188, 189, 212, 224–7, 235,
237, 258, 293n11, 294nn5–6, 301n4,
303n9, 305n28, 305n30
Vitebsky, Piers, 287n5

Warnke, Georgia, 16–17
Weber, Max, 6–7, 125, 140, 141,
302n12

weddings, 30, 46, 57, 112–13, 117,
224–41, 251, 275; invitations,
189–92. See also *manzaraka*

York, Graf, 288n11
youth, 41, 48, 104, 162, 192, 203,
251–2, 269, 299n8, 300n14, 303n10,
304n18

Žižek, Slavoj, 183, 300n21

Anthropological Horizons

Editor: Michael Lambek, University of Toronto

Kaleidoscopic Odessa: History and Place in Contemporary Ukraine / Tanya Richardson (2008)

Invaders as Ancestors: On the Intercultural Making and Unmaking of Spanish Colonialism in the Andes / Peter Gose (2008)

From Equality to Inequality: Social Change among Newly Sedentary Lanoh Hunter-Gatherer Traders of Peninsular Malaysia / Csilla Dallos (2011)

Rural Nostalgias and Transnational Dreams: Identity and Modernity among Jat Sikhs / Nicola Mooney (2011)

Dimensions of Development: History, Community, and Change in Allpachico, Peru / Susan Vincent (2012)

People of Substance: An Ethnography of Morality in the Colombian Amazon / Carlos David Londoño Sulkin (2012)

'We Are Still Didene': Stories of Hunting and History from Northern British Columbia / Thomas McIlwraith (2012)

Being Māori in the City: Indigenous Everyday Life in Auckland / Natacha Gagné (2013)

The Hakkas of Sarawak: Sacrificial Gifts in Cold War Era Malaysia / Kee Howe Yong (2013)

Remembering Nayeche and the Gray Bull Engiro: African Storytellers of the Karamoja Plateau and the Plains of Turkana / Mustafa Kemal Mirzeler (2014)

In Light of Africa: Globalizing Blackness in Northeast Brazil / Allan Charles Dawson (2014)

The Land of Weddings and Rain: Nation and Modernity in Post-Socialist Lithuania / Gediminas Lankauskas (2015)

Milanese Encounters: Public Space and Vision in Contemporary Urban Italy / Cristina Moretti (2015)

Legacies of Violence: History, Society, and the State in Sardinia / Antonio Sorge (2015)

Looking Back, Moving Forward: Transformation and Ethical Practice in the Ghanaian Church of Pentecost / Girish Daswani (2015)

Why the Porcupine Is Not a Bird: Explorations in the Folk Zoology of an Eastern Indonesian People / Gregory Forth (2016)

The Heart of Helambu: Ethnography and Entanglement in Nepal / Tom O'Neill (2016)

Tournaments of Value: Sociability and Hierarchy in a Yemeni Town, 20th Anniversary Edition / Ann Meneley (2016)

Europe Un-Imagined: Nation and Culture at a French-German Television Channel / Damien Stankiewicz (2017)